French Salons

French Salons

High Society and Political Sociability from the
Old Regime to the Revolution of 1848

Steven Kale

The Johns Hopkins University Press
Baltimore and London

© 2004 The Johns Hopkins University Press
All rights reserved. Published 2004
Printed in the United States of America on acid-free paper
9 8 7 6 5 4 3 2 1

The Johns Hopkins University Press
2715 North Charles Street
Baltimore, Maryland 21218-4363
www.press.jhu.edu

Library of Congress Cataloging-in-Publication Data
Kale, Steven D., 1957–
    French salons : high society and political sociability from the Old
Regime to the Revolution of 1848 / Steven Kale.
        p.   cm.
Includes bibliographical references and index.
    ISBN 0-8018-7729-6 (hardcover : alk. paper)
    1. Salons — France. 2. France — Social life and customs — 19th
century. 3. France — Social life and customs — 18th century. I. Title.
DC33.5.K35 2004
944'.03'08621 — dc21
2003006218

A catalog record for this book is available from the British Library.

053104-4224 H5

For Marla and Alex

Contents

Acknowledgments

Like the proverbial cat, this book has lived and died many times, although certainly fewer than nine. An enduring sense of the importance of the subject always overcame distractions, whether they be the birth of a son, other interests, or fears about my own limitations as a historian of women's experience. The original premise took the form of a conventional work of herstory, inspired by my graduate mentor's query during a seminar on the state of French women's history about what the wives, sisters, and mothers of the legitimist aristocrats on whom I was writing my dissertation were doing while the men were trying to restore the monarchy. To my uninitiated astonishment, they were doing quite a lot, but were mostly presiding over salons.

Two women persuaded me to pursue salons as the topic for a book: Mary Lynn Stewart, who insisted on the significance of the subject and encouraged me to stick with it, and Dena Goodman, who was skeptical about the importance of salons in the nineteenth century but nevertheless thought that there was a worthwhile story yet to be told about their persistence. Goodman not only gave me some excellent advice during the initial stages of my research, she also put salons on the historical map. Although I disagree with many of her central arguments, it has to be acknowledged that she more than anyone made salons a topic of serious research for French historians, convincing everyone that *salonnières* ought to be taken seriously and listened to attentively. Because of her work, the salon no longer belongs to *la petite histoire* and is no longer detached from what Jolanta Pekacz called "the big themes of the discipline."

A number of people have read parts of this work and offered helpful advice at various stages of its development: Whitney Walton, Edgar Newman, Rachel Fuchs, Heather Streets, Susan Armitage, Jo Burr Margadant, Ted Margadant, K. Steven Vincent, and Scott Haine. I found especially fruitful my periodic exchanges with Jolanta Pekacz, whose own work on the salons of the eighteenth century developed lines of inquiry in which we had a common interest. I would also like to thank the office staff in the Department of History at Washington State University, and the editors and readers at the Johns Hopkins University Press, who worked patiently and carefully to help me bring this project to completion.

During the writing of this book, my wife's melanoma returned. After two years of fruitless treatment, she died. Whenever she was feeling up to it, and sometimes when she was not, Marla read chapters, corrected errors, and, as a journalist and feature writer, complained constantly about long sentences. She found that the salonnières of the nineteenth century struggled with the contradictions of their society in ways that still resonate today. Like them, she tried to achieve autonomy but remained wedded to the conventions of motherhood and domestic life. Driven to excellence at work, she was also anxious to set an impeccable table; affronted in private by the latest political outrage, she did not hesitate to shoot me a glance if I expressed similar opinions too forcefully in public. I miss her very much and I hope that this book, on which she collaborated in her own way, carries something of her spirit.

French Salons

Introduction: The Persistence of Salons

"If an author wants to depict the *grand monde,*" wrote Stendhal, "he will have to have first seen it and lived there." As literary correspondent for the *New Monthly Magazine* in London, he warned his readers that their probable lack of prior knowledge of "the social mechanism of France" would make what he had to say unintelligible.[1] For historians, who under such strictures ought not even try to write about the salons of French high society, that seemed to be the good news. According to Count Rudolf Apponyi, a longtime attaché at the Austro-Hungarian embassy in Paris, one could spend years living among and talking to French *mondains* without ever being able to understand or predict their behavior. In order to formulate reasonable, sane judgments of the state of French politics in the 1830s, Prince Schönburg, an Austrian envoy to the government of Louis-Philippe, went into society often, spoke with as many people as possible, read everything, listened attentively to conversations, and could still not figure out why this one supported the government, why that one belonged to the opposition, or why everyone seemed always to be changing their opinions. For Apponyi, the French were inscrutable because they were all actors playing to the crowd, always looking for an adroit phase with which to please society, and therefore incapable of believing anything for a precise reason.[2] The aphorist Nicolas Chamfort (1740–1794) surmised that the French could not even explain their own behavior, commenting that they knew nothing of *le monde*, in the same way that a maybug knew nothing about natural history.[3] Perhaps French novelists wrote so extensively about high society because they were aware of a significant audience hungering for commentary on itself.

Salon sociability was a well-regulated practice embedded in a larger social formation, usually referred to as high society, or simply as le monde, which itself was governed by rules and conventions. Both salons and *mondanité* (society life) existed in close proximity to the worlds of politics, literature, art, fashion, and business, all of which preoccupied French elites. Anyone attempting to study this complex reality, or even the connection between salons and politics, which is the principal focus of this book, must ignore Stendhal's advice and be a better anthropologist than Prince Schönburg in showing how the system worked. Historians could better live in nineteenth-century French high society by knowing more about what was said in salons. Unfortunately, there are no extensive records of salon conversations and no regular administrative inquiries examining the precise number, location, and composition of salons. What we do have in relative abundance are the memoirs of salonnières and the testimony of their habitués, which do not report the content of salon conversations so much as offer a wealth of information about what was taken for granted, about the salon's centrality in French upper-class life, and about the intricate links between politics and traditional mondaine sociability. These sources are familiar but have not been used systematically to address the latter.[4]

In the seventeenth and eighteenth centuries, salons encouraged socializing between the sexes, brought nobles and bourgeois together, and afforded opportunities for intellectual speculation. During the reign of Louis XIII and the ministry of Cardinal Mazarin (1610–1661), they helped transform and homogenize the mores of the upper classes and provided a setting for feminine literary expression; in the Age of Reason, they focused and reflected enlightened public opinion by facilitating the exchange of news and ideas and by permitting the philosophes to display themselves to the "the world."[5] With the outbreak of the French Revolution and the emergence of parliamentary government, salons acquired a political vocation, becoming institutions of political sociability for French aristocratic and intellectual elites. The present study is an examination of this latter transformation.

The persistence of salons in the nineteenth century shows their remarkable ability to adapt to changing historical circumstances. During the French Revolution, salons were largely eclipsed in France, although they were partially reconstituted abroad by aristocratic émigrés. They revived in Paris shortly after the Terror ended, however, and Napoléon welcomed and encouraged renewed salon sociability in order to win the support of the traditional aristocracy and elevate the social prestige of his regime in monarchical Europe. After Waterloo, salons flourished, their interior life no longer being circumscribed by the imperatives of an authoritarian regime. During the Bourbon Restoration (1815–1830) and the July Monarchy (1830-1848), salons became the principal centers of elite political networking and discussion, structured by the conventions of mondaine sociability and managed by salonnières, whose traditional mediating function seemed all the more necessary in the face of growing political partisanship. The political role of salons grew alongside those of competing institutions such as political parties, voluntary associations, and mass-circulation newspapers. These institutions of modern political life eventually marginalized the political role of salons, made salon sociability more private and more specialized, and pushed women outside the mainstream of political life.

Salon sociability was resilient because it was simultaneously a sociability of leisure, a form of communication, and an arena for social encounters, providing opportunities for conviviality, intellectual exchange, and unconventional social relationships.[6] The basic features it acquired in the seventeenth century (a luxurious space, feminine governance, a select company, polite conversation) changed very little in subsequent years. Salons persisted because they were anchored to stable cultural norms defined by feminine attributes that were taking shape in the eighteenth and nineteenth centuries. Linked in the public mind to widely accepted "feminine" characteristics, they came to be idealized by generations of male writers, artists, intellectuals, and politicians as protected spaces for the reconciliation of differences whose neutrality was guaranteed by the self-effacement and devotion to propriety of the salonnière. At the same time, as a particular type of gathering place for the upper classes, the salon had an extraordinary flexibility; its size could be altered and its functions adjusted to fit a variety of circumstances, so that salons themselves changed less than the realities to which they managed to adapt. This adaptive capacity gave the salon a certain utility over the course of a series of social, cultural, and political transitions from the seventeenth to the twentieth century; it made possible both the persistence of the salon's premodern function as a medium of social fusion and cultural exchange, and its transformation into a political institution during and after the revolutionary era. Originally conceived by the marquise de Rambouillet (1588–1665) as an architectural framework for a new kind of sociability, the salon managed to survive the most turbulent circumstances, including its own dissolution and reconstitution.

This contrast between a stable form and a changing content makes salons easy to define but terribly difficult to characterize. As a flexible vehicle for the accomplishment of goals constrained by social and gender norms, but existing on the margins of public life, the salon was able to accommodate activities and anticipate forms of interaction that were being created by protracted historical pressures but had yet to be sanctioned by convention or law. This is why most attempts to move beyond definitions of the salon or descriptions of ideal types of sociability slip into analogy: the salon was like a royal court, a university, an academy, a republic, a monarchy, a publishing house, a medium of communication, or some other institution or practice whose function was ambiguous and to which contemporary society had yet to attach a name. Salons could be either marginal or mainstream, bourgeois or aristocratic, courtly or enlightened, hierarchical or democratic, mixed or exclusive, public or private, feminist or masculinist, leisurely or "work-like," frivolous or serious, literary or political, or both. In all this confusion, one thing seems clear: in the French context at least, salons always filled some sort of institutional vacuum at the intersection between public and private life left by the decline of certain cultural, social, or civic institutions and the rise of others that had not yet taken root. Salons did not replace things that had disappeared but invented some of the attributes and functions of things yet to be born. In that sense, they were less transitional institutions than expressions of an era of transitions.

I

A variety of French novelists have tried to depict life in a nineteenth-century Parisian salon. Some of these portraits are insightful, illuminating, and deftly drawn; others, however, are pure fantasy, managing to offer the historian vivid and credible anthropological evidence on matters of attitude and comportment only by dint of the author's probing cynicism, revealing social resentment, or talent for plausible exaggeration. Balzac's keen sense of custom and *usage* in French society was colored by his conviction that women were hopelessly frivolous and could find pleasure only in scheming. The gloom and hypocrisy of Musset's salons owe something to his skepticism regarding love and the opposite sex.[7] On the question of politics in salons, the literary evidence is absolutely inconclusive. Proust insisted that politics was scrupulously avoided in salon conversation, commenting in *La Prisonnière* that aristocrats wanted to keep it from invading le monde just as soldiers wanted to prevent it from penetrating the army. Stendhal explained the "drawing room constitution" as follows: "Provided you did not treat God, the clergy, the King, or anyone holding public office as a matter for jest; provided you did not speak in praise of Beranger, the newspapers of the opposition party, Voltaire, Rousseau, or anyone allowing himself any freedom of speech; provided, above all, that you never mentioned politics — then you were free to discuss anything you pleased."[8] Of course, writers will take literary license and cannot be expected merely to provide documentation. But the contrast between fiction and reality in the case of political salons seems remarkably stark. Other novelists not only contradicted Proust and Stendhal, they took matters to the opposite extreme, suggesting darkly that salons determined the march of events and controlled political life from behind the scenes. Lamartine went so far as to represent the salons of the Restoration as governing institutions, with Madame de Boigne's salon as the Chamber of Peers, Madame de Sainte-Aulaire's as the Chamber of Deputies, and Madame Récamier's as the monarchy itself.[9]

The connection between salons and politics was obscured by the fact that few salons in the nineteenth century were seen by members of high society as distinctively political. Virginie Ancelot, playwright and salonnière for more than four decades, labeled as *femmes politiques* only three women of the July Monarchy (the comtesse de Castellane, the princesse de Lieven, and the duchesse de Broglie) and questioned whether political salons were free enough or cheerful enough to be considered "true salons."[10] In fact, very few salons focused exclusively on politics, very few salonnières dedicated themselves solely to the political fortunes of a male associate, and many of the most prominent femmes politiques of Paris were foreigners, like the princesse de Belgiojoso and the princesse de Lieven. High society was slightly more open-minded than society at large about gender roles, but politics was still a man's business and women who appeared to take it too seriously were considered to be harboring nefarious motives or acting out of some illegitimate purpose.

There were many kinds of salons in nineteenth-century France. Some sought to continue the legacy of the eighteenth century by preoccupying themselves with philosophical matters; other salons, purely mondains, deliberately avoided matters of the spirit. In addition to various official or ministerial salons, there were literary salons, musical salons, and those identified with particular celebrities. Salons were primarily for conversation, but they were also places of distraction and amusement, where people went to gamble, sing, dance, play charades, listen to poetry, view art, or participate in a theatrical representation.[11] Among political salons, there was a good deal of variety as well — in the 1840s, Victor de Balabine, an employee at the Russian embassy, was astonished to find an assortment of opportunities for political chat in Paris: "Here we have political salons, literary salons, legitimist salons, salons of the *juste milieu*, diplomatic salons, and finally, neutral salons." The vicomte de Beaumont-Vassy divided the political salons of the July Monarchy into ministerial salons ("veritable branches of the Palais Bourbon") and those directed by former *hommes d'état* or femmes politiques.[12]

The problem with this sort of taxonomy is that virtually all salons were used for a variety of purposes. More often than not, the intimate conversations of the afternoon gave way to larger gatherings for dinner, or to some planned activity for the evening.[13] Indeed, the ideal established for salons during the Revolution by Madame de Staël envisioned the fusion of *la politique* and *les lumières*, so that constitutional debates would be informed by the most educated minds and the most rigorous philosophical considerations. At the same time, salons often considered uniquely literary were almost never immune to other preoccupations: writers often attended salons as celebrities rather than artists; in some cases, a writer was also an *homme politique*, lending the salons he frequented "a politico-literary character." Such was the case with the salon of Sophie Gay, whose guests included political figures, musicians, and men of letters (among them Lamartine, Balzac, the marquis de Custine, and Eugène Sue).[14] According to the comtesse de Bassanville, the salon of Princesse Catherine de Bagration simply defied characterization:

> With all the diverse personalities who came in and out of the salon of Madame Bagration like shadows, one could not find a particular physiognomy there. The princesse loved noise, commotion, and newcomers; hence the innumerable transformations that her house underwent. One day, it was a political salon; the entire diplomatic corps could be seen there, distinguished foreigners, men of state, indeed even princes and ministers, and, according to a rumor circulating quietly, the soul of Metternich, although absent, animated this lavish residence. Then, all of a sudden, one heard only laughter, song, joyous outbursts to the accompaniment of a grand orchestra; and charming young women, smiles on their lips and brightness in their eyes, crowded in to replace the grave and serious men, brilliant in their attire,

dripping with diamonds, in order to seek out the pleasures of a ball. . . . Later, another complete change occurred: the orchestra went silent, the echoes of the *hôtel* ceased to reverberate with bursts of joy, and one heard only verse more or less well rhymed, prose more or less well written; literature had replaced pleasure, the blue-stockings, the fashionable women.[15]

Such changes of scenery took place every night throughout le monde, or slowly, over the life of a salon. As Maurice Agulhon has pointed out, multifunctionality was a general and long-standing feature of French institutions of sociability, and politics was often at the heart of associations ostensibly established for another purpose.[16] In a climate that was both repressive and highly politicized, where the rules governing political association were shifting and unclear, salons could be political either by design or simply by default. In the flush of novelty and excitement that accompanied the advent of parliamentary government in the 1790s and during the first half of the nineteenth century, politics was fashionable in fashionable society and politicians were celebrities. As Balzac wryly commented, "The politician of 1840 is in some way like the abbé of the eighteenth century. No salon would be complete without its homme politique."[17]

No clear barrier separated politics and high society.[18] The political personnel of most of the regimes that succeeded 1789 overlapped with the clientele of the salons, where politicians, diplomats, artists, and journalists frequented the same salons and participated in the same system of social networks. Salons inhabited a sphere of unofficial politics from which women were never fully excluded, where gender constraints made "private" the political conversations that occurred prior to official political conduct, and where the ambiguities of gender and privacy among the rich belied the efforts of authorities to separate politics from the customary institutions of associational life. In the fashionable Paris of the early nineteenth century, the public statements and actions of princes, ministers, and deputies were "also the object of private commentary"; they were among the most popular topics of conversation, speculation, mockery, and jest for the elite. Upon becoming "members of the governmental majority" in 1830, wrote Charles de Rémusat, "we became gluttons. We led the elegant life of the times, inferior in good taste to that of the past, but agreeable and amusing." Everyone, he declared, was tempted by "this alliance of the preoccupation with weighty matters, ambition, and political activity with the careless pleasures of a brilliant and dissipated world."[19]

It is one thing to establish that salons were political; it is another to discover why, and to account for their role in French politics. Contrary to the testimony of contemporaries and the opinion of many historians, salonnières did not normally exercise an influence in affairs of state and the choice of ministers, determine the march of events, prepare electoral lists, or even procure theater boxes from powerful relatives. If salons and salonnières did take a hand in such matters, there is very little evidence to verify activity that would intentionally have been secretive and naturally the subject of less than disinterested conjecture. In fact, the assertion that salons and salonnières had an influence on political decisions and events, as opposed to a less tangible and ill-defined role, is almost always based not on direct historical testimony but on the assumption that the presence of women in places where important matters were discussed implies that they played an integral part in the decision-making process. Adeline Daumard characterizes as "legend" the notion that "women held the key to power and imposed their tastes, preferences, and ideas, notably in political matters." She concluded that the "women of the highest society and the best circles at court did not have . . . the power either to make the careers of a man they honored or to determine public affairs by friends interposed."[20]

Salons were crucial to the politics of early nineteenth-century France because they structured the political sociability of elites. After 1789, salons became increasingly politicized; they took on clearer partisan identities, gave a measure of coherence to the proliferation of political factions, and performed a number of social and communicative functions that came to be viewed as politically useful. French salons originated in the seventeenth century, and they have persisted into the twenty-first, but their political role was greatest during the Restoration and the July Monarchy, when French politics was open enough to allow for a certain degree of free debate and association, but closed enough to restrict active participation to a narrow elite. It was also a time when a more or less stable parliamentary regime operated in an atmosphere of bitter partisanship, requiring a complexity of political organization that could still be accomplished by the customary institutions of elite sociability.

II

The salon is best understood as an aspect of what Arno Mayer calls "the persistence of the Old Regime," which corresponded to the protracted decline of aristocratic predominance within the French elite. By "persistence" Mayer does not mean mere survival, as in Charles Morazé's characterization of the salon as the "last vestige of the Old Regime." Rather, he has in mind an active process of "ingesting, adapting, and assimilating" on the part of a slowly declining aristocracy trapped in "the relentless tragedy of historical perseverance," engaged in elaborate and "cunning" strategies of resistance and containment instead of fatalistic nostalgia, so that salon culture became a tool of survival in a time of adversity. Like the codes of honor studied by William Reddy, nineteenth-century salon culture demonstrates how the "values, attitudes, and . . . feelings of an earlier age" persisted as a means of stabilizing identities and establishing social rules at a time when social and cultural coordinates were unsettled, a phenomenon that gave enormous symbolic capital to older elites. Otto Dann sees the lack of formality in French forms of aristocratic sociability as a sign of profound habituation that explains their legitimacy, resiliency, and broad attraction. German associations, he observes, always needed formal rules and procedures for orientation and purpose. "In France," however, "forms of social organization appear marked to a much greater extent by informal arrangements, habits, and customs [so that] new forms of communication and association take root more within tradition and the dominant impression is that of a much greater continuity between traditional forms and new forms of sociability."[21] A whole world of social arrangements and attitudes supported the existence of French salons: an idle aristocracy, an ambitious middle class, an active intellectual life, the social density of a major urban center, sociable traditions, and a certain aristocratic feminism. This world did not disappear in 1789.

Salons were a historically specific expression of the aristocracy's determination to regulate and control the transition from a hereditary to an open elite. They emerged at a time when the justification of noble privilege in terms of a traditional military function was under attack, when circumstances promoted a more modern view of nobility based on a combination of birth, education, manners, and sociability, and when an increasingly wealthy bourgeoisie was gaining entry into an expanding service nobility and aspired to "live nobly." Carolyn Lougee has shown that salons appeared along with the need to regulate this transition in order to provide a space for social fusion and cultural homogenization among the diverse elements of an aristocracy in the process of domestication and restructuration.[22] The genius of salons, and of salonnières, lay in their ability to maintain a delicate balance between exclusivity and openness, between "inclusions and exclusions," so that the aristocracy could have both a means of producing social cohesion and a vehicle for the dissemination of traits meant to characterize a wider society of elites undergoing redefinition. As the French elite became larger and more diverse, the importance of salons grew, because the ability of the aristocratic element to manage social change came to depend more and more on its control over the criteria of elite status. Outside of marriage, such control was exerted primarily by making high society more distinctive and more attractive as a cultural model. The Revolution therefore temporarily strengthened rather than weakened the social utility of salons: nobles, who had already acquired a means to "determine nobility independently of the king's designation," emerged from the adversity of exile and repression with a greater sense of cohesion than the monarchy had ever provided; in these circumstances, the cultural authority acquired by salons was complemented by a level of social and political predominance that gave nobles a preponderance within the larger society of notables and accorded them more control over access to social prestige than they had had in the eighteenth century.[23]

The association of noble manners with high status was a *longue durée* feature of the French social landscape. Since the seventeenth century, those aspiring to elite status had "to go to the school of the ladies" in order to acquire that "*parfum de l'aristocratie*" to avoid being "a ludicrous figure."[24] The salon's success in helping to regulate the multiple transformations experienced by the French elite from the seventeenth to the nineteenth century can be seen in the homogenization of elite comportment in the eighteenth century and in the Revolution's failure to destroy the allure of courtly manners, despite the boost it gave to the social and political fortunes of the middle classes. According to Elizabeth Goldsmith, defining a noble class by its "cultural sophistication . . . probably helped to prolong rather than weaken the dominance of noble culture" because institutions such as the salon made non-nobles participants in an ongoing conversation about "what it meant to be naturally 'superior.'" Consequently, the popularization of the cultural values of the nobility disseminated respect for traditional forms of elite status, while allowing nobles to maintain a sense of distinction.[25] Marx might have scoffed at the spectacle of the nineteenth-century European nobility posing as "the dancing masters of Europe," but "the prebourgeois cachet of the French ruling class," as Mayer puts it, remained a powerful instrument of aristocratic social power well after 1789. Throughout the better part of the nineteenth century, aristocratic life fascinated the established bourgeoisie, for which the salon remained the supreme model of social elegance, making it a crucial form of "symbolic capital," embodying what Christophe Charle calls the "indirect power of domination over other factions seeking social legitimacy by imitation." In his study of French elites across the revolutionary era, Guy Chaussinand-Nogaret was struck by two things: the slowness of change from the eighteenth to the nineteenth century and

> the perpetuation of very old models, often put in place in the sixteenth and seventeenth centuries, and the fascination that they still exercised in the nineteenth. There is no secret whatsoever to this permanence. As factors of longevity for traditional elites, they would lend additional legitimacy to ascendant elites and give to all a moral benefit that would sustain their credit and assure their prestige: the prestige of knowledge over the ignorant, of luxury over the poor, of elegance and refinement over the boorish. Pure artifice, perhaps, but they carried a heavy load: they reinforced their own seductive power in public opinion and consolidated their mastery. Proof, if need be, that neither birth, nor money, nor power were in themselves enough to define elites who for the sake of their own indispensability demanded a combination of conditions that had no objective character whatsoever, and where the role played by imagination and symbolism was sometimes decisive. Elites nourish themselves on symbolism and exist only by virtue of an ensemble of semiotic representations that distinguish them from the masses, or, rather, the public, because they are above all a spectacle, and this spectacle creates a relationship that explains, better than the other attributes of power, the bonds of subordination.[26]

The Revolution increased the salon's importance to the old aristocracy because it had become the institution principally responsible for cultivating and maintaining what Norbert Elias calls the "social argument . . . that something is better because it is the usage of the upper class, or even only an elite within the upper class."[27] Consensus on this matter was a critical political asset for the nobility in the early nineteenth century because it sustained the idea that a ruling class required an aristocratic element, a sentiment that supported postrevolutionary hopes for a reconciliation at the top of the social hierarchy and that gave salons an important role in the social politics of the Napoleonic, Bourbon, and Orleanist phases of France's social and political restoration.

The fact that salons did not disappear despite the Revolution's assault on the nobility and women in the public sphere suggests that its role in the restructuring and redefinition of the elite had not ended. By dispersing the aristocracy, the Revolution had only interrupted *la vie mondaine*; during the Directory, and especially during the Consulate, conditions for the rebirth of salons congealed: émigrés returned and Napoléon and Josephine, anxious to win the support of the old aristocracy, founded a new court at the Tuileries and encouraged the reconciliation of royalists and republicans. The aristocratic salons of Faubourg Saint-

Germain and Faubourg Saint-Honoré acquired the status of established institutions under the Empire and remained central features of Parisian high society at least until the Revolution of 1848, despite the collapse of political consensus within the expanding and increasingly diverse world of the notables. Salons lasted as long as their social functions continued to be historically relevant, which is perhaps the best evidence of their aristocratic nature. They arose when hereditary hierarchies began to give way before the dominant criteria of social status in the modern world—money, talent, education, and *capacité*—and moved to the margins of social and political life as the process ran its course. The salon was unique neither to the early modern period nor to the world of letters. Its existence was conterminous with Jürgen Habermas's "bourgeois public sphere," from the time when the "social" could be "constituted as its own sphere to the degree that . . . the reproduction of life took on private form [and] the private realm as a whole assumed public relevance" to the advent of democracy "about the middle of the nineteenth century," when "an enlarged public . . . came to the fore as the subject of the public sphere" and traditional elites lost control over their own internal restructuring and turned their attention to matters of survival. The two centuries roughly from 1650 to 1850—from the Fronde to the waning years of the July Monarchy and the shock of 1848—saw the rise and consolidation of bourgeois society in France, and this was also an era when aristocratic women seem to have had a great deal of influence.[28]

Public and private spheres overlapped in aristocratic salons, where feudal traditions placed women at the center of a family's public responsibilities and status concerns. In this respect, today's scholarship generally reflects Elias's view that the separate spheres of the Victorian era are not applicable to early modern French aristocrats, because noblemen did not work, and noble households were not so much domestic spaces as public ones, dedicated to "the preservation of status through [the] public display of rank and wealth." The reputation, honor, and continuation of the family led nobles to eschew individualism and the norms of bourgeois marriage in favor of a collective effort to maintain prestige and connections, so that private decisions were routinely made for public purposes and public actions were readily influenced by private considerations.[29] Based in the private domicile and maintained by unspoken rituals rooted in the practices of an aristocratic milieu, the salon was a powerful tool for linking private interests to political power and public influence prior to the rise of professional specialization and the bureaucratization of public life. Networks and relationships formed by marriage and liaisons that were contracted for public purposes made each salon at once familial and mondain, where consanguinity and friendship produced publicly significant alliances.

The position of aristocratic women at the intersection between public and private concerns made the French aristocracy particularly resistant to the notion that women were an element of social disorder. Noble attitudes to women reflected the courtly traditions of the Renaissance and the codes of gallantry elaborated before and during the decline of feudal institutions, in which civilized attention to the ladies required magnanimity between the sexes, ascribing to women the role of teaching men how to act toward "the fairer sex." Pleasing women therefore became not only the font of mondain civility but an ethical cornerstone that complemented the importance of patrimony and lineage in noble society. The counterpart of *la galanterie* was the notion of women as civilizers. The salon eventually became the principal depository of this legacy of noble civility and sexual "commerce," embodying standards of refinement and *politesse* that contrasted with the coarseness of male society and made France uniquely sociable. By the nineteenth century, this legacy had become central to aristocratic identity, an identity that, according to the comtesse d'Agoult, required that women with the power to render "the final opinion on delicate matters of propriety and honor" receive "fervent and constant homages."[30]

Nobles saw women's ability to civilize not merely as a feminine attribute but as a social and political responsibility, which required noblewomen to perform the preeminently public task of guarding social conventions and maintaining the equilibrium, and consequently the advantages, of civilized life. Nobles in nineteenth-century France were convinced that times of upheaval were also times when women were most hidden from view, when violence replaced diplomacy, when demagoguery replaced private conversation, and when liberty gave way to the inordinate power of the state. Such sentiments resulted in a tenacious commitment to the notion of gender complementarity at a time when social trends, political ideas, and cultural attitudes were moving forcefully in another direction.[31] The aristocratic counterideology of gender complementarity accorded with what Suzanne Fiette has called a "noble religion of honor," characterized by "submission to the imperatives of lineage" and grounded in "a familiocentrism that above all privileges the renown and judgment of the group." As a nexus of this larger social and cultural universe, the salon, according to Jolanta Pekacz, could have "nothing subversive about it," because the values it was supposed to disseminate "did not violate the traditional social roles designated for women." Intended to "prevent anarchy caused by transgression," salons were "a more powerful repressive tool for women than for men," because they turned the salonnière into an enforcer of rules of propriety that limited her possibilities while being useful to the public activities of men.[32]

The size and composition of the elite who voted under the *système censitaire*, the traditions and dimensions of Parisian mondanité, the proximity of the court, the Chambers, and the ministries, and the intimate nature of political communications in an era of limited suffrage allowed salons to structure political sociability in the absence of modern political parties. Anxiety among the postrevolutionary generation of French notables about the fractionalism that accompanied the development of parliamentary government, long-standing aristocratic assumptions about the civilizing function of women, and the salon's ability to bring men with divergent personalities and opinions together in harmonious conversation encouraged French elites to look to salons to fortify social and ideological cohesion at the top of the social hierarchy. The harnessing of gender conventions to the interests of class had two important implications: it gave salonnières privileged access to politics, and it put women in the role of configuring the social world around aristocratic power.

As an institution of upper-class political sociability, the salon was not a target of France's repressive laws on association, which, beginning with the Le Chapelier Law of 1791, were aimed primarily at the burgeoning democratic movement and not at *réunions* that could be considered private. Subsequent revolutionary legislation banning "les clubs des femmes" in October 1793 and "sociétés particulières s'occupant des questions politiques" in August 1795 was partly aimed at the clubs and associations of the Right—the Directory closed the liberal royalist Club de Clichy—but had limited impact on the salon's traditional clientele, which had been dispersed by the emigration, imprisoned by the revolutionary tribunal, or killed by the Terror.[33] When the penal code was elaborated between 1808 and 1810, associations of twenty persons or fewer were exempted from the need for government authorization by *conseillers d'état* who, like Comte Berlier, wanted to protect "these small gatherings established by relations of friendship, family, and neighborhood."[34] Most Napoleonic officials knew from experience that salons met in private domiciles and were therefore notoriously resistant to surveillance. In a memorandum to Napoleon on gambling in 1811, Chancellor Etienne-Denis de Pasquier noted that "[t]he rich have *salons* into which it is difficult to gain admittance; but supervision can always be exercised with ease over the poor, for their places of meeting are necessarily public resorts."[35] The Napoleonic Code subjected women to a dependent legal status, but it did not exclude them from political participation or deprive them of a public voice to a greater extent than had been the case under the Old Regime. The Constitution of 1791 relegated women to the status of nonvoting citizens, and the Jacobins had tried to sweep them from the public sphere. By contrast, the notables who crafted the civil code consolidating women's inferior legal status protected traditional institutions of elite sociability by failing to define them as overtly political, even though they could comprise considerably more than twenty guests.[36]

The notables who governed France during the first half of the nineteenth century were hostile to the right of association, but they never deprived themselves of occasions to gather, eat, dance, and talk politics. The result was a paradox: a public sphere stamped by the patriarchy of the Napoleonic Code that nevertheless made room for salons and their influence in public affairs. Under the Restoration, the government often frustrated efforts by liberal elites to establish political associations but turned a blind eye when groups of deputies or officials gathered for political purposes in salons, creating a situation not unlike that of the Old Regime, when an ordinance making unauthorized assemblies of more than five people illegal was hardly ever enforced against salons and masonic lodges. French laws on association therefore embodied not only masculinist impulses but the privilege of class: while the former annihilated women's political rights, the latter granted women of wealth a certain exemption from the rigors of an otherwise gendered public sphere. That exemption excluded the rich from their own efforts to constrain political freedom and turned salons into informal political institutions.

III

The question of the relationship between salons and politics is important for two reasons: it offers an opportunity to examine the role of women in public life after a time when women are thought to have been excluded from the public sphere, and it allows us to rewrite the history of the salon from the perspective of the nineteenth century, thereby restoring continuities to the history of an institution that historians have for the most part failed to take into account in their interpretation of its nature and significance.[37] Shifting perspective involves a shift in analytical priorities: from women's seemingly abrupt exclusion from the public sphere by the Jacobins and the Civil Code to the persistence of salons during the emigration, their revival under the Directory, the Consulate, and the Empire, and their proliferation during the Bourbon Restoration; from the exceptionality of the salonnière as a semi-public figure to the commonality of salons as an institution of aristocratic life; and from the intellectual sociability of the eighteenth-century Republic of Letters to the political sociability of elites during a period of protracted social transition that witnessed the consolidation of modern political institutions.

This study is an institutional history of French salons rather than a history of women in salons per se. The intention is not to marginalize salonnières but to place their ideas and actions in the historical, social, and political contexts that gave them meaning. The first chapter discusses the institutionalization of salons in the seventeenth and eighteenth centuries, when they became an important feature of both polite society and the Republic of Letters. What follows is a chronological and analytical history of the rise and fall of the importance of salons in French politics from the Revolution of 1789 to the Revolution of 1848, in the course of which I examine the evolution of salons, the changing role of salonnières, and the functioning of salons as institutions of political sociability. I close with a consideration of the salon's decline, an account of its political marginalization, and an assessment of its status as a feminist institution.

CHAPTER ONE

Between the Republic of Letters and the *Grand Monde*

"In the good old days, before anyone had begun to think about national representation," recalled the marquise de La Tour du Pin, "a list of supper guests was a most important and carefully considered item! There were so many interests to be fostered, so many people to bring together, so many others to be kept apart! . . . One needed a very profound knowledge of convention and the current intrigues."[1] By the time the marquise entered fashionable society toward the end of the Old Regime, salons were well-established institutions of aristocratic life, functioning according to an elaborate set of conventions, and helping to integrate the worlds of letters, mondanité, and the royal court.

I

The most important salons of the seventeenth century, those of the *précieuses*, emerged toward the end of the Fronde (1648–1653), when powerful noblewomen had taken on extraordinary political and military roles. In an atmosphere critical of feminine assertiveness, the précieuses tried, like the marquise de Rambouillet before them, to foster civility and restore the image of women by reaffirming their right to consideration, independence, and learning.[2] As a result, salons became sites for two forms of innovation: the contestation of social conventions and the discussion of progressive ideas. Not only did seventeenth-century salonnières encourage novel social encounters, they challenged traditional notions of marriage and maternity, advocated unions based on love, and emphasized the importance of individual autonomy. At the same time, women-centered gatherings cultivated both the new science and the priority of female learning while testing discursive boundaries that were shortly to deny women equal access to intellectual life.[3] The result was an original creation: an institution in which the freedom and creativity necessary to generate new literary genres, fresh humanistic ideals, a feminist sensibility, and the opportunity to refine one's taste and sharpen one's wit existed side by side with an obsession with propriety, status, and *bienséance* that tended to constrain and modulate the subversive impulses for which it often provided an initial hearing. Even in its moderate form, the transgressive potential of the salon had difficulty asserting itself once the antifeminist backlash set in during the long reign of Louis XIV, when the founding of the Royal Academy of Sciences and the "exclusion of women from the new rationality," mockery of the précieuses, denunciations of women's role in the Republic of Letters, and the decline of the "feminocentric salon" coincided with the domestication of the nobility, the formalization of court rituals, and the stabilization of absolute rule. Consequently, the salon entered the eighteenth century as an institution in which the balance between subversion and constraint seemed tilted decisively in the direction of the latter by social forces hostile to political ferment and the autonomy of women, who, according to Erica Harth, "were left with the discourse of polite society."[4]

Salons changed in significant ways between the seventeenth and eighteenth centuries, becoming less "feminocentric" as conversation involving "literary and linguistic arbitration" gave way to the passivity of philosophical conversation "dominated by the great male writers," who used salons to showcase their talents and promote their literary careers.[5] In the process, salons became more "serious" and eighteenth-century salonnières more educated than their predecessors.[6] Because salons commonly offered time for a variety of activities, it is hard to discern a consistent and linear evolution from mondaine and literary salons to philosophical and political ones.[7] A salonnière could choose to engage writers in serious discussions on Tuesdays and entertain society friends on Wednesdays, or talk philosophy at dinner before enjoying a game of whist. Multiple utility gave prerevolutionary salons the longevity to allow salonnières to institutionalize a public role for women at a time when other avenues for feminine public expression were vanishing and when the salon's clientele among the elite were mobilizing intellectually and politically to challenge absolutism.

By the middle of the eighteenth century, the salon had become a regular and well-structured institution that brought working scholars and writers into a world of aristocratic *divertissement* in order to provide a framework for mondaine conversation. Madame de Lambert established the pattern of receiving guests two days a week on a regular basis and of providing different programs depending on the composition of her salon. Madame Geoffrin, who made sure that she was always home at hours set aside for her twice-weekly gatherings, instituted the practice of meeting for one o'clock lunches instead of the traditional late-night supper so as to open the whole afternoon to discussion. Julie de Lespinasse received guests every day from five to nine o'clock in the evening for twelve years. By the time Madame Necker's salon gained prominence in the late eighteenth century, a philosophe's social agenda had become so crowded that salonnières staggered their meeting days so as not to clash with those of others. Necker instituted a third weekly "day" to accommodate intimate friends but still left herself time to prepare between sessions.[8]

By the early nineteenth century, regularity had become such a common feature of Parisian salon life that the social map of the capital was dotted with a "crowd of houses open, on a fixed day, once a week" — under such circumstances, people could always find one another and life became "a sequence of conversations." The typical salonnière had an open house once or twice a week where invited guests could arrive at various times of the day, beginning at about four o'clock in the afternoon. "I have arranged my mode of life in a manner which pleased me extremely," wrote Madame de Boigne, recalling the Restoration. "I went out very little, but when I was away my mother received visitors, so that our *salon* was open every evening." Delphine de Girardin was so conscious of a salonnière's duty to keep to a regular schedule that she excused Madame de Boigne in advance from attending a reading of "my poor [tragedy] *Judith*." "You cannot be permitted," she acknowledged, "to leave your salon, where so many distinguished minds come daily to seek inspiration from yourself. I am not so presumptuous as to think that these advantages can be sacrificed for my sake."[9]

Institutionalization turned holding a salon into a time-consuming career involving considerable work and expense. Meals had to be provided for a dozen or more people on a regular basis, talented and distinguished guests had to be recruited, theatrical presentations had to be arranged, readings and music had to be scheduled, and an agreeable space had to be maintained. The effort required to sustain a lively, attractive, and pleasant assembly over the course of many years demanded what amounted to professional self-sacrifice.[10] Although the comtesse d'Agoult called the salon "the supreme ambition of a Parisian woman, the consolation of her maturity, the glory of her old age," many nineteenth-century salonnières spoke of their obligations as a form of social incarceration. The duchesse de Duras worried that the regularity of her existence was sapping her strength and confided to Madame de Staël that she considered "this world is a tissue of chains." The princesse de Vaudémont had a "salon en permanence," which stole her freedom and forced her "never to accept an evening invitation."[11]

Institutionalization also involved the development of a pattern of succession, complete with conventions of apprenticeship and inheritance. Members of Rambouillet's circle — Mademoiselle de Montpensier and Madame de Créqui — started their own salons in the late 1640s, anxious to preserve values they had already begun to think of as traditions. According to Joan DeJean, Rambouillet's "direct heirs" (Madeleine de Souvé and the marquise de Sablé) and those who experienced the "precious decade" of the 1650s "carried the torch until the end of the seventeenth century and, in the case of Anne Thérèse de Lambert, formed a bridge to the next." From there, the line of succession extended across the eighteenth century as it passed from Tencin to Geoffrin to Necker, and from Deffand to Lespinasse. Madame Geoffrin had apprenticed herself to Madame Tencin for twenty years before opening her own salon. Madame du Deffand learned the art from the duchesse du Maine at Sceaux before teaching it to Lespinasse. Most salonnières learned how to "hold a circle" by frequenting a celebrated salon and by participating in the duties of the hostess.[12] By the end of the eighteenth century, aristocratic girls commonly attended convent schools or worked with private tutors, whose lessons included music, dancing, and deportment, as well as history, geography, and catechism. Young initiates also learned the rituals and obligations of high society by attending balls, arranging theatricals, and even holding mock salons in the company of older girls. The comtesse d'Agoult underwent hours of training in conversational skill, dancing, singing, and piano, not for the sake of practicing a "great art," but only to impress a suitor, entertain the family, play for a neighbor, or "accompany some virtuoso."[13]

On occasion, the career of salonnière was open to talent, but it was more common for the succession from one salonnière to another to take the form of an act of inheritance triggered by the death of one woman and the ascension of another. Madame de Lambert's passing led her guests to migrate to the salon of

Madame de Tencin, whose death in turn gave Madame Geoffrin the opportunity to formalize her own salon. Madame Necker inherited the habitués of Geoffrin and Lespinasse before stepping aside in favor of her daughter, Germaine de Staël, who took over her mother's salon prior to opening her own at the Swedish embassy.[14] In retrospect, Madame Necker became the founder of a veritable liberal dynasty when her prerevolutionary habitués showed up at Coppet (the family estate in Switzerland) to stay with Madame de Staël, and when her grand-daughter, Albertine de Broglie, "inherited the debris" of her mother's society. Once the salon had acquired long-standing traditions, it was possible for succession to become less a matter of inheritance than conscious self-styling. Salonnières began to proclaim themselves the heirs of this or that predecessor in order to continue a particular salon tradition or capture the aura of a legend. Madame de Duras bequeathed her guests to her daughter, the duchesse de Rauzan, but thought of herself as the spiritual successor of Madame de Staël and behaved accordingly. The comtesse d'Agoult modeled her salon on an eighteenth-century *bureau d'esprit*, thereby creating a reference point for Juliette Adam and other republican society women of the 1860s and 1870s.[15]

The continuities created by these various forms of succession turned many nineteenth-century salons into living archeological sites, complete with fossils from another era and long institutional memories. Madame de Boigne traced "the social tone and conventions" in the princesse de Poix's salon to society "as constituted under Louis XV." At Coppet, Charles de Rémusat found "distinct traces of the spirit of French society in three memorable eras, that of the death of Voltaire, that of the Constituent Assembly, and that of the salon of Madame de Staël." He recalled hearing stories about the baron de Monthyon's (1733–1820) recollections of what Corneille had said to Fontenelle, and remembered Etienne Dumont's account of "the effects of the publication of the letters of Jean-Jacques Rousseau to Christophe de Beaumont." In the salon of Madame d'Houdetot at Sannois during the Napoleonic era, Suard liked to entertain guests by rehearsing conversations he had had with Grimm, Diderot, Holbach, and d'Alembert.[16]

II

Ideally, a salon was a deliberately composed gathering of individuals selected by the salonnière for compatibilities and contrasts likely to produce the most interesting and harmonious conversation. It was also a forum in which the salon-nière could locate and amplify the particular qualities of her guests. Salonnières therefore had to perform a difficult balancing act, cultivating individual merit without letting one guest overshadow the others, and maintaining decorum without dampening creativity or upsetting the spontaneity of conversation.

Salonnières were sovereign in their power "to greet or reject guests of their choice."[17] The power to invite gave salonnières the freedom to create select groups for a variety of different occasions. They determined whether and when to use their salons for an intimate conversation or a crowded society event and adjusted their guest list accordingly, using the power of selection to achieve the right mix needed to create an agreeable encounter. The power to invite was also the power to arrange, making each salon an act of self-expression with its own character, and each salonnière the author of its particular qualities. A salon, therefore, was similar to a work of art: it embodied the values of creativity, originality, harmony, balance, and proportion and required special abilities akin to those involved in writing or painting. Jean-François Marmontel compared Lespinasse's ability to create harmony among the disconnected guests of her salon to the playing of an instrument by an artful musician. Kathleen O'Meara likened the cultivation of a salon to a floral arrangement or the work of a skilled collector. The most apt metaphor, however, was that offered by Madame Ancelot, who described her salon as a *tableau vivant* that changed with the seasons of her life.[18]

The salonnière's art consisted in "knowing how to create a harmonious gathering of people who differed not only in temperament and intelligence but in their social background, whilst allowing them all to express their own personalities and to show themselves at their best." Consequently, she was required to rise above envious feelings that might stop her from receiving someone who might otherwise contribute to a perfect balance of elements. "One must know how to put enemies face to face, all talents in a good light, and the tedious out the door," wrote Sophie Gay. In arranging her salon during the Revolution of 1848, Ancelot invited General Schramm so that "military glory would be represented with dignity" in a gathering she hoped would mirror the qualities of the Roman Republic.[19]

As with any craft that involved the art of composition, clutter had to be avoided in favor of beauty, pleasure, and grace. That is why no salon worthy of esteem could be an open house. When Madame de Boigne extended invitations, she was "careful to run into those whom I wished to bring together and whom I knew would suit one another. In this way, I could avoid an excessive crowd and the necessity of receiving the great number of bores toward whom decency compels evasion, and who never failed to rush forward at the first sign."[20] The most celebrated salons were those that others considered well designed. The duchesse de Duras came in for special praise in this regard, receiving accolades from François Villemain for weaving her variegated guests together with threads of silk and gold to create a "collective being." The duchesse de Dino judged the princesse de Lieven's dinners to be "very well assorted." By contrast, Marmontel considered Madame Helvétius to be an ineffective hostess because she drew "about her the persons whom she liked best (and not choosing the worst) broke up society somewhat."[21]

A salonnière treated her salon as her own creation and took responsibility for what happened there — those entering her salon did so expecting to follow her rules. Conversational enjoyment and efficacy required the enforcement of certain rules of decorum and demanded the avoidance of topics that might be too thorny to ensure congeniality or too arcane to allow everyone to participate.[22] More than a hostess or entertainer, the salonnière was a moderator who had to use a rare combination of specialized skills to ensure her salon's survival, failing which habitués might grow bored, feel slighted, or succumb to the allure of an alternative invitation. After observing his mother-in-law at work in her salon, Baron de Staël concluded: "One fools oneself in believing that conversation between superior men was an unalloyed pleasure. On the contrary, the joy of it had to be purchased by continual labor, and an uninterrupted tension of mind."[23] Those who complained about feeling restrained in salons also knew that decorum was a necessary condition of polite conversation. Antoine Thomas likened Madame Geoffrin to a "wise legislator" and Baron de Staël described what Madame Necker did as "a kind of literary and social administration."[24]

Dena Goodman claims that disputatious philosophes who "groaned about the constraints placed upon them by the salonnières" continued to attend salons regularly because they "counted on the salonnière to support and uphold rules of polite discourse" in order to bring harmony to the Republic of Letters. Her argument is meant to contest the assertion that the politesse practiced in salons was a "barrier to spontaneous conversation" and a check on the audacity of thought, which certain philosophes hoped to escape by gathering outside the presence of women.[25] The evidence on this score is inconclusive: some salonnières were paragons of propriety who nevertheless entertained all subjects; others appreciated an animated conversation but insisted on circumspection in deference to the established order. Rules did not always ensure the orderly discussion of ideas, and intellectual sociability could occur outside of salons, which suggests that intellectuals attended salons for respectability and renown regardless of whether they could talk freely or were on a leash. The rules salonnières enforced were those of high society, and the propriety philosophes had to observe was meant to make an Encyclopedist fit company for a duke.[26] That is why Carolyn Lougee's characterization of the salon as both a school of manners and a social crucible seems more than sufficient as an answer to the paradox Goodman raises. Beginning in the seventeenth century, salons served to bring together nobles and intellectuals in an atmosphere of civility and fair play in order to educate one, refine the other, and create a common medium of cultural exchange based on a shared notion of *honnêteté* that combined learning, good manners, and conversational skill.[27] Salons were not responsible for the emergence of a new sociology that resulted from the sale of offices, misalliances, commerce, education, and literary achievement, but they did attend to the new reciprocity of cultural needs such forces brought about. Salonnières were not gatekeepers determining the composition of either high society or the Republic of Letters, and they did not admit newcomers to salons in order to given them a "proper education," as if any bumpkin could walk in off the street.[28] "I discovered two things," wrote Madame de Genlis upon entering the society of the duchesse d'Uzès, "first, that one ought not to enter into the great world but when one can be on a footing with others, as to dress, &c; and secondly, that, if it had not been for my talents, these persons would have had no wish to invite me." Fear of ridicule probably did more to modify behavior in the eighteenth century than the active pedagogy of the ladies. As Marc Fumaroli puts it, salons were the *écoles supérieures* of fashionable society, where instruction was conducted "by example and symbiosis, not by lessons," and to which access implied "an already remarkable degree of polish."[29]

Writers frequented salons during the Old Regime to enter the world of the rich and powerful, whose confidence and consideration they sought. It was only then that they could hope to have any influence over the principles and conduct of those who dominated the social and political order.[30] "Society people have cultivated their minds, formed their tastes and acquired new pleasures," wrote C.-P. Duclos in 1751. "The men of letters have gained no less advantage. They have found consideration, they have perfected their tastes, polished their minds, softened their manners and on several matters acquired enlightenment such as they would not have found in books." D'Alembert described the same process as one of perfect reciprocity, in which salons made *gens du monde* "more enlightened" and men of letters "more agreeable," but the encounter was not an equal one.[31] Nobles might have wanted an education, but they would never have met with writers in the latter's cafés or *cénacles*. By contrast, men of letters needed the protection, pensions, employment, and subsidies that resulted from social connections they could not have made on their own, and they coveted the insider status that set those invited to salons apart from those who were not. The encounter between writers and le monde in the eighteenth century, therefore, took place largely on the latter's terms: not only was it a "highly restricted affair," but it turned high society rather than men of letters into the tribunal of good taste.[32] Although men of letters might have been the principal attraction in many salons, the aristocracy never relinquished the power to determine the conditions of elite status, even if those conditions were becoming more modern and less rigid. Indeed, the prevailing system by which status was defined left nobles in a position to move the bar. According to Joseph-Alexandre de Ségur, fashionable women of the early eighteenth century pushed "the elegance of manners" to the level of "Attic perfection" to make them more difficult to acquire, a practice Genlis saw repeated in the 1770s, when there appeared "a very numerous party of both sexes, who declared themselves the partisans and depositories of the old traditions respecting taste, etiquette, and moral themselves" so as to "claim for themselves exclusively the high-sounding appellation of *good company*" in order to exclude from society "every person of bad *ton*, or licentious notoriety."[33] The point is not that men of letters were always subject to the dictates of the highest social circles, but that a system that gave aristocratic women the role of *arbiter elegantiarum* ensured that entry into society entailed a large degree of conformity.

Historically, the salon was an aristocratic institution that served the needs of the aristocracy in its encounter with other classes.[34] Salon sociability was closely tied to the redefinition of nobility from a title based on birth to an attribute based on behavior, but nobles were always in a position to determine such new definitions (for themselves and others) by integrating everything they touched into an aristocratic system of values. Salon sociability challenged the society of orders under the Old Regime by mingling members of the nobility and the bourgeoisie, but it was not an egalitarian institution. The divestiture of "all the concrete distinctions" of "real social existence" by those who entered salons did not simply eradicate habits learned in a corporative social order.[35] Laws of etiquette and theories of conversation elaborated in the seventeenth century established an aristocratic tradition of reciprocity and good will in private gatherings that became increasingly relevant once the symbiosis that took place between le monde and the Republic of Letters during the eighteenth century enhanced the need to disguise social distinctions and relations of power in the presence of men of low birth and modest fortunes who nevertheless possessed a valuable form of cultural capital. The harmony and mutual respect that reigned in the salons came not only from the talents of the hostess or the intrinsic nature of sociability but from the general ethos of aristocratic society. Politeness meant first and foremost that one treated as equals those whom one admitted into one's home. According to Madame de Genlis, "all enmities were suspended in society" by "a tacit and general convention" that demanded that even the bitterest rivals "treated each other with all the outward tokens of regard and politeness." Madame de Boigne found nothing wrong with "the English system of social gradation" while abroad during the emigration, but, as a Frenchwoman, her "social instincts were irritated when [she] saw that system in operation in the drawing room." "In France," she wrote, "such treatment would not endure for a moment" because "the mistress who issues invitations for a dinner or an evening party is under an obligation to those who come."[36]

The French notion of conversation involved a tacit exchange of confidence and trust based on the mutually assumed honesty of those with whom one interacted. Intimate conversation in salons imposed on invited outsiders the obligation to express something close to friendship in a manner that excluded the sort of rancor and jealousy born of inequality, without actually erasing the real inequities of power that made the encounter possible in the first place. Salons met in private homes at the salonnière's expense, so that writers frequenting le monde did so as guests entering a situation with a material dimension that implied at least the acknowledgment of existing social hierarchies and a degree of moral subordination.[37] Salonnières regularly performed a bit of magic by temporarily suspending the rules of social distance, but they neither sought to nor could abolish the social realities that forced writers to seek society's approval. When Rousseau resisted the co-optation to fashionable society to which so many of his cohorts had succumbed, he expressed his resentment by shooting at the wrong target: association with women neither emasculated writers, tempered their ideas, nor trivialized their conversation, but regular attendance in salons did make them part of the establishment.

Salons reinforced conformity, but they also served to identify, recruit, spotlight, and promote individuals of rare talent. Gender conventions attributed to women a singular ability to understand the human heart. Salonnières used the passivity imposed by their location in the domestic sphere to cultivate the art of observation and psychological analysis, giving rise to the distinctly mondain art of prose portraiture — perhaps best exemplified by the literary character sketches of Madame du Deffand — and leaving women the task of monitoring the integrity, talent, and authenticity of those admitted to society.[38] Salonnières often facilitated the insertion of newcomers into le monde by vouching for the credentials of an unknown writer or by helping a young wife make the acquaintance of a well-connected grande dame. Sometimes, salonnières helped young talent gain entry into a salon by supplying letters of introduction or by arranging for the son of a friend or a relative to be seen and heard in the right company. Such favors were crucial to eighteenth-century writers, because salons had long engaged in aesthetic evaluation and salonnières had long served as intermediaries between intellectuals and gens du monde. Since the judgment of those who met in salons could make or break a writer's reputation, the reception of a work there often determined its success or failure. While it is an exaggeration to call salonnières "power brokers" with the ability to make what amounted to "judicial decisions" in the world of letters, it is nonetheless true that salons were key to the creation and expansion of a new critical public, which drew its members from elite society, the Republic of Letters, and the court.[39]

Salons were important to the philosophes' success because they integrated this audience on an international scale, telegraphed news within it, and brought writers into contact with people who could promote their careers and ideas. Salons, in other words, represented the spectrum of public opinion at its most influential, well-connected, and socially conservative end, where one could gain access to rank, privilege, and even, perhaps, a royal pension. Turgot and the physiocrats frequented the salon of Madame Necker, but they looked to that of the maréchale de Beauvau to gain the approval of Parisian society. According to André Morellet, Geoffrin's principal ambition was not to provide men of letters "intellectual consecration" but "to be useful [by] bringing them together with men of power and position."[40] To seek the publicity afforded by salons, was to seek conventional success — notoriety in le monde. If salons were the theaters and the instruments of the philosophes' fame, it was because they were performing for *grands seigneurs* and had themselves become "men of the world."

The salon's central role in the Enlightenment depended on a "convergence of female and philosophical ambition": salonnières satisfied their educational needs in what amounted to a "surrogate university" and philosophes acquired an institutional base.[41] This mutual exchange involved the provision of a number of services to aspiring and accomplished writers, including publicity, news of politics and the literary world, opportunities to make fruitful connections and contacts to enhance careers, and financial assistance in the form of gifts, pensions, subsidies, and job offers. In addition, salons served as small private academies, affording men of letters venues in which to read new work, hear valuable criticism, gain editorial assistance, carry out the business of publishing, or simply work. But there was a more important reciprocity involved in the relationship between salonnières and philosophes, one in which the former acquired a station in the Republic of Letters as the latter gained an audience among influential people who could help them change the world.[42] In this respect, salons embodied an emerging system of public celebrity in which philosophes used salons to establish and strengthen their influence and reputation while salonnières used celebrated philosophes to magnify the importance, enhance the attractiveness, and ensure the success and survival of their salons. To criticize this position by saying that it assumes "the centrality of men in the actions of women" is beside the point: a salonnière could only attract the best society by providing a well-regarded place to meet, so that it was not men who were central to her actions but rather the fame and success of her salon, which was her own creation.[43]

A successful salonnière was one who could attract celebrities whom others wanted to see and hear. Madame Geoffrin, who was proud to have as guests the princess d'Anhalt-Zerbst (mother of the future Catherine the Great), Gustave III of Sweden, David Hume, and Benjamin Franklin, saw herself as providing writers and artists with a platform for their talents.[44] In this regard, Madame de Rambouillet set a very high standard, having attracted to her *hôtel* the likes of Richelieu, the duke of Buckingham, and the princesse de Conti, along with Bousseut, Corneille, and academicians like Voiture, Malherbe, and Desmartes de Saint-Sorlin.

The practice of organizing a salon around a principal guest had become well-established by the eighteenth century — as Horace Walpole commented, "Every woman has one or two [*auteurs du logis*] in her salon" on whom she "heaped praise." For Mesdames de Lambert and Tencin that role was filled by Fontenelle. Madame de Châtelet had Voltaire, and so did Deffand, who also had Chastellux, Turgot, and d'Alembert before she had to surrender the latter to Lespinasse. Madame d'Epinay had Grimm, Necker had Buffon, and the Holbachs had Diderot. In purely mondain salons, it was much the same: gatherings at the home of the duchesse de Gramont drew their fame from the presence of the duc de Choiseul, and Madame de Mauconseil coaxed society to Bagatelle by holding parties for King Stanisław II of Poland.[45]

III

How big was the social world in which the philosophes sought fame, fortune, and influence? Recent literature on Parisian public opinion in the eighteenth century has not been terribly clear about the social contours of the public. Although there is general agreement that the reading public was much larger in the 1780s than earlier in the century, its size and scope remain amorphous.[46] At the same time, studies of the Enlightenment speak of le monde as having a tangible institutional structure by identifying the court, the salons, and the Republic of Letters as among its constituent parts, but they offer no consistent description of the relationship between these entities, their commonalities, borders, barriers, and frontiers.

During the Bourbon Restoration, the aristocrats of Faubourg Saint-Germain liked to describe le monde as consisting of those received at court, but this appraisal reflected a desire to restrict its growing dimensions. No doubt, court and society had been synonymous in the sixteenth century, but courtly manners soon spread to the capital as the cultural influence of the monarchy grew beyond its grasp. According to Elias, court society underwent a process of decentralization between the last days of Louis XIV and the outbreak of the Revolution, with "a tightly knit social formation" evolving into a looser one as centers of "convivial life" migrated first from Versailles to a series of "small courts" presided over by princes and princesses of the blood, and then into the homes of innumerable aristocrats and financiers. The Goncourts paint a similar picture, contrasting the early days of Louis XIV's reign, when Versailles still dominated everything and le monde did not exist, with the middle of the reign, when social life broke away from the court and flowed into Paris, branching and spreading, throbbing and flowering "in a thousand drawing rooms." In 1689, the chevalier de Méré described le grand monde as extending "everywhere" but as being more "accomplished [in] manners of living and behaving" than the court, suggesting that the institutions of le monde were simply distillations of the latter, composed of courtiers who sought a select company in order to escape the court's din, but who did not want to remove themselves from the social world its expansion called into being.[47]

The contours of le monde have become harder to discern in light of recent scholarship suggesting that the distance between the court and le monde in the eighteenth century grew as the Republic of Letters increased its influence over the latter and tried to "define a new center" hostile to the existing order. Under this scenario, the Republic of Letters remained "a part of le monde" even as contact between nobles and intellectuals modified the content of an older sociability of divertissement by bringing "philosophy down from the heavens and into the drawing rooms of polite company" and by producing a general culture of casual learning and affability at odds with the rigidities of absolutism and the society of orders. As philosophical salons helped to create a critical public, they moved "beyond the sphere of the court proper," ceased to be mondain, and became institutions of the "public sphere."[48]

Efforts to delineate le monde from salons and the court tend to obscure the fact that le monde operated primarily as a great medium of social encounters and cultural exchange of which the court and the salons were a part. The problem is not to distinguish between its component parts but to analyze how this medium was structured and how it worked. The court, salons, and the Republic of Letters were three relatively well-defined areas of distinction within a larger and more amorphous world in which people and ideas circulated according to various pathways structured by distances, proximities, exclusions, and relationships. Such pathways made it possible for individuals who never encountered one another to be part of the same milieu. Madame de La Tour du Pin, who did not belong to the Republic of Letters, was nevertheless connected to the salon of Madame Necker through her aunt, Madame d'Hénin, a courtier married to the younger brother of the prince de Chimay, who was linked both to the very mondain maréchale de Beauvau and "a swarm of Turgot's followers." The circle of the princesse d'Hénin itself was made up of "the most elegant and highly-considered coterie of Paris" whose members were "by birth . . . all of importance and high rank." They were, nevertheless, "all what we then called 'philosophes,' or free-thinkers" who "upheld one another, defended one another, adopted one another's ideas, friends, opinions, and taste." Voltaire, Rousseau, d'Alembert, Condorcet, Suard, and other philosophes "were not of this circle," she explained, "but their principles and ideas were eagerly adopted by it and many gentlemen of these ladies' acquaintance did frequent this group of literary men, which in those days was quite separate from the world of the Court." Elsewhere in her *Mémoires*, when trying to situate Josephine de Beauharnais in le monde, La Tour du Pin was forced to describe an entire social cartography:

> Josephine had, in fact, given [Napoléon] to understand that she herself belonged to [the upper ranks of society]; this was not quite true. I do not know if she had been

presented at Court or had had the *entrée* at Versailles — though the rank of her first husband, M. de Beauharnais, would certainly have made this possible. However, even if she had been presented, she would not have belonged to that class of lady who, after their first presentation, returned to Court only on New Year's Day.

Between 1787 and 1791, I used to see M. de Beauharnais daily in fashionable society. As he had also seen a great deal of M. de La Tour du Pin while my husband was aide-de-camp to M. de Bouillé during the American War, M. de Beauharnais asked him to call so that he might meet his wife. M. de La Tour du Pin did call on them once, but not again. They moved in different circles from ours. M. de Beauharnais, however, was accepted everywhere, for during the war he had become acquainted with many of the highest in the land.[49]

Society, wrote Ségur, was a unity that nevertheless extended in a thousand directions to points where members might lack "habitual communication."[50] It was a world of comings and goings, where different circles might share the same acquaintances, where husbands and wives had their own circles of relations, which did not intersect, where the habits and rituals of the court found their way into the salons, and where the balance of influence between the court and the city could shift back and forth without one center ever eliminating or supplanting the other. The circulation of people and ideas in le monde required a lowering of social and cultural barriers, but it did not necessarily efface the distinctions and prejudices that gave rise to its various coteries, demarcations, and institutions.[51] Nor did it determine the content of what circulated there: le monde could be a conduit for civilized values and advanced ideas as well as the latest culinary fashion and the intrigues of the duc de Choiseul. The medium was not the message.

In its progressive guise, it was above all a force for the social and cultural homogenization that resulted from the novel encounters it made possible. Anne-Pierrette Paulze, the future Madame Lavoisier, met her husband in the salon of her father, a director of the Compagnie des Indes and the nephew of the abbé Terray, *contrôleur générale des Finances;* the maréchale de Beauvau, married to the daughter of a princess, saw the English poet and Whig parliamentarian Charles Fox in the salon of Madame du Deffand and exclaimed: "I shall have supper to-night with him at the Neckers, with [the English] ambassador and ambassadress; tomorrow he will have supper with me and Mesdames de Luxembourg, de Cambis et Boisgelin, at the Chevalier de Boufflers." Upon leaving a reception at the royal palace just prior to the Revolution, Madame de Boigne reported that some courtiers returned to Paris while others went to the various salons of Versailles; at the same time, Madame de Montesson, who yearned to establish herself there for the season and was anxious to be at "the center both of social life and business affairs," was not welcome at court and was forced to open a salon in the capital, where many courtiers mixed with those who had never been presented. Clearly, le monde could be traversed by many routes. High nobles, returning to ancestral homes in the summer or taking up residence in provincial capitals as administrators, acted as emissaries of the capital and received people whom they would never have encountered at Versailles. At the same time, lesser nobles who were not admitted to court were treated like *seigneurs* at home and were welcomed by local aristocrats who were familiar with Parisian society and with courtiers exiled to the provinces. Voltaire showed up occasionally at the salon of Mademoiselle de Rochebaron, who entertained the aristocracy of Lyon; at Besançon, Madame de La Corse, wife of the *intendant*, who held a literary salon in Paris, was at the center of local high society.[52]

Within le monde, salons functioned as points of refinement that gave a measure of organization and stability to what Madame de La Tour du Pin called "the social whirl."[53] Regularity, a fixed location endowed with the requisite material resources, and the practice of attracting a shifting collection of guests around a nucleus of habitués made salons perfect for providing ballast in a world of autonomous circles that came together and dissolved at different moments as people circulated between them. The duc de Saint-Simon recognized this aspect of salons as early as the seventeenth century when he called the Hôtel de Rambouillet a "gathering place for all that is most distinguished in condition and merit," as did the Abbé Galiani in the eighteenth, when he told Madame d'Epinay that high society in Naples needed "a woman to guide us, organize us, *Geoffrinise* us" so that it could acquire the intimacy and coherence necessary for the presentation of serious manuscripts.[54] Indeed, the tendency of salons to sort out features present in le monde was evident in the double meaning acquired by the appellation *grand* that was often attached to it. *Grand* could refer to le monde's general size and extent, or it could designate a select group within it, which was considered *grand* not because it was large, but because it was "the most choice and brilliant by the rank, personal estimation, *ton* and manners of those who compose it."[55]

Salons helped give le monde a measure of coherence in a time of social and cultural transition. The number of salons grew in the eighteenth century, and continued to grow in the next, not only because le monde became larger, but because a larger sociable world produced more sites of discrimination. That is why the size of le monde was ultimately in the eyes of the beholder: its potential dimensions could be calculated statistically by juggling figures related to literacy, the book trade, titles of nobility, the government payroll, and annual revenue, but its real dimensions were always changing because its members arrogated to themselves the right to determine its frontiers. For some, the grand monde consisted of a few select circles meeting in the salons of a single neighborhood; for others, it was made up of all who loved beauty and truth.

Salons proliferated in the eighteenth century as le monde grew — between the two there was a distinction, but no barrier. "The eighteenth century," wrote Baron Auguste-François Fauveau de Frénilly, "was the century of the word and especially of the spirit of conversation," when "innumerable salons flourished in Paris and in all the towns." It was, Gilbert Stenger asserts, "the most brilliant era of salons," when, according to the Goncourts, French society was "teeming and full-blown" with "a thousand drawing rooms." The society of the Paris magistracy alone, Chancellor Pasquier recalled, had "more than thirty *salons* where there was no lack of agreeable and solid conversation."[56] Goodman judges that in the 1780s, the number of salons was "necessarily small" because she confines her definition to those of the Enlightenment. In fact, salons were quite numerous, because le monde was much larger than the Republic of Letters.[57]

The same pathways of le monde that connected the court, the salons, and the Republic of Letters made eighteenth-century salon sociability a way of life. D'Agoult's entry into le monde at age sixteen and her subsequent years spent "in the most noble and elegant company" were the consequences of neither deliberation nor personal preference nor character but simply "the assent of general opinion": everybody did it, she recalled, and "we did as everyone else."[58] Nearly all salons opened onto the world of elegant society, like a window onto a garden, making salon sociability a habitual aspect of daily life. Women went into society almost every evening, calling on friends, going to a play, or attending a supper at half past nine. Even if a gentleman did not intend to go himself, he often met visitors in the salon after dinner or accompanied women to the theater at night.[59] Certain gens du monde were notoriously busy, passing through a series of salons in a single day. The comte d'Espinchal, an assiduous guest at the home of Madame Lebrun, was so adept at chasing down salon news about the theater, love, scandals, and politics that people said he was better informed than the police. A constant round of conversations and elegant socializing could leave time for little else. Deffand's drawing room was almost always in use, with afternoon guests giving way to a supper crowd of varying size before new arrivals came from other suppers to play backgammon or whist and prattle late into the night.[60]

A record of Madame de La Briche's activity from December 9, 1788, to April

1789 in the journal of the comte de Diesbach tells the story of a nearly unbroken chain of social events: it began on December 12 at the home of her good friend, Colonel d'Affry; on the fourteenth the party moved to the Diesbachs', and later "chez M. de Garville"; on the seventeenth, it was soup with the comtesse d'Houdetot. The New Year found her again at the d'Affrys' before she and her friends headed off to visit the Montbretons, where they enjoyed "innumerable receptions . . . almost daily." On January 19, Madame de La Briche attended a concert at the duchesse de Caylus's, along with "all society," before being re-united "chez Adélaïde" on the twenty-first with her closest friends at a reception featuring the duc de Crillon, whose eldest son had just been made a *chevalier de la Toison d'or d'Espagne*. Deisbach's tour with La Briche ended with a few musical soirées with the duchesse de Caylus in March, a costume ball with the prince de Salm-Kirbourg on February 9, and dinner with the d'Affrys, where a large group of guests heard a memorable concert.[61]

It is not that salons were rare but rather that the Republic of Letters was very small. The women who presided over the landmark bureaux d'esprit of the eighteenth century belonged to a very select group.[62] The tendency to conflate eighteenth-century salons with the Enlightenment has generally been sustained by two contradictory arguments: that Enlightenment salons and those of le monde ought not be confused, and that the former nevertheless took command of public opinion. Certainly, it became more fashionable in the eighteenth century to welcome artists and men of letters into salons, but literary guests had always been a part of salon culture, their presence was not necessary, and a writer did not turn each salon he attended into a philosophical workshop. Although salons brought together people from various walks of life, most were well-ensconced in a particular milieu. The typical bureau d'esprit belonged to the milieu of men of letters, but there were many other salons that did not. The salons of Mesdames de Sainte-Amaranthe, Sabran, Murinais, Bercheny, Montoissieux, Dufort, Chambonas, and d'Augivilliers were composed mainly of nobles; those of Madame Filleul and Madame de Marigny included artists and writers but catered mostly to the world of finance and commerce. There were salons associated with government officials (Mesdames de Montmorin, Necker, d'Aiguillon), journalists (Madame Panckoucke), the theater (Madame Careau, Mademoiselle Quinault), economists (Trudaine de Montigny), and the entourage of the duc d'Orléans (Madame de Genlis). There were even salons at court, like the one to which Madame de Polignac often invited the queen, which, according to the prince de Ligne, "received all of France on Mondays, Wednesdays, and Thursdays." The salons of Versailles might have been careless of events and absorbed in gambling, but they were still salons, and they were, wrote the vicomte de Reiset, quite à la mode.[63]

The Enlightenment did not appropriate the salons. It is probably more accurate to say that the salons appropriated the Enlightenment, which passed through this venerable institution like a seasonal wind.[64] There is no doubt that many nobles acquired a passion for learning and embraced many currents of modern thought during the latter half of the eighteenth century. There is also much to indicate that the new cultural values were communicated to the nobility through the salons, where, according to Frénilly, revolutionary ideas were "at ease" in some, marginal in others, "but everywhere honorably received" because "they entered in pumps and curls, bearing a name that always finds doors open."[65] Salons clearly contributed to an extraordinary degree of cultural homogeneity among the elite as people from diverse backgrounds read the same books, discussed the same ideas, used the same language, and acquired many of the same tastes. As a result, nobles "laughed at the foibles of their order along with the *philosophes*" and contemplated an end to privileges associated with birth. "We were," wrote Madame de Chastenay, "all brought up to think of men as equals, to mistrust vain distinctions, to feel the obligations to be worthy of [equality], to enjoy its benefits as well as the etiquette that increased the price."[66] As salon life demanded higher and higher levels of education, even for the acquisition of a superficial brilliance, learning became highly valued in elite circles and those without it were made to feel self-conscious. Pasquier recalled feeling both his ignorance and a strong desire to remedy it upon entering le monde and encountering many people "with a pronounced taste for the enjoyments of the mind." He subsequently acquired a "taste for assiduous and careful reading" and began to attend lectures to which "the best elements of Parisian society flocked." The status of writers had risen enormously in this respect since the 1670s, when the chevalier de Méré had condemned learning and warned nobles to avoid the *ordure* of the universities. As Malesherbes famously observed in his introductory remarks to the French Academy in 1775, "The public displays an avid curiosity about things to which it was formerly totally indifferent."[67]

The Enlightenment succeeded in expanding the boundaries of permissible public discourse by making itself acceptable in salons. Salonnières censored certain topics of discussion out of moral circumspection or in deference to royal officials and court society. Philosophes enjoyed the patronage of aristocrats and obtained public offices, despite incidents of persecution and a certain weariness of noble largesse and royal sponsorship of the arts.[68] As the moderate Enlightenment became semi-official in the 1770s, radical intellectual currents emerged outside of salons as a younger generation of marginal writers, fired by passion or jealousy, moved to the left and began to form alternative institutions of sociability. Salon culture did not disappear, nor were salons displaced, but an entirely new stratum of places for discussion and expression spread beyond their purview, and in opposition to their by now respectable criticism of the established order, blending into the "literary underground" described by Robert Darnton.[69]

Alexis de Tocqueville found it remarkable that the eighteenth-century aristocracy should have treated "the doctrines most hostile to their prerogatives" as "mere flights of fancy, entertaining *jeux d'esprit*" at a time when the spread of "new political theories" threatened its survival.[70] In fact, most nobles looked to the philosophes not for a political program so much as a coherent language with which to speak about realities they had already come to accept. The Enlightenment represented (not merely recommended) the cultural homogenization of the elite, and therefore made possible a way of talking about social relations that were already normal in salons, academies, and in the economy as well. The Revolution for a time disguised the makings of a social compromise that was already well under way.[71] It is this development, rather than the nobility's blindness or frivolity, that explains why so many nobles accepted a new way of thinking about the social assimilation of commoners while rejecting the idea that privileges of birth should no longer be recognized and guaranteed; why they clung to their "immunities and privileges [and] talked lightheartedly of the 'absurdity' of all the old French customs"; why they demanded individual liberties, accepted fiscal equality, and approved of promotion by merit, but remained attached to titles, honors, and *seigneuries;* and why they scoffed at traditional religion but sent their servants to church.[72] One ought not confuse intellectual commitment and the sociocultural import of an idea, erudition and the serious discussion of cultural products in salons; nor should one fail to distinguish between an attitude and an ideal. The Enlightenment was a matter of values for nobles, not philosophy: as Suzanne Fiette puts it, there is a very large gap between "the ideal society constructed by reason and culture considered only as a social quality." There was no unmediated relationship between the content of "public opinion" and what philosophers wrote in books; if the former was a "tribunal," there is no reason automatically to think of the latter as its "magistrates."[73]

The nobility was already well disposed to give a hearing to bourgeois concepts of individual merit and public service because such values were similar to older aristocratic notions of virtue, honor, and independence.[74] At the same time, nobles took a particularly selfish interest in such values by using them to articulate a new conception of nobility designed to assert the relevance of the Second Order in a period in which traditional values were in crisis and traditional definitions of nobility were under attack. This was a task made all the more urgent by the fact that the Second Order had become too large for cohesion and too restricted for those seeking social promotion in the face of the crown's failure to point the way toward a consensual social accommodation. The disunity of the Second Estate that resulted from the Ségur edict of 1781, which excluded recent nobles from the military, served to demonstrate that all efforts to shore up the society of orders would lead to social confusion and that the elites themselves would have to produce the criteria by which they were going to be ranked. It is no surprise, then, that the nobility played such a preponderant role in the Enlightenment, contributing many of its most important representatives and presiding over some of its most prominent salons. As Madame de La Tour du Pin noted on the eve of the Revolution, the upper classes denounced abuses and spoke passionately of a national rebirth, fully confident of their own security.[75]

IV

In 1834, the English writer Edward Bulwer Lytton proclaimed that "woman is queen in France," dominating everywhere, despite her exclusion from the throne, because she "reigned by a power greater than laws." A year later, Lytton's compatriot, Mrs. Trollope, dubbed France "le paradis des femmes," where the fairer sex had "more power and exercised a greater influence" than the women of England.[76] The two foreigners undoubtedly heard such assertions from their society friends in Paris, who themselves imbibed this unique and generally held form of French exceptionalism as a legacy of the aristocratic eighteenth century.

Lytton and Trollope were echoing aspects of a traditional representation of old-regime feminine power that found mature expression during the nineteenth century in Edmond and Jules de Goncourt's *La Femme au dix-huitième siècle,* although it had innumerable incarnations in earlier works. "Women," the Goncourts wrote,

> was the governing principle, the directing reason and the commanding voice of the
> eighteenth century. She was the universal and fatal cause, the origins of events, the
> source of things. . . . Nothing escaped her; within her grasp she held the King and

France, the will of the sovereign and the authority of public opinion — everything! She gave orders at court, she was mistress in her home. She held the revolution of alliances and political systems, peace and war, the literature, the arts and the fashions of the eighteenth century, as well as its destinies, in the folds of her gown; she bent them to her whim or to her passion. . . . From one end of the century to the other, government by woman was the only visible and appreciable government, possessing the consequences and mechanism, the reality and activity of power, without fail, apathy, or interval.

In this retelling of the political history of eighteenth-century France, women's power was portrayed as pervasive, but hidden from view. "Woman touched everything. She was everywhere," they explained. Her domination extended through the force of intrigue to the king and spread everywhere about him — to each minister, to their offices, and to every position and appointment at Versailles, until it reached throughout society and "descended to its lowest ranks." She "lurked in the shadows," conducted secret maneuvers, acted behind the scenes, "granting audiences, receiving reports from her spies, and attending the Council of Ministers." Devoured by ambition, she grew more masculine as she schemed, acquiring characteristics needed to rule the state, evincing, "a greatness superior to the instincts of her sex," and, in the process, emasculating men both politically and intellectually. In the end, women filled the void left by a degenerating monarchy: "And while the throne of France diminished and imparted disrespect to the people, the salons held the gaze and the attention of the public. In the interregnum of royal greatness, they tried to reign. In the era of Louis XVI, this latent, unofficial, but real and continuously active, domination grew by virtue of the voluntary abdication of a court, purified but without either spark or initiative."[77]

One version of this traditional representation depicted women as potent but ethereal, as sovereigns who reigned but did not rule. Often painted in the language of flattery, and usually associated with salonnières, such women were described as queens who presided over empires, who were surrounded by a bevy of admiring courtiers, who exercised a secret power through coquetry, personality, or magic, but who accomplished nothing in particular. In the other version, which was more common, women both reigned and ruled — mostly from behind the scenes. We see them leading political coteries and factions at court, planning strategy, dictating foreign and domestic policy, taking a hand in treaty negotiations, removing ministers, arranging alliances, and getting favorite men of letters elected to the Académie française. This fantasy of eighteenth-century France as a hidden matriarchy has had a successful run in literary studies and in historical scholarship as well.[78]

While the traditional discourse on feminine power allows distinctions between intriguers and goddesses, it does not distinguish between salonnières and the women of the court, between scheming royal mistresses and patrons of the Republic of Letters. This is because it conflates court intrigue with the influence salons supposedly wielded in the literary world. It does so by replicating in descriptions of women's influence in the arts the language used to describe their covert and illegitimate political power, and by using the participation of the court, the salons, and the Republic of Letters in le monde as proof that women dominated everything. On the one hand, salonnières used their authority to confirm literary reputations in private before they were publicly consecrated by election to the Academy. By exercising a form of "spiritual royalty" in presiding over the literary world and governing the Republic of Letters, women shaped public opinion. On the other hand, government during the decay of absolutism was directed by this same public opinion, which was made in equal measure at court, in the salons, and by men of letters. All of these entities taken together constituted a much larger one called le monde, which was controlled by women and intervened in every facet of political life. Consequently, "the most important decisions of national and international policy" were made not only at court, but in the city, at the Palais-Royal, in the *hôtels* of Condé and Conti, and "in the salons of an infinite number of grandes dames." The Goncourts themselves made more or less explicitly analogous the antechamber of a royal favorite, where favors were held and withheld, and that of an eighteenth-century salonnière, "this all-powerful mistress who decides on the value of a work and on the standing of writers." In this imaginary world, feminine sovereignty operated through women's control of the empire of conversation, which was solipsistically mistaken by French high society for the source of all things. As Sophie Gay put it with stunning pretension, the *maîtresse de maison* "has the right of life or death over all conversations; and, in France, the power to make someone talk about what one wants comes very close to the power to make them do it."[79]

This composite portrait of feminine power might appear anachronistic today if contemporary feminist scholarship had not revived a number of its central themes by repeating the analogy between salonnières and royal women and by insisting that women "exercised a considerable degree of power" in salons, where their "leadership" was similar to that "accorded royal women in matters of taste and pleasure."[80] Arguments of this sort tend to equate an anomalously high level of gender mixing in French institutions of sociability with a uniquely high degree of feminine political power.[81] But the traditional representation of feminine political power, whatever element of truth it may contain, cannot successfully be applied to eighteenth-century salons. It is not simply that most eighteenth-century salonnières lacked access to power; there is also little evidence that they practiced a courtly style of politics by scheming to advance the careers of their guests. Geoffrin may have patronized artists, and Deffand may have supported d'Alembert's election to the Academy, but this did not necessarily constitute intrigue. Haussonville specifically denied that Madame Necker befriended philosophes to implement "an ambitious design planned beforehand . . . to bring her husband to power." In the opinion of Madame de Genlis, "It would be unjust to class among intriguers all who engage in public affairs without holding public situations, for the love of the public good, and the desire of serving friends may govern the mind as well as avarice and ambition; I have known virtuous men and worthy ladies who had great talent for public affairs, and I approved of their conduct for interfering, because they were guided by honorable motives, and their disposition and talents were such as to lead to success in this career."[82]

The power of women in the eighteenth century is something of an optical illusion that magnified and made remarkable what was simply an aristocratic alternative to the dissipation of court life and the servitude of the Victorian private sphere, one that was subsequently effaced by the onslaught of bourgeois domesticity. A more circumspect characterization of feminine power in the eighteenth century does not, however, invalidate suggestions that there was a relationship between salons and politics under the Old Regime. Is it possible to describe salons as political before 1789? If so, what was it about eighteenth-century politics that gave salonnières access to the political sphere?[83]

There is no doubt that people discussed political matters in salons before 1789, and that interest in politics grew as the Revolution approached. The courtiers, nobles, and men of letters who gathered in the salon of Madame de Tencin openly criticized Louis XV; foreign affairs was a topic of great interest with Voltaire at Fernay. In the salons of the comtesse de Boufflers and the comtesse d'Egmont, where great nobles expressed their aspirations for a constitutional monarchy, a whole range of economic and administrative reforms were held up for consideration. When Lafayette returned after the War of American Independence, he was fêted there as well as in the salons of Madame Necker and Madame Helvétius, where Benjamin Franklin was a frequent guest. At the Suards', the

American War occasioned numerous exposés by members of the Academy on the state of French colonial affairs; Madame de Lespinasse oversaw discussions of constitutional reform in the company of Turgot. In the provinces, interest in politics was just as great: salons held by the wives of members of the parlements like Madame Duplessis at Bordeaux and Madame de Cambon at Toulouse attracted a distinguished company of governors, intendants, and especially magistrates for conversations that touched on "all the acts of the central government and local authorities." The marquise de La Tour du Pin found the amount of political talk to which events gave rise in the decades before the Revolution both tiresome and disconcerting.[84]

But is talking politics the same as politics itself? Were the campaigns launched in salons by the philosophes to capture the Academy political because the Academy was a state institution, because academicians had influence on public opinion, or because all politics at the time were discursive? Was there an important difference between a salon conversation about the grain trade among men of letters and one that took place in the presence of Turgot when he was controller general? Did Jacques Necker need to be present in his wife's salon when policy matters were discussed, or was it enough that she had her husband's ear? Ought politics not to imply a connection between opinions and the means to make them a reality in public life, a connection, that is, between theory and practice? Madame d'Hénin discussed the need for a constitution with the marquis de Lally-Tolendal in her salon after he had been elected to the Assembly of Notables in 1787 — did that mean her salon had "influence?" Upon becoming controller general, Turgot nominated Suard and Condorcet, fellow habitués at the home of Lespinasse, for official positions — did that make her salon a courtly antechamber? The Swedish ambassador, Baron de Staël, gave advice to his monarch from 1786 to 1789 about the French political scene based on conversations that took place in his mother-in-law's salon on the rue de Bergère and in his wife's drawing room at the embassy on the rue du Bac — does that mean that Madame de Staël and her relations had the power to shape Swedish government policy?

"All the literary myths that form the symbolic architecture of salons [*des sociétés mondaines de conversation*]," Fumaroli writes, "are myths of the life of noble leisure, set apart from daily business and public affairs."[85] That is why salonnières and their guests experienced the politicization of le monde as a difficult transition. At no time was the ambiguity of the salon's relationship to politics as pronounced as in the last years of the Old Regime, and in no salon was this truer than in that of Madame Necker. There, participants had to live through a profound change without having experienced the Revolution that would eventually give it meaning. They also enjoyed an entirely undefined and unofficial position halfway between the court and public opinion. Although Madame Necker launched her Paris salon to enhance the reputation of her husband, hers was a purely literary affair from its opening in 1776 until Necker's appointment to high office in 1781. Recognized generally as "the last of the great literary salons" of the eighteenth century, it was nevertheless more firmly tied to the political world and daily events than any other.[86] The transition from philosophy to politics was a matter of leadership, style, and personnel: it occurred not only during the interval between Necker's two ministries (1781 to 1788) but also at the time of Germaine Necker's marriage, the opening of her own salon on the rue du Bac, and her increasing centrality among the guests at the rue de Bergère. "Political matters, for which Mme. Necker had never felt any strong interest, gained the upper hand over literary discussions" as Germaine became "acknowledged as the queen of the drawing-room," according to Haussonville. A salon that "had been purely literary," he continued, "became nearly exclusively political," the daily meeting place of "the Liberal Opposition."[87] Whereas Madame Necker had gathered with Buffon, La Harpe, and Marmontel in order to help Necker gain renown in the eyes of the enlightened public, Madame de Staël enjoyed the company of Lafayette, Clermont-Tonnerre, Narbonne, Talleyrand, and Lameth and worked actively to win him the support of the philosophes, the opposition *parlementaire*, and members of the diplomatic corps. The transition was abrupt as well: in the 1770s, Madame Geoffrin had managed to banish political discussions, but Madame Necker could no longer hold back the flood. The latter had shown a certain "severity" toward nonliterary subjects, had tried to treat controversial matters academically, and regretted the politicization of her salon in the 1780s. Nevertheless, with the advent of Madame de Staël, according to Simone Balayé, the "era of the philosophes was over, that of the politicians had begun."[88] That is why commentators have never been able to decide whether Madame Necker's salon was the Old Regime's last literary salon or its first political salon.

Madame Necker was not a court intriguer, but Jacques Necker, unlike an English minister, had no power independent of the court. There is no doubt that Necker recognized public opinion as a new force in politics, but public opinion was not embodied in his wife's salon. On the one hand, Necker's political career clearly influenced Madame Necker's activities—not only were "new elements, social and political" introduced into her home, but the men of letters who had been paying their respects to the maîtresse de maison began to expect results.

When Marmontel read Necker's public accounting of royal finances in the *Compt rendu au roi*, he was not only filled with admiration, he was also filled with ideas. He had "advice upon everything, upon the government of landed property and upon the financial accounts of the navy," advice "you may throw . . . to M. Necker," as he said to the minister's wife. Diderot asked her to recommend his son-in-law to her husband for a job. Madame Necker might not have been an intriguer at court, but her proximity to power created the expectation that she had influence; "therefore it came to pass," wrote Haussonville, "that people attributed to Mme. Necker an exercise of power in determining academical elections."[89] In other words, the politicization of high society makes any useful distinction between salonnières and courtly women harder to sustain. Necker's salon anticipated arrangements created in abundance by the Revolution, and especially by the advent of representative government in the first half of the nineteenth century.

Salons became political in the 1780s because the public sphere was politicized in the final years of the Old Regime. At a time when new forms of political sociability emerged both inside and outside le monde, existing salons whose members had not paid attention to politics began to do so as politics insinuated itself into places where it had previously been excluded or ignored. At Versailles in the 1770s, most people were preoccupied with either intrigue, society events, or personal interest, but "[n]o one thought of national politics," according to Madame de Boigne. A decade later, courtiers were "content to talk of abolishing abuses" but politics never became an obsession at court and most gens du monde were oblivious to any approaching danger. "Amid all these pleasures," wrote La Tour du Pin, "we were drawing near to the month of May 1789, laughing and dancing our way to the precipice."[90] Elsewhere in high society, however, the clamor of political chat became deafening in the 1780s and the increased volume was experienced as an abrupt change. Chateaubriand recalled that it was not until Necker's first ministry and the publication of the *Compt rendu* that "women discussed expenses and receipts." Others, however, pushed the moment of politicization forward a couple of years: the duchesse Laure d'Abrantès observed that politics had not yet invaded the salons of Paris at the time of Madame de Staël's marriage in 1786, which tends to support Habermas's contention that the philosophes did not turn their critical attention to politics until "the years just before the Revolution."[91] For many contemporaries, the crucial turn occurred in 1787, with the meeting of the Assembly of Notables, the event that induced everyone to discuss political theories. "During the Assembly of Notables, which I found unbearably boring," wrote La Tour du Pin, "politics were the sole topic of every conversation. All who entered the drawing-room had some infallible remedy for the treasury deficit as well as for the abuses which had been allowed to grow within the state." According to Pasquier, "politics occupied a small place" in the concerns of Parisian society before 1788, the year Madame de La Briche started to complain about the "air of malevolence" and extreme partisanship that was causing "the alarms that preceded the Estates General," making the winter "unbearable." Whatever the exact date, it is clear that in 1789, politics was still a great novelty in France.[92]

It is impossible to determine what was and what was not political under the Old Regime because absolutism cast a veil of uncertainty around all forms of politics that did not emanate from the king. Either everything that impinged on public affairs that did not relate to royal initiative was political — and politically subversive — or everything was simply moot. Only the Revolution, which gave those with opinions the opportunity to act, cleared up the ambiguity and gave salons the chance to become more than forums of urbane conversation. That is why Habermas is justified in thinking that only the convening of the Estates General "created in France overnight . . . the institutions which until then had been lacking for critical public debate of political matters." As Augustin Challamel put it in 1895, "political clubs existed for a long time in England; in France, they opened at the time the Estates General held its first session, [when] the clubbists could attempt to imitate, follow, and counterbalance the discussions of the National Assembly."[93]

What role, then, did salons play in this protracted process leading up to the revolutionary opening of 1789? According to Keith Baker, the public of the prerevolutionary era "remained relatively ill-defined" in terms both of its social composition and its political and ideological dispositions. Salons assisted in the clarification that was forced on the public "by the political process set in train by the calling of the Estates General" amid the breakdown of the absolutist state.[94] Salons helped give public opinion more definite contours by providing an organizational structure for the upper classes. At the same time, other regions of the public were forming their own parapolitical organizations outside the sociable institutions of le monde and the opposition of the parlements. Le monde was merely the higher reaches of the public, and salons remained sites of refinement within le monde, as they had always been. As Madame de Chastenay said with regard to Madame Necker's salon during her husband's second ministry, "*le grand monde* was always a restricted framework, in which a coterie marks a more narrow circle." In retrospect, Haussonville called Necker's salon "an Opposition drawing-room." This was also the way Abrantès saw it from the perspective of the 1830s when she wrote that the

> hatreds and fanaticism that would cause the first effects of the Revolution took shape in our salons. In this era, people read very little. Each and every grocer did not have a newspaper to direct his opinion, as is the case today. But he had a cousin who was a *maître d'hôtel*, a sister-in-law who was a chambermaid, or a brother who was a valet, who told him the opinion of their employers. This opinion was often against the queen, because the party opposed to her interests was more numerous than hers; so opinion passed from the salon to the office, and from the office to the boutiques or into the workshops of Paris.[95]

What is striking here is not Abrantès's elitist and amusing trickle-down theory of public opinion. It is her use of the term *parti* to describe the salon's opposition to the interests of the queen and her assumption that public opinion was formed and expressed at the point where people met face to face. There was in the 1780s no language with which to speak about the salon's place in public affairs. The language both Haussonville and Abrantès chose to borrow from a different era seems significant in this regard.

In an era before the advent of the technologies of modern communication, collective political action had to begin at the point where like-minded people could congregate and assess the events of the day, whether in the streets, in cafés, in clubs, or, as was often the case in the early nineteenth century, in the editorial offices of the opposition press. Such beginnings also occurred in private homes, as long as they contained a large drawing room that their owners or inhabitants were rich enough to decorate. In 1789, salons were for the upper classes a principal site for congregation, where information and ideas converged at the point at which people met, and where members of the elite became conscious of the indispensable connection between conversation, an intimate knowledge of public affairs, and the freedom to act on their convictions.

CHAPTER TWO

Liberals and Emigrés (1789–1799)

The French Revolution neither destroyed the salon nor radically altered the social realities that had made it an institution of elite sociability; it did, however, complete the salon's politicization. The form remained the same, but the Revolution changed the conversation: public affairs became a principal preoccupation and salonnières put at the disposal of those who sought active participation in the newly emancipated public sphere the services they had earlier provided men of letters.

The salon's new political vocation gave salonnières and habitués an unprecedented opportunity to merge disinterested critical reflection with the shaping of public opinion; at the same time, the divisiveness of politics challenged the French sociable ideal. It had been easy to equate the salon's aptitude for social mixing and regulated conversation with the search for a unitary public opinion when the public had had no hope of writing legislation, but how would the salon fare in the factional turmoil of ideological politics? How could an institution that had been part of an emerging and autonomous public sphere survive in the face of growing Jacobin hostility toward pluralism, social intermediaries, and the participation of women in public affairs? And how could those who hoped to put the enlightened sociability of the salons at the service of creating a liberal society avoid partisanship themselves in the face of clubbists who rejected their version of the Revolution's potential?

I

When the Revolution "created in France overnight . . . the institutions [necessary] for critical public debate of political matters," it also kindled an explosion of political sociability. Habermas identifies "[c]lub-based parties," associations linked to politicians, and "a politically oriented daily press" as the instruments of the new public sphere. But the list should also include salons. Older forms of elite sociability existed side by side with newly founded ones during the first years of the Revolution and served as ready-made *réunions* for those among whom such sociability had already become an established social practice. Throughout Parisian society in 1789, wrote Chateaubriand, "there were literary gatherings, political societies, and spectacles; the renowned of the future wandered unknown in the crowds, like souls on the banks of the Lethe before taking possession of the light." In the three years between the meeting of the Estates General and the ratification of the constitution of 1791, no fewer than 1,100 *sociétés politiques* were created in France; by the spring of 1793, there were close to 6,000. The same process that gave rise to such associational effervescence also provoked the blossoming of a new aristocratic political sociability.[1]

In May and June of 1789, most gens du monde continued to see one another daily in society. Mondains gatherings were generally more animated than usual: the first émigrés had not yet departed, people were conscious of the importance of events, they were hopeful for reform, and they believed that the crisis would be of short duration. Initially, salon habitués discussed issues, made proposals, or simply gathered to follow the events of the day, listening to news of a speech by Vergniaud, a response by Barnarve, or a declaration by Mirabeau before there was time for them to be reported in the press. Many of the most prominent aristocratic salons of 1789 initially welcomed the Revolution. An Orleanist faction took shape in Madame de Genlis's blue room on the rue de Bellechasse. In the salon of Madame de Tessé, who, according to the Goncourt brothers, had been formulating plans for a constitutional monarchy for twenty years, "the most advanced opinions" found themselves amid what Guizot later called "a small group with elegant manners." The list of aristocratic households that the Goncourts labeled as won over to the Revolution was truly impressive, including those of the marquise de Laval, Madame d'Astorg, the baronnne d'Escars, Madame de Coigny, Madame de Murinet, the duchesse de Gontaut, Madame de Gouvernet, and the prince de Salm, to name just a few. Gouverneur Morris, the American ambassador, described the salons of Mesdames de Broglie, Lafayette, Staël, Beaumont, and Beauharnais as "nearly republican." Meanwhile, deputies of the Right met in the salons of the duchesse de Luxembourg, the maréchale de Noailles, the princesse de Poix, and a number of other aristocratic women before the emigration temporarily relocated la vie mondaine to urban centers abroad.[2]

Salons were politicized when the revolutionary crisis compelled habitués to affirm a particular political orientation.[3] In the process, salons did not change in any formal sense and many salonnières hoped to carry on as if nothing had happened. Madame Panckoucke wanted her salon to remain literary and philosophical after 1789 but was forced to make concessions when her husband, the editor and proprietor of the *Mercure de France*, began to publish the *Monitor universel* and have dinner regularly with Barère. Still, the maîtresse de maison set aside Thursdays for academicians who consented to talk of anything but politics. Madame Necker, who had put up with her daughter's political friends and the transformation of her salon into a sort of public reception hall thanks to Necker's position, tried to confine political discussions to Mondays after eleven o'clock.[4] At the same time, a number of established salonnières eagerly received deputies of varying political hues: Madame de Beauvau met with the leaders of the Third Estate in order to persuade them to rally behind Necker; constitutional monarchists gathered in the salons of Madame de Bailly and Germaine de Staël; and noble deputies with more advanced opinions went to the homes of Madame de Tessé, the princesse de Hohenzollern, and the duc de Rochefoucauld.[5]

Politicization made salons more boisterous and conversation more argumentative. It also turned politicians into celebrities.[6] It did not, however, dramatically alter the customary social practices of salon sociability, because salon habitués who gravitated to monarchist clubs continued to meet in salons. Indeed, the duc de Lévis blamed salons for undermining aristocratic effectiveness in the National Assembly by producing in the representatives of the Second Estate an incapacity for forceful public speaking bred in political society, where everything had to be said softly in a measured and respectful tone.[7] Of course, certain habits had to be altered: habitués spent more time in other réunions or at the National Assembly; salonnières found the pleasures to which they had previously devoted their time displaced. Nevertheless, the basis patterns of mondain sociability remained surprisingly durable in the first two years of the Revolution. Various forms of political sociability tended to coexist, although their functions might differ.

The aristocratic political clubs that emerged between 1788 and 1790 did not replace salons, because they were generally formed for specific reasons or for a limited purpose. The Society of Thirty was created primarily to disseminate the writings of its members, all of whom were salon habitués. Clubs formed by deputies elected to the Estates General, according to Raymond Huard, were the first specifically political associations. Like the Club Breton, they were organized for the purpose of planning parliamentary strategy, influencing public opinion, and recruiting support outside the Assembly. Similar motivations were apparent in the formation of clubs created exclusively by members of the Second Estate: the Club de Viroflay, led by the comte de Clermont-Tonnerre, was formed at Versailles in 1789 to prepare conservative orators who could lead and give greater cohesion to the noble delegation; the Salon français, one of the earliest and largest counterrevolutionary clubs, with nearly 600 members, was founded in 1790 specifically to protest the decree of April 3 in which the National Assembly refused to recognize Catholicism as the state religion. The other important club of the Right, the Club monarchique, was established in 1790 to protest the treatment of the king and to publish the *Journal de la cour et de la ville*.[8] Members of both the right-wing Salon français and the more liberal Club de Viroflay found themselves in the homes of the same aristocratic salonnières after the Assembly moved to Paris, where they could rendezvous in the afternoon or the evening. Madame Helvétius's habitués showed up at Auteuil in the evening after a day of politicking with Mirabeau. Individual deputies, especially nobles, had forged connections with one another in salons (as well as lodges and academies) long before making the decision to form a club. As the duchesse d'Abrantès pointed out, "relations in society [had] contributed to the establishment in this period of an infinity of political relations that might otherwise never have existed."[9]

Clubs and salons inhabited the same political space during the liberal phase of the Revolution, but they were nevertheless distinct. Salons may have played a complex and subtle role in politics, but politics was never their singular or original purpose. As a ritual of sociability rather than a political organization per se, salons continued to bring together people who had begun to attend them regularly before political disagreements might have prompted them to gravitate to rival clubs. Hence, while clubs tended to have homogeneous memberships and clear ideological colorations, salons remained more eclectic. The division of the Assembly into parties did not necessarily bring about a similar political division among salons. A salon usually had a particular orientation or clientele — either liberal or conservative, noble or bourgeois — but a salonnière could easily widen and diversify her society by lengthening her guest list. Moreover, customary practices and self-interest discouraged salonnières from taking sides: dogmatism was considered impolite, coteries were less attractive to a cross-section of society, and instant political celebrity had to be accommodated, as did the universal search for connections. Consequently, the salons of Paris contained many ideological nuances and gradations. For example, the salon of Madame de Pastoret, whose husband was a deputy and minister of the interior in 1790, entertained very mixed company, including conservatives like M. de Vaisnes, despite the couple's well-known moderate views. Madame de Coigny, whom Marie-Antoinette called "the queen of Paris," welcomed conservative aristocrats as well as Lafayette, whose wife also frequented the Convent of Miramiones, "one of the principal foyers of royalist fanaticism."[10]

By mingling elements of the new political sociability with the formalities that regulated le monde, salons could be political coteries, but they could also become neutral terrain. This made them especially useful in political circumstances in which one faction hoped to build bridges to another. Indeed, the queen secretly received members of the National Assembly whom she wished to win over in the salon of the princesse de Lambelle at the Tuileries, which at other times served as a site for conferences "the object of which," according to Joseph Weber, "was to unite the leaders of the different parties in order to plan together and listen to each other in the interest of saving the Constitution, the State, and the King." As for royalist clubs, they acquired a sort of hybrid quality as well: their mostly aristocratic clientele maintained links with the court in a manner similar to the old salons of Versailles and were never fully cut off from a feminine presence. The Club français met in a house on the Butte Saint-Roche belonging to Madame Level, and the Club de Viroflay was in permanent contact with the comte d'Artois, Louis XVI's youngest brother, through the duchesse de Polignac, whose salon its leaders had frequented before the Revolution. Members of the Club monarchique and its successor, the Club des impartiaux, communicated with the court through the salon of the king's aunts at Bellevue and gathered routinely in the aristocratic salons of Paris. Members of the largest royalist club seemed determined to emphasize their connection to the preexisting world of aristocratic sociability by calling their association the Salon français.[11]

The sudden politicization of salons at the beginning of the Revolution provoked diametrically opposed responses. Most gens du monde seemed to join those who, like the duchesse d'Abrantès, believed that political friction caused irreparable harm to France's sociable tradition. Before 1789, she wrote, the philosophes had introduced into the calm of the grand monde an "annoying and contentious spirit," which "confounded all our old and beautiful customs" and threatened to "trampl[e] under foot everything that flourished around the arm-chair of our *maîtresse de maison.*" Once the Revolution began, "[s]ociety changed completely in its usage and its manners," inasmuch as the "revolutionary move-ment communicated a rising power to all who were constrained to follow a path in which they found themselves awkward at first, but then so at ease that it was quite difficult for a maîtresse de maison to impose any sort of consistent regula-tion on her salon." Initially, the trouble was minimal: talented men anxious to prove their patriotism engaged in animated discussions that bore elements of "the excellent tone of former times." Enthusiasm, however, soon gave way to "noisy clashes" and "resounding words." Disputes and duels replaced discussion until "all those delightful reunions which formerly constituted the charm of intimate acquaintance no longer existed, or were poisoned by politics." As a result, women suffered a serious loss of esteem. No longer able to control the contentious spirit that had invaded the salons, the salonnières of the Revolution became "queens without realms" whose power to grant or withhold approval vanished without a trace. Political passions extinguished gallantry in men and made it impossible for women to mediate disputes and call others to their higher nature. In the end, it was no longer possible for a man to flatter a political rival by seating him next to his wife because "the party spirit does not compromise, especially not with *politesse.*"[12]

Such views seem to have been rather common at the time, or to be a widely held retrospective perception, which descriptions of salon life in the early 1790s suggest was at least partly accurate.[13] Madame de Flahaut, who paid attention to political matters despite her tastes and inclinations, felt that her life had been overturned by events. Her salon eventually split in two because of irreconcilable differences between opponents and supporters of the constitution. Madame de La Briche, who found "this air of malevolence" created by political disputes insupportable, was forced to stay away from the salon of the princesse de Poix, who considered her a democrat because of her willingness to have "new doc-trines" discussed in her salon. The Suards' salon was battered not only by politi-cal disagreements between old friends but by Madame Suard's regret at the declining "joy of conversation," her distress over the cost of living, her fear of mounting household debt, and the gloom cast by news of daily arrests. According to the vicomte de Broc, Madame de Kerjean (later the marquise de Falaiseau) became so upset one day by the stormy debates that occurred in a friend's salon over the question of whether or not to emigrate that she fainted.[14]

In contrast to Abrantès's characterization of 1789 as a social disaster, Madame de Staël saw the early years of the Revolution as high society's finest hour. Although she acknowledged that it was harder to mix members of opposing parties when "things became too grave," she nevertheless saw 1789 and 1790 as a time when pluralism reigned, "the scaffold had not been erected," and "the spoken word was still an acceptable mediator." At the end of her life, she recalled the years of the constitutional monarchy as the last time "that the French spirit showed itself in all its luster; the last time, and in some ways also the first, that the society of Paris had succeeded in offering the idea of this communication between superior minds, the most noble enjoyment of which human nature is capable." More important, she believed that the salon life of the time announced the long-awaited marriage between *la philosophie* and *la politique:*

> [O]ne can say with complete honesty that never was this society as brilliant and as serious all at once as during the first three or four years of the Revolution, comprising 1788 to 1791. As political affairs were still in the hands of the elite [*la première classe*], all the vigor of liberty and all the grace of the old *politesse* merged in the same people. The men of the Third Estate, distinguished by their enlightenment and their talent, joined together with those gentlemen who were more proud of their own merit than of the privileges of their estate, and the greatest questions to which the social order has ever given rise were treated by the minds most capable of hearing and discussing them.[15]

Tocqueville argued in the nineteenth century that the problem with the politics of the Old Regime had been that "precepts and practice were kept quite distinct and remained in the hands of two quite independent groups," the actual administrators and the makers of public opinion.[16] Madame de Staël saw the Revolution as ending this schism by creating an opportunity to transform thought into action. Already in 1788, she saw her father as representing the potential of men of genius and good will to realize *la philosophie des lumières;* she drew inspiration from "talent that hopes to be useful." In 1789, she came to see politics as the arena of rational intelligence — during the storming of the Bastille, according to Abrantès, she seized the hand of a friend in her salon at the Swedish embassy and proclaimed that everything was occurring "by the sentiment of conviction." But where could a woman be useful in such times? For the rest of her life, Madame de Staël worked to make her salon a new Athenian symposium where those responsible for the government of men could cultivate the wisdom necessary to bring reason and virtue into the art of making policy and writing legislation. In so doing, she constantly tested the boundary between private and public by trying to bring the values of enlightened sociability into political life and by making women responsible for seeing that the public actions of men would always be informed by the most rigorous commitment to enlightenment and the public good. She thought that this alliance could be consummated in families as well as in salons, so there was no reason for her to assume that women would ever be entirely cut off from the public sphere. Indeed, at times, Madame de Staël seemed to ascribe to French salons a sort of semi-constitutional status, as when she argued under the Directory that women were necessary for public virtue in a free society, or when she described representation as "the political combination that causes the nation to be governed by men selected and combined in such a way that they possess the will and interest of all," suggesting that a people ought to chose its legislators in the same way a skilled salonnière composed her salon.[17]

Habermas claimed that "the Revolution itself combined the two sundered functions of public opinion, the critical and the legislative," but that left women on neither side of a divide that was no longer to exist. Madame de Staël thought long and hard about this exclusion and sought to avoid the fate of *une femme inutile* by writing literature that treated the great issues of the day and by conducting her salon in a way that would have an impact on public affairs.[18] That commitment made hers the first truly political salon. After the convocation of the Estates General, the Swedish embassy on the rue du Bac was a meeting place for constitutional monarchists like Talleyrand, Louis de Narbonne, and Mathieu de Montmorency, who were later joined by Sièyes, Lafayette, Barnave, and the brothers Lameth. According to Abrantès, it "was filled each morning with an immense crowd that flocked to her side seeking not only news, but advice and direction."[19] Although she was associated with the so-called *parti constitutionnel*, and later with the Feuillants, Staël did not make her salon the base of a particular political faction because she knew that ideological exclusivity would restrict its influence and eliminate its function as a neutral space; exclusivity was also incompatible with her view of the Revolution as a process of national regeneration. At first, she used her salon to multiply her father's supporters and make conversation an instrument for change. Eventually, it provided the various leaders of the constitutional Left with a place to meet, exchange opinions, and elaborate a strategy for discussions in the Assembly. Gouverneur Morris observed that her gatherings were always "very mixed" and that she often gave "un dîner de coalition" designed to unite constitutional monarchists around a common program.

After the royal family's flight to Varennes in June 1791, she and her friends used her salon to promote stability by putting together an anti-Jacobin coalition capable of consolidating the gains of the liberal Revolution and winning the king's confidence by supporting a revision of the constitution in favor of strengthening royal authority. At the time of the Legislative Assembly, she and Madame de Condorcet tried to facilitate negotiations between Fayettistes and Brissotins, using their salons to help the two groups coordinate tactics. Staël also used her contacts in the legislature and at court to help secure the appointment of Narbonne as minister of war and, in a related effort, tried to build support in the Assembly for his foreign policy, believing that a war with Austria and an alliance with England and Prussia was the best way to bridge the gap between liberal aristocrats who wanted a war to bolster royal authority and the Girondins, who wanted one in order to strengthen the revolutionary settlement and restore France's international prestige.[20]

Madame de Staël's salon was not the only mondain gathering of liberal aristocrats to make its mark during the first years of the Revolution, only the most famous. In addition, it was able to live on as a model for the liberal salons of the early nineteenth century. Why this should have been so had a great deal to do with Staël herself, who was not only a formidable personality but a prolific writer and a major political thinker in her own right. Moreover, the traditions of her salon were carried forward by her daughter, Albertine de Broglie, and consciously imitated by others. But her salon's reputation was also a result of its particular nature: although, like others of its kind, it did not survive past 1792, it struck the right balance between politics and intellectual pursuits, it never became a coterie, and it never moved too far to the left to be overshadowed by the clubs.

The contrast with Madame de Condorcet's salon at the Hôtel des Monnaies is instructive. Originally dominated by men of letters (Suard, Dupaty, Grimm), distinguished foreigners (Thomas Jefferson), and liberal nobles who, like Condorcet, had frequented the society of the duchesse d'Enville, the salon was eventually drawn into the cauldron of republican politics. By the spring of 1791, it was notable primarily as a place where Girondins and liberal constitutionalists could exchange ideas. Throughout the following year, Sophie de Condorcet and her husband worked at cross-purposes: she wanted to maintain the traditions of an eighteenth-century bureau d'esprit, while he was increasingly preoccupied with his political career and hoped to use the salon to build bridges between the partisans of Lafayette and his new republican friends. As a result, the salon became a debating society that offered little strategic direction; its earlier priorities (educational reform and philosophical discussion) were replaced by advocacy of a liberal republic, especially once Condorcet drew close to Thomas Paine, whose writings Sophie translated and who became the central figure in her salon. With the overthrow of the monarchy and Condorcet's election to the National Convention, moderate republicans lost the initiative, and they were eventually silenced by events. At the end of September 1792, Condorcet's salon was "decimated," according to Abrantès, and Sophie relocated along with her mother and sister to Auteuil, longing for security and calm, and regretting that "popular vengeance [had] profoundly afflicted true patriots." The salon of Madame de Sainte-Amaranthe suffered a similar fate: a mixture of Orleanists and Girondins, it saw a nearly complete "change of inhabitants" as the Revolution became more radical. In the end, the Sainte-Armanthe family was implicated in the conspiracy of Baron du Batz and its women were executed for participating in the *affaire des chemises rouges.*[21]

The other influential salon of the Revolution was that of Madame Roland at the Hôtel britannique on the rue Guénégaud, but it had virtually no imitators in the following century. The reason for this astonishing contrast with the legacy of Madame de Staël, it seems, is that a greater commitment to the ideology of separate spheres, combined with less interest in compromise with nearby factions on the bourgeois Left, made hers not a salon in the traditional sense but a political conference for men that took place in the home of an attentive and well-informed hostess who was married to an important member of the group, who served as minister of the interior when the salon reached its full notoriety. With the exception of Madame Roland, women were excluded, making the Roland home a nice corollary to arrangements republicans contemplated for the public sphere.[22] As such, the salon was built around male initiative and was largely a partisan affair. Dominique Godineau claims that it was open to "the entire patriotic milieu," and Gita May describes it as a place where "men who had similar views on a number of issues" could express a shared dedication to republican principles, but for most contemporaries, it was closely associated with the Girondin faction. Rather than a réunion of diverse groups on the Left, the salon was dominated by Brissot, Roland, Pétion, Barbaroux, and Buzot; although it commonly accepted notable guests (Condorcet, Paine, Robespierre), it served primarily to give consistency to the Girondins' inner circle. According to Abrantès, Roland's salon was a "center" that helped "centralize" a party.[23]

Madame Roland's status as a salonnière is rightly a matter of controversy.

Mona Ozouf is willing to consider her "coterie" a salon as long as we recognize that "it never reeked of the Ancien Régime," given its Spartan food, "tense, studious atmosphere," and exclusion of women. Gita May suggests that Madame Roland was a successor to the "supremely well-mannered and polished hostesses" of the past but nevertheless calls hers "a new type of salon" that bore "little resemblance to the genteel refinements of the salons of the Old Regime" because it was "a political salon with a Spartan flavor" whose hostess did not engage in "gallant chitchat" and "did not care to display the social graces and amenities so highly prized" during the eighteenth century.[24] But these references to other salons are beside the point: the salon was a feminine space used in a political context for promoting alliances between different factions in a manner that exploited the association of women with wholeness and conciliation. The meetings at the home of Madame Roland did not serve this function because they were presided over by men and were designed to foster a particular agenda. "If sometimes men of different opinions found themselves invited," May says, "they immediately became aware of the preference shown to those who were in accord with the Rolands. Such favoritism, it goes without saying, resulted in the prompt withdrawal from these gatherings of all those save the most docile disciples." That is why Madame Roland's private overtures inviting Robespierre to visit in the spring of 1792 were met mostly with silence: whatever his faults, the Montagnard leader knew that as a partisan, she did not speak entirely for herself; he could therefore be excused for identifying her salon with his political enemies, especially once the Brissot ministry deliberately excluded his faction from power.[25]

Unlike the salonnières of the past — and unlike Madame de Staël — Madame Roland did not participate in the conversations that took place in her home. Instead, she sat in silence or removed herself from the circle in order to do needlework or write letters. "Seated before a table on which there were some newspapers and brochures," wrote Abrantès, "[she] did not appear at first sight to have any part in these conferences [and] did not want to influence the sentiments of those whom Brissot introduced to her." Of herself, Roland observed that "[t]his disposition suited me perfectly; it kept me abreast of things in which I took an active interest, but I never went beyond the limits imposed upon my sex." May argues that what set Roland apart from Madame de Staël was that she "did not crave to be the center of attention at all times."[26] But the real distinction was not one of temperament but of class and milieu: like Madame de Condorcet and other women of aristocratic origins, Staël did not think of herself as an entirely private individual when at home and therefore refused to be either silent or passive in a private space when public affairs were being discussed. She not only presided over her salon but used it as an instrument of political activism. Roland, in contrast, thought that women ought not "show themselves" or appear "to contribute to political work," and she criticized Staël as well as "nos aristocrates" in November 1789 for giving the impression that the National Assembly was being led "by a dozen women."[27]

Despite Roland's silence, Abrantès imagined that she nevertheless imposed "her hidden direction" on the men assembled in her salon and was therefore responsible for many of the laws that later found their way into the civil code. Godineau is even less convinced by Roland's own testimony, insisting that she "not merely received company but directed the discussions and exerted a real influence on the guests." In fact, Madame Roland's political interventions took place not in her salon but only after her company had left, in the absolute privacy of conjugal collaboration. Godineau calls the salon "a place in which Girondist politics were worked out," but in reality such collective strategizing was accomplished in the Comité Valazé, a weekly meeting of about forty deputies at the home of Madame Valazé, where the Girondins deliberated on public affairs and planned joint action in the Assembly.[28]

Madame Roland's salon points to an emerging division of labor in the political sociability of the Left. On the one hand, political clubs met in the daytime and were reserved for activities directly related to political work; on the other hand, salons, which usually met in the evening, provided a distinctive venue for the leadership of a larger group to which visitors from other factions could come for political discussions of a more philosophical sort. In politics, such a division was only remotely analogous to the modern distinction between business and leisure, because people of means involved in public affairs with no other regular employment were not likely to leave their work at the office. Originally, in 1791, the deputies from the Gironde met three times a week at informal *déjeuners politiques* organized by Brissot and Vergniaud, which took place in the apartment of Madame Dodun, the wife of a rich businessman and the daughter of a former minister under Louis XVI. According to Armand Gensonné, the Girondin president of the Convention in 1793, these meetings occurred in the hours before the Assembly opened its sessions and generally involved discussion of the issues to be dealt with that day. In the evening, the same deputies often met with a more diverse crowd in the salon of Madame de Saint-Hilaire. Although invited to Dodun's apartment, Roland did not attend, because his home on the rue Guénégaud was too far away. Later, Pétion inaugurated more formal strategy sessions in the form of political dinners at the home of Madame Valazé for a larger groups of deputies, which Chaumette called a *conciliabule nocturne*. The Comité Valazé was part club, part festival: Dumont reported that on occasion, guests were treated to the spectacle of the *conventionnel* François Chabot in a red bonnet performing crude pantomimes mocking the king and was astonished "to see Condorcet enjoying company so ill-suited for him." It was this gathering, rather than the salons of the Old Regime, that inspired Madame Roland to establish a place to hold similar *conférences amicables*. When Roland entered the ministry in March 1792 and such dinner-time socializing moved to the Hôtel britannique, buffoonery gave way to the decorum of a semi-official reception where the Girondin leadership could hold discussions with members of other parliamentary factions. Conviviality, the work of strategic planning, and the enforcement of parliamentary discipline took place elsewhere, either in the Comité Valazé or the Club de la réunion, founded in 1793 to coordinate "federalist" opposition to the Montagnards.[29]

The logic of Girondin political sociability pointed toward the marginalization of women in traditional salons. The Jacobins took things a step further. By placing all private sociability under suspicion, they shut down or dispersed the old *cercles mondains*, integrated the convivial aspects of salon life into a new popular mondanité, and expelled women from informal yet active political involvement.

Although the old sociability of traditional elites did not collapse until the summer of 1792, a sense of gloom set in among moderates and aristocrats at least two years earlier. With the emigration picking up steam daily, and with the closure of the royalist political clubs in the spring of 1790, Parisian society was no longer gay, according to Victorine de Chastenay, who felt as if she were living in the crater of a volcano about to explode. Society lived on, she wrote, but her desire to attend balls and go to the theater had waned, and she could only recall one memorable evening spent in *le monde élégant*, at the sumptuous home of the baron de Grandcour, a wealthy Swiss who was known for giving magnificent suppers.[30] Private society balls were still held in 1791, like the one given in early March by the Société des sylphs at the home of Lord Bedford, but such gatherings by the rich were increasingly suspect.[31] In 1792, Chateaubriand recalled, Paris turned ominous: the appearance of the people was no longer tumultuous or curious, just menacing; the variety of dress gave way to uniformity; and "the old world was effaced." For the remaining salonnières, the pattern of normal existence ceased and their salons decomposed. Staël's company melted away in August, when liberal nobles who had refused to emigrate faced arrest. Before fleeing to Coppet in September, she was reduced to seeking passports and asylum abroad for her friends; once in Switzerland, she offered refuge to several émigrés and used part of her fortune to aid victims of the Terror, but her ability to play an active role in political life was interrupted. Madame de Flahaut's habitués dispersed in search of security, some ending up in the provinces and others taking trips abroad. Madame de Sainte-Amaranthe ran out of money and took to renting rooms, while Madame Helvétius, who had buried a small fortune in a park, which was supposedly never found, spent months holed up with Madame de Condorcet at Auteuil, talking constantly about friends who had disappeared.[32] At nearly the same time, Hébert told the readers of *Le Père Duchesne* to get ready to move into the evacuated mansions of Faubourg Saint-Germain, which were in fact sold as *biens nationaux* or used for balls, as gaming halls, or as asylums during the first years of the Republic, along with those of the opulent Faubourg Saint-Honoré.[33]

Many witnesses testified that the Terror annihilated *toute société* and caused all traditional sociability to collapse.[34] According to Abrantès, however, it was only in the worst moments of 1794 that "the respectable inhabitants of Paris shut themselves up in their homes, concealed their valuables, and awaited the results with fearful anxiety." Once each new crisis had passed, she wrote, "balls were resumed, and the theaters were filled every evening." "It may truly be said of the French," she continued, "that they met death singing and dancing. Balls, theaters, and concerts were crowded nightly, while famine was staring us in the face, and we were threatened with all the horrors of anarchy." The salons of Madame de Lameth, Mathieu Dumas, and the comtesse de Beauharnais remained open well into 1793.[35]

But even though a convivial sociability continued with a new clientele, traditional salons would have been hard to find under the Jacobins. La vie mondaine of the radical republic was open rather than private, festive, socially diverse, and often connected with the official theater. The premier salon at the time was that of Julie Careau, the wife of the great actor François-Joseph Talma, on the rue Chantereine, which was much more like a perpetual society ball than a Staëlian political salons or an old-regime bureau d'esprit. Large numbers of visitors, including prominent Jacobins, stopped by at any hour of the day to feast at an open buffet, listen to a piano concert by Julie Candeille, or meet celebrities from the arts like David or Chénier. Mademoiselle Montansier, the owner of the Beaujolais theater and the Café des chartes, received Cordeliers, Jacobins, and even sansculottes in her apartment in the Palais-Egalité (the erstwhile Palais-Royal), where guests "talked of the theater, victories, gambling, pleasures, war, politics, and diplomacy all at once." In short, the Jacobins preferred public festivals and balls to old-fashioned salons. As Abrantès put it,

> There were often gatherings, dinners, and suppers at the homes of the men of the Revolution, but the remarkable thing is that there were few private receptions [*fêtes particulières*] during this disastrous period of 1792 and 1793, even in the homes of members of the Committee of Public Safety. They met because it is in the nature of the French to abhor isolation, but it seems that they were afraid of awakening happy voices within themselves and of provoking laughter in the midst of so much crying and mourning! Balls, elaborate celebrations, all that was public, [was] given to the people in order to keep it from hearing the cries of the victims when death was too bitter for them to take. . . . Such saturnalias sufficed for these people, who, like those of Rome, would see heads fall and would applaud the games at the circus, crying "Hail Caesar!"[36]

Private sociability was counterrevolutionary because it shielded factional interests from public scrutiny and therefore undermined the sovereign will of the people as a whole. Jacobins exalted privacy as a condition of domesticity, they counted on it to be productive of salutary public virtues, but they also feared it as a shelter for secrecy and intrigue. When the Jacobins denounced salons as dens of conspiracy, they implicated gender twice by associating women with both hidden maneuvers and reactionary intent. The image of the salon as harboring conspiring aristocrats exploited the traditional discourse on feminine power to insinuate that women supported counterrevolutionary activity from behind the scenes. On the one hand, they were implicated in the salon as a symbol of an opaqueness that concealed feminine influence exercised through the magic of seduction.[37] On the other hand, they were implicated in the salon as a symbol of a politics that had not broken with the practices of the Old Regime and an aristocracy frightened of revolutionary change. The double rhetorical import of gender in the revolutionary discourse on salons gave the Jacobins a potent means of vilifying Madame Roland as "the Circe of the Republic," while pummeling the Girondins as cunning, devious, and secretive *révolutionnaires du monde*, reeking of the past.[38] In addition, salons were incompatible with a politics that saw no role for intermediary bodies. Since the popular will could only be expressed by those purportedly capable of speaking in the name of the people, or by associations equipped to monitor the execution of the laws and the conduct of public officials, the very existence of salons represented a danger to popular sovereignty, because all politics demanded publicity, the people could not be subsumed by a faction, and private associations could not usurp the representative aspect of the exercise of public authority.[39]

The only havens the Jacobin Republic afforded to the old sociability were prisons and the emigration. Abrantès claimed that the Terror all but destroyed "what we call society in France," but that elements of it survived "in the prisons of the Luxembourg, Les Carmes, and Saint-Lazare," which were the only places one could hope to find those who knew how to carry on a decent conversation.[40] Apparently, the Luxembourg was the most comfortable: prisoners paid for their cells like hotel rooms and were able to preserve some of the habits of private life, with access to reading rooms, a small orchestra, and good meals. According to Beugnot, women detained in the courtyard of the Conciergerie did not neglect their *toilette* and took frequent promenades. The aristocrats at Madelonnettes came to prison as if they were going to court: they maintained elegance and good manners; wore powdered wigs and well-polished boots; and tucked their hats under their arms. At Port-Libre, the former Port-Royal, inmates even held what Alméras called a "prison-salon" in the evening, where men read and wrote at a large table and the women did embroidery. On one occasion, the poet Vigée, brother-in-law of Madame de Vigée-Lebrun, organized a poetry reading contest in which the women crowned the winner. When the Comédie-Française actor Jean Mauduit de Larive was there, he charmed residents by singing portions of *Guillaume Tell* and a hymn by André Chénier.[41]

II

The Jacobins did not shatter the old sociability of prerevolutionary France, they just sent it abroad, where the emigration gave it shelter, preserved its continuity, and kept it intact for its return once the Revolution was over. During the Terror, many of those who had participated in the sociability of the eighteenth century went to the provinces to wait out the storm, but its leading lights — not to mention the royal family — fanned out across Europe, where they encountered a cosmopolitan mondanité modeled on their own.

Although many émigrés lived modestly or faced real hardship, some of the 150,000 individuals who comprised the emigration by 1793 possessed great fortunes, spent lavishly, and were able to maintain themselves and their companions in elegant style. This was certainly true of Louis XVI's brothers, the comte de

Provence (subsequently King Louis XVIII) and the comte d'Artois (subsequently King Charles X), who established a court at Coblenz, where for a few years they managed, under the protection of the local elector and with the help of other wealthy friends, to reproduce many aspects of life at Versailles. Bigot de Saint-Croix noted that it was common for grands seigneurs to arrive at Coblenz with their flatware and 300,000 livres, equivalent to more than one million francs. Madame de Matignon paid her dressmaker 24,000 livres per year to reserve his latest creations, and Madame de Kersaint lived more than comfortably in London on an income of 25,000 francs drawn from properties in Martinique.[42] Those without such resources found among sympathetic foreigners familiar with the rituals of French sociability an infrastructure of mondanité already in place. German princes, English gentleman, Austrian courtiers, Russian nobles, and even Jewish hostesses in Berlin were often more than happy to offer hospitality to the French. At the exiled court of Gustav III of Sweden in Aix-la-Chapelle, émigrés not only enjoyed security and comfort but the chance to serve as *chambellans* to a foreign prince. As a rule, émigrés of high birth were sought after by local notables in the places where they had taken refuge and were admitted to the most exclusive society. For those who spent 1790 and 1791 in the spas and winter gathering places they had frequented in the past, or in French salons reconstituted abroad, the emigration hardly disrupted the rhythms of the social season.[43]

At Brussels, which greeted the first wave of émigrés, many nobles acted as if nothing had changed.[44] Most contemporaries attributed such behavior to the shortsighted presumption that the ordeal of emigration would be of short duration. Chastenay ridiculed as "matadors" the hotheads at Coblenz who sent home letters predicting the month they would be returning triumphantly to Paris. The comte d'Espinchal reported from Brussels that "nobody could have imagined in 1791 that this flight beyond the frontier, this bird's life on a branch, would last very long," a fact to which Chateaubriand attributed the first émigrés' preoccupation with fashion and socializing and their imprudent refusal to economize. At Spa, Espinchal counted numerous French visitors from Liège, Aix-la-Chapelle, and Brussels, who spent their days "in the midst of the whirlwind of the grand monde" as if "Versailles was waiting for them to return to their ordinary games." According to the marquise de Falaiseau, most women brought only two or three dresses; Madame de Montsoreau had missals for only one season.[45] Equally unflattering explanations for émigré imprudence and frivolity include vanity, blindness, and an inability to abandon the traditions of the idle life. The comte d'Haussonville and the comtesse de Rochechouart, however, saw the matter in a more positive light, suggesting that the struggle to uphold established social traditions served to compensate for the privations of voluntary exile, preserve dignity, and help people remain cosmopolitan.[46] In any event, the will to maintain the habits of the past led the women of the emigration to resuscitate abroad the many distractions of daily life — soirées, receptions, dinner parties, and salons — to which they had been accustomed at home, with whatever resources were available. Indeed, so common was mondain sociability in émigré circles that a cottage industry emerged here and there to sustain it, complete with clothing and fabric stores, *parfumeries*, florists, hat makers, ribbon makers, jewelers, bookbinders, and typographers. The marquise de Chabannes ran a girls' school in London; the comtesse de Boisgelin and Madame du Camper gave piano lessons; and the duchesse de Lorge mended shoes.[47]

Salons were more than just a way to pass the time. Those who gathered in the salons of the emigration engaged in familiar activities, conversing, exchanging news and ideas, listening to literary works read aloud, and discussing the latest books.[48] But the spontaneous manner in which the salons of the emigration were created suggests that they had become central to the way aristocrats organized their collective lives, and that women played an essential role in reestablishing and integrating a dispersed and uprooted community. Shortly after a group of émigrés converged in a given location, relations usually formed quickly and easily. Prior acquaintance, family ties, social compatibility, or the desire to seek out those in similar circumstances combined with habits nurtured in good company to turn courtesy visits and offers of mutual assistance into regular meetings in a small number of salons. Upon arriving in Hamburg, Madame de Flahaut received numerous invitations, and she was soon able to establish her own salon with some of the same friends who had frequented her home in the past.[49] Commonalities often attracted people to the same neighborhoods, where salons served to anchor communities of nobles who had managed to retain a certain bondedness despite their physical displacement. In London, associates of the comte d'Artois formed a distinct French colony near Manchester Square, which assembled every evening in the salon of Madame de Polastron on Thayer Street. In the West End, around Baker Street and Spring Street, another colony formed, made up primarily of provincial nobles from Brittany, Poitou, and Anjou, who gathered at one another's homes and at Flahaut's salon on Half Moon Street for the few months she was there. At Aix-la-Chapelle, according to Falaiseau, a contingent of between two and three hundred émigrés saw one another daily for visits and then assembled in groups of fourteen or fifteen for tea, dinner, and cards. "*Les habitudes mondaines,*" she wrote, "maintained their empire over this errant colony. Upon arriving, women made their *visites de présentation,* then stayed at home to receive those who wish[ed] to render theirs." At Coblenz, where the French population was larger, less well acquainted, more masculine, and "more military than mondaine," general visits did not occur, women formed more intimate circles, and it took a bit longer for proper relations to become established. To overcome these obstacles, the duke of Brunswick opened his salons three times a week for billiards and music so that the émigrés could meet one another.[50]

As the emigration persisted, dwindling resources often made the sharing of meals a daily ritual, which was eagerly anticipated through long days of hunger, work, or sheer boredom. While in Altona during the invasion of Holland, the comte de Rochechouart spent his days waiting for nightly soirées with the marquise de Bouillé, where he was sure to enjoy supper and the pleasures of good company. According to Haussonville, the people with whom his father spent the emigration "employed a thousand ingenious ways to continue in miserable circumstances the same life of distractions to which they had become accustomed," like potluck dinners and movable tea parties, where guests had to supply their own sugar. Even in far-off rural Russia and the interior of the United States, émigrés managed to keep aspects of la vie mondaine alive.[51]

The spontaneity with which salons were reconstituted during the emigration has led some to claim that the women of the aristocracy found their "historical role" in the task of preserving traditional French sociability. Victorine de Chastenay went so far as to insist that this act of conservation put a brake on the Revolution after the fall of Robespierre and signaled "the return to the first notions of order."[52] It is true that the women of the emigration were anxious to reestablish a sense of normality and that sociability was an important aspect of what they hoped to salvage from the past.[53] But there is no reason to essentialize women's role in the preservation of la vie mondaine — most émigrés, even those of limited means, were eventually able to establish a stable residence and a generally idle routine, of which salon sociability had long been a part. As time passed, financial difficulties tended to fix émigrés in one place and therefore encouraged the progressive stabilization of their experience. Women were not naturally sociable, but they were better situated than men to accommodate the desire of émigrés to seek one another out.

But the problem doesn't end there. Jean Vidalenc puzzled over whether this insistent mondanité represented a "struggle against isolation" that expressed the French aristocracy's inability to live without *cette vie de société,* or more properly psychological motives born of adversity.[54] Were French aristocrats innately sociable or was it simply that misery loves company? The marquise de Falaiseau noted without passing judgment that "since the emigration, [the French] had more need than ever to seek one another out, to see one another, and to gather, all interests having become the same, as had hopes, fears, and misfortune." In common circumstances, she argued, all individual needs were similar: people craved news, sought reassurance, and so on.[55] Some have chosen to interpret this comment to mean that the émigrés gathered primarily to cope with poverty and hunger or confront sadness and regrets.[56] Others, however, have taken Falaiseau's observation as evidence of a "certain gregarious instinct" that was distinctively or essentially French, so that the presence of salons during the emigration represented a way to reconstitute the absent *patrie.*[57]

Such arguments, it seems, borrow much too generously from the self-representation of the émigrés themselves and are grounded too deeply in the pretension that French salons were oases of civilization in lands sadly lacking the conditions necessary to sustain true sociability. Still, it is significant that French aristocrats with common interests and a shared taste for "the pleasures of French society" spontaneously established salons abroad. The salons of the emigration became more than ever institutions of class cohesion by reinforcing among nobles a sense of distinctiveness and community, which did not carefully distinguish among social ties, political allegiances, and a commitment to preserve cherished sociable traditions. In rural Switzerland, the marquise de La Tour du Pin observed among the émigrés a stubborn unwillingness to shed old habits, noting that they "all brought the airs and the insolence of Paris society," mocked everything, "and were everlastingly amazed that there should exist in the world anything besides themselves and their ways."[58] Such cultural arrogance registered not only a certain chauvinism and a devotion to habit, it also expressed something similar to ethnic identity. One could view the formation of such an identity as an act of political defiance, as does Ghislain de Diesbach, who argues that the émigrés living with the comte d'Artois at Coblenz "amused themselves as much as possible" because "pleasure became a form of courage, an affirmation of royalism."[59] But the emigration's reinforcement of identity can also be understood if we consider the ordeal as a sociological experiment: in a condition of dispersion and in the absence of many of the accouterments of Parisian life, the émigrés managed to recreate their former world by establishing salons, as if to suggests that in a state of nature, the French aristocracy appears as a primitive community with the salon at its hub.

Emigrés created salons wherever they went. Some were necessarily improvised, but many embodied an element of continuity, either because they were headed by an established salonnière or because they reassembled the same society that had met regularly before the Revolution. At Brussels, where the French nobility gathered to be close to France and the popular thermal baths near Aix-la-Chapelle, Parisian high society met in salons presided over by such familiar hostesses as the princesse de Vaudémont, the marquise de Coigny, Madame de Béthizy, Madame de Matignon, and the duchesse d'Escars. In London's West End, the nobles of Versailles assembled with women of the court (Mesdames de Balbi, de Breteuil, and de Bouillé), while in Lausanne, aristocratic supporters of Necker (the princesse d'Hénin, Madame d'Aguesseau, Lally-Tollendal) dined with the marquise de la Guiche. A handful of famous salonnières could rely on their reputations to continue their vocation abroad; such was the case most notably with Madame de Staël at Coppet and Juniper Hall, but also with Madame de Genlis, whose salon became one of the centers of émigré life in Hamburg, and Madame de Flahaut, who attracted a small colony of liberal constitutionalists to her home in Mickleham, near Richmond. The salon of Gustav III at Aix-la-Chapelle was popular with men of letters thanks partly to his association with Madame Geoffrin twenty years earlier.[60]

Emigrés could be found all over Europe but were concentrated in Germany, the Low Countries, and England. Certain locations within this inner zone, however, were considered more attractive than others. Forty thousand French émigrés were drawn to Hamburg, the Venice of the North, which offered easy access to Russia and England, relative freedom and prosperity, and a rich urban culture of dance halls, theaters, newspapers, and cafés. Holland, by contrast, despite the wealth of its leading citizens, was regarded as somber, drab, and uncomfortable. Vienna and Saint Petersburg offered all the sumptuous enjoyments of court life but were considered too remote.[61] Two destinations were preferred above all: Coblenz, the political capital of the emigration, and London, where hospitality and decent accommodations offered the best circumstances to maintain the old sociability. Both locations offered émigrés aspects of the society life of the past. Coblenz, with its brilliant seigneurs and its fashionable ladies, its luxury, gaming, debauchery, intrigue, and ambition, most closely approximated the rhythms of Versailles. After being received *au château* by the comte d'Artois, émigré-courtiers could take in the pleasures of the city—a promenade along the Rhine, a café, or a salon featuring musical or literary entertainment.[62] In the latter part of the emigration, the center of émigré political affairs shifted to London when the British took up the counterrevolutionary cause in the west of France, but it was less the attractions of a court than the promise of a mondaine existence most like their own that drew 25,000 émigrés across the Channel — the life of the princes at Hartwell and Holyrood was more domestic and informal than had been the case at Turin and Coblenz. In England, the most fortunate émigrés enjoyed the generous hospitality of a curious and sympathetic social elite, among whose members the French nobility had many personal friends. The pleasures of a large and bustling city, coupled with the positive reputation the London social scene had acquired in French high society, made the British capital very much à la mode. Haussonville's father was impressed by the "ostentation" shown the French by "the best English society," and Falaiseau was gratified that richly attired women "of my rank" living in superb houses with numerous servants would take such interest in her plight. The fact that a good portion of the old court nobility inhabited the area around Manchester Square added to London's ability to offer a sense of familiarity. Madame de Duras later recalled her stay in London during the emigration as one of the two happiest times of her life.[63]

The emigration further consolidated the place of the salon in aristocratic life, but what impact did it have on the place of politics in the life of the salon? There was nothing new about the rivalries and ambitions that swirled about the court at Coblenz. In fact, the main players included some who had earlier become adept at jockeying for position at Versailles, like the Polignacs, Madame de Calonne, and Madame de Balbi, whose salon brought together the allies of the comte de Provence. Fernand Baldensperger records the shock of one newcomer who, upon his arrival, was astonished to see that the need to undertake "grand enterprises" had done nothing to suppress the thirst for intrigue.[64] Although Madame de La Tour du Pin emphasized a similar taste for "gossip, petty intrigue and scandal-mongering" among the émigrés of London, the real political innovation of the emigration was the deepening of political demarcations inherited from the constitutional phase of the Revolution and the role such fissures played in the formation of salons. As ideological divisions intensified under the pressure of events, salons tended to turn into coteries of homogeneous opinion. In London especially, royalists, intransigents, and "constitutionnels" generally avoided one another in society and kept to their own in a manner that anticipated the division between Faubourg Saint-Germain, Faubourg Saint-Honoré, and the Marais during the Restoration. The most fundamental split among nobles was between the *intégaux* who regretted all aspects of the Revolution and the *monarchiens* who had been partisans of reform and had supported limitations on the power of the king. Such divisions did not necessarily extinguish superficial contact between émigrés, but there was a distinct tendency for the intimate company of salons to be organized more exclusively according to political preference. In London, for example, friends of the duc d'Orléans (Walsh, Narbonne, the abbé de Cabre, Talleyrand) gathered at the home of Madame de Genlis, constitutional monarchists more generally made up the society of Adélaïde de Flahaut (and later Madame de Staël), and the future ultras met for dinners and receptions in a handful of salons around the King Street district, where they played cards, listened to Louis de Fontanes read verse, and pondered the counterrevolutionary writings of Antoine de Rivarol and Jacques Mallet du Pan.[65]

Noblewomen responded to the Revolution by preserving and reaffirming the place of the salon in aristocratic life, along with its ambiguous relationship to the division of social space into public and private realms. As in the past, that ambiguity offered aristocratic women access to public affairs, and the Revolution had clearly made the public more political.

III

The devastation wrought by the Revolution on the Parisian social scene was best symbolized for returning émigrés by the abandoned and sequestered hôtels of Faubourg Saint-Germain — silent edifices of a once glorious aristocratic past, now vandalized and neglected, with weeds pushing up through the paving stones.[66] In retrospective accounts, the spiritual desolation of post-Thermidorian social life is commonly made to reflect the material decrepitude of the noble *quartier*: both Madame de Staël and the duchesse d'Abrantès concluded that the hypocrisy that allowed the tormented to live alongside their tormentors gave rise to habitual dissimulation, pervasive mistrust, and a general sense of loss. Abrantès even imagined that in the aftermath of the Revolution, the French character had changed its nature from confidence to "somber anxiety," that women had lost the aptitude for sociability, and that men had forgotten how to be polite.[67]

Upon closer inspection, however, it seems that Abrantès, like many others of her class, was reacting less to the absence of social life than to what she considered the crime of bad taste. The image of deserted hôtels in Faubourg Saint-Germain was not nearly as troublesome to her as the fact that some had been purchased by "these same army contractors, the newly rich, who believed that they would take on the manners of the *beau monde* by admiring themselves in the same mirrors." Abrantès knew that the Revolution and the emigration had not destroyed French sociability, she only regretted that it was being reconstituted under the auspices of the nouveaux riches of Faubourg Saint-Honoré and the Chaussée d'Antin, where the frivolous *merveilleuses* presided over a world of puerile conversation, ridiculous Greek fashions, and "jargon patoisé." As the duc de Raguse observed, "the social order was beginning to take shape again" under the Directory, but its "most flagrant characteristics" were pomp and corruption. Although returning émigrés generally regarded the opulence and extravagance of post-Thermidorian society with contempt, they also understood along with Madame de Chastenay that the new search for pleasure and the public display of wealth meant that "the revolutionary regime was absolutely finished." Upon returning from the United States in 1796, Talleyrand reported that "balls, spectacles, and fireworks have replaced prisons and *comités révolutionnaires.*"[68]

As high society revived after Thermidor and under the Directory, its principle of development was not so much crass bourgeois display as a hesitancy and uncertainty regarding the expression of status. How would it be possible to embody aristocratic forms of distinction in an age that still considered itself republican, and what standards of organization would determine the relationship between a new elite recently enriched and a traditional social leadership of diminished means that nevertheless intended to remain on top? Although returning émigrés and other nobles were determined to resume the sociable habits of the past, they were financially strapped, reluctant to draw attention to themselves, and consequently resentful of the new power of money. Such circumstances helped give post-Thermidorian sociability a socially chaotic and almost exclusively public nature. Salons were rare immediately after Thermidor, and social life was concentrated in balls, restaurants, gardens, theaters, cafés, and tearooms.[69] Benjamin Constant recalled only "immense gatherings" in those years and attributed the lack of salons to a general atmosphere of political repression in which "all closed meetings were suspect." Chastenay blamed the preference for subscription balls and the scarcity of "private parties" (*des fêtes particulières*) among "the best company" on a lack of money, but others pointed out that people of means were afraid of appearing wealthy by habitually receiving company.[70]

By most accounts, the famous balls of the Directory were both diverse and exclusive at the same time: diverse in that the guests included both Jacobins and royalists, victims and executioners, the conquerors and the conquered — in short, "persons of all opinions"; exclusive in that they were reserved for those belonging to "the best society," where, according to Madame de Staël, the so-called *salons dorées* brought together "the elements of the old and new regime" without reconciling them. Chastenay reported that such balls were attended by numerous Vendéens and émigrés who, in seeking reintegration, demonstrated a remarkable adaptability to the new situation, which contrasted sharply with the rigidity and haughtiness they had displayed during the emigration. In circumstances where traditional modes of status demarcation were risky or contested, those who considered themselves privileged were forced to search for novel means of expressing distinction. "When it was recognized that there would be no private receptions for some time," recalled Abrantès, "the most fashionable young people . . . decided to go and dance at public balls where, if all of good society went en masse, there would be no risk of encountering individuals not of one's own set." Although lacking decorum and a "mistress of the house to preside over them," such entertainment offered a chance to reconstitute the boundaries of *la bonne compagnie*, which began, in Staël's recollection, to seem "very redoubtable to those who were not admitted." The balls held at the Hôtel de Thélusson came to be known as the Bal des victimes, where guests, who danced with their hair tied up or cut short and a small red ribbon around their necks, were required to have lost at least one relative on the scaffold to be admitted, turning what had been a mark of social and political proscription into a status symbol. As Baron de Frénilly quipped, there was neither salvation nor consideration for those who had not been imprisoned during the Terror; it was enough to make one regret not having been guillotined.[71]

The desire for pleasure, the search for distinction, and amnesia regarding the immediate past all combined to make Thérésa Cabarrus (Madame Tallien) "Notre-Dame de Thermidor," the quintessential representative of Thermidorian high society. Married in December 1794 to a regicide who nevertheless subsequently played a key role in the overthrow of Robespierre, Thérésa welcome a "very mixed society" of directorial elites and old-regime aristocrats to her house, La Chaumière de Chaillot, where she presided in her famous *coiffure à la victime* over what was neither a ball nor a salon but a series of extravagant supper parties and high-stakes card games. "Politics," wrote Gabriel-Julien Ouvrard, a war profiteer of the Republic and the Empire, formed "the staple of the conversation" at the Talliens' but did not occupy it completely: "It often happened that, in the midst of the most animated conversations, people would go aside and form little groups, where they forgot in light and careless talk the grave matters that oppressed their thoughts."[72]

By 1796, venerable features of the old Parisian social scene had begun to reappear, like the exhibition of the works of contemporary artists at the Salon (which had not been held in 1794) and promenades at Longchamps. Not even the crisis of 18 Fructidor broke the momentum of high society's reconstruction. Still, in the eyes of those who had been leaders of le monde under the monarchy, post-Thermidorian society offered only a framework for sociability, not the real thing. True society, they insisted, could not be improvised and would have to wait until its former members had gotten back on their feet. In the meantime, only the nouveaux riches enjoyed a stable situation, and polite society would have to be content with the "nucleus of sociability" offer by the likes of Tallien, Madame Récamier, Madame Hamelin, and Josephine de Beauharnais. The women of Thermidor presided over the renaissance of the Parisian world, but "the salons *du vrai monde* did not open all at once" because "the society dispersed by the Revolution" was still in the process of reconstituting itself.[73] Abrantès repeatedly emphasized the incompetence of the parvenus who tried to relaunch society under the Directory. "The first réunions that took place," she wrote, "were almost all the butt of jokes. Those who *knew how* to receive did not yet dare to do so. It was therefore the newly rich who began to reopen this delicious French society. . . . They did not serve proper suppers[, and] they dined too late. They would give teas: these teas were more or less ridiculous, being served with such luxury that they could be mistaken for suppers."[74]

Private salons did indeed begin slowly to reopen as aristocratic families began the process of rebuilding their fortunes and women with established reputations took the initiative of choosing guests and posing as maîtresses de maison. The first to do so were those whose fortunes had remained intact, or had even been augmented during the Revolution. Madame de Caseaux, the wife of the former president of the parlement of Bordeaux, occupied a suite of apartments in the Hôtel de Perigord on the rue de l'Université where she and her daughter Laure — recently the recipient of a vast inheritance — were the first to open their doors in Faubourg Saint-Germain. Madame de La Briche, who was fortunate enough to have retained her estates during the Terror, reopened her salon on the rue de la Ville-l'Evêque in 1796 and began to entertain in a grand style three years later, after her daughter's marriage to Comte Louis-Mathieu Molé brought the family an inheritance of 300,000 francs.[75] According to Abrantès, circumstances at first required the best society to accept a "forced melange," but the divisions provoked by proximity made such an arrangement "more insupportable even than solitude" and led to a growing desire on the part of hostesses "to separate the pure gold from the alloy." In that sense, the revival of salons under the Directory represented the determination of those who considered themselves part of the best society to inaugurate the hierarchical restructuring of le monde. Once former salonnières began to open their doors, members of the old elite, many of them returned émigrés, separated themselves from the society of the Directory in a process of social and ideological collation. Pasquier remembered the salon of Madame de La Briche as a place of rendezvous for "all those who did not want to frequent the *salons* of the Directoire and the society of contractors who had suddenly acquired wealth." The salons of Madame de Staël, Madame de Condorcet, and Madame de Montesson brought together liberal nobles who had remained in France and émigrés anxious to reestablish connections. Madame Lebrun collected "the debris of the old court." In Auteuil, the former members of Madame Helvétius's salon quickly reassembled.[76]

Hostility between *honnêtes gens*, as the monarchists called themselves, and the *buveurs de sang*, their adversaries, was too great to keep the world of the Parisian elite from splitting into factions, especially when the former ceased to feel outnumbered and were no longer willing to accept the latter's rules. "People of the old regime," wrote Baron Arthur Léon Imbert de Saint-Amand, "plunged into amusement like the rest, [but] . . . who could pass through the Place de la Révolution without recalling the scaffold?"[77] Since the still-vivid political memories that separated men and women under the Directory were complemented by social differences, animosities were often expressed in the language of snobbery and social contempt. Sharp political distinctions first reappeared within high society in the form of private acts relating to dress and intimate sociability — the private was politicized first because the public sphere was not free. Monarchists linked to the Club de Clichy and their Jacobin rivals met in different cafés, gathered in separate neighborhoods, and wore distinct clothing (long black waistcoats versus red pants stuffed into boots). Police grew suspicious of the salon of Madame de La Briche, despite the absence of any preoccupation with political affairs, when guests started to be announced by their former titles. Royalist aristocrats first began "to ridicule the new institutions" and sneer at the Directory's personnel from the privacy of their salons in Faubourg Saint-Germain.[78]

Because their location in the private sphere shielded them from the rigors of the law, salons became, as they had been under the monarchy, one of the few sanctuaries of free exchange. The Directory was wary of both the Club de Clichy and the salons in which its members met — it kept both under surveillance — but when it moved after 18 Fructidor to make good on its previous ban against "all private associations occupying themselves with political questions," it closed only the former, hesitating to treat private salons as political associations.[79] Juridical realities, therefore, converged with the politicization of the private sphere and the growing expression of animosities in le monde to produce salons distinguishable by political tendency: former Girondins assembled with the marquis d'Antonelle; royalists of various nuances sorted themselves between the salons of the duc de Fitz-James, Madame de Montesson, the marquise d'Esparbès, and the duchesse d'Aiguillon; Madame de Pastoret provided refuge for a number of *députés fructidorisés*. Meanwhile, Mathieu Dumas tried to use his *salon mixte* to build bridges between the regime and its opponents on the right, while those favoring the fortunes of Napoléon Bonaparte gathered at the salon of Talleyrand and at the home of the abbé Sièyes on the rue du Rocher.[80]

Still, the most famous salonnière of the period, Madame de Staël, upheld the distinction established early in the Revolution between a mondain gathering of assorted guests that sought to influence the general orientation of politics, and ideologically homogeneous clubs that worked to organize a parliamentary faction, shape legislation, or promote particular candidates for ministerial office. When she reopened her salon in the Swedish embassy upon her return from abroad, Staël immediately found herself in a politically sensitive position. Accused by royalists of having contributed to the overthrow of the monarchy and not yet regarded by the new leadership as a supporter of the regime, she was nevertheless anxious to make a contribution to the stabilization of the Revolution by using her salon to reconcile moderate republicans and constitutional royalists. According to Madame de La Tour du Pin, who reported seeing Staël in her salon nearly every day, "she was working for the royalists, or rather, for some form of compromise."[81] As a consequence of her political agenda, Staël maintained ties to both the constitutional monarchists of the Club de Clichy and the liberal republicans of the Cercle Constitutionnel (also known as the Club de Salm after its location in the Hôtel de Salm on the rue de Lille), where Benjamin Constant presided over an impressive assembly of hommes politiques and *idéologues*, including Daunou, Garat, and Cabanis. A few members of one club frequented the other, and members of both commonly mingled in Staël's salon. The duc de Pasquier was convinced that as a result of these connections, Staël's "little coterie . . . enjoyed a somewhat important influence" at the time because it gave her the opportunity to manipulate affairs from behind the scenes through Constant and Talleyrand, her "prop in the government." In fact, the two clubs and the salon to which they were linked preserved a consistent division of labor: the former was mostly preoccupied with specific legislative matters (changes in electoral laws and the use of deportation instead of the death penalty for political crimes) while the latter was designed to create a forum for discussions primarily about the general political choices facing the regime.[82] Such a division was roughly consistent with the distinction Staël repeatedly made between political acts undertaken in the short term out of vanity or ambition and those conceived in high-minded deliberations and motivated by a desire to serve the common good. Under the Directory, Staël's salon included a wide array of members of the government, returned émigrés, journalists, diplomats, men of letters, revolutionaries, and celebrated society women.[83] On her own initiative, Staël did try to exploit her political connections to achieve specific ends: she intervened with the authorities to remove the names of friends from the *liste des émigrés*, obtained assistance for those put at risk by the events of 18 Fructidor, tried to influence discussions concerning the Constitution of the Year III, and encouraged Barras to appoint Talleyrand as minister of foreign affairs. But the favors she obtained were more a result of personal intimacies or fame and did not derive from her activities as a salonnière.[84]

Private interests compelled Staël to solicit favors from the vicomte de Barras, who maintained the most notorious of the Directory's official salons. Located at the seat of government in the Palais du Luxembourg, the salon combined elements of a ministerial reception with those of a private réunion. Contemporaries described it as an opulent court, with Barras himself acting like a new sovereign, surrounded by intriguers, speculators, parasites, and flatterers of all kinds. Staël testified that former émigrés stood in line for hours in the hope of receiving an audience and elegant ladies from Faubourg Saint-Germain fawned over a former Jacobin "in order to obtain the return of brothers, sons, and husbands." The spectacle reminded her of the court of Versailles and heralded the restoration of all its abuses.[85]

The official salons of the Directory were neither bureaux d'esprit nor political coteries; they offered access to power and favors amid the attractions of entertainment in order to support a policy aiming at the fusion of elites. At the parties given by Talleyrand at the Ministry of Foreign Affairs in the Hôtel Gallifet, in the heart of Faubourg Saint-Germain, repentant republicans like General Bonaparte "met those of the old nobility who had come over to the Revolution," including Madame de Beauharnais.[86] The Directors wanted good public relations and came to view both salons and official receptions, along with a controlled press, as means with which to influence the opinion of elites. Salons could act as autonomous centers of opposition, but they also could serve as accessories to an authoritarian regime interested in overseeing a union of the old and new elements of high society for the sake of stability. The Directors probably gained more from Staël's solicitations than they gave in return, offering bureaucratic favors in exchange for connections and prestige under conditions in which administrative benevolence could be withdrawn from one person without harming the good will it had purchased from others. The official salons of the Directory reversed the flow of political input from the government toward the public sphere. In that regard, they anticipated the new relationship between the government and high society that would be more fully developed under the Consulate and the Empire.[87]

IV

Barbara Pope has argued that most aristocratic women and *grandes bourgeoises* used the hiatus offered by the Revolution to reflect on the meaning of events: having interpreted their own misfortune as a condemnation of feminine influence in the politics of the Old Regime, they concluded that the "concentration of women's talents outside their proper sphere of home and family was in itself dangerous."[88] Although there had been a growing sentimentality about marriage and family among elite women in the eighteenth century, which was reinforced by the progressive normalization of bourgeois values, aristocratic women were hardly ready to abandon la vie mondaine for the joys of domesticity. What upper-class women yearned for was not home and hearth but what they imagined to have been the elegant sociability of the eighteenth-century salon. The most common reaction of aristocratic women to the Revolution was best expressed by Abrantès, for whom sociability was the universal antidote for sadness and adversity. After the ordeal of political upheaval and emigration, she insisted, women wanted nothing more than a true salon, "a gathering place for the arts and muses," where those "who had suffered . . . [could] begin a new life" by rediscovering "the light of that intellectual existence which alone can make a woman's life happy." The great crime of the Revolution, she believed, was not the exclusion of women from politics but the substitution of "solitude" for sociability and the degradation of "the immense sociable resources" that had made Paris the envy of all Europeans. Writing her massive *Histoire des salons de Paris* in the 1830s, Abrantès helped create the postrevolutionary myth that the eighteenth century had been the golden age of pure sociability, when elegant men and women had mingled to engage in refined conversation about matters of the spirit, and not about public affairs. It was the decline of such sociability, she insisted, that did the most to harm the position of women in French society.[89]

Salons survived the Revolution and emerged at the end of the 1790s almost entirely unchanged. They continued to be an essential element of a sumptuous *mondanité*, offering *salonnières* and *habitués* a combination of convivial and intellectual sociability. The myth that most upper-class women found convincing was not the one that viewed domesticity as punishment for the cultural ascendancy of the salon, but the one that equated the disruption of pure sociability with the ascendancy of politics. For high society, the triumph of Napoléon over the Revolution was embodied in the social success of the duchesse d'Abrantès and the exile of Madame de Staël.

CHAPTER THREE

Ralliés and Exiles (1799–1815)

In the spring of 1794, the revolutionary government moved to deprive popular societies of their autonomy and make them official institutions subordinate to the Convention. These societies had been the focus of the new sociability of the people, made possible by the opening of the public sphere and made potent by the assertion of popular guardianship over the Revolution. Now they became cogs in the machinery of government, approving directives and expressing a public opinion whose content was determined by the state.[1] In a strange analogy to the experience of the sansculottes, the upper-class sociability that had reappeared under the Directory underwent a similar fate during the Consulate: Napoléon annexed it to the government and turned it into an instrument of a social policy designed to bolster the stability and legitimacy of his regime.

I

The years of the Consulate and the Empire represented the first sustained effort to work out a postrevolutionary accommodation between the state and traditional sociable institutions. The revival of salons lent the Consulate and the

Empire a measure of social prestige, but it also enhanced the social power and political autonomy of the aristocracy and gave wealthy women access to the public sphere. As a result, the struggle to control mondanité became a crucial part of Napoléon's efforts to consolidate an authoritarian Empire.

Napoléon had a number of reasons for reviving Parisian high society, including economic recovery, political pacification, and the restoration of France's reputation as the capital of elegance and pleasure. He also wanted France's traditional institutions of sociability to promote the fusion of old and new elites, a goal that required the return of émigrés who had been familiar with the social life of the eighteenth century and who alone knew how to make high society acceptable to what the old nobility had called la bonne compagnie. By all accounts, the first task was accomplished successfully. After the Napoleonic coup d'état of 18 Brumaire (November 9, 1799), high society rallied to a government whose magnificent fêtes were "a signal not only to Paris, but to the whole of France, for balls, dinners, and social assemblages of every kind." Victorine de Chastenay noted that the famous ministerial balls of 1801 and 1802 were "very animated" and "followed one another with rapidity." Abrantès estimated that there were as many as "eight to ten thousand balls and five to six hundred thousand dinners . . . given in the course of the winter at Paris." As a consequence, the luxury market returned, textile merchants prospered, shoemakers, florists, hairdressers, perfumers, and dressmakers got back to work, and society events gained distinction from a rising tide of foreign visitors and diplomats. Chateaubriand's perception was that the revival of private sociability signaled a return to order: "the cafés and the streets were deserted, and people stayed at home; scattered families were reunited; they gathered the fragments of their inheritance, as troops assemble after a battle and find out how many are lost. . . . Gradually, I began to enjoy the sociability that is a characteristic of the French."[2]

The successful fusion of elites, however, was a much more difficult task to accomplish. Returning émigrés were gratified with the closure of the *liste des émigrés*, the amnesty granted to the victims of the Directory's various coups d'état, and the commemoration of the death of Louis XVI. But they understood that the policy of appeasement from which they benefited was part of a larger strategy of pacification, which unfolded painfully according to a series of gradual and discriminatory concessions designed to maximize the government's advantage.[3] The rhetoric of fusion favored by the First Consul and his supporters implicitly acknowledged that the Revolution and the emigration had seriously undermined whatever cohesion le monde had achieved in the eighteenth century under the unifying influence of the Enlightenment and the regulated social mixing of the salons. The Consulate, according to Madame de Staël, was a time of competing interests, jealousy, and rancor.[4] After 18 Brumaire, the aristocracy was no longer (or not yet) in a position to determine the rules governing the social world. The emigration "still depopulated Faubourg Saint-Germain[, and t]hose of its inhabitants who had remained or returned, for the most part seriously injured by the Revolution in their affections and their fortunes, wanted to go into mourning for their past grandeur."[5] Circumstances under the Consulate, therefore, were not much different from those under the Directory: the nouveaux riches of the Chaussée d'Antin still dominated the Parisian social scene, and socially and ideologically diverse salons were rare.[6] Despite official encouragement, consular society did not witness a spontaneous *rassemblement*. Members of the old aristocracy insistently maintained attitudes and habits expressing nostalgia for all they had lost and were easily vexed by the behavior of the nouveaux riches, which they piteously ridiculed as either clumsy or vain, faults they attributed to profound insecurity. "[T]he people of the old society of Faubourg Saint-Germain," wrote Madame de Saulx-Tavanes, "preserved the same language and the same formulas of politesse at the same time as they dwelled on economic details necessitated by the state of their fortunes with a sort of complacency carried to the point of exaggeration."[7]

By lifting the ban on the elegant life of the past, Napoléon inaugurated, not the fusion of elites, but the reassertion of aristocratic preeminence within le monde. High society during the Consulate was the theater of a thousand little coteries divided by rivalries and jealousies. In the face of efforts by those in charge to co-opt them, those who had led it in the past sought, from a position of relative weakness, to resurrect old boundaries and rules. Their principal weapons in this campaign were tradition and exclusivity, and since the by now mythical model of the eighteenth-century bureau d'esprit could lend any salon a little of both, men of letters were typically enlisted in the cause and made part of a new cultural politics designed to replace the primacy of money and power with that of intelligence and birth. A good example of this strategy is the salon the Madame de Pastoret, which met in the home of her wealthy uncle, M. de l'Etang, and sought to reestablish the equation between *civilisation* and bonne compagnie by uniting returned émigrés and conservative intellectuals like Georges Cuvier, Abbé François-Xavier de Montesquiou, and Jean-Baptiste Suard, who themselves hoped to transmit the traditions of the eighteenth century and the Académie française to a new generation. The priority given to literature, poetry, and music in the aristocratic salons of Mesdames d'Argenson, Beauffremont, Beaufort d'Hautpoul, and La Briche was part of a larger shift in cultural tastes favoring the return of madrigals, Latin poets, bouquets, and portraits, all of which recalled the ambiance of the baroque court. As Gilbert Stenger pointed out, rhyming verse, newly à la mode, was extremely popular in aristocratic salons.[8]

Aristocratic resistance to Napoléon's advances made the salon of the marquise de Montesson on the rue de Provence a valuable resource from the regime's point of view. Neither related to the Bonaparte family nor part of the official world, the marquise was an authentic representative of the society of the Old Regime who was both an enthusiastic supporter of the First Consul and intimately acquainted with his wife. Although members of the old nobility like Madame de Saulx-Tavanes did not think much of "her attempts to obtain by surprise some of the prerogatives attached to the rank of princess," the sixty-year-old Montesson was nevertheless the morganatic widow of the duc d'Orléans, the stepmother of the late Philippe-Egalité, and the aunt of the comte de Valence. She had been treated like a relative by Louis XVI after the duc's death in 1785 and had lost her property and gone to prison during the Terror because of her association with the royal family.[9] Moreover, she was the type of salonnière who embodied the survival of the manners of the old aristocracy, receiving every evening without fail seated on a couch, her feet on a *tabouret* hidden by a *couvre-pied* — hers was the first salon of the era to require sheer silk and shoes and Madame d'Abrantès considered her receptions models to be imitated.[10] Such qualities made it possible for her to attract returned émigrés and members of the former court to the dinners she gave every Wednesday night and to her celebrated fêtes, which "recalled the most splendid entertainments of the Monarchy." At a time when the receptions given by members of Napoléon's family were restricted to the official world, Montesson's salon was entertaining representatives from across the spectrum of society: royalists (the duc de Guines, M. de Noailles, and Archambaud de Périgord), liberals (Madame de Staël and Madame de Vaudémont), and luminaries of the new regime (Talleyrand, the duchesse d'Abrantès, and Hugues-Bernard Maret). By throwing a *grande fête* for eight hundred guests in February 1802 in honor of the marriage of Louis Bonaparte and Hortense de Beauharnais, the marquise was able to enlist the various elements of the French elite in a collective gesture of respect for the First Consul; by subsequently giving a ball for the king and queen of Etruria she did the same for a member of the Bourbon family and showed that mondain sociability could be a site of social ecumenicity.[11]

According to Abrantès, Napoléon hoped that the revival of old-regime sociability would attract the old aristocracy to his government while propagating values favorable to a new absolutism among those who had acquired status during the Revolution.[12] On the one hand, this strategy reflected an astute understanding of the social function of salons: Napoléon knew that a traditional salon had an inherent tendency to integrate high society because salonnières aimed for a perfect mixture of guests; he also saw that they could give nobles who rallied to his cause access to those who did not, and at the same time help initiate parvenus in the traditions of exquisite politesse. On the other hand, Napoléon displayed a profound contempt for the historical autonomy of the salon by narrowly equating politesse with the ability of the old monarchy to command obedience and by interpreting the refined manners of the aristocracy as an expression of its social authority. The First Consul wanted to annex and control these resources, but he had no use for what Habermas might have called the oppositional content of the prerevolutionary public sphere. Consequently, his instrumental conception of the salon went hand in hand with his condemnation of the libertine social atmosphere of the Directory, which he viewed as a sign of disorder, and his embrace of a rigid moral traditionalism that mirrored his views regarding the coercive function of politesse and court etiquette. As First Consul, Napoléon denounced the immorality of Barras's *fêtes galants* at the Luxembourg Palace and spoke openly of his distaste for the new *modes grecques*. According to his brother Lucien, he was "horrified by courtesans" and insisted on the need "to purify" the company Josephine kept at the Tuileries, going so far as to post spies at the entry to her salon in order to make sure that certain individuals, like Madame Tallien, were not admitted.[13] Although Napoléon thought it appropriate that women should oversee the influence exercised by "[e]verything that concerned etiquette, the life of society, [and] *le monde*" in the interest of reestablishing order "not only in general and in political life, but in the private life of each family," he did not want them to be powerful and spoke openly in the Council of State of the need to "contain women." He envisioned salons without salonnières, where the political interests of the regime would be supported by women willing to act as guardians and enforcers of a new culture of subservience.[14]

Napoléon's behavior toward aristocratic salons reflected his general attitude toward the old nobility—a complex mixture of envy and hatred. He was convinced that the men and women of Faubourg Saint-Germain detested him, but he was willing to go to great lengths to win their support, which made their ridicule hard to bear and their very existence a sort of permanent humiliation. The First Consul believed that his regime needed the historical legitimacy that association with the great families of France's past would bring. He also admired the nobility's confidence and sense of honor in the face of financial ruin, and interpreted the revival of their influence in high society as a sign that they still commanded the sort of respect necessary to the restoration of social hierarchy.

Observers have often attributed Napoléon's desire to surround himself with nobles to some irrational impulse, like vanity, prejudice, or sentiment.[15] Psychological factors undoubtedly played a part, but they were probably less important than the fact that he drew his conception of monarchy from historical precedent and could therefore not conceive of an alternative to the manifestations of authority that had prevailed in the past. Having taken noble presumptions for granted, he ended by ratifying their mystique: the higher he rose, the more he invested in the belief that aristocratic manners were a form of magic, capable of warding off mockery and commanding respect. When Abrantès's returned from Portugal, where her husband was the French ambassador, the emperor pointed out to his family that her manners had improved "since her sojourn in a foreign court" and commented that "it is only there, in fact, that one really gets to know le monde." She pointed out that Napoléon had to learn about *les vieux usages* secondhand because he "knew nothing of the high society of Paris" in his youth and "therefore could only know through oral tradition what we called la bonne compagnie and what he wanted to have around the throne."[16] Unable to communicate directly with those whom he held in such high esteem, Bonaparte was always eager to receive news of Faubourg Saint-Germain from noble courtiers who had access. When the object of his obsession refused to give up its secrets or showed ingratitude for the favors and protection it received, Napoléon lashed out in violent exasperation, threatening to exile every woman who spoke ill of him, his family, or his court. The royalist grandes dames of Paris, whom he liked to refer to as *des gros bonnets*, were special objects of his frustration—not only were they the guardians of an authenticity he could not possess, but their entrenchment in private life shielded them from the normal sanctions of the law to which men were vulnerable and allowed them to criticize with impunity.[17] Madame de Staël saw such anger as "a certain Jacobin antipathy against the fashionable society of Paris, over which women exercised a large measure of ascendancy" and blamed Napoléon for exposing himself to mockery by making himself "a parvenu king, a bourgeois gentleman on the throne," but her attitude only underscores the problems to which his outbursts were a reprehensible response.[18] The dozen or so aristocratic salons that tormented Napoléon were largely products of his own prejudices and insecurities. Unable to subjugate a class whose power he never failed to inflate, the emperor had to be satisfied with the spectacle of gentlemen and women begging for positions at the imperial court in an attempt to repair their finances. He was happy to accept their service, but he could never really trust them.[19]

Instead of rewarding Napoléon's overtures with gestures supporting the amalgamation of elites, the returning émigrés promptly repopulated their old neighborhoods, repurchased or reoccupied their former hôtels, and began to establish what Chastenay called "a sort of colony," anchored by a series of aristocratic and royalist salons. Madame de Falaiseau described these salons in 1808 as characterized by a network of shared relationships and a conformity of opinions.[20] Preferring to reconstitute an exclusive aristocracy, the elegant society of the Old Regime shunned both official receptions and the balls given by Lucien Bonaparte at the Hôtel Brissac, thereby threatening the policy of fusion. In response, Napoléon moved into the Tuileries on February 19, 1800, and set out to establish a monarchical court modeled on that of Louis XVI. The effort required a bit of historical reconstruction: Napoléon consulted musty books of etiquette, talked to former valets, and sought the advice of old courtiers like Madame de Montesson and Madame Campan, who before the Revolution had been one of Marie-Antoinette's *femmes de chambre*, and who subsequently ran a finishing school for girls in Saint-Germain-en-Laye where "all parvenu families hastened to [send] their daughters" to imbibe "the elegant manners of the old court." The First Consul also learned a great deal about the customs of Versailles from Madame de Genlis, whose letters and memoirs were suffused with details of court etiquette, courteous language, and descriptions of the mannerisms of the past.[21]

It was Josephine, however, who was principally responsible for managing "the feminine side of the Court." Although Napoléon generally excluded women from political affairs, he wanted his wife to supervise the process of *radiation* because he hoped to enhance her ability to win the allegiance of the upper ranks of society.[22] Napoléon needed nobles at the Tuileries in order to acquire the prestige of a European chief of state: if he were to receive people of rank, he would have to restore protocol and banish undesirable elements. This would not only make the palace an appropriate venue for solemn receptions, it would distinguish the new court from the official salons of the Directory and elevate it above those of the two other Consuls, Cambacérès and Lebrun. Napoléon expected Josephine to be a valuable asset in this regard. Although not a member of the elegant society of the Old Regime, Josephine had nevertheless been born into a noble family and had been married to the vicomte de Beauharnais, who was guillotined during the Terror. In her youth, she had acquired the manners and many of the prejudices of the young nobles with whom she liked to socialize both before and after her marriage to Bonaparte in 1796. It was among the remnants of the former society of Faubourg Saint-Germain that Napoléon first met her in the salon of Madame Permon, where she also established connections with such noblewomen as Madame Caffarelli and the comtesse d'Houdetot, who would eventually help establish the social legitimacy of her receptions at the Tuileries. Josephine acquired a number of similarly useful acquaintances at the spas of Aix-le-Chapelle, where she was installed at the prefecture while General Bonaparte was in Italy, and where, according to Sophie Gay, she held grand receptions for "the principal functionaries and inhabitants of the city, including foreigners of distinction" who were taking the waters. In Paris, living in a small hôtel on the rue Chantereine, she moved in a more varied circle, but her salon was generally seen as contributing to the revival of elegance under the Directory and was able to attract such nobles as Madame de Vergennes, who used her relationship with Josephine to secure positions for her daughter and son-in-law, Charles and Claire de Rémusat, at what became the imperial court. All told, active participation in la vie mondaine had given Josephine access to a wide variety of women with important pedigrees. Consequently, when Napoléon married her, he thought "he was allying himself to a very great lady." He would later write from Saint Helena: "My marriage to Madame de Beauharnais brought me into relations with a party which I required for my plan of fusion, which was one of the most important principles of my administration, and one of the most characteristic. Had it not been for my wife, I should not have had an easy means of approaching it."[23]

Napoléon believed that he could marginalize autonomous sites of sociability and discourage the critical discussion of public affairs by making his court the uncontested center of la vie mondaine. Once installed in the Tuileries, the First Consul ordered the generals and civil servants to whom he had distributed pensions, positions, and hôtels to "maintain not only a credible, but a splendid establishment." Young officers were required to marry — quickly — and establish themselves at court, where their wives were encouraged to open salons and receive guests. After marrying General Junot in 1800, Laure Junot (the future duchesse d'Abrantès) and her husband acquired a house on the Champs-Elysées suitable for entertaining guests "with convenience and creditably to fulfill the duties of the post Junot occupied." Even Foreign Minister Talleyrand was forced to marry his mistress, Madame Grand, when the First Consul discovered that certain ambassadors's wives declined invitations to the salon at his hôtel.[24] Few members of

Napoléon's original entourage had had much contact with the bonne compagnie of the past: in addition to former Jacobins, it consisted of soldiers and their wives who hailed mostly from the provincial bourgeoisie and were too young to have acquired much knowledge of either the old court or its *usage du monde*. That is why Napoléon placed such value on the collaboration of society women like Madame Junot and Madame Ney, who could serve as teachers and models. Josephine addressed the problem by holding frequent informal breakfasts for between five and fifteen young women of the court in her private salons at the Tuileries and Malmaison in order to familiarize them with the customs of good society in an atmosphere free of the intimidating presence of men. Shortly after the establishment of the Empire, Napoléon proclaimed that he wanted his court to be "one of the most brilliant in the world" and called on the women associated with the household to support him. In 1804, he ordered all those with an official position to have a salon in which to receive guests, especially foreigners of distinction.[25]

Napoléon's contradictory attitude toward the nobility was reciprocated with a combination of admiration and mistrust. Regarded as a vulgar usurper, the "little corporal" was nevertheless applauded for the restoration of order and the return of military glory. Royalist women like Comtesse Charlotte de Boigne and Madame de La Tour du Pin repeatedly allude to his genius. Nobles easily succumbed to feelings of antipathy toward Bonaparte because he had never been part of their world: they ridiculed his family, found fault with his wife, and sniped at the dictator who tried to make himself their patron and protector — they unfavorably compared their own manners with those of his parvenu courtiers, who "did not know how to walk on a waxed floor."[26] At the same time, however, his policy of fusion was grudgingly acknowledged as a partial success. In general, most observers agree with Chastenay's assessment that the former émigrés were taking advantage of "the pleasures of neutrality" in order to "marry, inherit, accept positions of all kinds, so that the income, and the title of *émigré ruiné*, would suffice to make them honorable."[27] A number of prominent nobles joined Napoléon's court during the Consulate. Many more rallied after its expansion with the proclamation of the Empire and Napoléon's marriage to Marie-Louise of Austria.[28] Jean Tulard has estimated that the old nobility made up only 22.5 percent of those who received titles during the Empire, although a large number of those who served at court were old-regime dukes.[29] Nevertheless, the contemporary impression was of a massive *ralliement*. The future Louis XVIII was stupefied to see the lion's share of the *ancien amorial de France* listed in the *Annuaire de la noblesse impériale*, and Madame de Boigne claimed that "the great majority of the nobility attached themselves to the Empire," especially after Napoléon's second marriage. Within Parisian society, Boigne met few "ladies who do not go to court" and insisted that "if the Emperor's prosperity had continued a few months longer, there would have been none of them." Abrantès concurred, noting that by 1808 there were only two or three noble households that remained in what the emperor like to call "the enemy camp."[30] More important than either statistics or perceptions, however, was the fact that the emperor did not need to win the adhesion of a majority of the former elite — it was enough that his policies created a mass of *attentistes* who had neither the passion nor the inclination to oppose him.

II

The exile of Madame de Staël and the closing of her salon was the obverse side of Napoléon's campaign to monopolize elite sociability in the interest of consolidating his regime. Madame de Staël supported the coup of 18 Brumaire and was enthusiastic about the conciliatory measures taken by the new leadership toward the émigrés and the moderate royalist opposition. Over the next six months, however, she began to see that Napoléon's ambitions were compromising liberty and thwarting the establishment of parliamentary government. Her salon, now located on the rue de Grenelle-Saint-Germain, remained what it had been under the Directory: a gathering of liberal republicans and moderate royalists, among whom Staël wished to create a consensus favoring an English-style constitutional regime. It was also an extraordinarily illustrious réunion, attracting numerous diplomats, ambassadors, artists, and men of letters, as well as such political notables as Camille Jordan, Mathieu de Montmorency, Benjamin Constant, and the comte de Narbonne. Although the salon maintained its characteristic ideological mix — Napoléon's brothers, a few ministers, and a handful of journalists allied to the regime were guests for a time — Staël's close ties with Constant and the idéologues linked it to the liberal opposition inside the Tribunate. When, with Staël's encouragement, Constant used his first speech in the Tribunate in January 1800 to test the limits of debate within the new institutions by denouncing the threat of tyranny, the association between Staël and the opposition was confirmed, her salon was placed under surveillance, and Joseph Fouché, the minister of police, summoned her to his office to suggest that she spend some time in the countryside. A year later, Napoléon purged the Tribunate of unreliable elements; he also tried to buy Staël's silence by offering to give her the two million livres her father had lent to the royal treasury. When the First Consul announced to the court his displeasure with her salon, "people deserted it," according to Abrantès. With the publication of Necker's *Dernières vues de politique et de finances* in 1802, which included a critique of the Constitution of the Year VIII, and the appearance of Staël's own *Delphine* a year later, with its appeal to "la France silencieuse mais éclairée," Napoléon had had enough — he forced her to stay away from Paris.[31]

At first glance, Napoléon's banishment of Madame de Staël seems easy to understand: her celebrity made her support for the liberal opposition a threat. Such a dramatic confrontation between two compelling personalities has encouraged contemporaries and historians to personalize the struggle.[32] There is no doubt that the two disliked each other intensely and almost right away: she found him rude and was disappointed with his policies; he believed women ought to be modest and not pretend to be "something other than their sex."[33] The matter is clearly more complicated. Even if we view her banishment in the context of a general crackdown on the opposition, problems remain. In one sense, Staël was a victim of timing: Napoléon's power was not yet secure in 1802 and 1803, and the increasing visibility brought by her writings coincided with his efforts to tame the Tribunate and reorganize the Institut de France, where the idéologues had their base. At the same time, she was suspected of complicity in the conspiracy of General Jean-Victor Moreau because a number of his accomplices were habitués of her salon. Years later, when Napoléon had little to fear from a few quiescent intellectuals, Madame de Staël might have been considered a minor irritant. After becoming minister of police in 1810, René Savary, who called the idéologues "boudeurs d'Auteuil" and the Institut "a retreat for philosophes," reported to the emperor that "the government is strong and its principle is national: it has rallied all opinions and all parties. One would regard as foolish those who would preach discord."[34] Napoléon had little tolerance for either traditional salonnières or women who spoke their minds, but that does not explain his persecution of Madame de Staël. A few old salonnières weathered the Empire unmolested, as long as they concentrated on social amusements or submitted to Napoléon's demands. Such was the case with Madame de Vaudément, who allowed Fouché to use her salon as a listening post, and Madame de Genlis, who kept things strictly literary at the Arsenal and wrote Napoléon letters denouncing the immorality of Staël's writings, while accusing her of conspiring against the government.[35] In 1802, Madame de Champcenetz and Madame de Dumas were exiled for participating in a royalist conspiracy, but Napoléon had nothing as concrete on Madame de Staël. Jean-François de La Harpe was dispatched to a village some distance from Paris for holding what Abrantès called "a mysterious political confabulation," but his fate was more a consequence of the vigor with which he expressed his views than of the fact that he had a salon. Napoléon exiled courtiers such as Madame de Balbi and Madame de Chevreuse for impertinence and "jesting remarks," but he left liberal salonnières like Madame de Condorcet alone, despite her opinions, because her salon at Auteuil was not overtly political and was frequented by a relatively homogeneous group of intellectuals.[36]

Madame de Staël saw herself as a victim of Napoléon's inability to tolerate her "untimely conversations" and her "unnatural" interest in politics. Being a man who hated "all independent beings," she reasoned, he could not abide expressions of nonconformity. Consequently, when she pleaded for the chance to return from exile in 1810, she hoped that he would accept her promise to think of nothing but "friendship, poetry, music, and painting" as a sufficient act of "submission owed to the monarch of France."[37] To be sure, Napoléon considered her insubordinate and unfeminine, but he seems to have been more disturbed by the fact that she agitated public opinion. Paris was still a *grande petite ville*, in which salons had acquired considerable importance as a means of communication. As he told Metternich, he did not care whether she was republican or royalist, but he could not have her in the capital, because she was "a perpetual motion machine, who stirs up the salons."[38] Simone Balayé emphasizes the ideological and cultural dimension of Staël's relationship to public opinion by arguing that her status as a writer was "the key to the problem." Literature, she pointed out, has "a social and political function" and required freedom for its exercise. There is no doubt that Napoléon regarded *Delphine* as antisocial and dangerous: it not only defended ideas, such as divorce, that he considered immoral, but it treated political matters he did not want publicly discussed. It is also clear that he wanted literature to serve power.[39] It does not follow, however, that Madame de Staël was exiled for her political writings. Publishing alone invited neither routine condemnation nor "systematic discrimination against writers on the basis of their gender," not even during the Terror and under Napoléon, when "public anxiety about the public influence of women" crested.[40] Censorship rather than exile was Napoléon's usual response to the publication of views deemed harmful by the regime. The emperor routinely manipulated the political press, but he let pass most literary and technical publications; he failed to exile any of the idéologues associated with the liberal opposition and told Savary to "[t]reat men of letters well," hoping that contented writers would "bring honor to France."[41]

Staël's role as a salonnière, rather than her insistence on the freedom to write, constituted the greatest threat. The Directory had previously told her to leave France because her salon was a meeting place for factions opposed to the regime. Under the Consulate, her salon was once again a *salon de fusion* that brought together nobles and men of the Revolution in the company of opinion makers in the worlds of diplomacy, letters, and the arts. "When in Paris," wrote Madame de Rémusat, "Mme. de Staël received many people, and all political subjects were freely discussed under her roof. . . . Men of letters, publicists, men of the Revolution, great lords, were all to be met there." According to Sophie Gay, her salon frightened Napoléon not only because it was "composed of the leaders of the opposition," but because it attracted "many people attached to the government."[42] In short, her salon arranged a fusion of the very forces Napoléon hoped to bring together for his own benefit and hindered his efforts to rally the aristocracy at a time when support for the Consulate was still fragile and factionalism had left public opinion vulnerable to disarray. Napoléon had already demonstrated an understanding of the role salons played in building coalitions among elites by the way he regarded the value of his marriage to Josephine. In conversations with his brother Lucien, he equated Staël's status as "an intriguing woman, accustomed to defying Governments" not with her writings but with the salon she had run at the time of the king's trial, "the orgies of the Directory," and the troubles that had led him to purge the Tribunate. In 1802, when Madame de Staël wrote the emperor asking that she be allowed to return to Paris on the strength of her promise to "never write a single word relating to public affairs," her request was denied on the basis of police reports that pointed to the large number of visitors she was receiving in Maffliers. Six years later, when her son, Auguste de Staël, asked Napoléon whether she could return if she devoted herself to literature, he was told that the combination of her salon and her opinions constituted the root of the problem: "To talk of literature, morals, the fine arts, and everything under the sun," said the emperor, "is to indulge in politics. . . . Women should knit. If I let her come to Paris she would make trouble; she would lose me the men around me." Once in exile himself, he admitted that he had found Staël "very dangerous, because she gathered together in her salon . . . all the partisans, republicans, and royalists. She put them in each other's presence; she united them all against me. She attacked me from all sides. . . . Her salon was fatal." He filed the same complaint against the salon of Madame Permon, the mother of Abrantès, scolding General Junot for spending too much time there: "People who detest me meet in her drawing room; people who, before my return from Egypt, were prisoners in the Temple for their opinions—these are her friends. And you, great blockhead! You make them your friends also . . . you make friends of my enemies."[43]

Politically subversive sociability among elites was harder to suppress than other forms of opposition—like a critical press—because it took place in the privacy of the home under the auspices of women who were less vulnerable than men to the subtle forms of repression prescribed by the law. Madame de Staël was keenly aware of the costs and benefits of her situation: on the one hand, women were "less accessible than men to the fears and hopes which power can bestow" and therefore harder to coerce; on the other hand, they were more vulnerable to a dictator's irrational ire.[44] Banishment was a crude instrument, but it had two advantages—it drove a wedge between Madame de Staël and those who feared Napoléon's disapproval, and it swiftly decapitated her salon. If it was her salon that made her powerful, then it was enough to exile her in order to destroy it; exile, however, seems only to have enhanced her literary career.

Napoléon considered Staël's salon a political club because he associated salons with frivolous amusements undertaken in the company of women who behaved as he expected. Staël's salon, however, did not fit his preconceptions: it was not just a place of benign sociability, it was a forum where his adversaries met to criticize the regime.[45] Under authoritarian systems, private associations tend to be either official or illegal. Madame Récamier's salon was a case in point. Although a fixture of high society under the Directory, it was not until the time of the Consulate that the immense fortune of her husband allowed the couple to entertain on a truly lavish scale. By 1802, she had acquired a reputation as an incomparable hostess with a special gift for creating amity and sympathy among men with opposing ideas. Napoléon closed her salon in February 1803 by prohibiting her regular Monday receptions. Although it was generally believed that this was the price she was made to pay for associating with Madame de Staël and General Moreau, it was the sociability of her salon that was at issue, rather than her ideas. Récamier published no political writings, but she had access to fashionable society and was thus able to provide Napoleon's rival Moreau with exposure to a diverse crowd of notables. In addition, her varied social network made the relatively mild punishment she received an effective warning to others. Although she was not exiled until after returning from a visit to Staël at Coppet in 1809, her salon remained under suspicion from the beginning of the Empire; not only did she have friends in the opposition, but the circumstances surrounding her husband's financial ruin estranged her from the emperor.[46] By all accounts, Madame

Récamier was apolitical. Constant wrote that she "occupied herself with politics only out of her general concern for the vanquished of all parties," and Chateaubriand insisted that she "would have never entered into political matters without the irritation that she experienced over the exile of Madame de Staël." Stendhal, who met her in 1803, saw her salon as completely benign — "There is music, the mothers play at *bouillotte* [the card game "three of a kind"], their daughters at other games, and they nearly all finish by dancing."[47] The problem was not her personal attachments, however, but her association with just about everyone in a salon that was not within the ambit of the court. If Récamier had been closely identified with the regime, then her social ecumenicism would have been an asset. As it was, her neutrality made her a threat because inclusiveness in the absence of an affirmed ideology meant a lack of control. Accounts by the duchesse d'Abrantès and Madame de Rémusat show repeatedly that Napoléon resented associates who were willing to get along with his enemies and was on guard against anyone who was "careful to conciliate all parties."[48]

By demanding the support of those with an independent status whose prestige he needed to consolidate his regime, Napoléon created a problem he could not entirely solve: how to control the rich and powerful once he had helped restore their wealth and social position? It was a problem to which he attended immediately by turning the granting of amnesty to émigrés and the withholding of unsold biens nationaux into tools of social appeasement and political pacification. The persecution of Madame de Staël and Madame Récamier were part of a larger strategy of intimidation that took a variety of forms — exile, imprisonment, and execution were only the most extreme. Indeed, Napoléon selectively exiled or banished quite a few nobles in a manner that most observers judged relatively effective. Madame de Boigne called exile "the chief restraint upon . . . Faubourg Saint-Germain" and attributed the scrupulous prudence of the nobility to the fear it provoked. Staël thought of her own ordeal as a clear warning to others, and Chastenay believed that the threat alone induced many to present themselves at court. The emperor, however, used a variety of other means to obtain similar results: he dispatched government agents and military personnel to society balls, placed spies in salons, drafted nobles into service at court, and arranged marriages between his associates and the daughters of the rich. If these failed he could always execute a royalist conspirator as "an example to Brittany" or suspend the sentences imposed on convicted rebels to win their gratitude and indebtedness.[49]

Madame de Rémusat was undoubtedly correct in arguing that Napoléon regarded women as inferior, but he also acknowledged their power by seeking their counsel and by using intimidation to silence them or make them submit. He once told General Junot that aristocratic women thought themselves "privileged by their sex" to lure his supporters away from him. In this sense, his misogyny paralleled and frequently expressed his feelings toward the aristocracy, whose authority provoked in him the desire to humiliate, and whose eventual submission invited contempt. The most memorable episodes of imperial spite occurred in public and were calculated to emphasize a woman's deviation from the conventional norm — as when he told Madame Regnault de Saint Jean d'Angély at a ball for the grand duchess of Berg that she looked old, or when he named the lover of each woman attending breakfast with the empress. When Madame de Staël first met him in society, he told her that the greatest of all women were those with the most children.[50] Madame de Rémusat attributed such behavior to a fear of women's social skills, and Talleyrand thought it expressed his rejection of their civilizing role, but it seems more likely that he needed constantly to reenact and reinforce what he regarded as his victory over traditional elites. On one occasion, when he refused to pardon a group of royalists condemned to death, he told Madame de Rémusat that his resolve would "give M. Chateaubriand an opportunity of writing some pathetic pages, which he will read aloud in Faubourg Saint-Germain. The fine ladies will weep, and you will see that this will console him!"[51]

III

The imperial court dominated high society to a greater degree than had the court of Versailles. To some extent, its centrality was a reflection of its size: by 1814, the court had nearly 3,000 officials and over 100 chamberlains, making it both the largest in Europe and the largest in French history.[52] Napoléon wanted a brilliant court befitting the grandeur of a ruler whose conquests stretched from Hamburg to Rome. Few observers doubted the court's splendor, but many also considered it a crashing bore. Victorine de Chastenay found it strained and unpleasant, despite "the magnificence of its fêtes." At Fontainebleau, wrote Madame de Rémusat, prudence and custom stifled spontaneous conversation and led to ennui.[53] A variety of factors contributed to excessive formality: Napoléon was alternatively aloof, imperious, or rude, and he discouraged private friendships between courtiers who were already less well known to one another because of their more diverse social backgrounds than had been the case at Versailles. Most observers, however, blamed strict protocol and the reintroduction of the rigid etiquette of the past. The emperor placed the court under martial law: etiquette was "regulated with extreme precision" and ceremonies "were gone through as though by beat of drum." The situation worsened after Napoléon's marriage to Marie-Louise in 1810, when excessive courtly politesse became disconnected from its prior social function and served only to embellish an endless series of mechanical routines. Madame de Staël pointed to such practices as proof of the intellectual nullity of those who tolerated Napoléon's despotic rule: "When there were four hundred people in his salon," she wrote, "a blind man could have believed himself alone, so profound was the silence that one encountered there. . . . The oriental etiquette that Bonaparte established in his court blocked all the light that one reaped from easy communication in society."[54]

In the latter half of the eighteenth century, the distance between the court and the city had widened as the salons of Paris increased their autonomy from Versailles. Under the Empire, the process was reversed as Napoléon sought "to confiscate . . . *la mondanité parisienne*" in an effort to control the elites.[55] By suppressing autonomous sociability and by having government officials open salons, he eventually succeeded in giving the so-called "official salons" of the Empire a predominant place in le monde — the policy of fusion, coupled with authoritarian rule, tended to make high society and official society one and the same.

The most prominent official salons were ministerial receptions that attracted a clientele made up mostly of diplomats, officeholders, and *gens de la cour*, a group that by then included quite a few old nobles. By the end of the Empire, according to Victor de Broglie, official society was distributed among three salons currently or formerly associated with the Ministry of Foreign Affairs, those of the duc de Bassano (Hugues-Bertrand Maret), who became foreign minister in 1811, Armand de Caulaincourt, his rival, and Talleyrand, France's disgraced but indispensable grand dignitary.[56] Official salons centered not on a woman but on a powerful male figure, and they originated not in the salons of the eighteenth century but in the receptions held by the directors and the consuls of the previous regimes. Second Consul Jean-Jacques Cambacérès opened the drawing room of his hôtel and received company every Tuesday and Saturday for six months of the year during the Consulate; visitors, mostly magistrates, functionaries, and returned émigrés, remembered these gatherings as boring, albeit cordial, but had high praise for the gourmet dinners he gave. When Madame d'Abrantès became an official maîtresse de maison as wife of the governor of Paris, she took Cambacérès's receptions as a model, asking the famous epicure Laurent Grimod de la Reynière to recommend a chef of the same quality as his. Official salons were also prefigured by the *salle de audience* of ministers like Fouché, where casual meetings in which people with official business gathered to chat were turned into regular receptions that allowed the government to attract and unite those it hoped to convert.[57]

By the time Bassano became foreign minister, there was no longer much difference between the government and the court. Ministers and grand dignitaries were also officers of the imperial household and those seeking jobs or favors had to go to the imperial palace. Broglie heard of his nomination as a chief *auditeur* for the *maître des requêtes* of the Armée du Nord in Bassano's salon, and the comte de Chabrol attributed his promotion to prefect of the Seine to the fact that Napoléon had noticed him one day at the Tuileries.[58] The institutional and political proximity of the court and the official salons meant that those who attended the latter could not criticize the regime. Official salons could not exist for purposes unrelated to the policies of the government and became in effect physical extensions of the court into the social spaces of le monde. The only politics that were possible under such circumstances were court politics — hence, the contest for the emperor's favor that erupted between Bassano, Talleyrand, and Caulaincourt after 1809 was echoed in the official salons. At the Hôtel Gallifet, Bassano worked to gather support for an invasion of Russia, while his wife staged puppet shows mocking Talleyrand's and Caulaincourt's preference for peace. According to Broglie, the company kept by Bassano and Caulaincourt "mutually scoffed at and denounced one another."[59] Under these conditions, the role of the hostess was not that of a salonnière who presided over an exchange of ideas but a maîtresse de maison who did the honors of the house, supported her husband, and cultivated respect for the emperor by enforcing civility and silencing *frondeurs*.

Napoléon equated women and politics with intrigue, and he did not want women interfering, or even taking an interest, in "serious matters."[60] Salons, he surmised, were best designed to provide amusements that would divert women from emulating such salonnières as Madame de Staël. Although he gave his male chamberlains control over access in order to deprive court women of the influence he imagined them to have possessed in the past, he was also quite willing to use the women of the court to influence high society. On the one hand, "anything resembling intrigue was almost unknown" at court, according to Madame de Rémusat, because "each individual was convinced that everything depended on the sole will of the master" and the affairs of state "were absolutely confined to the cabinet." Napoléon refused to have a favorite, because he did not want "the empire of women" to control the court. "They have done wrong by Henri IV and Louis XIV," he wrote. "My *métier* and I are much more serious than that of these princes, and the French themselves have become too serious to pardon their sovereign for public liaisons and mistresses-in-chief." On the other hand, the efficacy of using women associated with the regime to set examples with regard to taste and fashion was consistent with his policies — apparently matters that were "unimportant" could be political as well. After establishing the Continental System in 1806, he told officials to have their wives serve Swiss tea and chicory coffee in their salons and cautioned against their wearing dresses made in England.[61] Napoléon, wrote Claire de Rémusat, was convinced that "the influence of women had harmed the kings of France," and he considered "the power they had acquired in society as an intolerable usurpation." He wanted them to be little more than ornaments of his court, a development Madame de Staël registered in 1800 when she observed that "since the Revolution men had thought it politically and morally useful to reduce women to the most absurd mediocrity." Chastenay refused a position at court because she didn't want to stand around like a "mannequin." She was no more impressed with the sexual asymmetry of Bassano's salon, where she found the men standing and talking or playing billiards while the women sat behind them looking at their backs.[62]

The duchesse de Bassano, reputedly the most elegant contemporary *femme du monde*, and well known for her spectacular parties, preferred her husband's charming stories or the company of artists to political discussion. Napoléon, who paid the duc de Bassano a salary of 400,000 francs, was especially anxious for the duchesse to have a magnificent open house in order to lure the diplomatic corps away for the Hôtel de Luynes in Faubourg Saint-Germain.[63] But it was Talleyrand's salon on the rue d'Anjou that showed most thoroughly how official status warped the distinctive features of the original institution. Talleyrand's wife (the former Madame Grand), who did the honors of his salon, was by all accounts an intellectual nullity, whom her husband overtly ignored. The company was a mixture of diplomats, old nobles, and government officials, although it included a number of Talleyrand's relatives. It also tended to be politically homogeneous, since those with pronounced royalist opinions were usually unwelcome. Guests were often served dinner, after which they were more likely to play cards than engage in organized conversation. Talleyrand rarely spoke and preferred to listen to amusing stories, like those of the duc de Choiseul-Gouffier, France's ambassador to Constantinople, who often treated his guests to lively descriptions of the customs of the Turkish Empire.[64]

IV

It is hard to say at what point Napoléon no longer considered the old aristocracy a threat. His marriage to Marie-Louise suggests that he had conquered Faubourg Saint-Germain and was now intent on gaining access to the family of kings. By then, the old aristocracy of the faubourg was marginalized and constrained. *Ralliés* were usually confined to the military and the court to ensure their vulnerability to sanctions. Although the creation of the imperial nobility was intended as the culmination of the policy of fusion, it had the added benefit of placing potential opponents in positions of subservience. Of the 950 old-regime nobles who accepted imperial titles, only 18 percent were *hauts fonctionnaires*, and many of those worked in the emperor's household. When Madame de Chevreuse, daughter of the duc de Luynes, criticized the government in high society, she was forced either to become a *dame de palais* or lose her family's estate; when she refused to attend the captive queen of Spain, she was exiled to the provinces. Meanwhile, members of the nobility awaited news of war and peace with interest, "because every family was more or less connected with the army."[65]

François Villemain describes the faubourg in 1808 as a society "on a second plane, a society of leisure and independent thought in this busy century; a society of elegant simplicity and witty grace under the reign of the sword and algebra."[66] Royalist salons were held in check not only by fear of exile and the police, but by the fact that many old nobles had relatives who had rallied to the regime. Even the duc de Luynes, whose grand hôtel on the rue Saint-Dominique was the center of gravity of Faubourg Saint-Germain, maintained a respectful restraint toward the regime.[67] Having rebuilt their patrimony through savings, cunning, and the emperor's largesse, the aristocracy wanted above all to live in peace and comfort. Intrigue with "inferior conspirators" and "paid agents of disturbance and disorder," as Madame de Boigne called royalist militants, was generally forbidden in salons at a time when the regime's most active opponents had already been chased from France or isolated in the provinces. The remaining *irréconciliables* of the nobles' quartier usually met not in hôtels but in the Café de Valois.[68] In private salons, aristocrats unmercifully ridiculed, mocked, and sneered at the emperor, his family, and his court in printed lampoons, satirical verses, and biting stories; high society indulged the most outrageous rumors about Napoléon's illegitimate birth, Josephine's affairs, and his brother Joseph's attempt to poison his wife. But opposition of this sort was strictly verbal, a sign of weakness, confined to epigrams and bad jokes behind closed doors.[69]

Although open political partisanship seems to have died out by 1806, the absence of a vocal opposition did not mean that the policy of fusion had been a complete success.[70] The old aristocratic society might have been rendered impotent in its muffled acrimony, but it had also come to form a largely separate world that resisted most of the emperor's advances. Napoléon's efforts to create a new ruling class had paradoxical results: on the one hand, they established the juridical and institutional framework for a fusion of interests at the top of the social hierarchy based on property and access to appointive and elective office; on the other hand, they deepened a sense of difference among the notables by promoting distinctions among supporters, victims, and "deserters," which were refined and extended each time a nomination or an act of coercion prompted anguished discussions and recriminations in le monde. To be sure, returned émigrés, habituated by family and social relations to insist upon sensitive points of honor, were bound to nurture resentments and pretensions, but Napoléon added fuel to the fire by playing elites off against one another and by using tactics that often required people tied to more than one camp to sever previous connections. The result was a petty war of coteries that put the salons of the past in a more positive light, while anticipating the "rancor and hatred" that would be given free reign during the Restoration.[71]

The political geography of Paris was reshaped in consequence. Posh neighborhoods became associated with the ideological preferences and social antecedents of their principal inhabitants: Faubourg Saint-Germain was ultraroyalist and aristocratic; the Chaussée d'Antin was the home of the Bonapartist nouveaux riches; and in Faubourg Saint-Honoré, liberal nobles struggled to reconcile their nostalgia for the both the Enlightenment and the monarchy by cultivating a royalism consistent with the early accomplishments of the Revolution. Although demographic realignments since 1789 contributed to the spatial differentiation of le monde, the neighborhoods that constituted its basic elements gained their rhetorical significance only under the Empire, when they acquired the power of symbols capable of designating an entire sensibility and a way of life.[72] Once neighborhoods became politically distinct, they could be anchored in a set of ideologically distinctive salons; members of the most elegant aristocratic society could then begin to travel between more or less exclusive private salons, where they would encounter mostly their own, and other mondain gatherings, where they mixed uneasily with others. Each neighborhood under the Empire began to be associated with a specific set of salons whose social and political nuances were generally known: those of Adélaïde de La Briche, Louise de Boigne, and Marie-Anne de Rumford in Saint-Honoré; those of the duchesse de Luynes, Madame de Vintimille, and Madame de Pastoret in Saint-Germain. In retrospect, Saint-Honoré was the seat of a nascent Orleanism under the Empire, while the salons of Saint-Germain harbored the future leadership of the ultras.[73]

Ordinarily, "the two societies of the old and new *régimes* were habitually separated," but they sometimes met in official salons, at ambassadorial residences, or in homes of foreigners, where they would not have to be on one another's turf. Even on these occasions, however, relations were strained: at the Foreign Ministry receptions Chastenay attended, people kept to their own circle; when Caulaincourt attended a ball given by Madame Récamier to mark the end of Carnival, he was embarrassed to encounter guests who believed him to have been complicit in the kidnapping of the duc d'Enghien. Abrantès concluded that no amount of imperial splendor was capable of putting members of society at ease with one another; in the end, the Empire failed to establish the "mutual respect necessary for society to be more than a momentary gathering of individuals who no longer know one another as soon as they return home." "[G]atherings were possible under the Empire," wrote Chateaubriand, but only because the emperor had "fashioned a society of passive obedience" in which Bonapartists and their adversaries were prevented from discussing public affairs. Napoléon "would willingly have put an stop to [the] jesting" about manners and appearances that took place when different elements of society were apart, "but this was beyond his powers."[74]

The Napoleonic experience showed that society life could be annexed for political purposes and that the manners cultivated in salons could serve to embellish and legitimize a dictatorial regime. It also demonstrated that criticism of the state could be emptied from salons when le monde became contiguous with the political class and authoritarian politics turned institutions of sociability either into accessories of the court or exclusive, secretive coteries. Salons emerged from the Napoleonic era less overtly preoccupied with political questions than they had been in 1789, but more clearly partisan than in 1800. They had become vehicles of factionalism rather than instruments for the creation of enlightened public opinion, more suitable for expressing the desire for advantage or revenge than for engaging in a collective reflection on the common good, the constitutional order, and the nature of the state.

V

Madame de Staël reentered Paris in May 1814 and took up residence in Faubourg Saint-Germain, where she revived her salon around a core of habitués who had met with her in exile at Coppet. Madame de Montcalm, sister of the duc de Richelieu, saw her from time to time surrounded by admirers and noted that even for those who detested her, she was an object of general curiosity. Her two most famous novels, *Delphine* and *Corinne*, were still in print, and would remain popular at least until the July Monarchy, when the latter continued to receive critical attention.[75] Although she was discouraged and frightened by the Hundred Days, her waning years, by most accounts, were happy ones—Madame de Rémusat had the impression that she was "overwhelmed with joy at being once more in her own land, and at seeing the dawn of the constitutional regime for which she so ardently longed."[76] Montcalm claimed that her "admirable conversation" suffered from the onset of a fatal illness, but Broglie testified that she nevertheless rejoined le monde with aplomb and made her salon on the rue de Grenelle "the rendezvous for all the foreigners that the Restoration attracted to Paris."[77] As a leader of liberal opinion, Madame de Staël was sought out by ministers and princes; she met with the comte de Provence and the comte d'Artois before arriving in Paris and was even able to arrange an interview between Lafayette and Emperor Alexander I. Broglie, who would soon marry Albertine de Staël, used her salon to discuss pending legislation, such as the new electoral law, and helped make Staël's home a rallying point for liberal parliamentarians. Madame de Staël's personal initiatives concerned mostly foreign policy and concentrated on efforts to limit the French indemnity and reduce the number of troops occupying the capital. The latter question not only became the subject of an extensive correspondence with the duke of Wellington, it made her salon a center of opposition to British policy, to the extent that Lord Canning and Charles Stuart thought it necessary to warn their government about the "dangers inherent in Mme de Staël exciting national passions by her language."[78]

Madame de Staël's celebrity status and her public activities as a salonnière contrasted sharply with her pessimism about the mingling of salons and politics in the last years of her life. She was convinced that the triumph of the Empire and fifteen years of military despotism had destroyed the enlightened sociability of the eighteenth century by "enervat[ing] the public spirit" and by changing "everything in the mores of the country."[79] The Revolution had created circumstances favorable to Napoléon's designs, and he had in turn destroyed the sources of intellectual curiosity and humanitarian "enthusiasm" by killing liberty and choking off all communication between individuals on serious matters. Staël tied these consequences not only to a general desire to avoid chaos, which Napoléon exploited, but more specifically to the emperor's contempt for humanity and his fear of honest social interaction, characteristics he seemed to have communicated to the entire French elite.[80]

Staël's belief that Napoléon had brought about a fundamental change in

French sociability is evident in the skepticism with which she regarded the sociability of the Bourbon Restoration. Although she died in 1817, she saw enough of the new era to formulate a consistently unflattering impression. By reviving "the old habits of the court," Napoléon made "the hope of obtaining jobs the principle of life animating society" and bequeathed to the Restoration salons that, in her opinion, endangered the consolidation of parliamentary institutions.[81] High society, she wrote, had become a "labyrinth of interests and ambitions" that found expression in the intense political factionalism of the Chamber of Deputies, where the parties found it impossible to compromise. Political leaders treated one another without cordiality, lacked integrity, and were incapable of being sincere.[82] In the past, women had softened men's passions, and salon conversation had subjected public issues to the most rigorous intellectual scrutiny, but by the time of the Restoration, "women no longer felt the need to be superior to men." The grandes dames of the Old Regime had maintained the seriousness and good manners of the past, but they were now elderly, embittered, or had voluntarily withdrawn from public life. The center of gravity in high society had shifted to the *hommes nouveaux* who had been active in public affairs during the Empire, and who "had all the passions of the Revolution and all the vanities of the Old Regime." On the one hand, the "grand jurisdiction" the aristocracy had once exercised over the size and tone of la bonne compagnie had been broken by the invasion of "the less refined class," cheapening the price of admission and filling the salons with young people lacking in "serious instruction." On the other hand, "the fear inspired by the imperial government had destroyed any practice of independence in conversation."

> [T]he French, under this government, had almost all become diplomats, so that society spent its time in insignificant talk that in no way recalled the audacious spirit of France. Assuredly, no one had anything to fear in 1814, under Louis XVIII, but the habit of caution had become a reflex, and besides, courtiers had determined that it was not good form to talk politics, or to deal with any serious subject: they hoped once again to have a frivolous — and therefore subjected — nation; but the only result they obtained was to make conversation insipid and to deprive themselves of all the means of knowing the true opinion of each.[83]

Such doubts about the political influence of salons centered on two forms of deception, one involving the use of elegant manners by charlatans to give themselves an "illusory importance" and the other concerning the ability of the mediocre to silence merit with ridicule and lower the general political intelligence of society. She was not the first to notice that la vie mondaine was susceptible to artifice and frivolity, but she was more adamant than most in linking such vices to what she saw as the degeneration of the salon. It was as if she had discovered all of a sudden that every positive attribute of the salon had its antithesis: manners could indicate good character, but they could also deceive; intimacy could enhance the exchange of ideas, but it could also lead to clannishness and bigotry; equality in conversation could support generous sentiments, but it could also cultivate a sense of exclusivity; the salon could serve as a news bureau, but it could also be used to manipulate public opinion. Viewing the salon as a product of its moral environment, she was forced to conclude that it was a chameleonlike institution whose essential nature was no better than that of those who made use of it. Salons could serve to improve humanity in certain circumstances, but they would always register the defects of the prevailing political and social system. When the enlightened sociability of the eighteenth century failed to assist in the triumph of liberal institutions, Madame de Staël began to see salons less as Athenian symposia and more as small villages, with all the venal passions, jealousies, seductions, and material desires that existed in the real world. Gens du monde, apparently, were no better than anyone else.[84]

If women were morally superior to men, then they would have to bear the greatest degree of responsibility for society's moral decline. Salonnières, she believed, were supposed to bring out the best in people and cultivate genius. The women of the Restoration, however, were remiss in their duties and were failing to oppose the rising tide of corruption. They had become a "kind of artificial third sex, a grim product of the depraved social order," and were apparently no less factious, frivolous, and vain than the men. Instead of demanding "attentive listeners," they feigned innocence or dwelled on trivial matters in order to please; they competed for attention, engaged in hateful rivalries, and sought out celebrities to bolster the reputations of their salons.[85] In the end, they harmed not only themselves but also the common good: they exposed themselves and society to flattery, deception, and betrayal at the hands of men whom they had failed to influence in a positive way.

The disillusionment of Madame de Staël was just one more indication that the Enlightenment was over. Her death, like those of Jean-Baptiste Suard in 1817 and André Morellet in 1819, contributed to a sense of loss among young liberals that helped inaugurate a persistent nostalgia paralleled by an ongoing process of idealization. In imagining the eighteenth century as both superior and dead, the generation that frequented the Parisian salons of the early nineteenth century was prepared to disdain the present and struggle to recapture a vanished ideal. Staël's pessimism at the end of her life reflected this state of affairs and gave those who identified with her legacy a language with which to deplore the folly of their time. It was not that the salon was dead—high society grew in size, popularity, and complexity throughout the first half of the nineteenth century—it was just that the social elite that had grown up in the shadow of the Revolution and Napoléon never tired of saying that it was. "My God! What a pitiful thing is the conversation in these large assemblies," wrote the duchesse de Duras in 1817 after dining in the grand monde. "You could just sense the joy of those who only lived by ridiculing others. Poor nourishment. Their spirit benefits no one. . . . It was the first [party] of the year: the stupidity, the foolishness, the gossip, the frivolity was in all its glory."[86] According to the marquis de Custine, the art of bringing out the best in others, which he considered "the great charm of ancient French society," was "scarcely known" by the 1830s "because it requires greater refinement of mind to praise than to depreciate." By 1837, it seemed to Delphine de Girardin that everyone had been complaining about the sterility of salons and the puerility of high society for twenty years—she insisted that there was more to it than beautiful duchesses, insignificant gossip, and dandies, although she too was forced to concede its artifice, hypocrisy, silliness, vanity, pretension, and "exceptional tolerance for what is really bad."[87]

The other side of this coin was the search to regenerate society by reconstructing the old sociable ideal, an ideal that by now owed much to Staël's conception of rigorous, refined, and regulated conversation as the path to political reconciliation and civic improvement. But it was also an ideal that crystallized in an age of reaction and romanticism among a generation that was tired of politics and yearned for its erasure. For François Villemain, French sociability regained its earlier perfection in a handful of salons during the Restoration, "where politics had not set aside *politesse*, where ranks, and even opinions, were brought together by the best and truest equality, that of knowledge and noble sentiments, where men, engaged in great matters, could still find improvement, where men of science were greeted by men of leisure, and all were more or less inspired by the good taste that the influence of women has contributed to high society, and that often added less to the progress of useful truths than to the grace of the conversations."[88] Villemain and Sainte-Beuve saw the postrevolutionary sociable ideal actualized most clearly in the salon of the duchesse de Duras, where Sainte-Beuve found "a chivalrous alliance of legitimacy and liberty" under the supervision of "a rare woman, who naturally caused to take place around her a marvelous compromise between taste, the tone of the past, and the new forces."[89] By her simplicity, grace, and intelligence, Duras was able constantly to focus the attention of her guests on the higher qualities embodied in the arts — when the conversation veered into politics, she gently but firmly nudged it back. Determined to dispel the acrimony left by memories of the Revolution, Duras worked to create in her salon an atmosphere where politics would simply vanish; she never allowed her salon to become a sort of club, as did other grandes dames, where "one leaves exalted by the bluster of deputies rushing in from the Chamber after a fiery speech." When Lord Stuart raised the possibility of dissension in the cabinet between Chateaubriand and Villèle, Duras shifted the mood by asking the comte de Capo d'Istria his views on the former's latest literary achievements. According to Villemain, she welcomed the novelist Alexandre Duval, despite his reputation as a revolutionary, because she judged him a man of honor and talent. She also frequently invited Delphine Gay to read verse, convinced that the young woman's charm and beauty would silence the diplomats, politicians, and scientists in her circle and put all opinions seemingly in accord.[90]

Madame de Boigne considered Duras to have fancied herself a more diffident version of Madame de Staël, whose former position in the world she sought to claim. She wrote novels that displayed "a thorough knowledge of salon customs" and copied the mannerisms of her exemplar by twiddling a sprig of green in her fingers. Chateaubriand thought that Duras "had the imagination and even something of the expression of Madame de Staël," and Villemain believed that her celebrity came in part from their highly touted friendship.[91] Under the Empire, in letters to Staël's Swiss neighbor Roselie de Constant, Duras expressed admiration for the Staël's books and curiosity about her life at Coppet. When the Bourbons returned, she acted on her oft-expressed desire to get to know Madame de Staël by initiating correspondence, occupying an adjacent residence, and attending her salon.[92] But it is not clear whether Duras loved Staël or Corinne, the heroine of Staël's most famous novel, about a woman of genius driven to despair and death by social conventions. To be sure, their friendship owed as much to what Villemain called "certain affinities of mind and heart" as it did to Duras's attraction to Staël as an author. Villemain and Chateaubriand describe her desire to play the muse as requiring a posture of devotion and intellectual passivity, but she was a well-educated woman who considered the cultivation of merit as serious work and who criticized other salonnières for occupying themselves with "petty things that [are] incompatible with what is simple and elevated." In this sense, she would have agreed with Marie d'Agoult's insistence that women could "exercise a serious influence outside of private life" by capturing people's imaginations, stimulating their minds, and encouraging them to reexamine received opinions.[93] But when it came to politics, Duras took as her model the celebrated fictional muse who supported liberty by questioning conventions, rather than Staël herself, the salonnière who acted politically to promote enlightenment. Whereas Staël wanted to transform sociability into action by placing transcendent reason at the disposal of free institutions, Duras hoped to transcend politics entirely through a concerted admiration for something more beautiful and more ideal. Like many of her generation, Duras misread Staël, who criticized Restoration society, not because politics had destroyed sociability, but because salons and salonnières had failed to create a better politics.

Madame de Staël's legacy to the nineteenth-century salon was to situate politics ambiguously at the center of its preoccupations. On the one hand, her life justified the image of the salonnière as a woman with strong political opinions who was eager to act forcefully on the periphery of the parliamentary game. On the other hand, her eighteenth-century sensibilities, reinforced by long-standing gender conventions, led her to refuse to make her salon a political coterie. She continued to see the reconciliation of antagonists as the salonnière's unique and transcendent role. During the Restoration, her salon was closely associated with liberals who were skeptical about the character of Louis XVIII and openly hostile to the ultras; at the same time, she "admitted all opinions and all ways of expressing them," because "she did not care to deprive her *salon* of anyone adept at [the] kind of fencing [that] could bring it variety."[94] Staël's daughter, by contrast, invited mostly liberals and ex-Bonapartists and did not mind seeing the rancor and passions of aristocratic society transported into her home. As Madame de Boigne explained, the women of her generation "lived in the narrow ideas of party spirit" and considered Staël's indulgence toward those with whom she disagreed "very shocking."[95] At the same time, it was a generation that sought to salvage the French sociable ideal, along with a public role for upper-class women, by associating the salon with reconciliation.

CHAPTER FOUR

Le Pays féminin (1815–1848)

By the time the troops of the Quadruple Alliance entered Paris on March 31, 1814, the salons of Faubourg Saint-Germain were already helping to create a current of opinion strong enough to persuade Allied leaders to support a Bourbon restoration. Even before the fall of the Empire, the salons of Saint-Germain had been considered active coteries of royalist intrigue.[1] The crossing of the Rhine by Field Marshal Blücher in January was Saint-Germain's signal to awake. Within days, royalist agents arrived in Paris with the king's proclamation from Hartwell promising to respect acquired positions and give France free institutions. Copies of the document were distributed to the salons, where society women quickly got to work furtively slipping them under doors and sticking them into the shutters of boutiques. After the French capitulation, lampoons against Napoléon and his family were sold openly on the street. The duchesse de Duras, accompanied by her daughter and two servants in livery, passed out white cockades and armbands to passersby. As Allied troops approached the French capital, conflicting news regarding the coalition's plans convinced royalists of the need to demonstrate that the country favored the Bourbons. Consequently, the arrival of foreign troops on the 31st unleashed a veritable aristocratic *journée:*

amid considerable enthusiasm, young royalists ventured out into the streets wearing white cockades; women waved white handkerchiefs out windows and shouted "Vivent les Bourbons" at passing soldiers; smartly dressed *gens de société* paid crowds to chant royalist slogans or read the king's proclamation to the public. "[W]omen of the finest circles," according to the duchesse de Maillé, "set the best example," abandoning their normally retiring lives to walk the streets and harangue the people. That evening, as Saint-Germain celebrated, a group of royalists from the neighborhood followed Sosthène de La Rochefoucauld to the Vendôme column and tried to pull down the statue of Napoléon.[2]

The role of salons in early nineteenth-century French political life was already clear to Madame de Staël in 1814, when she warned that their influence would be a problem for Restoration governments to overcome. A year later, when Louis XVIII reentered Paris after the Hundred Days, Madame de Montcalm had the same impression, noting that a few salons could already be considered "a deliberating power in the government" with the right to judge her brother's ministerial appointments "according to the nuance of their opinions."[3]

I

Aristocratic high society was at its pinnacle during the Restoration. According to the comtesse de Bassanville, Paris took on "an unaccustomed air of celebration" in the winter following the second return of Louis XVIII as the pleasure that had faded in the last years of Napoléon's endless wars began to return, "younger, livelier, and more animated than ever." From the vantage point of the Second Empire, Virginie Ancelot remembered the Restoration as a time of rebirth, when men of letters and politicians alike were more urbane and distinguished than before, and when society was more united than would have been conceivable in the 1860s. For Duras, the society of the Restoration came closer than any other to that of the eighteenth century, when the old *douceur de vivre* allowed gens du monde to breath free. In short, aristocratic society came to life with renewed vigor, and the sociable traditions of the past were easily restored.[4]

When the Consulate revived la vie mondaine, salons that had existed before 1792 reopened only slowly as émigrés returned, tested the waters, and displayed themselves with caution. In 1814 and 1815, by contrast, there was no such hesitation — the rich and powerful were mostly on hand and former émigrés had had time to repair their finances. Consequently, when the Empire fell, previously established salons opened their doors effortlessly and new ones were constituted in rapid succession. Each class, each party, and each political nuance, it seemed, had its salon. By 1819, François Villemain wrote, the salons of Paris had become "une puissance considérable." Guillaume de Bertier de Sauvigny claims that Faubourg Saint-Germain was never greater nor more brilliant than in this period, when, counterposed to a lackluster royal court, its salons became "the center of social life."[5]

The advent of broad civil liberties and the end to the enforced silence of the Empire made the Restoration favorable to the reemergence and proliferation of salons.[6] Salon sociability also benefited from peace, material prosperity, the desire to impress foreigners, and the mondain prospects created by the establishment of a new royal court.[7] The most important factor, however, was the Charter of 1814, which created the conditions for a sustained development of parliamentary government. Alphonse de Lamartine made an explicit connection between sociability and politics when he noted that "[c]onversation had returned with the Restoration, with the court, the nobility, the emigration, liberty, and leisure. The constitutional regime, by [virtue of] its continual party controversy, [and] by the very novelty of a regime that allowed people to speak freely in a country that had experienced ten years of silence, accelerated the expression of ideas and the steady and lively murmur of Parisian society more than at any other time in our history."[8]

The Charter contributed to the vibrancy of salons, because the new institutions made public opinion a real force in politics, created a framework for perpetual debate, and allowed party politics to spill over into le monde, as it had in the early 1790s. Karl Marx noted the relationship in *The Eighteenth Brumaire of Louis Bonaparte* when he wrote that the parliamentary regime "lives by discussion" and that "the debating club in parliament is necessarily supplemented by debating clubs in the salons." The vicomte de Beaumont-Vassy pointed out that during the July Monarchy, each session of Parliament produced "a perpetual exchange of relations, combinations, and ideas" between the Chambers "and a great number of Parisian salons."[9] Before 1814, the royalists and liberals of the faubourgs could talk in private, but now they had projects to offer and legislation to pass — as a consequence, the gatherings over which the grandes dames of the aristocracy presided suddenly became sounding boards that registered the deliberations of the Chambers.[10] At the same time, the Charter's associated electoral laws defined a *pays légal* roughly the size of le monde. In the absence of modern forms of political organization, participation in government involved participation in preexisting institutions of elite sociability, in which a small yet socially heterogeneous society of notables steeped in aristocratic values tried to regulate the slow expansion of the ruling class, while passing judgment on those who wished to govern the country.

The Restoration was also a time of bitter partisanship among an elite preoccupied with threats to its unity. Memories of the Revolution and the emigration, intensified by the resentments cultivated during the Napoleonic era, created divisions in high society and coteries within le monde. Meanwhile, the Charter and the *cens* made no distinctions among members of the ruling class with regard to political rights and required notables to collaborate and coexist in order to prevent the collapse of an advantageous political settlement. Fear of another Jacobin republic or a return to dictatorship established a relatively strong foundation for consensus: members of the electorate, at least until 1828, were monarchists and supported the regime; they accepted the Charter and the new composition of the society of notables, and had thereby tacitly agreed to refrain from the kind of bloody or intractable conflicts that had previously made it impossible to achieve constitutional stability.[11] Haussonville found society to be more tolerant during the Restoration than it was to become in subsequent years. François Guizot, who praised the Restoration for its "liberal tolerance for the diversity of origins, situations, and ideas," admitted that it was the only time when conditions prevented *ancienne France* and *la France révolutionnaire* "from oppressing each other."[12]

The men and women to whom the Charter granted responsibility for governing the nation were preoccupied with preserving solidarity in the face of the many forces that served to pull them apart. These included not only ideology and politics but the heterogeneity of the nobility, regional differences, the variable composition of fortunes, and egotism itself.[13] Obsessed with stability and hopeful of removing politics from "the domain of the passions," the generation of the Restoration preached against intransigence and "was easily frightened by anything that smacked of excess and violence."[14] In such an atmosphere, long-standing assumptions about the civilizing power of women and the ethic of polite society made the salon seem an antidote to the characteristic divisiveness of partisan politics. Political discussions begun under the influence of "habits of the most exquisite politesse," claimed Madame de Bawr, could be piquant and lively, but "would never turn into disputes."[15] This general image of the salon as a remedy for disunity gained its political specificity under the Restoration when contrasted with the partisan bloodletting that occurred in the Chamber of Deputies, which the duc de Richelieu characterized as an "annual focus of delirium and agitation." Once the salon was made a direct counterpart to the process of parliamentary deliberation, it became what Marc Fumaroli calls "a cogwheel in the political machinery, a sort of diplomacy preliminary to the combinations of assembly or cabinet."[16] Villemain was certain that salons "tempered the polemics of sect or ambition, and assisted in the debates of representative government by rectifying them through a tradition of elegance and finesse." Guizot regretted the partisan spirit of the time, but insisted that it "hardly ever penetrated the house of Madame de Rumford," where urbanity reigned among "the most diverse party politicians," who, "by a tacit convention, it seemed, left their disagreements, antipathies, and anger at the door of this salon." For Madame de Staël, Madame Récamier was "an angel of peace," outside whose presence the partisan rancor that divided her friends could not otherwise have been calmed. It was her unique ability to make friends of political enemies that led Sainte-Beuve to suggest that she was the most prominent woman of her time: "Party spirit was then in all its violence. She disarmed anger, softened asperities, smoothed over all the roughness, and inoculated everyone with indulgence. She would not rest until she had made her friends of opposite sides meet at her house, and had conciliated them under her clement mediation."[17]

Under both *monarchies censitaires*, the history of salons was dominated by the need to balance increasing partisanship with a persistent ethic of conciliation. Although memories of the recent past favored the search for stability, the Restoration inaugurated a process of political structuration among elites that extended throughout the period of French democratization. The need to define the criteria of political differentiation was particularly acute once the Empire fell and a whole complex of issues replaced a more general opposition to dictatorship among groups supportive of representative government. Political liberty permitted the rise of an opposition and the formation of various tendencies on both the Right and Left; at the same time, the advent of regular elections required at least some rudimentary forms of political organization, if only to allow electors of the same opinion to meet, discuss issues, forge alliances, and ridicule the opposition. Since this process took place among a narrowly defined elite in the absence of changes to existing regulations prohibiting the formation of political associations, traditional structures of sociability were used to accommodate developments that would eventually require greater organizational specialization.[18]

The necessity for partisan organization in an era obsessed with stability made salons particularly well suited to structure political sociability. Salonnières could transform their salons at will from coteries into mixed gatherings by selective invitations. The salons of the Restoration and the July Monarchy could be either partisan, ideologically mixed, or both, depending on the political preference of the salonnières or the goals and interests of the social circle with which they were associated.[19] The more salons were politicized, the more salonnières embraced the ideal of pacification. Consequently, the salons of the nineteenth century were more political than those of the eighteenth century, but they did not differ dramatically in structure, function, or design. The political relevance of early nineteenth-century salons, however, rested on a delicate and precarious balance of factors. Salons benefited from a level of partisanship that made them seem necessary, but they could also be harmed by tensions that were too great to overcome. Salons drew favor from assumptions about gender that assigned women a certain public utility, but not everyone held such opinions, and gender conceptions were in flux. Political gatherings that took place in the customary institutions of elite sociability were sexually mixed, but the new institutions that arose from pressures necessitating the organization of the public sphere were not. Men and women could easily choose not to discuss politics in salons. The political salons of the early nineteenth century were, therefore, a mixed blessing for salonnières: they afforded women a role in politics, but they put salons at the mercy of political passions and events; at the same time, they made aristocratic women co-executors of a political settlement that embodied class privileges and thereby kept gender alive as a weapon of political abuse.

II

Despite a certain momentary unanimity on constitutional matters, members of high society were nonetheless separated by political loyalties, social origins, and memories of the recent past. Royalist spite and Bonapartist anxieties, compounded by the tensions arising from the general scramble to secure titles, recover lost property, or obtain financial rewards, added to existing animosities. On the surface, supporters of Napoléon seemed to have forgotten the emperor overnight — they quickly switched allegiances, entered the administration, and solicited positions at court. At the same time, circumspection rather than conviction forestalled the early emergence of a Bonapartist opposition, and the Bonapartist press was full of sarcastic comments about "old ghosts" arriving from the provinces with antiquated ideas, encumbering the salons of the Tuileries in their ancient uniforms, and awaiting the return of Louis XV.[20] The ultras, for their part, felt a bitterness that seemed amplified by an obvious sense of satisfaction.

They heaped abuse on the former emperor and his followers and grumbled about the number of imperialists who remained in the new administration. Royalist society women constantly made fun of imperial fashions, manners, and names, and spread rumors intimating that the diamonds worn by Bonapartist women had been stolen from the churches of Italy and Spain. According to the duchesse de Maillé, Restoration society never let the Bonapartists forget their "revolutionary origins" and never opened the doors of its salons to them.[21]

The widespread perception among liberals that the court was an exclusively noble and royalist institution made it difficult for the government to discourage such dissension. Initially, the spontaneous fidelity of former household officials, the inclination of the princes, and the attachment Louis XVIII felt for his own courtiers favored the reconstitution of the prerevolutionary court—in 1814, imperial nobles at official functions were few and far between. By 1820, however, things began to change: the mutual hostilities occasioned by the assassination of the duc de Berry persuaded the king that the court had to be seen as more inclusive and strictly nonpartisan. For the duc de Richelieu, who served as prime minister from 1815 to 1818 and from 1820 to 1821, the reconciliation of the old nobility, the imperial aristocracy, and liberal *doctrinaires* was the key to stabilizing the constitutional monarchy. Such a goal would require the monarchy to continue Napoléon's policy of amalgamating elites. Richelieu hoped to create a durable moderate royalist majority within the electorate by demonstrating that the Charter could provide a government that was firm, efficient, and liberal, combining the best of the Old Regime with the most important gains of the Revolution. By undertaking a complete reorganization of the Maison du Roi during his second ministry, Richelieu and other leading moderates wanted to make the court a pole of attraction for all parties by ending "the almost total exclusion of new families." Richelieu, who saw service at court as a way to "attach rich and powerful families" to the regime, hoped to align the court with the principles of the Charter by making positions in the royal household, like those in the government, "open to all social successes, without exception."[22]

Under the new policy, service to the monarchy overrode class, pedigree, or ideological zeal as the basis of selection for court appointments. This allowed the new regime to accomplish two goals simultaneously: it could continue the fusion of elites while making the Restoration court a model of ecumenical sociability for high society as a whole. Court employment and invitations to official ceremonies were calculated to integrate the imperial nobility and satisfy the vanity of the elite—consequently, the royal household became as socially heterogeneous as high society but much less overtly partisan than its salons. Of the 107 new court officials appointed after the reforms of 1820, 22.5 percent were non-nobles, 39 percent were nobles who had not met previous requirements for presentation, and 38.5 percent were from the *noblesse présentée*. Of these, 60 percent had served the Empire and were neither especially rich nor solidly royalist.[23] Louis XVIII was most strongly attached to those who had demonstrated their personal loyalty to him, but he went out of his way to protect the dignity of imperial titles. After the Austrian ambassador refused to allow Maréchal Oudinot to be announced as the duc de Reggio at an official reception, the king instructed all diplomats to respect the rights of nobles created by the emperor. When the Empire's most famous actress, Mademoiselle Mars, appeared on stage wearing in her sash a bouquet of violets — used as a rallying sign by Bonapartists during the Hundred Days — the king is said to have commented that "even violets are included in the amnesty." Although courtiers attached to the household of the comte d'Artois in the Pavillon de Marsan, such as the duc de Fitz-James and Jules de Polignac, had a reputation for partisanship, Artois himself was easygoing and generally tolerant of diverse opinions. As king, he carried on the policy of his brother by maintaining a heterogeneous court and striving for equilibrium between the two nobilities.[24]

During the Empire, the mondaine influence of a magnificent and populous court was amplified by the political and social interests of an authoritarian regime. Under the Restoration, however, the court had neither the resources nor the will to dominate Parisian society; its ability to impose order and unity on le monde began to falter and decline.[25] This is not to say that the Restoration court was neither splendid nor well attended. But popularity and centrality are not the same — the court could not organize le monde, because its neutrality put it at odds with the trend toward partisanship, while its respect for the autonomy of the public sphere prevented it from effectively reducing the tensions that arose from the contentiousness of parliamentary life. The Revolution of 1830 only confirmed and accelerated the court's progressive political decline, making it anathema to the legitimist aristocracy, while marginalizing it with regard to the expanding mondanité of Tout-Paris.[26] Officially neutral, and forced by the Charter to play a limited role, the court could no longer act as a center of power and intrigue and consequently ceased to be the focus of political attention. Napoléon had tried to wield power from the Tuileries, but the monarchs of the Restoration preferred the traditional distinction between the government and the royal household and tried to maintain a certain distance between the court and *la ville*.

Louis XVIII left most decisions to his ministers and did not let informal soirées become opportunities for intrigue. Household rituals ceased to be "career-making opportunities" and became purely social. After 1830, the legitimists deprived Louis-Philippe of the entourage and personnel that had lent prestige to the courts of the past and discredited his household with accusations of vulgarity and bad taste, sentiments widely echoed in a bitterly partisan press. As a consequence, the court of the July Monarchy acquired a bad reputation: visitors routinely commented on the banality of the conversation in the royal salon and complained of being "prodigiously bored" at official functions. Political power drifted to the Chambers and into the hands of independent politicians.[27]

Between 1815 and 1848, France rapidly recapitulated the process Jürgen Habermas has detected in eighteenth-century England, when the capital grew in stature while "the Court grew dim" and political criticism moved into the salons, cercles, clubs, and assemblées before entering the institutions of modern political life.[28] To a significant degree, this shift registered the rising power of ministers in relation to an increasingly ceremonial court, along with the growing importance of parliament and the press. A nationalized monarchy was simply incapable of accommodating the partisanship of an elite that viewed politics as a principal element of mondain excitement. Meanwhile, the rapid dispersion of power into new institutions after 1815 was evident in the growing prominence of ministerial salons, which, although ostensibly official, were physically embedded in la vie mondaine and hosted by salonnières not directly affiliated with the court. The ministerial salons of the monarchies censitaires did not monopolize high society as Napoléon's official salons had, but they did give the government a means of influencing public opinion in ways that would have compromised the neutrality of the royal family. Although they excluded no one, and therefore could not satisfy the need for partisan organization, they nevertheless offered the sort of access to power that people had previously sought at court. According to Thiers, the court receptions of the July Monarchy could not compare to the regime's ministerial réunions, where elegance and bonne grâce joined with power to produce "public life . . . at its apogee." Charles de Rémusat observed that although people of different backgrounds and habits were uncomfortable in "les salons du gouvernement," they were nevertheless drawn to them by the business of politics and by a certain relaxation of etiquette.[29]

Beginning in 1815, there emerged in the eyes of society a firm contrast between a tedious court and a sociable world where people could dance, amuse themselves, and talk freely. Even courtiers, who felt duty-bound to attend court, "left as soon as possible to spend the rest of the evening in a salon of the Faubourg," where evidence of court influence, according to Villemain, was nowhere to be seen.[30] After 1830, le monde achieved its definitive independence: the legitimist aristocracy separated itself from the court and created an alternative center of political sociability in Faubourg Saint-Germain, while leading Orleanist politicians opened their own salons. Among the biggest mondain events of the 1830s were the balls organized each year by the marquis de Balincourt in the Salle Ventadour to benefit pensioners of the former civil list of Charles X. Meanwhile, according to Rudolf Apponyi, "very few grandes dames of the old court assisted" in the grand balls hosted by the new king at the Palais-Royal in 1831. Political sociability outside the court had become so important that the duc d'Orléans and the court proper had to use the salons of Madame Flahaut and Madame de Massa as outposts. In 1833, Balzac announced that the old opposition between *cour* and *ville* had been replaced by the fusion of *le monde* and the *capitale*; a year later, he compared Faubourg Saint-Germain to the Louvre during the reign of François I and to Versailles during the seventeenth and eighteenth centuries.[31]

III

The decline of the court left society without a single pole of attraction, while the rise of partisanship in a liberalized public sphere shattered the unity of le monde. The duchesse de Dino recorded the consequences in 1836 from the perspective of her own liberal social circle:

> Paris is likely to become increasingly difficult as a place of residence. Apart from the two great dynastic divisions which separate society, we shall now have to deal with all the factions caused by disappointed ambition, the Molé, Broglie, Guizot, and Dupin factions, and finally the Thiers faction. These will be as bitterly hostile to one another as the Legitimists are to the Moderate Party. All these factions will never find any such common point of amalgamation as the Château might and should become; on the contrary, some object to the King, others to our house.[32]

In his novel *Ethel*, published in 1837, Astolphe de Custine has the hero orient a young Irishwoman in Parisian society by pointing out that in the absence of aristocratic influence, it "no longer had a center, or, at least, the center is everywhere and the limits nowhere." In 1843, Victor de Balabine made roughly the same observation: "We speak so easily of Parisian society, of French society. But is there really a French society? And, if it exists, where is it? Properly speaking, there is none: any society needs a center; here, this center does not exist; there are consequently only coteries without any bond between them."[33]

Once the "*centre mondain* was no longer confounded with the center of political power," le monde became "a conglomeration of sectors" differentiated by the various political, social, and cultural inclinations.[34] In this context, it was left to the salons to give coherence to le monde by organizing the political sociability of elites. The Parisian social world had stable features of its own that had already made it possible for high society to structure itself. The most important of these were the regularity of the social season and the existence of distinctive neighborhoods: Faubourg Saint-Germain, Faubourg Saint-Honoré, the Chaussée d'Antin, and the Marais.

The upper-class social geography of early nineteenth-century Paris had begun to take shape before the Revolution, when court nobles took up residence in Faubourg Saint-Germain during the months spent away from Versailles. At the same time, robe nobles entrenched themselves in the Marais, while financiers and artists inhabited the Chaussée d'Antin. The Revolution disrupted the establishment of Saint-Germain as a high aristocratic enclave, but the Consulate saw the beginning of its partial reconstitution.[35] Under the Restoration, each district came to designate a political orientation, a social affiliation, a language, and a way of life, constituting what the comtesse d'Agoult called a "voisinage d'esprit."[36] Aristocratic, legitimist, loyal to the traditions of the emigration and the Vendée, and reeking of class egotism, Faubourg Saint-Germain was most often contrasted with the wealthier and more liberal, but just as thoroughly aristocratic, Faubourg Saint-Honoré, which Charles de Rémusat characterized as politically moderate, generally opposed to the Bourbons, and comfortable with the "honest" Revolution and the philosophy of the Enlightenment.[37] By contrast, the Chaussée d'Antin was sumptuous and unambiguously Orleanist, home of the families of the nouveaux riches, such as the Lafittes and the Rothschilds. The Marais, meanwhile, continued to represent old wealth. The physical parameters of the quartiers gave le monde barriers and signposts in a growing and tumultuous city where such things were constantly eroding — each neighborhood was a discernible moral entity because it was also a *voisinage de fait*, where everyone "met one another, knew one another, and submitted to the rules of propriety and politesse."[38]

The salons that anchored social life in the fashionable neighborhoods of Paris were themselves regulated by abiding and predictable rhythms. The social season extended from December to Easter and was divided into two periods — before and during Lent. It had its official overture with the reopening of the salons and its official closure with the last show of the Théâtre Italien and the *promenade de Longchamps*. From May to December, members of high society deserted Paris and retired to their country estates; mondanité in the capital quieted down considerably, although the roughly 15 percent of nobles who owned estates in the Paris region continued to meet. The months from July to September were the low-water mark during which aristocrats and *haute bourgeois* alike colonized the thermal spas. Nearly 80 percent of nobles living in Paris had a secondary residence in the provinces. "Six months of château, six months of Paris, the ball to the carnival, concerts and the sermons of Lent, marriages after Easter, very little theater, no traveling, card playing all the time," the comtesse d'Agoult observed with studied weariness. In the society column she wrote for *La Presse*, Delphine de Girardin described the preparations of le monde élégante in the winter of 1836 as if they were clockwork; in May, she sent her column from Chantilly, where the social season ended with races. Her mother, Sophie Gay, portrayed the typical *salon au mois du décembre* as a place of quiet anticipation — "the ministerial salons were full, the government confronted fewer opponents, and kings were less likely to be assassinated."[39] In provincial cities like Grenoble and Toulouse, the patterns of society were repeated on a smaller scale, with nobles living in urban hôtels during the winter and vegetating all summer on their country estates. Even foreigners living in Paris habitually obeyed the social calendar, which neither great events nor the much-exaggerated internal emigration of legitimists seemed able to alter or amend.[40]

The integration of specific salons into distinctive neighborhoods tended to organize le monde into definable social groups, but it did not make each neighborhood strictly exclusive. Balzac and Etienne Jouy insisted that Paris was socially segregated, the latter comparing it to Peking and Lahore, but Beaumont-Vassy testified that there were "salons that belonged to Faubourg Saint-Germain by *société*, if not by *quartier*," because the demarcations in aristocratic society were less a matter of wealth than "une affaire de coteries, de sociétés, d'individualités même." Delphine de Girardin granted that in order to participate in the grand monde of Faubourg Saint-Germain, one had "to belong to an old family," but she also listed a few less categorical qualifications, including connections, an important government position, a lot of money, and relations with foreigners. Indeed, there was a permeable membrane between Saint Germain and Saint Honoré because from a sociological perspective, they were not entirely distinct: members of the two societies had similar backgrounds and mixed easily, especially under the Restoration; it was possible to live in one neighborhood while being part of the other; aristocracy, in Anne Martin-Fugier's estimation, was more a matter of style than geography or class.[41]

Le monde was structured by social distances, but it could be navigated along the alternative vectors created by political opinions. People of different backgrounds encountered one another frequently in society, especially at foreign embassies, at court, and in government salons and salons de fusion, but they might on such occasions be "completely unknown to one another" and therefore sensitive to what others might think of their class origins.[42] At the same time, the relationship between social affiliations and political sympathies was clouded by marriage alliances and by the successive ralliements to different regimes, which tended to create novel associations and stir the social pot. Class affiliation and family background undoubtedly played a powerful role in upper-class life, but they did not give coherence to le monde. Instead, they established barriers and distinctions that were both well demarcated and violated time and time again in the name of political conviction and ideology. Nobles had long since stopped interrogating one another with regard to titles and genealogy and had accepted the principle of meritocracy in those areas of life that were most publicly significant: politics, business, and artistic achievement. "Aux rivalités sociales, les rivalités politiques ont succédé," Delphine de Girardin proclaimed while attending the races at Chantilly in 1841. The consternation caused by the king's attempt to control the upper house by nominating seventy-six new peers in 1827 was more political than social, according to Abrantès, because titles had become "worthless designations" unrelated to privilege. At the beginning of the Restoration, Madame de Staël divided its elite into political rather than social categories: "arrogant" aristocrats, whom she also called "incensed royalists"; Bonapartists; and "friends of liberty." In retrospect, the comtesse d'Agoult concluded that the Faubourg Saint-Germain and Faubourg Saint-Honoré of her youth had been "separated only by nuances of opinions" and a few other trivial matters.[43]

As partisanship increased in stages in association with specific events — the dissolution of the "Chambre introuvable" in 1816, the assassination of the duc de Berry in 1820, the Martignac experiment of 1828, the crisis of 1830 itself — le monde became divided ever more clearly along party lines. Haussonville wrote that partisan divisions in "the best Parisian society" did not reach a critical stage until "the last months of M. de Polignac's ministry," when moderates reached "the end of their patience" and purely political disagreements separated old friends. But Haussonville was only a child at the time and did not remember similar moments in the immediate past. Madame de Boigne traced the origins of irreconcilable differences in society to the months following the assassination of the duc de Berry. The duchesse de Maillé cited the exasperation among ultra-royalists provoked by the dissolution of the Chambre introuvable in September 1816 as the decisive rupture, causing "society to become divided by opinion" and ultras to consider all who were not with them as revolutionaries. Charles de Rémusat had the same perception from a liberal perspective, calling the ordinance of September 5 "a sort of dividing line, from whence the waters would flow in different directions according to their natural inclination." From the vantage point of her salon, the marquise de Montcalm could already sense "an intolerance and excessive bitterness" in May and observed as early as October 1815 that "imaginations seemed exalted in the Chamber and more still in the salons, where far from seeking to calm or soften attitudes, people worked only to animate them beyond measure." In general, it seems, partisan bickering had severely strained relations by the winter of 1817–18, when Madame de Rémusat began to regard the level of animosity she witnessed in society as something painful and new.[44]

By 1840, "party spirit" had become "the scourge of society," Guizot declared.[45] Partisanship undermined personal relations even in intimate circles and made it hard to converse freely.[46] As partisan convictions became so strong as to override social ties and personal affection, habitués began moving around society like pieces on a chessboard. By Montcalm's calculation, political motives alone accounted for the changes that took place in the composition of her salon: some "old and intimate acquaintances" distanced themselves, while newcomers requested to be presented in the hope of meeting her brother. In 1818, Frénilly began to feel he had become a stranger in the salon of Madame de Montefontaine, where two years earlier he had been an intimate guest; the maîtresse de maison having embraced liberalism, began to favor the Left within her circle "while pretending to hold the balance between extremes." The duc de Raguse migrated from the salon of Duras to that of Boigne after members of the former froze him out for his role in the affair of M. de La Valette, postmaster general during the Hundred Days, who was condemned after Waterloo, but who had escaped from the Conciergerie on the eve of his execution by exchanging clothes with his wife. When Madame de Staël died in 1817, the habitués of her salon distributed themselves among those of her successors: Madame Récamier inherited the royalists (Custine, Montlosier, Montmorency, and Chateaubriand) and the duchesse de Broglie got the liberals (Lafayette, Constant, Royer-Collard, and Jordan).[47]

In the closing years of the July Monarchy, observers had begun to depict le monde as alternatively exhausted or paralyzed by party strife. For Balabine, Parisian society at the time was a "political volcano," from which Europe awaited periodic clashes to erupt between a "strange medley" of ideological stereotypes. In 1847, Delphine de Girardin compared the tranquility of Paris's political salons to a respite between storms: no one dared to write, people hesitated to send out invitations, and everyone was afraid of sparking a new round of conflict by committing a political act—months earlier, passions had reached another boiling point with the publication of Lamartine's history of the Girondins. When the comtesse d'Armaillé made her entry into society in the same year, she reported that "people were very preoccupied with politics, never with games, and very rarely with pure society talk."[48]

As a consequence of increased partisanship, salons in general became easier to distinguish by function, and political salons in particular became firmly identified with organized partisan opinion.[49] This was what Balabine observed in 1843 when he wrote: "We have here [in Paris] political salons, literary salons, legitimist salons, salons of the *juste milieu*, diplomatic salons, and, finally, neutral salons," each with their own color and nuance, and each representing "a page torn from the great book of national history." Villemain made much the same point, arguing that the salons of Paris "delineated themselves almost like the parties that composed the Chamber. There were purely *liberal* and quite *democratic* salons, except for the elegance that they lacked, *ultraroyalist* and even *congregationalist* salons, monarchical salons, and, finally, doctrinaire salons, which, despite their awkward name, were not any less endowed with orators, publicists, and even beautiful and witty people."[50] Sainte-Beuve, too, described high society in terms of its political topography, identifying "a doctrinaire zone," purely aristocratic circles, and ones devoted to an alliance of liberty and legitimacy. In gauging reaction to the resignation of Talleyrand as ambassador to London in 1834, the duchesse de Dino listed the principal centers of opinion as the Bourse, "the Boulevards," and the salons of Mesdames de Flahaut, Massa, Broglie, and Boigne, representing the duc d'Orléans, the court, the doctrinaires, and the ministry respectively.[51]

Certainly, not all salons were primarily political: those of Madame Ancelot, Etienne Delécluze, Charles Nodier, and the princesse Belgiojoso were mostly filled with intellectuals, novelists, and painters eager to discuss literature and the arts. But for most of the inhabitants of Parisian society, political opinion became both the glue and solvent of sociability. "Everything in France is a party matter," Apponyi wrote in 1832. "Today there is no action possible without a political aim: people eat, amuse themselves, get bored, love one another, and detest one another according to politics."[52] Fearing himself alone among his peers in 1815 by virtue of his liberal opinions, Rémusat expressed great relief upon becoming a habitué in the salon of Madame de Catellan, where everyone he encountered "reaccommodated" him to Parisian society, "at least in the sense that I understood that my philosophical and political ideas would not be condemned to preserve me in my solitude." Guizot similarly appreciated the salon of the duchesse de Broglie, calling it in his *Mémoires* "notre cercle propre et intime." Salonnières still set the tone by selecting *invités* and by determining topics of conversation, but they themselves had strong partisans convictions that gave the contacts and mediations they sponsored and developed more than merely an unintended political character. According to Horace de Viel-Castel, three questions greeted those who sought entry into the society of Faubourg Saint-Germain: what is your birth, which religion do you profess, and what are your political opinions?[53]

Political salons were not "the General Headquarters of the *political parties,*" as Villemain claimed, but they did acquire a degree of political instrumentality. Beaumont-Vassy found that they both echoed parliamentary debates and served as extensions of "des coulisses" of the Palais-Bourbon, where speeches were prepared, ideas elucidated, and majorities formed.[54] According to Noëlle Dauphin, *La Biographie des dames de la Cour et du Faubourg Saint-Germain* cites roughly one hundred salons, of which only about fifteen were "the theater of political conversations." Not one of them was like the salon of the princesse de Cardignan, the invention of Balzac, where the Carlists assemble at night in what amounts to a clandestine *salle de conseil.*[55] Like the salons of the royalists and the Girondins in the early years of the Revolution, the salons of the monarchies censitaires maintained a complex division of labor — the variable preferences of salonnières allowed political business to be separated from the work of mediation or the pleasures of philosophical debate because different activities occurred in different salons, or at different times in the same one. During the Restoration, Rémusat was able to join the liberal faction in the Chamber, discuss the imperfections of French representative government, and gather with political allies and friends after an exhilarating day in the legislature by participating in three salons, those of Elie Decazes, Madame de Catellan, and Madame de Broglie. The ability of salons to accommodate both partisanship and novel combinations gave every nuance of public opinion a home. Madame Swetchine, who had "a horror of groups and coteries," formed friendships with men as diverse as Tocqueville, Comte Alfred de Falloux, Joseph de Maistre, and Jean-Baptiste Lacordaire by making her salon a unique point of convergence for liberal Catholics. Bonapartist court officials who wanted to reminisce about the Empire and cultivate their hostility to the Bourbons could meet with Mesdames d'Abrantès, D'Hilliers, or Saint-Leu; those who preferred to serve the new regime went to the home of M. de Bourrienne; and those wanted to maintain connections in the diplomatic corps frequented the salon of the princesse de La Moskowa.[56]

A number of historians have argued that profound differences separated the two major categories of political salons during the Restoration. On the one hand, there were the salons of the ultras, reserved "to a very narrow patriarchate of birth," allied to the court, and threatened by social mobility. The principal political function of women in this milieu was the exclusion of parvenus through the deployment of social and discursive conventions. Hostile to the ideals of the Enlightenment and convinced of the righteousness of their cause, the "women of ultraism" engaged in a defensive politics of denigration and slander against their adversaries, justified by an intolerant ideology and rooted in a passionate affectivity that discouraged rational discourse. On the other hand, liberals who recognized personal merit and the equality of rights practiced an openness in their sociability aimed at diffusing progressive ideas and respect for parliamentary government among an ever-wider *corps politique*. In the liberal salon, women with austere political and religious principles performed an educative and mediating function by presiding over and participating in reasoned and critical debate.[57]

Such characterizations are far too categorical and tend to mirror Sainte-Beuve's famous distinction between salons that were "studious" and "doctrinaire," and those that were purely "aristocratic and frivolous."[58] Liberal salons could also be isolated coteries in which habitués spoke disparagingly of those with whom they disagreed.[59] At the same time, Faubourg Saint-Germain and Faubourg Saint-Honoré were equally inhabited by nobles and were distinguishable less by their social composition than by their attitude toward political change and cultural innovation.[60] Ultra salons, moreover, could be very political: the very partisan princesse de La Trémoïlle presided over interminable political conversations and provided a place for deputies like Abbé Nicholas MacCarthy and Comte François de La Bourdonnaye to rehearse speeches for the Chamber; the comte de Pontécoulant recalled that "the aristocratic salons of Faubourg Saint-Germain" and "the plebeian salons of the rich bankers of the Chaussée d'Antin" in 1818 were equally preoccupied with "important" political discussions.[61] At the same time, liberals knew how to have fun — Madame de Broglie's salon might have been austere and politicized, but that of Madame de La Briche was not. Stendhal even complimented liberal salonnières such as Vintimille, Dino, and Castellane for providing as much amusement as the women of Faubourg Saint-Germain, in contrast to the "bankers' wives" who put their guests to sleep.[62]

There were, nevertheless, important distinctions between the salons of the Right and those of the Left. Both were partisan, but ultra salons were more ideologically exclusive because the sociability of the extreme Right was driven by a quest for counterrevolutionary purity. As a result, the term *le faubourg Saint-Germain*, or simply *le faubourg*, became political shorthand for organized ultraroyalist (and later legitimist) public opinion, designating for all, according to d'Agoult, "the emigration, the Vendée, the 'Pavillon Marsan,' the 'Congregation,' the 'Bord de l'eau,' all the defenders of *altar* and *throne*, all the devotees of *Vive le roi quand même*." The public knew by instinct that the term referred not just to the concrete reality of a predominantly aristocratic neighborhood but "to all those who wanted to revive prerevolutionary France."[63] In *Les Misérables*, Victor Hugo depicts the typical ultra salon as "purely royalist," composed of guests who "veered toward elegy or dithyrambs, groans or cries of horror, at the age, the Charter, the Bonapartists, the prostitution of the Blue Ribbon to untitled persons, and the Jacobinism of Louis XVIII."[64] Legitimist society after 1830, it seems, was equally cramped and exclusive: Balabine observed that the society of Madame de Girardin, whose husband had been Charles X's *maître des chasses*, was limited to "legitimist notables, some noteworthy foreigners, and some members of the diplomatic corps"; in the 1840s, Madame d'Armaillé described the society of Faubourg Saint-Germain as made up of "family phalansteries" that usually "remained purely legitimist."[65]

Membership in ultraroyalist society was open to people with a variety of views provided they had the right pedigree or social rank, but access was not denied to ardent royalists of undistinguished birth. The ultra salons of the Restoration each had their contingent of obscure provincial deputies whose zeal, talent, or circumstances allowed them to serve the royalist cause — men like Henri Bernier and Henry Brenet, both doctors, or Jean-Pierre Piet, a lawyer from Nancy whom La Trémoïlle put on a pedestal until her interest in politics waned. According to Villemain, "the provincial gentlemen" who "formed the base of the royalist majority" and who frequented royalist society when the Chamber was in session "did not have much of a penchant for an aristocratic hierarchy," expected full equality to exist among nobles, and "did not recognize grands seigneurs."[66] A repudiation of the liberalism of the eighteenth century did not necessarily entail a rejection of the sociability of the Old Regime: the dowagers of Faubourg Saint-Germain had once received the philosophes and were living monuments to an age of moral indulgence and open conversation that had prized Voltaire's stories and the racy narratives of Abbé Claude-Henri de Voisenon. Greater moral circumspection might have stiffened the conviction that France was going to the dogs, but Comte Alexis de Saint-Priest testified that the faubourg still loved art and artists and sought out celebrities of all sorts.[67]

Liberals and moderates did not consider ultra society to be frivolous and apolitical — on the contrary, they blamed it for injecting an unprecedented degree of partisan bitterness into public life. "In the past," wrote Madame de La Briche, "the aristocrats permitted themselves to hate only democracy, demagogues, republicans, [and] everything that assailed the king and royalty, but currently they have been giving freer range to their antipathies."[68] The inflammatory nature of right-wing political invective was clearly at odds with the spirit that had informed the sociability of the past. During the trial of Marshal Ney, according to Lamartine, "the salons of the aristocracy . . . clamored around the King's ministers, demanding the hero's blood as if for a personal favor. Women of the highest rank, young, beautiful, rich, laden with gifts, favors, titles and dignities by the court, forgot their families, their pleasures, their indolence, and their amours, and ran about from morning till night if so be they might prevent a single vote in favor of mercy or secure one in favor of punishment."[69] At the time of the dissolution of the Chamber in 1816, the duc de Richelieu was depicted in a caricature circulated in Faubourg Saint-Germain with the Charter in one hand and a knout in the other. Subsequently, the faubourg set its sights on Decazes, first to imply that a liberal was the real power behind the ministry and later to accuse him of aspiring to be a dictator. In the furor that followed the assassination of the duc de Berry, libelous songs calling Decazes a traitor made their way through the salons, along with rumors implying that he had ordered de Berry's death. When the Chamber of Deputies was in session, aristocratic women regularly attended, "shouting as if in the street" from the gallery when they disapproved of what was said. During the session of January 15, 1820, the comtesse Balbi commented audibly that M. de Courvoisier's speech was "insolent" and announced that "M. d'Argenson would be better off cultivating his lands," prompting the duchesse de Broglie to wonder how the elderly women of the Old Regime could have such good taste and such bad manners.[70]

Whereas ultra salons cultivated a new political orthodoxy and engaged in personal attacks, those of the liberals were verbally less derogatory and socially more diverse because they sought a basis for accommodation between the various elements of the elite. Animated by the eighteenth-century practice of taking pleasure in the harmonious exchange of serious ideas, salonnières like Madame de Rumford and the duchesse de Broglie tried to assemble an eclectic crowd of liberal intellectuals and gens du monde in an effort to unite philosophy, politics, and high society. But that did not mean that liberal society was consistently tolerant, nonpartisan, or democratic. The doctrinaires of the Restoration wanted to create a new aristocracy of superior capacity composed of pre- and postrevolutionary elites, a "classe pilote" that would "unite all the merits of the nation" and give public opinion the impartial universality of judgments reached by the most enlightened segment of the population.[71] In short, they wanted not to diffuse *des lumières* to the nation at large, but to redefine the ruling class on their own terms. This combination of political sociology and moralizing intellectualism gave liberal society its distinctive and contradictory characteristics. It was, wrote Rémusat, "a mixture of the Hôtel de Rambouillet and Port Royale," at once agreeable and forced, free and scholarly, like a *"seminar doctrinaire."* Guizot saw the problem as typical of those who came of age during or shortly after the Revolution: "Although not part of the revolutionary action, they were dragged into it — all in all, the revolutionary spirit dominated them with all its merits and faults: more independence than loftiness; more acridity than independence; a love of humanity and its progress, but suspicious, envious, and unsociable toward whoever did not accept [their] yoke; uniting the prejudice of a coterie with the hatreds of a faction."[72]

Madame de Broglie's salon on the rue de Lille was in an apartment that had once been occupied by Marie-Antoinette's friend Madame de Polignac. Her weekly receptions, held on Tuesdays and Saturdays, brought together royalists, doctrinaires, and liberals for discussions that were serious, impartial, and unpedantic. They were also rather tense, "subjugated to ideas already formed," according to Rémusat. Since guests often disliked one another and had battled in the press, the conversation could sometimes be like walking on eggshells: Guizot observed that the hostess was very discreet and preferred to keep silent rather than inveigh against the reactionaries who surrounded her; Haussonville wrote that "the strict command was to speak only diffidently [*du bout des lèvres*]." At one reception in 1835, Apponyi witnessed an argument between Pasquier and Guizot "en plein salon." Broglie's habitués were all liberals of one sort or another, constituting what Rémusat called "a school or party." Liberal deputies would assemble there after the end of a session, as if it were a club.[73] The same combination of diversity and partiality was to be found in the salon of Madame de Sainte-Aulaire, where moderates and liberals met with a salonnière who was openly hostile to the ultras and the grands seigneurs. The mondain Left might have regarded itself as congenial to all *les supériorités acquises*, but the ultras saw their adversaries as "caustic, hateful, and exclusive."[74]

The July Revolution did not dramatically alter the nature of legitimist salons, which became more exclusive than ever, but it did tend to identify the salons of Orleanist society with what Pascal Ory aptly called the *caciques* of the regime: Guizot, Molé, and Thiers were the main attractions in the salons of the princesse de Lieven, the comtesse de Castellane, and Madame Dosne respectively.[75] Other political salons of the July Monarchy were more directly tied to specific factions at court or in the Chamber. According to the comtesse d'Armaillé, the salon of her brother, Paul de Ségur, came together in the late 1830s to counter Molé's ministry. One night in Dino's salon, Thiers surveyed the political landscape of le monde as follows:

> The *salon* of Madame de Lieven is the observatory of Europe; that of Madame de Ségur is purely Doctrinaire, with no concessions; that of Madame de La Redorte is entirely in the power of M. Thiers; with Madame de Flahaut the convenience of the Duc d'Orléans is the general desire, and with M. de Talleyrand the convenience of the King; the house of Madame de Boigne is for the 11th of October and for the concession, though the most bitter of concessions; the cabinet of Madame de Dino is alone guided by the most perfect independence of mind and judgment.[76]

When factional leaders entered the ministry, the salons with which they were associated became semi-official and combined what Beaumont-Vassy called "this political nuance with the governmental nuance." Thiers's salon, presided over by his mother-in-law, Madame Dosne, collapsed the distinction between politics and mondanité entirely by becoming a political bureau. According to Comte Edmond de Lignères Alton-Shée, deputies and journalists went in and out of the salon on the place Saint-Georges all day, preparing parliamentary campaigns and talking tactics and strategy. The hostess took an active part in all such conversations and wrote Thiers copious letters full of keen political advice when he was away from home.[77]

IV

Le monde of the early nineteenth century was big or small depending on one's point of view. Eugène Guinot estimated that it consisted of a "sacred battalion" of no more than four or five hundred individuals. Balzac, by contrast, counted "two thousand people who believed themselves to be *tout Paris.*" At the same time, le monde could be cut down to a more human scale: Mesdames de Lauriston, Oudinot, Marcellus, and d'Istrie liked to coordinate their morning and evening activities so as to end up in the same salons. "Paris is great and there are many roads between Faubourg Saint-Germain and the Chaussée d'Antin," wrote Balabine. Still, everyone, soldiers and clergymen, liberals and the devout, managed to find an intimate circle of their own.[78]

Parisian society was small enough to be familiar, but large enough to occupy a considerable portion of one's life. Tocqueville was a habitué of no fewer than eleven prominent salons between 1815 and 1848, including those of the duchesse de Rauzan, Madame Récamier, and Princesse Belgiojoso. Some mondaine personalities were known primarily for their ubiquity, like Prince Tufiakin, a Russian by birth, who for twenty-five years attended every fête and theater opening Paris had to offer.[79] It was common for assiduous mondains to visit a number of salons and a series of society events each day. In the 1830s, Apponyi, who complained of being overwhelmed by "dinners and invitations of all sorts," which obliged him to go "from one salon to another," attended five salons on a regular basis. In just one evening, on December 23, 1832, he had tea and dinner with the marquise de Bartillat, attended a concert at the home of the chevalier de Puisieux, accompanied the duchesse de Valençay to the Opéra-Comique, and ended at the Café anglais for supper at one in the morning. On one Tuesday evening during the social season of 1845, Balabine put in an appearance at the Ministry of Foreign Affairs before making the rounds, first to Madame de Castellane's and Madame de Circourt's, and then to a ball with Madame de Chastenay at midnight; on February 22, 1847, he dined at the Normanby's, where he found the princesse de Lieven, and visited Madame de Boigne, before attending a *bal monstre* at the Neapolitan embassy and a late soirée with the Turkish ambassador. According to Madame Ancelot, the days of the comte de Castellane were filled with an "insane activity" — "each evening he went to a multitude of gatherings, and boasted to me of once having been at forty houses from nine at night to one in the morning."[80]

In such a world, it was more dangerous to be anonymous than ridiculous. As a consequence, Frenchmen who wanted to participate in politics were all but required to go into society.[81] Boigne's father, Comte René d'Osmond, had to retire from political life because the years he spent as ambassador to Turin (1814–1815) and London (1815–1819) had severed all his relations. "He was a stranger to the influential people of his country, he no longer had an intimate knowledge of those small details that preoccupy men in power, because they gossip as much as we do." Boigne advised politicians against serving even a few months in a diplomatic post:

[N]o other kind of absence more rapidly and definitively breaks [one's] connections with [one's] clientele. We have seen Monsieur de Serre, the best orator in the Chamber, unable to secure his reelection after an ambassadorship for two years at Naples: he died of vexation as a result. . . . The more sociability one's country offers, the more striking are these disadvantages. This is especially true of the French, who live in coteries formed more by personal sympathies than by family allegiances or rank. No bond can be stronger, and yet none can be more fragile. They are like glass — they can last forever, or be broken by a trifle. They cannot resist a prolonged absence. . . . Frenchmen are so well aware of this social tendency that our diplomats will always be found anxious to revisit their native society at frequent intervals, and thus to keep in touch with it.[82]

High society was a whirlwind, as contemporaries liked to say, but it was also grounded in intimate and stable gatherings.[83] The role of women in society was to knit le monde together by giving it a certain social density. This was less a voluntary service than a social fact, one that arose from women's position at the center of a multitude of crisscrossing relationships that defied and modulated the centrifugal force introduced by politicization. Each salon embodied a social convergence that women themselves created through the ties they had to family and friends. To frequent more than one salon at a time, as was typical, was to be part of a network of relations that ran in many directions and that "led into [se commandait]" political ones, like one room leading into another. As a consequence, salons that were apolitical in content nevertheless performed political functions of a specifically practical import, like mediation or career advancement.[84] On the one hand, women had access to public affairs through the men in their lives, who provided connections and information. On the other hand, men forged their political liaisons partly through women and salons. Members of the old aristocracy had an advantage in this regard, because they entered society already assured of encountering relatives who were part of established kinship networks. Liberal society, although more open, had the same quality of familiarity, bound together by what George Armstrong Kelley calls "the dense texture of connubial relations among liberal aristocrats."[85] In a sociable world suffused by ties of matrimony and consanguinity, women and salons represented an antidote (and alternative) to the fragmentation created by partisan politics — gens du monde divided by political affiliations almost always had connections in every camp. Haussonville's maternal grandfather was a nobleman from Dauphiné who had served the Empire; his mother had friends from the courts of Napoléon and Louis XVI. Rémusat befriended influential liberals in the salons of Madame de Rumford and Madame de La Briche, but he also frequented the salon of Madame de Catellan, where he met Alexis de Noailles, Sosthène de La Rochefoucauld, and Juliette Récamier. La Briche's family ties pointed in two directions: toward liberals and Bonapartists on her sister's side, and toward the legitimists among the friends of her maternal aunts. When Comte Molé was not occupying the Ministry of Foreign Affairs, he could be found on the place de la Ville-l'Evêque in a salon presided over by his daughter, Madame de La Ferté, whose husband belonged to the *parti légitimiste*.[86]

André-Jean Tudesq once commented that the Chamber of Peers under Louis-Philippe was less like a parliamentary assembly and more like a cercle made up of men who were part of a small number of "great family alliances."[87] The power of women to reinforce and secure such alliances made the combination of women, mondanité, and class one of the pillars of the monarchist Right. In the eighteenth century, when salon sociability implicitly contested the principles of absolutism, mondanité could have mildly subversive connotations. In the nineteenth century, that was no longer the case: the salons of the Restoration generally supported the regime and embraced the social hierarchy of the day. As Bertier de Sauvigny points out, the nobility of the Restoration was distinguished from that of other eras above all by "the role it played in the service of the state, a role regarded as both a privilege and a duty." Old nobles not only occupied their traditional places in the households of the royal family but colonized the government and the administration.[88]

Unlike its eighteenth-century predecessor, the Restoration nobility was socially and politically conservative, having concluded that the Revolution had been punishment for the sins of the Enlightenment. This counterrevolutionary idea strengthened the nobility's attachment to the monarchy, aligned it with the Catholic Church, and made it generally more class-conscious, intolerant, and parsimonious. Margaret Darrow has argued that the nobility's turn to the right was accompanied by the sudden adoption by noblewomen of domesticity as a class ideal "in an effort to answer middle-class criticism of the nobility and, consequently, to forestall the political triumph of the bourgeoisie during the Restoration." To be sure, noblewomen participated in the formulation of a discourse that held their class responsible for the calamities of the past, but they did not draw from it the conclusion that they ought to embrace bourgeois motherhood and confine themselves to the home.[89] Counterrevolutionaries like Joseph de Maistre and Bonald, who frequented Faubourg Saint-Germain, criticized the salonnières of the Old Regime for entertaining philosophes and engaging in licentious behavior, not for having salons. If upper-class women had begun to evince a certain *passion maternelle*, it caused them neither to abandon society nor to eschew public affairs. Indeed, there is plenty of evidence to suggest that aristocratic women liked politics and felt entitled to assert themselves in the public sphere. Noblewomen not only talked politics in salons, they openly cheered Napoléon's abdication, demonstrated for the return of the Bourbons, and routinely sat in the gallery of the Chamber of Deputies.[90] Many salonnières derived pleasure from political involvement and were determined to make their salons part of the tumult and excitement of events. Madame de Boigne considered it normal for salons "to take a keen interest in all the events," and Rémusat reported that he sometimes found Madame de La Redorte at home with his wife when he returned from work "dying of envy to be in politics" and avid for news of the day. According to Abrantès, the law on female congregations passed the Chamber of Peers on May 24, 1825, after a stormy day of oratory, "amid the great applause of the young and old women of the Faubourg St. Germain." When the comte de Ségur published a pamphlet critical of Napoléon's actions during the Russian campaign, "it was seen everywhere in the Faubourg Saint-Germain" and in the Saint-Louis quarter of Versailles, where ultras "devoured [the] work with such avidity that the two reading rooms were crowded out."[91]

The most prominent aristocratic grandes dames of the early nineteenth century were not violating gender norms by occupying their traditional position in Parisian society. The problem was not their refusal to conform to an emerging ideal of domesticity but their association with a broad reassertion of aristocratic power. During the Restoration, salons became identified with reaction and ceased to be in the cultural avant garde. At a time when Faubourg Saint-Germain was at the height of its influence, no one could have known that the old aristocracy was reaching the apogee of its power, so close to what would be its final defeat. Many observers feared, rather, that the Old Regime was about to be restored. Faubourg Saint-Germain's place in high society was reinforced by the apparent restoration of the nobility's economic and political power — the weight accorded to landed property in the electoral system helped give nobles roughly 60 percent of the seats in the Chamber in 1821, 40 percent in 1827, and 35 percent as late as 1835. Nobles dominated the lists of the highest taxpayers in most departments and regained a significant position in the military, the Church, and the magistrature. The nobility acquired "a social rank in the early nineteenth century for which it had been incessantly reproached during the eighteenth," Pierre Serna observes.[92] Even before the Revolution, cultural assets were replacing birth in determining access to the top of the social hierarchy, but the aristocratic monopoly over the symbols of status was somewhat compromised by the convergence of new descriptions of nobility and the values of the Enlightenment. The abolition of noble privileges and new possibilities for social advancement elevated the importance of the nobility's symbolic capital at a time when progressive ideas no longer competed with elegance and manners to define aristocratic prestige. The Revolution of 1830 deprived the legitimists of political power but did not undermine the aristocracy's cultural cachet.[93] By the 1840s, the partial democratization of high society had introduced a profusion of new social types, but Delphine de Girardin could still point to grands seigneurs and duchesses as the ideals; she compared Faubourg Saint-Germain to the Chamber of Peers in 1839 by virtue of its power to consecrate. Four years later, Balabine referred to the duchesses de Gramont and de Maillé as "eternal oracles" for the way their salons combined *esprit*, elegance, good taste, urbanity, and politesse. It was this ideal toward which Stendhal's Madame Grandet, the wife of a rich manufacturer in *Lucien Leuwen*, constantly aspires, convinced that her husband's wealth makes her nothing more than a "merchant's wife," whereas she wants "to become a Montmorency."[94] Members of the aristocracy reinvested this social capital every time they spoke of tradition, recited their memories, or evoked their illustrious names; and they conjured up the power such traditions afforded them every time they received guests in their exquisite salons. By embodying the past, the famous dowagers of Faubourg Saint-Germain claimed a sort of social jurisdiction that lent them great ritual authority: they alone had direct access to the spirit of France's ancient sociability; they alone possessed a profound knowledge of its customs and decrees.[95]

It was impossible to enter a world whose rules and practices were based on the wisdom of those venerated as guardians of tradition without already paying homage to the putative cultural superiority of the aristocracy, whose members were always apt to be its most confident, secure, and socially accomplished. Madame de Staël observed that non-nobles regarded the society of Faubourg Saint-Germain with a strange mixture of jealousy and resentment, but most calculated that it cost less to embrace aristocratic manners than to forgo the benefits of participation in le monde. Those who scoffed at "the bourgeoisie's rage for co-optation" routinely condemned sordid middle-class ambition without acknowledging that the nobility was still able to make itself the privileged focus of elite recruitment. Madame Dosne testified that her self-respect was not diminished by the prevailing association of elegance and high birth, and she regarded the tendency to deride the value of aristocracy by contesting the "superiority of birth" as a symptom of "bourgeois foolishness."[96] Bourgeois values may have been ascendant in nineteenth-century France, but the outlook of the French bourgeoisie was marked by a clear reverence for aristocratic traditions and a strong anti-bourgeois and anti-materialist sensibility, especially in matters of literary and artistic taste.[97] It is not surprising, then, that the aristocracy maintained a sort of monopoly over the salon as a cultural form. The leisure class par excellence, the aristocracy set the tone for la vie mondaine, and its salons provided a standard for elite sociability. In 1837, according to Viel-Castel, Faubourg Saint-Germain was still "le monde, the grand monde, high society, from which derives all others, and on which all other societies seek to model themselves." Ten years after the fall of the Bourbons, Balabine continued to see the salons of the legitimist aristocracy as "the imperishable mold."[98]

The ascendancy of the aristocracy during the Restoration prompted Stendhal to repeat Rousseau's complaint that salonnières had become the arbiters of fame, capable by virtue of their dominance over opinion of reducing both artists and the wives of businessmen to abject humiliation.[99] Like Rousseau, who also accused women of overweening and illegitimate power, Stendhal mistook the roles particular women played in limited social circumstances for the conditions that afforded such women an exceptional position. Nevertheless, the persistent equation of salonnières with real power demands a serious consideration of the real power of salonnières.

Salons and *Salonnières* in the Politics of the Restoration and the July Monarchy

Salons were able to organize political sociability because they were institutions of elite society, although the practices they embodied and the circumstances that gave them a political role did not necessarily make them centers of political power. Salons were part of la vie mondaine, but that did not mean that they were exclusively devoted to idleness and frivolous entertainment. They were also structures for getting things done, but the political functions they performed did not give salonnières significant political influence.

I

In the postrevolutionary era, the salon was still primarily a place to gather and talk. At a time when politics attracted great interest, habitués naturally spent a lot of time recounting and commenting upon the events of the day. In the nineteenth-century, the salon continued to play its eighteenth-century role as a clearing house for information on which people relied to remain in touch with the world.[1] Altogether, the numerous salons of Paris formed a dense communicative network. Within this medium, conversations informed by a steady flow of news and information (as well as gossip and rumor) contributed to the formation of public sentiments that sometimes found an echo in the Chambers or at court. In times of crisis, salons became listening posts where friends gathered to follow the unfolding of momentous events. During the Revolution of 1830, fresh news arrived every quarter hour at the home of Madame de Boigne, where "[t]he same people who had gathered . . . the evening before came in one after another" bringing stories "of a character more and more alarming." The duchesse d'Abrantès learned details of the trial of the ministers of Charles X "through friends of Madame Récamier, whose salon was always filled with persons taking a direct interest in the events of the day." Récamier's salon was linked to the proceedings by a network of couriers who "kept coming and going all the time with news," informing her about everything from the testimony of witnesses to Polignac's pallid expression. Toward the end of the trial, warnings that acquittals would bring "another bloody revolution" circulated in Faubourg Saint-Germain.[2]

Contemporaries spoke of making ideas and opinions *circuler dans les salons* or of rumors traveling through them as if along a telephone line or, more properly, a grapevine. Salon conversation was frequently said to "echo" a larger body of opinion, or to be itself echoed in journals, brochures, and cafés.[3] Talleyrand seems to have been especially adept at using salons in this manner. After 1830, he made a point of visiting the salon of the marquis de Lafayette "to purify his old sins against liberal politics" and sent letters to Madame de Vaudémont in his capacity as ambassador to London asking her to circulate his flattering observations about the British royal family throughout Parisian society.[4] According to the duc de Laval, it was Madame Récamier who had the greatest talent for "showing off [her] friends to advantage, and serving them at the right moment." Her most famous work as a publicist involved her efforts to create a climate of opinion in society favorable to Chateaubriand's political career. While ambassador to London in 1822, Chateaubriand launched a many-sided campaign designed to convince the government that he should be a member of the delegation to the upcoming Congress of Verona. After notifying the foreign minister, Mathieu de Montmorency, that he wanted to be sent to the conference, he asked the duchesse de Duras to persuade the prime minister, Villèle, that his presence there would enhance the reputation of the ultras in the courts of Europe. At the same time, he encouraged Récamier to lobby Montmorency directly and to circulate in society information he hoped would bolster his cause. On June 11, he posted to her a copy of the initial notice he had sent to Montmorency and told her that she could "now say to him frankly that I appear to have a strong desire to go." A week later, after hearing that Lord Londonderry, the British foreign secretary, might go to Verona, he began to suspect that Montmorency would want to do the same and let float the idea that he might take over Montmorency's portfolio in his absence. He instructed Récamier to "throw out" this proposal "in advance to Sosthènes [de La Rochefoucauld] and his friends," who were known to be intimate with Villèle and with Madame de Cayla, the king's favorite. When a decision regarding his role was delayed through the summer, he asked Récamier to suggest widely that the Russian government's willingness to send its ambassador, the Corsican-born Pozzo di Borgo, created the expectation that France would send an ambassador as well. As his desperation mounted, he suggested to her that she make use of the fact that the king of Prussia had given him a snuff box bearing the royal portrait set in diamonds, and that he had expressed the conviction that Chateaubriand's presence at Verona would be "the most favorable augury for the success of the labors of the Congress." Meanwhile, Chateaubriand worked to persuade Récamier that her happiness was bound up with his success, because participation at the Congress would elevate his reputation, position him for a "most honorable retirement" or the Foreign Ministry, and thereby allow the two of them to spend evenings together at the Abbaye-aux-Bois.[5]

Salonnières occasionally possessed inside information because a dense network of foreign and domestic contacts gave them access to remarkably good intelligence on ministerial decisions and the intentions of foreign governments. Madame de Staël already knew of Russian and Austrian plans to scale back the Allied occupation force when she tried to persuade the duke of Wellington to be more conciliatory toward France.[6] Salon news was often taken seriously, and salonnières were thought to be uniquely well informed. More often than not, however, gens du monde overestimated both the accuracy and the quality of the information they acquired in salons. Politicians and diplomats rarely circulated important news in society for fear of divulging sensitive information or provoking the inevitable distortions of constant repetition.[7] Haussonville was convinced that Madame de Boigne was "always well informed of what was happening in the upper reaches of politics and *le monde*," even though Boigne confessed that she rarely "took the trouble to inquire into the authenticity of the information" she received and tended to believe "without examination such news as pleased my wishes." Although she admitted to receiving "some special information or some secret piece of news" from time to time, she considered herself "little better informed" than anyone else. The duchesse de Gontaut admitted that "nothing ever transpired" with regard to the things she was allowed to reveal in public, despite her "intimate acquaintance with the different members of the aristocracy of all countries," who "furnished [her] with interesting and reliable information."[8]

Gens du monde generally considered salon news more recent and more truthful than the information reported in the press. Salons often received early rumors relating to the composition of ministries or the deliberations of government councils. As a result, wrote Stendhal, "A man who mingles in Parisian high society ordinarily knows all the news twenty-four hours before its publication in the newspapers," and he himself read the latter "only to see what spin [*tournure*] was given to facts already known to him."[9] Salon news was not only firsthand, its credibility was vouchsafed by the respect society had for a salonnière's ability to assess the character of the personalities involved. The written word was opaque as to the feelings and motives of those who used it to convey information — consequently, public opinion as expressed in the press needed what the comtesse de Bassanville called "a theater to be the interpreter of its sentiments."[10] The largely oral and semi-private culture of aristocratic sociability gave women the role of reading character in the tone and sincerity of speech, accompanied by telling gestures, meaningful references, and sometimes insights drawn from physiognomy. Feminine discernment was especially important with regard to weighty political news, because privileged information could only be fully reliable if it was conveyed in an atmosphere suffused with the trust cultivated by family ties or habitual social contact. On the one hand, women were believed to have a special talent for judging temperaments, values, and affinities. On the other hand, the press was not supposed to delve into private matters.[11] Although society rumors gave the duc de Laval the impression that Chateaubriand was conspiring to replace him as ambassador to Rome in 1828, he was reassured by Madame Récamier: "Certainly, the language that you say your friend uses, and the proper expressions that you quote, are very different from those the public attributes to him, and from the sentiments and designs he has been supposed to hold with so much assurance and obstinacy. But, in spite of appearances, you must be right, as you know what his secret thoughts are better than anybody."[12]

Newspapers in the early nineteenth century were generally held in very low regard, particularly by aristocrats, who often hesitated to collaborate in founding a journal and who disdained even the papers for which they wrote. Not only was the press untrustworthy, but journalism was considered to be a dishonorable profession, because it required a writer to sell his services to the highest bidder while claiming to speak the truth.[13] French sociable traditions, moreover, taught that private conversation was genuine, while public discourse often turned to deceit — that which appeared in cheap newspapers and pamphlets was by definition untempered by reflection or politesse. "When religion or philosophy have not enlightened or consoled a man who feels injured," wrote Virginie Ancelot, "the envy, hate, and vulgarity locked in the heart will soon reveal itself in the form of irony, sarcasm, and slander, thanks to the liberty that permits him to express himself in the newspapers." Many mondain political figures had contempt for popular government and made a point of insisting that the personal attacks to which they were subject in public were unworthy of a response. Dino, who called the 1830s "the most libelous age of journalism," explained that she and her friends were well aware of their own faults and saw no reason to acknowledge "the gutter calumnies of all kinds" directed at her and Talleyrand. She insisted that no one in her circle took the press seriously and testified to the "great merriment" that ensued in the salon of Madame de Chastellux when the aging Madame de La Briche sternly related to guests what she had read about Louis-Philippe in the "low-class" press. Chateaubriand felt similarly about reports in *La Quotidienne* and *Le Globe* calling him a Jesuit and a Bonapartist respectively, and told Récamier that "on principle I never reply to the papers."[14]

Information, especially of a privileged sort, did not empower a salonnière to act in public, because the importance of the news she received was directly proportionate to her discretion. Men divulged political secrets to women of whose confidence they were assured. The greater a woman's reputation for discretion, the more secrets she was believed to know. The tantalizing details and bits of news that came from a close acquaintance with society rarely amounted to more than food for thought, because they were not conveyed in confidence and were regarded as inconsequential. Salonnières who gossiped freely or who casually disseminated sensitive information were likely to be comparatively lonely and singularly ill informed. For salonnières, therefore, confidentiality was axiomatic. "There is no security in society, when any person belonging to it is a tattler or a satirical or scandalous person," wrote Madame de Genlis. Gens du monde, she warned, were required to keep "with inviolable fidelity the secrets which are [e]ntrusted to us," and were never to repeat anything that could only be said in select company. According to Delphine de Girardin, indiscretion was an unpardonable crime, because "it is not permitted to say in public confidential things that have been said to a prince alone in his palace or a minister in his salon." The press, by contrast, was impersonal, manipulative, and corrupt: it was routinely used as a means of shaping public opinion by politicians writing incognito and was widely regarded in aristocratic circles as a medium for libel and deception.[15]

The code of discretion forbade women to use information on their own behalf and confined them to the role of intermediaries, whose impartiality was considered to diminish along with their active participation in events. Individual women could be channels of communication, but their salons could not become marketplaces for secrets conveyed "behind the scenes." At best, women who enjoyed the confidence of men in power were better informed than society at large, as Rudolf Apponyi learned in 1835 when Madame de Bondy and Madame de Rumford told him that a pamphlet he admired arguing for an interpretation of the Charter that favored the power of the king had been written in part by Louis-Philippe himself. "If, in consequence of my exceptional position, I have been well informed and have even been asked my advice and have exerted some influence upon the decision of important matters," wrote Dino, "I have at any rate not lent either my name or my energies to an intrigue, nor do I desire to play the part of a political woman."[16] Information, in short, could make a woman a worthwhile consultant, but it did not make her a player. Its greatest value for a salonnière was the help it provided in attracting prominent guests to her home. A *salon politique*, after all, was not a governmental institution — it was, rather, a drawing room in which the conversation was dominated by political news. Those who aspired to have one therefore had to attract people in the know. The reputed master at this game was the princesse de Lieven, whom Charles Grenville credited with a particular talent for knowing how "to glean some useful and interesting information." Her liaison with Guizot "kept her *au courant* of all that was going on in the political world." At the same time, she would sometimes interrogate guests and often liked to invite foreigners to dinner along with various French "political notabilities" in the hope of getting the former to divulge information on matters of diplomacy. Apponyi went to see her almost daily, because he concluded that she knew a lot; she, in turn, ensured his return by satisfying his desire for an insider's perspective.[17] Many sought an introduction to a salonnière's drawing room so that they could benefit from the information and the contacts she had at her disposal. Others made a point of knowing everything they could in order to gain access to as many salons as possible.

Aside from organizing sociability and facilitating communication, salons and salonnières performed a number of other functions in the political life of the early nineteenth century that echoed the roles played by salons in the prerevolutionary era. The preliminary reading of speeches intended for the Chamber was common in political salons during the Restoration and was analogous to the traditional prepublication *lecture* practiced most famously by the philosophes in the eighteenth century.[18] Male public figures not only tested their political oratory in salons, they also read historical or literary works with politically relevant themes. Pierre-Paul Royer-Collard tried out a speech on credit policy in the salon of Madame de Castellane, which Molé judged to be adroit and full of paradoxes; Chateaubriand, by contrast, read a short piece on Fontanes for Duras's guests in the presence of the duchesse d'Angoulême as a way of improving his reputation with the royal family and increasing his chances of becoming president of the royalist Société des bonnes lettres. The collective reading of controversial pamphlets, histories, or memoirs was also a common feature of political sociability. By the nineteenth century, such a reading was as much a performance as a search for editorial comment, a form of entertainment as much as a collective effort at composition. Benjamin Constant's presentation of his novel *Adolphe* in Madame Récamier's salon during the Hundred Days was remembered more for the sobs and the laughter that filled the room than for the book's plot, although its status as a performance text undoubtedly helped shape its structure and content. All the same, readings of this sort, whether literary or political, still served to establish or expand an individual's reputation and give publicity to his works and his ideas.[19]

The active involvement of a salon's clientele in public life turned the salonnière's traditional role as an agent of publicity more clearly toward coaching and advice.[20] The public side of Lieven's relationship with Guizot centered almost entirely on the princess's efforts to burnish Guizot's image and make him presentable to the British and European aristocracy. Having spent years in English high society as the wife of the Russian ambassador, she was in a position to give Guizot detailed instructions on what to do and say when the latter was appointed French ambassador in 1839. Such advice always combined a profound knowledge of English customs with a keen eye to the requirements of Guizot's political career. "As for places at dinner," she wrote from Paris in April 1840, "it is annoying, but you shall be obliged to have the chancellor on your right and Lord Landsdowne on your left. Ask Lord Palmerston to take the seat across from you between the duke of Wellington and Lord Melbourne." When the Eastern Question erupted in June, she told him that everyone in Europe knew that France would be inflexible — "Pronounce it like that (*in-fle-xi-ble*), and repeat it. In England, only Lord Palmerston has an opinion that is contrary to everyone else's." When he committed a social and diplomatic faux pas, like dining with the Maberleys, she was not afraid to point it out: "Truly, my husband would rather have swum in the Thames than dine with these people, and he had much less of a reputation for gravity than you." She subsequently told him to send her his schedule so that she could warn him against invitations not worth his while: "No one knows London society better than I do. . . . You have no idea how much one profits by this economy. I am an expert at this business: No little people! If in doubt, one gains everything by abstaining. There are so many grand social and political events in England. Reserve yourself for these." Guizot, for his part, generally welcomed such advice — "I have as much confidence in your discretion as in your judgment" — and solicited it often, not only in London but throughout his long premiership. When negotiating with the English in 1846 over the political situation in Spain, he asked her not only about matters of etiquette but about what ought to be said: "Tell me your opinion on this. Is it necessary to wait until Palmerston has spoken to Jarnac on Spanish affairs and has indicated his disposition, or would it be better for Jarnac, taking the initiative, to go right to Palmerston and to say to him: 'Don Enrique is arriving in London; the *progresistas* wish to make of him their instrument and your candidate.' "[21]

The duchesse de Duras played an analogous role in Chateaubriand's circuitous ascent to the Foreign Ministry, briefing him on the latest news, coaching him on how to bolster his importance in the eyes of others, and helping him improve his image with those who were skeptical about his political worth. As Chateaubriand rather disingenuously and unfairly put it: "Madame de Duras was ambitious for me: she alone knew my political value, but she grieved . . . over the obstacles that my character placed before my fortune. She chided me, she wanted me to be less careless, less frank, less naive, and to make me adopt the habits of a court toady, which she herself could not stand."[22] When the moderate royalists were in power, she encouraged him to display his independence and advertise the "liberality" of his views. When he requested springtime leave from his post in Berlin to visit Madame Récamier in Paris, she warned him that his behavior "spoiled [his] diplomatic gravity" and suggested that he "could not live without chains." Upon his arrival back in Paris in April 1821, she advised him that his reputation as a liberal would harm him as the political winds shifted to the right, and when he was finally named to head the French delegation to the Congress of Verona in 1822, she warned him against flaunting his triumph and to be "modest in success."[23]

Salonnières were able to act as political advisors to the extent that they remained guardians of aristocratic propriety. By assisting public men with matters of image and with the etiquette surrounding delicate personal encounters, they often contributed to the success of policies in whose confection they took no part. The political advice they gave was therefore less an attribute of power than an extension of the traditional role they played in preparing aspirants to enter society. The princesse de Lieven thought that the responsibility for training newcomers for society gave her more "direct influence" over political events than a position at court, because it afforded her the independence that went along with having a distinguished and agreeable salon.[24] The importance of an *education mondaine* increased as the spread of good manners and greater access to society entailed a greater scrutiny of comportment and appearance.[25] As in the seventeenth century, salonnières continued to enforce a uniform code of conduct that "erased visible differences among individuals from diverse backgrounds." All the most famous bourgeois politicians of the Restoration and the July Monarchy — François Villemain, Guizot, Thiers, Victor Cousin, Frédéric Ozanam — acquired a knowledge of le monde by attending salons. The republican salons of the 1870s provided the likes of Gambetta and Jules Ferry with the same benefits. But it was not only *routiers* who needed to be introduced to the world: upon leaving school or getting married, young men and women of aristocratic birth routinely served their social apprenticeship under the direction of an older woman.[26]

Access to high society made available to gens du monde the politically valuable "services" salons traditionally provided: introductions, connections, and patronage. A salon's reputation had a lot to do with its social utility, or the quality and quantity of the useful contacts that could be made there. Some people were even shameless enough to frequent a particular salon in the hopes of getting a political appointment. Chateaubriand went to see Madame de Montcalm twice a day during the early part of her brother's first ministry with the goal of obtaining a cabinet position. For financial assistance, he turned to the duchesse de Duras, who, in the tradition of Madame Geoffrin, raised money on his behalf to help advance his career.[27] Guizot wrote *Du gouvernement de la France depuis la Restauration* in 1820 at a country house provided by Madame de Condorcet. Services of a specifically political nature included the use of a salon as neutral terrain for a meeting of rival factions and reliance on salonnières as intermediaries. In the cabinet crisis that led to the formation of the Villèle ministry in December 1821, Corbière used Duras's salon to inform Richelieu and Pasquier that the ultras would demand ten new prefects as the price of their support. During the Revolution of 1830, Madame de Boigne kept Pasquier, Pozzo di Borgo, and the duchesse d'Orléans in contact with one another.[28]

Influential salons that mediated a wide range of contacts and were centered on a publicly prominent guest became veritable political bureaus to which politicians hastened each evening as if going to the office. The "duties" of these so-called *égéries* was never exactly the same: Madame Récamier mostly handled Chateaubriand's personal affairs, dealing with literary agents and holding off his numerous creditors; Madame de Castellane, by contrast, took a more direct role in Molé's political work, organizing receptions, polishing his oratory, and marking passages in books that she thought he would find interesting. The princesse de Lieven and Madame Dosne were for Guizot and Thiers respectively much closer to executive secretaries: Lieven introduced Guizot to her English friends and gave him detailed reports on political developments in Paris relevant to his career. Dosne handled Thiers's correspondence, advised him on political strategy, and managed his electoral campaigns.[29]

A salonnière never gained any personal advantage from these services, because the assistance she rendered was never accomplished on her own behalf. Her ambition never went beyond her own salon.

II

Salonnières continued to regard the maintenance of civility and the conciliation of conflict as their most important social and political functions. Montcalm saw the rapprochement of those she loved and esteemed as an obligation that belonged to her as a consequence of her sex, her family relations, her country, and her loyalty to the Bourbons.[30] Salons were deemed successful if the hostess could blend and balance a variety of guests and opinions. It was the ability to conciliate for which salonnières usually received the warmest praise and the most solemn eulogies. Women in elite circles often had personal reasons for not wanting to see political animosities break the bonds of friendship and divide families. According to Madame de Staël, women's fondness for influence was nothing more than a condition of their desire to please and to be surrounded by friends "whose attachment to them is heightened by the feeling of obligation."[31] Many in high society believed that such attachments grew stronger, more durable, and more consoling as political passions became more extreme. The fact that salonnières inevitably had friends and relatives in more than one camp reinforced the belief that the reconciliation of factions was a patriotic duty imposed on all those who, in Montcalm's words, wanted "to repair the evil that so much upheaval has caused" and bring the Revolution to a definitive close.[32] In either case, sociability was the cure, and salon conversation, which was prized more for the relationships it cultivated between individuals than for its relevance to the outside world, became a putative antidote to the politics of slander and hate.

Salonnières could undertake the reconciliation of political differences on their own initiative because they usually controlled a salon's composition and had the authority to direct its conversations. Their autonomy in this regard was also sanctioned and reinforced by the salon's historical and institutional identity, gender expectations, the desire of women to preserve the advantages of high society, and the center-right political leanings of most prominent salonnières. According to Charles de Rémusat, Madame de Boigne "willingly" used her good reputation "to prevent ruptures and affect conciliations." Her invitations, she explained, went to those whom she "wished to meet one another and whom I would harmonize." The duchesse de Maillé took advantage of the fact that politicians liked to talk among themselves to practice "a little diplomacy" — she brought together Bonapartists, liberals, constitutionalists, and *royalists exaltés* in her salon in the hope of causing animosities to dissipate. She was especially proud of the fact that disgraced ministers and those currently in office would eventually approach one another there. The princesse de Lieven liked to exercise her talent for negotiating the most potentially explosive encounters by putting enemïes in the same room. She would often have the legitimist Antoine Berryer and the Orleanist Louis-Mathieu Molé to dinner at the same time, and once introduced the British foreign secretary, Lord Clarendon, who had a reputation as a radical, to "my [legitimist] diplomatic friends" on the theory that "there is nothing so salutary as personal contact with the thing one is most afraid of."[33] Sometimes women tried to patch things up between two rivals whose cooperation was deemed politically beneficial, as when the marquise de Montcalm worked to mend fences between Chateaubriand and Villèle before the ultras took power in 1820, or when she helped to bring about a rapprochement between her brother and the ultraroyalist Hyde de Neuville to improve Richelieu's standing with the extreme right. In general, however, salonnières contained political passions by enforcing limits: Ancelot would interrupt conversations between her royalist and liberal friends if they became "too lively"; Boigne gave all opinions a hearing as long as they "were not too violent"; Madame de Castellane prevented enmity by making the discussions she directed interesting and simple; the duchesse de Duras welcomed guests of every point of view provided they were respectful of those with opposing convictions. "I understand the good fight that goes on between political men," wrote Lieven, "but I also understand that it can go much too far. This sort of attack strikes me as entirely below personal dignity and is of *la plus mauvaise compagnie.*"[34]

It was Madame Récamier who, more than anyone, gained a reputation for turning what the duc de Montmorency called "a sweet passion for affecting reconciliations" into a science. According to Etienne-Jean Delécluze, she would typically arrange the chairs in her salon into five or six circles at a fair distance from one another; the women would be seated, while the men were free to move from one cluster to another. As newcomers arrived, Récamier would direct them toward friends, or toward those with whom they had tastes and ideas in common, in order to create what Cynthia Gladwyn characterized as "planned harmony." Sainte-Beuve was convinced that "[s]he would not rest until she had made her friends of opposite sides meet at her house, and had conciliated them under her clement mediation." Récamier was credited with a unique, almost mystical, ability "to communicate to everyone her soft moderation." She and her salon were said to have pacified the stormy relationship between Chateaubriand and Mathieu de Montmorency, served as an "arbiter and a link" between liberals and moderates, and provided the neutral ground upon which Carlists and Orleanists could meet soon after 1830.[35]

The task of conciliation justified the salon's diverse composition. The blending and harmonizing of social conditions and ideological perspectives remained the ideal toward which the most prominent salons continued to aspire, a goal that was made easier to reach in the first years of the Restoration, according to Rémusat, by the diverse opposition the Empire had drawn together.[36] The classic salons of the Restoration, like those of Duras and Rumford, mixed old aristocrats, newer elites, foreigners, and men of letters in view of combining tradition and innovation, effacing worldly distinctions, and cultivating a tolerance for what was new. The duchesse de Rauzan, Duras's daughter, had as habitués Berryer, Falloux, Salvandy, Sainte-Beuve, and Eugène Sue. Although a few salons harbored some truly striking contrasts — Madame Ancelot's included Victor Considerant of *La Démocratie pacifique* and Honoré de Lourdoueix of *La Gazette de France* — many that strove to be politically inclusive had relatively narrow clienteles. Under Louis XVIII, guests in the great ecumenical political salons of the Right (Montcalm, Duras, Maillé, and even Madame de Staël) ran a very short gamut from ultraism to moderate royalism and always met under what François Villemain called "strongly aristocratic auspices." After 1815, partisanship made salons that could ideally encompass all ranks, talents, and ideas increasingly rare; the classic salon came more and more to be characterized as a *terrain neutre*, as if it were a demilitarized zone, atypical and difficult to maintain. Once the Revolution of 1830 cleaved society in two, according to Apponyi, efforts by salonnières to conciliate political rivals often failed or had to be aborted; the salons de fusion he visited at the time, like those of Madame de Ségur, the baronne de Meyendorff, and the comtesse de Sainte-Aldegonde, were "horribly cold." By the 1860s, Madame Ancelot was complaining that the mixed assemblies that would have been called salons in the past were the exception rather than the rule.[37]

The fragmentation of society into finer and more sharply drawn divisions was accompanied by a search for alternatives to purely conversational sociability. One approach, exemplified by the salon of Duras, was to turn the clock back to a prepolitical ideal, when literary and philosophical debates between politicians and men of letters styled on those of the past were intended to elevate men beyond their baser nature, or at least to distract them momentarily from discord. According to Villemain, diplomats, politicians, and scientists fell silent in Duras's salon before the poetic voice of Mademoiselle Gay reading the *Veuve de Naïm*. It was there, too, that Pozzo di Borgo and Capo d'Istria forgot their rivalry in the presence of distinguished literary scholars. Gay's mother recalled that guests at the salons of Baron Gérard and Mademoiselle Contat achieved a similar serenity by continually seeking out new topics of conversation or by forgetting the past, abandoning politics, and "deliver[ing] themselves over to light-hearted conversation." In 1825, after returning from Naples, Récamier declared her salon to be neutral ground and turned it into temple to the genius of Chateaubriand, to whom she required her *invités* to pay deference.[38] A related strategy involved the use of musical performances as a means of entertaining guests, preventing political arguments, and signaling a salon's neutrality. The popularity of musical salons seems to have grown in the 1820s and 1830s, following the example of the duchesse de Laviano, Madame Orfila, and the comtesse Merlin, who frankly acknowledged that men of letters were bored by concerts and recitals, which prevented them from discussing ideas and shining before an audience.[39] The shift from talking to listening in salons suggests that the cure for political conflict could be worse than the disease: salonnières could either banish political conversation entirely, as did the comtesse de Circourt, or invite only those with similar opinions, like Madame Aubernon. The other alternative was to have no soirées at all, which is what the wife of the English ambassador, Lady Cowley, was forced to do in 1835 so as not to offend the legitimists, with whom she wanted to meet, or the Orleanists, whose displeasure she could not afford to provoke.[40]

As the willingness or the ability of Frenchwomen to sponsor and encourage political cohabitation diminished, foreign hostesses stepped into the breach and foreign ambassadors offered their embassies as neutral terrain. Upon returning to

France in the middle of the July Monarchy, after five years abroad, the comtesse d'Agoult was alarmed to find that the most prominent salons in Paris belonged to three Russian women and one Italian: the princesse de Lieven, Madame Swetchine, Madame de Circourt, and the princesse de Belgiojoso.[41] Of all the foreigners hosting noteworthy receptions in Paris, the British were the most numerous (Bertier de Sauvigny found that there were more than twenty-thousand English citizens living in France in 1821), and they were credited with introducing big parties to the French. The most memorable and highly praised gatherings, however, took place at the Austrian embassy on the rue Saint-Dominique. According to Beaumont-Vassy, the balls, *déjeunes dansants*, and grand receptions given by Count and Countess Apponyi were the most brilliant and most popular *fêtes diplomatiques* of the July Monarchy. Although the embassy had close ties with the grand monde of Faubourg Saint-Germain, "[t]hat did not stop the notables of the new court from showing up in large numbers." In the early 1830s, when high society was most sharply divided, the ambassador was asked by the duc d'Orléans to serve as an intermediary between the Orleanist princes and the women of Faubourg Saint-Germain.[42]

Foreigners had less at stake in the conflicts that sowed dissension in French society and were therefore in a better position to maintain their neutrality. Michelle Perrot points out that foreign women were freer than Frenchwomen to engage in politics, because many were living in exile and had ready access to a politicized émigré community—such was the case with the princesse de Belgiojoso and various Polish countesses, who actively supported patriots from their own countries.[43] Like the bourgeois salonnières of the eighteenth century, who operated in a largely aristocratic world, the foreign women of nineteenth-century Paris were free to go anywhere and did not fit effortlessly into exclusive coteries or long-established social groups; as a consequence, they were better able to engineer unconventional encounters, bringing together people who would not otherwise meet. At the same time, foreign aristocrats and diplomatic personnel usually had strong Orleanist or legitimist sympathies and therefore could not entirely ignore the barriers and detours erected by French quarrels. In the opinion of Madame de Girardin, there was no such thing as *un terrain neutre*, because all sociable gatherings in which nobody fought were just politics in suspended animation, when rivals met to take the measure of one another, and where it was possible to observe "the new political chemistry" coming into being, as if viewing a still photograph taken immediately before the commission of a crime.[44]

III

If the power of women to harmonize the political world was largely a fiction, so was their ability to influence policy and events from behind the scenes. Women who maintained political salons in the early nineteenth century and who were also linked to a prominent male figure were usually referred to by contemporaries as *égéries*, after Egeria, the nymph who advised Numa Pompilius, the second king of Rome, according to Livy. The appellation was applied to all the most important salonnières of the time: Madame de Boigne (Pasquier's Egeria), the duchesse de Duras (Chateaubriand's), the comtesse de Castellane (Molé's), Madame Dosne (Thiers's), the duchesse de Dino (Talleyrand's), the princesse de Lieven (Guizot's), the princesse de La Trémoïlle (Villèle's), and Madame de Staël, who was considered to be the Egeria of sovereigns once she entered into a personal correspondence with Alexander I.

As a political metaphor, the legend of Egeria is ambiguous. She is said to have been the source of many laws, and Numa supposedly told the Roman people that he sought her legislative sanction and approval. The ambiguity relates to whether the source of power lay in its exercise or its inspiration, because historically women have only had the capacity to provide the latter. As a result, it was easy for the evocation of Egeria's name to obscure the difference between mere advice and the power to make things happen. Henri Malo assumed that Madame Dosne influenced Thiers's conduct because he consulted her on political matters, but it is actually impossible to know. Gabriel Pailhès argued that Duras's influence over Chateaubriand was very great, but that it only manifested itself "in his titles" and "in his doctrines," which suggests that she could help him acquire positions and formulate a point of view but could not control his public actions. The point is that feminine power was by definition indirect, secretive, and discreet, not subject to evidentiary verification. The influence attributed to Egerias was always mysterious and occult, transmitted nocturnally, or at least far from view, and consummated in an intimacy suggestive of sexual intercourse — it was in the depths of the forest that Numa listened to the celestial revelations of his nymph. Duras was said to have met with Chateaubriand in numerous *visites matinales* reserved only for him; Guizot exchanged "interminable notes" with the princesse de Lieven and was seen arriving at her house three or four times a day — "no one dared to stay when he got there."[45]

Proximity to power is not the same as its possession; it is to mistake apples for oranges to compare the sort of advice nineteenth-century salonnières gave to men — concerning whom to contact and how to behave — with the kind of advice that could be translated into policy or legislation. Those who confused salonnières with the *femmes politiques* of the Old Regime were also apt to make irresponsible assertions: Delphine de Girardin insisted that "[n]early all the acts of our politicians respond to the name of a woman"; Balzac called Madame Dosne "a sort of Father Joseph in a dress" who was "almost the queen of France" because she played "an immense role in [Thiers's] life"; the *Dictionnaire de la conversation et de la lecture*, first published in the mid 1850s, characterized Récamier's salon as a "politico-literary Areopagus" and charged that Récamier herself had had "all-powerful influence" over academic elections, ministerial appointments, and professorships at the university by virtue of her ability to offer protection and make recommendations.[46]

Although the princesse de Lieven saw herself an innocent spectator of the political game, her influence was the subject of the most elaborate suspicions and far-reaching exaggerations. During the July Monarchy, Dino spread rumors to the effect that she was making ambassadorial appointments, and Balabine called her Guizot's "stepladder."[47] Compounding the problem caused by Lieven's nationality and her obvious affinity for politics was that fact that gender norms encouraged the assumption that Egerias were required to hide their ambitions behind a male host capable of fulfilling their agenda — as Delphine de Girardin put it, women were made to command rather than to act. If Egerias had goals of their own, then it was easy to insist that they were the real movers and shakers. That is why Guizot's "scandalous intimacy" with a Russian princess caused great resentment among French politicians and "a violent outcry" in the French diplomatic corps: whose diplomacy was he practicing? As far as the marquis de Custine was concerned, "there is scarcely a capital in Europe without two or three of these Russian ambassadors: one public, accredited, recognized and clothed with all the insignia of office; the others, secret, irresponsible, and playing, in bonnet and petticoat, the double part of independent ambassador, and spy upon the official envoy."[48]

The myth of Egeria lent credibility to the notion that political decisions were made in salons, despite all evidence to the contrary. Salonnières on their own possessed neither the standing to overturn ministries nor the influence to lobby for academic appointments. They might on occasion use their good offices to help friends or relatives secure positions and favors, but these were the acts of private individuals and were not undertaken in salons. Madame de Duras, who devoted a great deal of time and energy to satisfying Chateaubriand's appetite for political fame, acted in this capacity as a courtier—married to a *premier gentilhomme de la chambre*—rather than as a salonnière, even though she was then one of the most famous in Paris. The secrecy that marked her efforts on his behalf clearly echoed an earlier tradition of courtly politics. In 1814, he asked her to intercede with the duc de Rohan, her brother-in-law, to gain an audience with the king for a deputation of candidates for the Chamber from Orléans that his *collège d'arrondissement* had nominated, believing that the quality of its members would rebound to his credit. A few months later, she was encouraging the duc de Blacas to make him ambassador to Sweden. In the double game he played prior to his selection as France's representative to the Congress of Verona in 1822, Chateaubriand exploited Récamier's neutrality and her more varied contacts to influence public opinion, while using Duras to furtively pressure Villèle:

> [Montmorency] has positively said that if I do not address myself to him directly, he would rather leave the Ministry than let me be nominated to the Congress by the Council [of Ministers]. You can say this confidentially to Villèle. But I beg you not to speak of this affair either to Polignac, or in your salon, or to anybody. . . . Arrange everything with Villèle! Proceed with everything. But I implore you, with Villèle alone and in secret. Do not even mention the Congress to my enemies or friends. I believe in success if the matter is completely ignored, and if it doesn't get all mixed up in chatter, reports, jealousies, and gossip.[49]

Influence of this sort consisted chiefly in the opportunity to intercede with powerful associates and protect patrons from the vulnerabilities resulting from their opinions or mistakes. Chateaubriand needed women to shield him from retaliation or neglect, because his behavior and his writings angered or alienated those who were in a position to deprive him of a rendezvous with history, including Louis XVIII and the duc de Richelieu. Such power was not inconsequential, but its efficacy was far from guaranteed, and the outcomes it helped produce could not be directly attributed to feminine intervention. In 1817, Duras talked repeatedly to Montcalm of Chateaubriand's desire to please the king after provoking his ire with the publication of *La Monarchie selon la Charte*. At the same time, Chateaubriand visited Montcalm twice a day, hoping to obtain a ministry. Montcalm conveyed the substance of these conversations to Richelieu, who, as a result, formed an unfavorable view of Chateaubriand's character because of his lack of frankness and his use of women as intermediaries. In his own account of Duras's earlier efforts to win him the Swedish post, Chateaubriand could not tell whether the success she achieved on his behalf was due to her courage and persistence or to Louis XVIII's desire to get rid of him.[50]

In light of such considerations, inflated claims regarding the power of salonnières invite only skepticism. What are we to make of the assertion that Récamier obtained ministerial audiences for her porter and the bastard children of her apothecary, or of Lieven's suggestion that Madame de Flahaut was "working as hard as she can" to force London to change ambassadors in order to have someone at Paris more inclined than Granville to intrigue? "Every Parisian salon has its inspiring muse who dictates to each the manner in which to think," intoned Joseph Turquan, in a passage typical of the blather written for mondains around the fin de siècle. "[S]he imposes on this one what he will say at a club, and on that one what he must say at the tribunal of the Assembly." Only in his youth did Rémusat imagine that salon success could lead directly to a salaried position; as a mature politician, he could only scoff at Casimir Périer's sincere complaints about the intrigues concocted by Madame de Boigne: she had, he admitted, "an agreeable salon; she liked political conversation, but no one dreamed of distributing portfolios."[51] Everyone in Paris seemed to agree in the 1830s that the princesse de Lieven was a spy working on behalf of the Russian court, but no one could figure out whether she was a mastermind or a puppet. Apponyi thought that she was turning Guizot against Austria and that she wanted to see her brother, General Alexander de Benckendorff, replace Nesselrode as Russian foreign minister. At the same time, Balabine thought that she and her salon were controlled alternatively by the English and the Russians, with the two influences canceling each other out. According to Custine, Russia possessed "a completely organized female diplomacy" run by a "concealed army of amphibious agents" made up of "political Amazons with acute masculine minds and feminine language" who were nonetheless content to gather information, obtain reports, and give advise to the czar's court. The duchesse d'Abrantès displayed a much more realistic sense of proportion when she told Napoléon that men were the worst intriguers, that women with true power were "exceptions to the general rule," and that it was "you men [who] dispose us; who compel us to move like pieces on a chess-board; who, in short make mere machines of us."[52]

The great political salons of the nineteenth century were often depicted as matriarchies in which important men surrounded a grande dame like "satellites beaming around the most important star."[53] In fact, women in politics were more often than not instruments of male ambition who could be compromised without risk and disavowed without consequence. The participation of women in the political life of the nineteenth-century French elite, Claude-Isabelle Brelot asserts, was "mediatized" by their roles as spouses, mothers, mistresses, or friends — women owed the possibility of political collaboration to love, conjugal or otherwise. Madame Dosne was plainspoken enough to say as much when she admitted to being perfectly aware "that my relations with so many important personalities is due only to the marriage contracted between my daughter and one of the most eminent men of his era."[54] The political salons of the Restoration and the July Monarchy tended to form around prominent men and served primarily to promote their careers, support their policies, and present them to le monde in a favorable light; the salonnière's principal role was to ensure their assiduous presence. People were drawn to the salons of Boigne, Lieven, Castellane, Montcalm, Dino, Dosne, Genlis, and Flahaut to be in the presence of Pasquier, Guizot, Molé, Richelieu, Talleyrand, Thiers, General de Valence, and the duc d'Orléans respectively. "The day my brother became a minister," wrote Montcalm, "everyone was of the opinion that I was an intelligent woman." Anne Martin-Fugier places Madame Récamier outside this "classic situation" because she acquired influence by her charm, whereas others, like Montcalm and Duras, came by it through family relations. But such "influence" (in Chateaubriand's behalf) amounted to the same thing — Récamier, like the others, adopted a model of sociability that put men at center stage. Even a woman as independent and self-assured as Lieven had to arrange her life for Guizot.[55]

The centrality of men in political salons, so well established by 1830, seriously compromised a woman's control over her salon's composition and conversational content. Salonnières could still "hold a circle" and invite a varied list of guests, but there were always a number of pressing considerations that had nothing to do with pleasure or aesthetics. Richelieu's position added his former colleagues and political allies to Montcalm's list of daily visitors and gave her salon a strong political hue, despite her inclinations. D'Agoult's mother usually socialized with her friends from the provinces and her husband's old comrades from the days of the Vendée and the emigration, but when her son entered the diplomatic service, she began to invite his superiors, colleagues, and those whom society took to be the shining lights of the foreign policy establishment.[56] After Molé was appointed minister of the navy in 1817, his mother-in-law, Madame de La Briche, had to begin to pay attention to his political interests. When he resigned from his post in 1818, the tone of her salon changed dramatically: "all the ministerial coaches" evacuated the courtyard, Molé's colleagues from the Chamber replaced government officials, and moderates and ultras began to quarrel more intensely.[57]

A number of subtle and well-policed distinctions kept salonnières from play-ing a direct political role. Such distinctions had less to do with the separation between public and private than with the convenience of men. French politicians expressed contempt for feminine intrigue, but they welcomed the assistance of an intelligent women, who was permitted to give publicly useful advice in private but was discouraged by ridicule from showing an obvious interest in politics. As a consequence, the intelligence of politically active women like Madame de Staël and the princesse de Lieven was bitterly criticized.[58] Men denied such women opportunities to act upon their knowledge and convictions and then treated their ideas as trivial and inconsequential. Negotiating such contradictions required woman to use their sense of the permissible to defend themselves against charges of meddling and partiality. Lieven, who "loved politics more than sunlight," had to be coy when Czar Nicholas I objected in 1836 that her Parisian salon was too politically involved. "Yes," she told her brother, "some political personalities go there," but they were people of distinction from all parties. Deputies, ministers, and diplomats arrived looking for distraction and for the pleasures of the "gentle life" — they talked about matters of political import, but they did not discuss affairs of state.[59]

Madame de Montcalm's relationship with her brother brought these contra-dictions sharply into focus. The duc de Richelieu put up a solid barrier between his professional self and the women in his life; his wife remained on the family estate and his two sisters, Montcalm and the marquise de Jumilhac, lived in hôtels in Faubourg Saint-Germain and were kept out of the ministerial residence. As a consequence, according to Montcalm, he was "little accustomed to the society of women," whose influence he feared and whose "intimacy he seemed to want to keep at arm's length in case anyone supposed they had some sort of control over him." At the same time, he often dined with Montcalm and considered her worthy of a role beyond that of a maîtresse de maison; he talked to her frequently, valued her advice, and let her manage his relations with a number of his political foes — but he refused to tell her about important political decisions. She seems to have accepted the limitations he imposed on her role, but not without comment. On the one hand, she questioned the political competence of women and insisted that it was "dangerous" to accord them "a deliberative role in the different opera-tions of the government." On the other hand, she doubted the political skills of many leading politicians and wondered how men could complain about the influ-ence of women after reducing them to complete nullities. She honored her brother's desire that she not meddle in his affairs, but she enjoyed directing the "substantial and animated conversations" that took place in her salon as a result of his work. She suggested that his tenure in office would have gone more smoothly if he had welcomed the company of women and complained that his unwillingness to accept petitions from her guests put her in an embarrassing position.[60]

The conventions that governed a salonnière's participation in nineteenth-century political life rendered her essentially powerless. The courtly model of feminine power was slowly dying as a result of the professionalization of politics. Gone were the days when women could organize and advance the claims of a political faction that aspired to the crown itself, or at least to the direction of foreign policy. Gone, too, were the days when a woman could pursue a purely personal agenda through the appointment and promotion of a male surrogate. The intrigue that foreshadowed a change of ministry might very well have taken place against the backdrop of salon conversations, but the part women played always escapes us, and any salonnière who closed her door to give asylum to secrets raised suspicions about her virtue. A salonnière was only as "powerful" as her ability to enhance the power of the men who took advantage of the mondain contacts she afforded them for the benefit of their careers. Once she tried to exercise influence in the light of day, she ran the risk of committing an indecency.[61] When the duchesse de Duras tried to get Chateaubriand to appoint her son-in-law, the duc de Rauzan, as his political officer when he was ambassador to Berlin, she was told that her obvious hand in the nomination "might compromise her and make enemies." Madame de Boigne testified that the episode was "the general object of blame and ridicule, and greatly marred [Chateaubriand's] reputation," making him in the eyes of society a victim of Duras's "imperious influence."[62]

The power of salonnières, in short, was merely a rhetorical phantom, a hazy abstraction built on resentment and conjecture. Aristocratic gallantry, the political potency of misogynist innuendo, and the crass pursuit through flattery of a mondaine female readership inspired opposition politicians, journalists, and society columnists to offer such conjecture routinely and without fear of contradiction. In reality, salonnières were rendered politically impotent by a systematic decoupling of those unities of power and knowledge, conscience and participation, that grounded and guaranteed male political initiative in the nineteenth century. Since women were supposed to be motivated by sympathy, affection, and a general desire for conciliation, they could not take sides in a dispute without being accused of ambition and self-interest. Since they could only act for others, there was no necessary relationship between their aspirations and the outcomes they helped bring about. Salonnières, therefore, routinely assisted in the accomplishment of political ends that ran counter to their personal views and convictions. Rémusat's aunt, Madame de Nansouty, was Pasquier's counselor and confidante in the early years of the Restoration, even though she was an ultra and he a moderate. Madame de Genlis, also an ultra, looked after the affairs of a liberal peer, General de Valence, for which the ultras never forgave her. Madame de Duras assisted in Chateaubriand's selection as France's representative at the Congress of Verona; once there, he championed a war with Spain that she opposed, believing that it would hurt the monarchy's popularity in France, while gaining credit for the revolutionaries in Spain.[63]

The emerging demarcation of public and private spaces that characterized nineteenth-century gender relations resulted not in the disappearance of salons but in the representation of their public function in language that pointed more insistently toward their association with the domestic sphere. In the eighteenth century, salonnières were generally characterized as magistrates or legislators by philosophes who had a penchant for using political language when eulogizing their favorite drawing-room hostesses. Jean-François Marmontel endowed Julie de Lespinasse with analogous managerial qualities when he described her guests as "the strings of an instrument played by an able hand."[64] In the nineteenth century, however, contemporaries liked to wrap salonnières in the metaphorics of restorative consolation. Delphine de Girardin believed that men expected salonnières to conduct themselves like mondain Sisters of Charity, reconciling hostile interests, calming implacable resentments, and reanimating the courage of the wounded. Women seem to have internalized this discourse to a remarkable degree, generally accepting the representation of the salon as a convalescent ward for the politically infirmed. The duchesse d'Abrantès described the salon of Madame de Staël as "a political hospital [where] one sees the wounded of all parties"; Théobald Piscatory compared Madame de Broglie's salon after a good floor fight to "a sick room"; and the comtesse de Bassanville called Lieven's salon "the Hôtel des Invalides of the monarchy" after the Revolution of 1848.[65]

Eighteenth-century philosophes, worried about the internal cohesion of the Republic of Letters, turned to salonnières to contain disputes and regulate conversation. By contrast, nineteenth-century politicians went to salons looking for shelter from a world characterized by combat and agitation. Gens du monde in the 1820s and 1830s still identified a salon with its partisan proclivities, but they saw it as a place of rest rather than a base of operations. Like the home, the salon had become a refuge, but with a specific relationship to the tribulations of political life. "Parliamentary mores," Virginie Ancelot wrote, "were not the chivalrous mores by which the French would only fight one another with *courteous arms.*" Instead, politics had become an endless round of ministerial crises, and Parliament a site of constant agitation. "Nothing in our day could give by comparison an exact idea of what parliamentary existence was like [under the July Monarchy]," Beaumont-Vassy wrote during the enforced calm of the Second Empire: deputies underwent "vivid and painful emotions" and felt a "perpetual tension of nerves," along with "inflammation of arteries" and "progressive and rapid changes of health."[66] In the wake of such travails, men craved what the duchesse d'Abrantès called "an oasis in a wilderness" among women who would renew their confidence and nurture their self-esteem. Richelieu reportedly went to Montcalm's salon to "calm his soul" and found her small réunions "less agitated, more attractive, and more agreeable" than the ministerial receptions he was obliged to attend. Her other guests liked to discuss literary matters to distract themselves from politics, according to Villemain. Tocqueville made a direct connection, and drew a sharp contrast, between politics and salons by noting "a lot of insolence" in the former and "an extreme benevolence" in the latter—he and Théodore Jouffroy considered Ancelot's house "a sanctuary." Guizot believed that the conversation in Broglie's salon gave his soul respite "from the work and sadness of life."[67]

And yet, a serene and comforting salon was to a certain extent a betrayal of an older ideal, because it undermined the salon's historical association with the life of the mind and made the salonnière little more than a caring friend and an obliging hostess. Men still wanted agreeable conversation, but they seemed less willing to be challenged. Madame de Staël had built her salon to incubate genius and thought of inspiration as much more than the ability to listen. Jean-Charles-Léonard de Sismondi compared her unfavorably to Madame de Duras because she did not always keep the conversation on track, followed her own line of thought, and failed to keep silent. He acknowledged, nevertheless, that both women presided over intellectually demanding conversations—in November 1824, Alexander von Humboldt excused himself from one of Duras's gatherings because a cold made him "too dull to show myself in a salon." Trends, however, were moving in a less promising direction as the salon's progressive metaphorical domestication banished public life to the world outside its walls. Chateaubriand paid tribute to Duras for turning his faults into qualities and making his imperfections charming but gave her no credit for the development of his art; he considered her difficult and preferred the company of Madame Récamier, whose little room in the Abbaye-aux-Bois he regarded as a "pleasant retreat" where he could forget all his trials. "Like you," he told her, "I need quiet and rest: I need tranquil studies and peaceful leisure. It is you who will procure me all this."[68] Was the salon becoming a refuge from the rough and tumble of public life, or from politics per se? When the duc de Broglie returned to his wife's salon in a state of agitation after having to explain to the Russian ambassador why he supported Polish self-determination, he found his friends engaged in a continuing discussion of the question. It was one thing to withdraw into familiar company, it was quite another to want to escape from politics entirely — if only for the evening. But escape is precisely what Chateaubriand was looking for at the Abbaye-aux-Bois, not a refuge from politics, but its total annihilation: "Agitated from without by political preoccupations or disgusted by the ingratitude of royal courts, the placidity of the heart awaited me in the depths of this retreat, as the fresh scent of wood escapes from a burning plain. I would find calm with a woman from whom serenity reached out."[69]

Madame Récamier was celebrated by her contemporaries because the Abbaye-aux-Bois exemplified the way in which the salon had become a sort of consolation for the coarsening of the public sphere.[70] Her friends echoed Chateaubriand's appreciation in praising the way in which her salon was cut off entirely from the cares of the world. The duke of Wellington told her that he especially liked to visit when he was least disposed "to turn my attention to politics," and the duchesse d'Abrantès testified that her salon alone "had escaped the contagion" of political talk that had overtaken society in the 1820s. Sainte-Beuve saw hers as an exemplary salon de fusion and cast her in the role of Orpheus, accomplishing a "work of civilization" by taming savage life and conciliating contradictory opinions.[71] Madame Récamier had many incarnations: young and beautiful hostess and rich banker's wife; confidante of Madame de Staël; celebrated literary salonnière; and, finally, curator of Chateaubriand's cult. It was this latter role, in which she was most hidden from view, that afforded her the most fame. Contemporaries seem obsessed with her absolute devotion to the brooding writer: every day for more than two decades, Chateaubriand arrived at her apartment at three o'clock so that she could soothe his wounded pride and put him on display. "[A]ll her faculties," wrote Boigne, "were concentrated upon the task of softening his violent conceit, calming the bitterness of his character, ministering to his vanity, and dissipating his weariness."[72]

In the end, Madame Récamier was both praised and eulogized not for her own qualities — except her beauty — but for her complete self-effacement. She was the nineteenth-century's version of the ultimate public woman: the closer she came to the public sphere, the more she erased her existence, whether by her dedication to Chateaubriand or by her selfless efforts at pacification in the name of monarchical unity. Goethe ascribed great influence to her by virtue of her "capacity to love and understand talent, and to have her soul catch fire by sharing its success." Women, however, found it much harder to account for all the fuss. Madame de Boigne considered her "coquettishness personified" and regretted that her talent for flirtation led those around her to ignore the independence of her character and the impartiality of her judgment. Madame de Montcalm admired her devotion to others but feared that she often made herself "the victim of those she loved." The duchesse de Dino had trouble understanding her willingness to service the ego of a man who was "barren and vain." For Marie d'Agoult, Récamier's fame was a complete mystery — there was, in her view, nothing to indicate why she should have had the most frequented salon in Paris: "Not only do I not find Madame Récamier intelligent, in the proper sense of the word, but there is nothing particular about her, nor is she very interesting. Her speech warbles a bit; her elegance cajoles; there is nothing to suggest either naturalness or a superior art, and nothing, above all, of the grande dame, assured in her deportment and able to carry her age with dignity: her voice hesitates, her gestures are halting, and she has all the encumbrances of an old pensioner."[73]

IV

The political hostess of the nineteenth century had the power to preside over and administer an unofficial point of access into a world that encompassed the political sociability of elites. As a maîtresse de maison, her role was to prepare a sociable space in which to receive guests recruited for their mutual interests and compatibilities. As a salonnière, she tried by her manners, her seating arrangements, and her conversational leadership to perform a bit a alchemy by turning discord into peaceful harmony. Since most political salons featured a single prominent guest, they became so many little courts for powerful individuals whom many people wanted to see. In that sense, most political salons were similar in function to official or ministerial salons, and indeed, they were often associated with former or future ministers. Courtly metaphors were frequently used to describe such salons and to characterize the behavior of those attending them: people went to "pay court" to Guizot, who was said to "reign" at the home of the princesse de Lieven; party leaders "ruled" France from "the corner of a salon."[74] The salons of "great men," so prevalent during the July Monarchy, represented a sort of democratization of the courtly model in an era of multiple centers of power and overlapping political networks. The same model could be used by almost anyone to whom others wanted access, or who wanted to be seen: government officials, party leaders, ambassadors, bankers, or artists.

Access to high society provided gens du monde with exposure and a hearing, resources that were especially valuable to ambitious provincial politicians and young men leaving school. It was therefore essential for strategies of social ascent and for the maintenance of aristocratic prestige. For insiders, salon sociability accorded the status of affiliation; for everyone else, it provided opportunities to rub shoulders with the sort of people who had access to la bonne compagnie. Salonnières were generally known for whom they knew, rather than for what they had done. Their authority was usually equated with their ability to shame vulgarity and was considered especially formidable if it was accompanied by the power to exclude those unworthy of good company. In the end, however, such power amounted to little more than the ability to deprive someone of the limelight or let them bask in prestige under conditions in which such mondain exposure was relevant to reputations and careers.

For their labors, along with the excitement and the advantages of being in "daily contact with those who are most noteworthy," women got access too.[75] Proximity to power gave them three opportunities to participate directly in politics: they could take part in great events as intermediaries; they could try to shape the thinking of those who had decision-making power; or they could use their culturally sanctioned powers of observation to assess and comment on the character, skill, and political fitness of those in office, or those who aspired to be. The first sort of influence amounted to very little: Madame de Boigne's access to Pasquier, Pozzo, and the duchesse d'Orléans allowed her to play the role of messenger during the July Revolution, but that made her little more than a fly on the wall. The second was nothing more than courtly power, based solely on access and intimacy and no different in kind than the power exerted by queens and royal mistresses. In the case of salonnières, courtly power can only be inferred — the fact that the politically powerful frequented high society did not make *femmes du monde* politically powerful. Montcalm believed that most people who complained to her about the budget or military recruitment lacked the proper competence to do so; she made a point of ignoring requests from those who wanted "to induce me to propose ideas about managing grain to my brother." When Hyde de Neuville asked her to appeal to her brother on behalf of his political ideas, she repeatedly told him that she had no influence; he refused to believe her, preferring to think that the problem lay, not in her unwillingness to talk, but in Richelieu's unwillingness to listen: "Your brother is smart not to accord anyone influence; but it is not, Madame, a question of exercising influence but of revealing the truth." Brelot argues that the ability of Céleste de Vaulchier to refine and develop her husband's political decisions in "conjugal exchanges" was a form of power that went beyond the strictly mondain and was therefore more substantial "than that which was habitually devolved to the wife of a great notable and that ordinarily limited itself to the management of social relations imposed by belonging to a network." And yet, the kind of things that Céleste talked about with her husband — conversations with friends and colleagues, salon rumors, hopes and worries engendered by audiences with important men of state — were the result of access.[76]

The third kind of participation derived entirely from salon sociability, because it was based on a combination of feminine passivity, assumptions about women's capacity to judge personalities, and the salon's association with the private realm, all of which allowed salonnières to observe powerful men in the most socially demanding, and hence revealing, situations. Observation, wrote Delphine de Girardin, was the métier of women who inhabited le monde — they were expected to practice it with finesse and were habitually praised for doing so. "Forty years spent in the whirlwind of society," according to Viel-Castel, had made the duchesse de Challux "prodigiously perspicacious in her judgments" and an arbiter of opinion in Faubourg Saint-Germain. Lord Grenville believed that the princesse de Lieven was "able to form a juster estimate of the characters and the objects of public men" once she had moved to Paris, away from the "passions and prejudices that complicated and disturbed her position in England"; he praised her for having "a nice, accurate judgment, and exquisite taste in the choice of her associates and friends."[77]

Salons were the domain of conversation, and conversational eloquence was assumed to be indicative of intelligence and oratorical skill; feminine observation had political import because success in salons was a predictor of success at the tribune. Consequently, men frequented salons to learn how to improvise effortlessly and salonnières commented widely on the language and demeanor of men in order to pronounce upon their suitability for public life. As a rule, those who were thought to be bad company were also considered bad politicians: Montesquiou, judged by Duras to be disdainful, petty, and evasive in conversation, was also "one of the most mediocre politicians of the Restoration"; Boigne considered Joseph Lainé to be splendid in opposition but thought that "his eloquence was not governmental" due to his "cold, measured, and uninteresting" conversation and his tendency to become "too irritated by partisan arguments advanced in bad faith"; Comte Louis de Sainte-Aulaire, by contrast, spoke wonderfully in the Chamber, vanquishing his enemies with courage, nobility, and moderation, "as if he were in a salon."[78]

Such powers of observation were valued and respected because character judgments were considered important in a political culture that saw the conduct of individuals as the key to understanding events. But they did not constitute political influence in any but the most ephemeral sense. The best orators might have made the most desirable salon guests, but the best *causeurs* were not necessarily a political success. On the one hand, Berryer, Thiers, and Odilon Barrot each overcame aristocratic disdain for their social origins by their intelligence and conversational skill, but they gained entry into the best society because of the prestige they earned in the Chamber. On the other hand, Comte J.-B. de Martignac, Achille de Salvandy, and the duc de Raguse were all three considered agreeable company but were regarded as ineffective public officials—the first could not control the Chamber, the second was a mediocre cabinet minister, and the third was widely criticized for inconsistency. At the same time, the putative connection between conversational brilliance and political capacity was dubious at best and easily subverted. Maillé thought M. de La Ferronnays was a scoundrel with little political talent who had nevertheless managed to persuade everyone of his frankness and loyalty. Pasquier, who was not *sympathique* and more adroit than intelligent in Bassanville's estimation, enjoyed an especially long political career despite a reputation in society for egoism, slyness, and deception. Exposing unknown talent or underappreciated virtue was a thankless task, according to Ancelot: "The benefits of society go to the clever, while the truly estimable people rarely get their due. Judgments made about them are often contrary to the truth. The crowd does not understand their virtues. The envious deny them, the spiteful persecute them as enemies, and the dignity of delicate souls is an obstacle to their success."[79]

Salonnières could neither shepherd their favorite guests into positions of power nor prevent rascals from entering high society—they presided over le monde, but they did not control access to it. Public opinion, momentary celebrity, social status, and acquired situations seriously impaired their power even to determine the composition of their own salons. Scholars disagree on whether salons assisted in the process of social mobility by substituting behavior for social distinctions (Norbert Elias, Carolyn Lougee), or whether they promoted class discrimination by restricting entry into le monde (Karl Mannheim, Joan Landes). In both cases, however, salonnières are wrongly cast in the role of social gatekeepers, a role that attributes too much independence to women and too much importance to salons.[80] This sort of plausible exaggeration ignores a variety of factors that overrode a salonnière's power to be selective. Noblemen and women with the right pedigree were almost never excluded from society, despite whatever foibles might have made them poor company. Even if it were true that a salonnière accorded recognition only to those with established titles, it would have been no less a limit on her discretion. In any event, aristocrats were born for society — they learned how to dress, walk, talk, and present themselves nobly at an early age. The certainty that they would count in society helped give them the confident manners that everyone else sought to imitate. They also had mothers, grandmothers, or aunts who were grandes dames, through whose salons they easily entered le monde. Haussonville gained access to high society through his mother's salon and entered the diplomatic service as Chateaubriand's attaché as a very young man. For Chateaubriand himself, it was family and provincial relations, as well as his literary and political opinions, that "opened the doors of society." According to Ancelot, Tocqueville had an advantage over other politicians because "he entered life great," being descended from Chancellor Henri-François d'Aguesseau and Malesherbes.[81]

Aspiring artists, talented provincials, and the young in general needed recommendations and the sponsorship of a insider to gain access to Parisian salons. Minor figures in the world of letters usually found a niche in society, but they were not invited to the best salons, and the company they kept was not considered entirely mondain. Men without social distinction who had acquired reputations on their own, however, did not need the approval of a salonnière to be sought after by good company. True celebrities were always in demand; they had already acquired a degree of social polish and had forced themselves on the attention of contemporaries through government service, higher education, journalism, or literary success. The famous were more interested in approbation than approval — Villemain, Guizot, and Cousin had made names for themselves at the Sorbonne before becoming habitués of the salons of Madame de Rumford and the duchesse de Duras. Thiers eventually built a base for himself in the salon of Madame Dosne, but he was already a political dignitary at that time — it was his pre-1830 journalism and his *Histoire de la Révolution* that made him an honored guest in the salons of the liberal aristocracy.[82]

As in the past, commoners still had to learn a code of conduct that was considered foreign to their experience, but by the 1820s, fame had begun to trump breeding and class; salonnières had always liked to recognize and admit all men of talent regardless of their origins, but now their personal discretion was being heavily supplemented by public opinion. In *Les Misérables*, Hugo explains that the difference between the sociability of the petite bourgeoisie and the rich was that the former esteemed virtue while the latter considered themselves above moral laws and were concerned only with class: the poor would shun "despised persons," but among the aristocracy, "A robber is admitted, provided he be a god." But Hugo's interest in developing a new mythology of the common man led him to miss the extent to which the old high society was undergoing a subtle form of democratization. By the 1840s, Delphine de Girardin noted, "people arrived at lofty positions by themselves, by work, business, or by the capricious combinations of politics." Rich and famous commoners could engage in aristocratic mondanité and acquire the signs of a superior social position, less as marks of refinement than as symbols of power and prestige. Wealthy men with beautiful, charming wives could win reputations for affability and good taste by receiving a few literary celebrities, especially ones with royalist credentials, like Pierre Ballanche or Lamartine. At the same time, Faubourg Saint-Germain wanted to see those "monsters" whose talent had enabled them to enjoy certain mondains privileges. Balzac and Eugène Sue might have made token expressions of dynastic loyalty, but their presence among "the best company" pointed to a certain relaxation of social relations and the persistence of an aristocratic taste for the slightly taboo. In this emerging culture of celebrity, connections and a name were almost never enough to draw attention to a provincial noble: Tocqueville's family origins provided him with a natural entrée into the great legitimist salons, but only *Democracy in America* made him fashionable; Comte J.-B. de Villèle and Comte J.-J. de Corbière did not attract the attention of Faubourg Saint-Germain until they began to acquire prominence in the Chamber of Deputies.[83]

Mondain celebrity was the result of a reciprocity of interests — celebrities enhanced their own notoriety in the presence of a famous salonnière, whose salon acquired even greater prestige. Celebrities and salonnières, therefore, engaged in a mutual transfer of benefits involving the exchange of notability and access for connections and opportunities for positive display. Récamier, known for gathering around herself only the most renowned, made Chateaubriand "the god of her salon," which in turn captured his reflected glory. As a result, the reading of fragments of Chateaubriand's *Mémoires* at the Abbaye-aux-Bois was nothing less than a major social and cultural event.[84] There were those who believed that only women benefited from such relationships; others insisted that the cult of celebrity helped only men, and that women could expect nothing but endless work and self-negation.[85] In fact, celebrity was a product of teamwork, a two-way street: the salonnière and her principal guest drew in different types of people and contributed to the pleasure and quality of the salon as a whole. Celebrity alone was never enough. Lafayette's stature brought crowds to his salon in 1830, but the absence of feminine governance left it deserted after he resigned as the commander-in-chief of the National Guard in 1831. Madame Dosne was not a particularly good hostess; as a consequence, Thiers's salon was well-attended but guests were subjected to "inexhaustible monologues" by a host who "knew neither how to listen nor how to discuss." Madame Lehon, on the other hand, had "a curious and amusing house," but she had "few liaisons in good company," and her salon was thus "less distinguished."[86]

By the early nineteenth century, there was clearly a hierarchy of salons, with the top salonnières being the ones who could attract the most famous guests. At the summit of le monde, there was no distinction between merit and fame — the greatest salonnières did not have to compromise their commitment to the ideal of pure talent in seeking to attract the most celebrated writers and politicians. Salonnières who inhabited the uppermost reaches of high society had instant entrée and were the most successful at cultivating contacts with the momentarily famous. They could consequently be very demanding in their choice of invités: Delphine de Girardin had ties to the duchesse de Duras and was able to meet the princesse de Ligne, the duchesse de Galliéra, and members of the diplomatic corps; Madame de Staël entertained Emperor Alexander, the duke of Wellington, and Lafayette and felt privileged enough to request an invitation from Montcalm when her brother became prime minister. At the same time, the existence of a mondain hierarchy spawned a star system for the cultivation and the creation of celebrity, which, by the 1820s, was becoming the primary animator of high society. To succeed in this system, salonnières had to attract or recruit guests who could add status or draw attention to their salons. Even Madame de Broglie, despite the advantages of her name, convened regular weekly dinners to which she expressly invited "persons with a reputation for *esprit* whom contemporary events had put most in evidence." A well-developed talent for trolling among what Apponyi called "prominent people in government and those in the Carlist opposition" made Lieven one of the most outstanding hostesses of her day; lineage established her mondanité, but sheer effort made her a Parisian salonnière, truly a product of the star system, a self-made grande dame.[87]

The mythology that allowed salonnières to claim talent as the only criterion for access persisted long after notoriety had become one of high society's principle attractions. As Martin-Fugier points out, nineteenth-century Paris had fallen in love with *vedettes* and had let itself be seduced by their prestige.[88] Salon society in the eighteenth century had not been so different in principle, but the earlier version of the star system had been less flagrant, because the public sphere was smaller and less commercial, absolutism gave philosophic celebrity a more serious and subversive quality, and the aristocracy maintained a virtual monopoly over elite status, while insisting that it had earned the right to occupy the top of the social hierarchy. As the values of the marketplace progressively took precedence over the dictates of social and cultural discrimination, salonnières imperceptibly lost the ability to select guests according to talent, intelligence, or *esprit*. The triumph of the star system made it harder and harder to tell the difference between innate ability, earned reputation, and the kind of glory conferred by public success; writers, savants, politicians, and aristocrats all entered the salons under the title of *hommes célèbres*. Moreover, the logic of the salon as an institution had always been consistent with the interests (if not the absolute autonomy) of the salonnière: she gained either way, whether invités came to her home because of the reputation of her salon or because of the celebrity of her guests. Fame, therefore, was almost certain to generate numerous invitations, because salonnières had a vested interest in pleasing society and ensuring their own success.

Salon tended to facilitate the democratization of le monde because they embodied a certain pragmatism that was never entirely compatible with social exclusivity. Ideally, salonnières hoped to attract stars whose renown rested on a solid base, but the star system made it impossible to police society against those who were willing to chase such momentary curiosities as lions, dandies, exotic travelers, magnetizers, somnambulists, and dwarfs. The Comtesse Dash even proposed a sort of ethical code for the star system, recommending that salonnières invite celebrities who really wanted to be on display, and only one at a time. Under the star system's pragmatic dispensation, there were no parvenus, only arrivistes — stringent rules of exclusion would only deprive society of those who might otherwise embellish it. In Paris, Custine wrote, the work of creating new attractions begins again each day and in each salon. Nobody recognizes the authority of another. Yesterday's success spares no penalty today. The man who is à la mode with one person is unknown on the other side of the street. If you reign in one house, go next door and see how much your glory is worth. In each circle, people are admiring another Richelieu, another Lovelace, and are celebrating a woman of genius superior to Madame de Staël.[89]

According to Girardin, even Faubourg Saint-Germain understood "that it must recruit from all the celebrities."[90]

The star system changed the relationship between salons and le monde. No longer simply islands of refinement and distinction, salons had become engines transforming high society into Tout-Paris. In the process, salons made themselves vulnerable to the criticism of insiders who wanted a political sociability that was less distracting and more exclusive.

CHAPTER SIX

The Decline of Salons (1830–1848)

The decline of French salons was a nineteenth-century cliché, repeated steadily throughout the Restoration, the July Monarchy, and the Second Empire. The salon was said to have been a casualty of a vulgar age, of cultural decadence, social equality, coarse manners, newspapers, cercles, socialism, materialism, bad art, and the denigration of nobility in general. In our own time, the list of culprits has been extended to include Jacobins, republicans, misogynists, and contentious feminists unable to appreciate the advantages of gender mixing and sexual accommodation.

The salon's decline was an eclipse rather than an extinction, more like the diminishing importance of the textile sector than the rise of ghost towns in the American West. Although vulnerable to protracted sociological and political change, the salon was not normally subject to violent repression: its history is one of the resiliency of a social practice and a cultural mystique, the revolutionary suppression of feminine associations being a bad model for analyzing its fate. Undoubtedly, the salon had its enemies, but it had the most to fear from its friends. At their hands, it was not so much murdered as marginalized, the victim of changing priorities rather than misogynist or anti-aristocratic sentiments.

Contextual factors undermined the salon's place in French political sociability, but so did the concerns both habitués and salonnières had about the interaction between politics and mondanité, concerns that made salons increasingly vulnerable to attacks from within.

I

Everyone agreed that salons ceased to exist in the nineteenth century but no one could say exactly when. Estimates ranged from the Napoleonic period, when the last grandes dames of the Old Regime faded from the scene, to the Second Empire, when the last traces of the traditional society of the Restoration could still be faintly identified. Most joined Balzac in citing the late July Monarchy as the point of no return.[1]

Such chronological indeterminacy reflected the fact that judgments concerning the health of salons were rhetorical rather than descriptive; to pronounce the salon dead was to condemn a degraded present, not record an actual event. A precise date is beside the point — what mattered was the erosion of the values and practices that sustained the salon and its world. On that score, salonnières were nearly unanimous in pointing to the rise of political factionalism as the primary cause. Madame de Staël had set the tone for a mondain critique of "the party spirit" in the 1790s by noting that partisanship united people around common hatreds rather than feelings of friendship and mutual esteem. The morality of mondain relations, she argued, suffered when those with "the same political religion" excused the vices of their allies and ignored the positive qualities of their foes; society lost its intellectual vigor when dogmatic thinking and the passions of partisan solidarity prevented judicious compromise and stifled the search for truth.[2] These themes were taken up in the early nineteenth century by those who witnessed the embitterment of social relations by partisan politics and worried that political animosities were destroying reputations and making impossible the honest recognition of true merit. The marquise de Montcalm was vociferous in her insistence that political acrimony threatened the values of the salon by agitating guests, making them surly, and dividing those she hoped to unite. The desire to criticize and shame opponents, she wrote, "denatured characters," corrupted feelings, and tarnished those otherwise worthy of esteem. Guizot voiced similar views, arguing that politics in salons had to remain an object of reflection, because active partisanship circumscribed intellectual horizons, coarsened manners, and undermined the free exchange of ideas.[3]

Salonnières were particularly upset by the fact that politics took the oxygen out of all other interests and pursuits, dominating conversation, and smothering other topics in its wake.[4] They complained that power made men grave, that politics made conversation somber, and that the "minute purges of society" occasioned by partisan exclusions made salons uniform and dull.[5] When political passions were at their most extreme, the rhythms of society were disrupted and salonnières found their personal lives overturned. According to the comtesse d'Armaillé, "the echoes of the political discussions that marked the agony of monarchical sentiment in France [in the 1820s] divided the most solid families and split all of aristocratic society into hostile clans." Under the July Monarchy, matters worsened: a bitter "war of the salons" broke out between the Carlists and their Orleanist foes, inflamed from time to time by controversies such as the Pritchard affair and visits by legitimists to the comte de Chambord in Belgrave Square.[6] Worst of all from a woman's perspective was the fact that the centrality of politics inevitably encouraged the domination of salons by men and pushed salonnières further into the background. Abrantès blamed "the contentious spirit" inaugurated by the Revolution for upsetting "all our ancient and beautiful customs," arguing that in the long run, politics had turned women into "queens without realms."[7]

The tendency to blame the decline of salons on partisan politics was reinforced by the conviction that the death of French sociability could be traced to the *bouderie* of the legitimists and the rivalry that erupted between monarchists in the aftermath of the 1830 Revolution. How, many wondered, could the cordial relations on which sociability depended withstand both the withdrawal of society's most elegant members and the full intensity of French political hatreds. Ancelot's perception was that the July Revolution had destroyed the very foundations of trust, because so many people had experienced an abrupt change of political fortune: "All positions changed hands. Those new to high offices feared losing them, while their former occupiers hoped to reconquer them. Under such conditions, how could one even think of gathering for amusement?" The apparent collapse of mondanité was amplified by a massive interior emigration as legitimists retreated to their country estates, a movement whose size seemed all the greater in that it coincided with the low point of the social season. Once sociability rebounded in the mid 1830s, people continued to deplore the sociable consequences of the July Revolution, blaming political events for disrupting the salons of the Restoration, destroying the aristocracy, isolating Faubourg Saint-Germain, and leaving society to the riffraff.[8]

Historians have largely seconded the position of contemporaries who argued that the July Revolution appreciably diminished the importance of salons, and who insisted that the Orleanist elite failed to replaced the salons of the Restoration with ones of similar energy and animation. Once Faubourg Saint-Germain retreated into isolation, so the argument goes, upper-class social life contracted, and the few surviving salons of the old aristocracy became "conservatories," lacking all creativity.[9] These positions are not entirely inaccurate, but they tend to make sociological interpretations out of sour grapes. As Beaumont-Vassy pointed out, the effect of each successive political shock on le monde had been akin to dropping a stone into a lake — the first ripples were immense, but those that followed became smaller and less agitating, until the surface returned to its former state. So it was with the Revolution of 1830: "The disorder and agitation were enormous at first, but then the disunited parties rejoined, the gaps were filled, salons were opened again, and, if their aspect was no longer absolutely the same, at least people found each other there and got to know each other again."[10]

From July 1830 until the winter of 1833, the legitimist aristocracy shut the doors of its Paris hôtels or remained in the provinces, where many of its members first heard news of events in the capital. When the duchesse de Maillé arrived in Paris eight days after the fall of Charles X, Faubourg Saint-Germain "seemed very lonely; its hôtels were all closed." Viel-Castel said that it was like "an immense tomb."[11] A few salons showed signs of life: Lafayette's on the rue Saint-Honoré d'Anjou, an Orleanist salon at the Palais-Royal, and Madame de Rumford's, which was reopened on February 12, 1831, for a concert and *grande soirée*. Meanwhile, a younger generation of nobles happily ventured into what they considered a more freewheeling and less restrictive society. For two years, the new aristocracy of July enjoyed a virtual free reign, creating an opulent society life centered on embassy balls, the theater, the Palais-Royal, and the crowded receptions of the Chaussée d'Antin. Beaumont-Vassy called it a rare mondanité without "the daughters of *ducs* and peers." Madame Dosne described it as luxurious, distinguished, and young, and recalled that upon their return to the capital, Carlists found more elegant carriages, diamonds, and magnificent urban exteriors than when they had left. Open displays of new wealth provoked vituperative commentary on the part of journalists for *La Mode*, who scoffed at those who would make a revolution against the upper class only to become one themselves.[12]

High society slowly began to take on its former habits in the winter of 1832–33, when a number of prominent grandes dames (the duchesse de La Bourdonnaye, the duchesse de Maillé, Madame de Bellissen, the duchesse de Rauzan) returned to Paris and reopened their salons. As early as May 1831, Chateaubriand was complaining to Récamier that the revolution had done too little to disturb salon life and interrupt court balls. Apponyi commented after a particularly well attended concert at the Austrian embassy in November 1832 that the Carlists who came were saved from being compromised in their party by the opportunity to blend into the crowd. "They want to be sad," he wrote, "but we shall see how long they will be able to carry it off."[13] On the whole, the process of reconstitution was not unlike that which had occurred under the Directory, when la vie mondaine came back in stages, starting with a vibrant public sociability of balls and fêtes and ending with regular receptions in private salons.[14]

With the salons largely closed in the winter of 1831, Paris was enlivened only by official gatherings, the subscription balls given by the National Guard in the salle d'Opéra, and evening dances organized in every quartier except Faubourg Saint-Germain. Although legitimist high society resisted the temptation to attend such social events, the women of the faubourg were already working to maintain the customarily familial sociability of the quartier by organizing intimate *petites soirées*.[15] Detachment from the court meant a loss of income for a number of old noble families. As under the Empire, many confined themselves to their hôtels and established an aristocratic citadel that liked to scoff at the government and its supporters from behind closed doors. Nevertheless, by 1833, elements of Faubourg Saint-Germain were already engaging in strategic acts of accommodation, encountering members of the new court (including the duc d'Orléans) on neutral territory, maintaining contact with relatives in other political camps, and searching out the company of newly crowned celebrities in the literary world in order to retain influence and remain in the game.[16]

Salons did not disappear after 1830, but the world they had served to anchor failed to cohere, as it seems to have under the Restoration, when society rallied behind the Bourbons, the old aristocracy held sway, and le monde was still homogeneous enough to fight back the ravages of partisanship and the gathering pressures of rapid urbanization. Those who spoke of the death of French sociability were responding to the increasingly composite nature of a social world undergoing diversification, in which it was no longer possible for the exclusivity of la bonne compagnie to enforce a common ethos. In a social world characterized more and more by factions and coteries, exclusivity implied not privilege but isolation — one had either to engage the new mondanité on its own terms or accept its indifference. Politics destroyed the coherence of le monde not so much by dividing it as by giving ideological commitments the power to erode or modify its values, rituals, practices, and traditions.

The "war of the salons" that erupted after 1830 was real enough. Arriving at the baths in Dieppe in August 1830, Apponyi found "[o]ur little Parisian society" already so divided that it had to split into two groups, with legitimists meeting in the salon of the princesse de Léon and Orleanists gathering in that of the duchesse de Noailles. "Discord," wrote d'Agoult, "inserted itself in families and among friends. Between those who remained loyal to fallen royalty and those who followed the fortunes of the new reign, there were now few means of encountering one another [in good company]."[17] The trials of former ministers of Charles X, continued popular unrest, the aborted uprising in the west of France, and the imprisonment of the duchesse de Berry only deepened animosities and plunged mondain relations into a state of crisis. Foreign embassies, normally considered neutral terrain, became embroiled in partisan controversy and found it nearly impossible to entertain. The Austrians were rightly suspected of Carlist sympathies, and the wife of the British ambassador scared off legitimists by receiving liberals — the former scheduled no balls in the winter of 1832–33, and the latter held only one. Legitimists refused to dance at society functions as long as the duchesse de Berry was in prison and were determined not to encounter members of the royal family in public.[18] By the latter part of 1832, tempers were at their height and mondaine sociability was at low ebb: Madame de Boigne remembered it as a time of "unimaginable vituperation" and the duchesse de Dino characterized Faubourg Saint-Germain as indescribably insolent and more irreconcilable than ever. The duchesse de Rohan lashed out at the duchesse de Valençay for causing her to run into the duc d'Orléans as she was entering Valençay's salon, nearly forcing their husbands into a duel. Madame de Chastenay abruptly left the salon of Madame de Jumilhac when the hostess suggested that she had lied about seeing the prince de Léon at the salon of Madame de Saint-Aulaire, at which point, Chastenay declared to the women, "Vous êtres toutes commes des furies" and murmured something about Parisian society becoming more intolerable every day. When Madame de Flahaut wrote an article critical of the Austrian ambassador for the English press, the Carlists deserted her salon; when the ambassador's secretary told Madame de Rumford that there would be no balls at the embassy in 1833 because the Carlists would not dance, she told him: "We don't need them to have a good time." In January 1832, the grandes dames of Faubourg Saint-Germain, who were already boycotting official receptions, organized the first society ball devoted to raising money for those who had been receiving pensions from the personal funds of Charles X. The event, held every year until 1848, combined politics and philanthropy and eventually became a highlight of the social calender.[19]

By the winter of 1834–35, society was still sharply divided, but the war of the salons had become a stalemate, and both sides gave evidence of a will to compromise. Even at its most intense, the war was characterized by contradictory impulses that pitted bitter partisanship against the determination to socialize. On the one hand, old aristocrats were still absent from court, legitimists did not invite Orleanists to their fêtes, and the women of Faubourg Saint-Germain would not go into the homes of partisans of the *juste milieu*. On the other hand, M. de Rambuteau, prefect of the Seine, attended charity balls organized by legitimists, who themselves encountered "governmental society" at the Opera and the horse races. Madame de Gontaut, seeking reconciliation, proposed that the duc d'Orléans marry the daughter of the duchesse de Berry, and Madame de Bartillat floated the idea of putting Louis-Philippe's eldest son at the head of the legitimist party by winning him over to its cause. For his part, the duc d'Orléans had asked the Austrian ambassador, Comte d'Apponyi, to act as intermediary between himself and the women of Faubourg Saint-Germain. The suggested encounter in the salon of Baron Delmar never materialized, because of unacceptable conditions on both sides, but it was clear that mondanité was once again seen as a possible *trait d'union*.[20]

The prohibition against interparty socializing seems to have been lifted by the winter of 1836–37, when legitimists and Orleanists were again attending the same salons. Although Faubourg Saint-Germain "literally turned its back on the society rallied to Louis-Philippe" at the Austrian embassy, at least both parties were present.[21] What had once been a war had now become an uneasy truce, broken occasionally by highly charged symbolic events that momentarily rekindled resentments. As the July Monarchy moved decisively to the right after 1840, open hostilities were replaced by greater calm and halting efforts at reconciliation: Madame de Flahaut, who regularly entertained the duc d'Orléans, worked tirelessly to attract the elite of Faubourg Saint-Germain to her house; salons devoted specifically to fusion emerged in the Chaussée d'Antin, where Madame Boscari de Villeplaine and Madame de Béhague tried to engineer a rapprochement with the old aristocracy. For its part, Faubourg Saint-Germain began to end its isolation. "The old hôtels were refurnished little by little," wrote Balabine in 1843, "and each winter for the past two or three years has seen a few old families open their houses to Parisian society"; he concluded that the legitimists were making concessions in order to regain political influence. In 1840, "two women of Faubourg Saint-Germain" invited Napoleon's illegitimate son, Comte Alexandre Walewski, to dinner to satisfy a burning curiosity. The gathering included Thiers, the duchesse de Grammont, the comtesse Alexandre de Girardin, Berryer, the comte d'Alton-Shée, and the marquis de Brézé, all of whom after his departure pronounced their guest of honor "dazzling, stunning, and adorable."[22]

The coherence of le monde was undermined as much by generational change in the 1830s as it was by the era's extreme partisanship. D'Agoult regretted the declining importance of salons, but she also credited the Revolution of 1830 with liberating her and her cohorts from the authority of elders and the etiquette of a restricted society. "[N]o longer under the eyes of the dauphine and our old dowagers, we felt ourselves delivered from a surveillance that had not until then permitted us to open our salons to new people, to men of a lesser condition, bourgeois, the newly ennobled, writers, and artists, whose celebrity had begun to pique our curiosity."[23] The disruption of Restoration society allowed established liberal salonnières like Rumford and Flahaut to move to center stage; it also let younger women like Madame de Caraman, the vicomtesse de Vaudreuil, the marquise de Courval, and the comtesse de Saint-Priest heighten the visibility of their salons and take the lead in organizing social events. At the same time, younger members of the old aristocracy seized the opportunity to invigorate their salons with new blood. According to d'Agoult, the duchesse de Rauzan led the way, welcoming "the eccentricities of romanticism" (Sainte-Beuve, Eugène Sue, Liszt) alongside "the relics of her mother's salon." Rauzan, in turn, inspired the likes of d'Agoult, Madame de La Grange, and the duchesse de La Bourdonnaye to break with the habits of their elders and "modify the tone and the allure of [their] salons." Under Louis-Philippe, new literary salons were en vogue, attracting such writers as Balzac, Hugo, Dumas, and Musset. In the end, even the "grave salons" of Faubourg Saint-Germain caught the spirit of youthful innovation, incorporating the new elements that gave contemporary society an air of "agitation, noise, cerebral fever, and universal ebullition." "Wit and politics," wrote Dino in 1835, "have strangely intermingled all society, good and bad."[24]

Aside from partisan politics, the decline of salons was commonly attributed to the rise of a partisan and sensational press.[25] It seems clear that salons suffered in the transition from oral to print culture. The seventeenth-century advent of printed material addressed to the public increased the distance between intellectuals and audiences, formalized the relationship between authors and readers, and undermined the ability of interactive conversation to shape literary style. During the nineteenth-century, a consensus developed around the notion that salons had been displaced as arbiters of public opinion by the rise of the modern press. Restoration salons, according to this view, lost their authority after 1830 to modern journalists, whose partisanship was geared toward the demands of the marketplace, animated by the quest for personal success, and productive of an individualistic appreciation of ideas and interests that helped fragment the political world.

The best explanation for the decline of salons is the functionalist argument that salons were undifferentiated, informal gatherings that performed tasks for which modernity subsequently invented a whole array of specialized institutions. Newspapers were just one aspect of an emerging public sphere in which "institutions of the public reflecting critically on political issues" proliferated. Eighteenth-century salons were able to play such a powerful role in shaping public opinion because they preceded the modern press, parliaments, railroads, and the telegraph. As Deborah Hertz observes in her study of Jewish high society in Berlin, the "eventual disappearance of the salon as a public space" was directly related to the growth of big cities and the evolution of "an array of other intellectual institutions [that] fulfilled some of the salon's functions."[26] The functionalist argument is both plausible and demonstrable; it convincingly presents the decline of salons as a complex, protracted historical process, and it provides a means of distinguishing between salons and other forms of sociability. It seems clear, for example, that the rise of commerce, the professionalization of government service, and the expansion of secondary and higher education would inevitably make inconsequential whatever place salons had traditionally had in modalities of elite recruitment and strategies of social advancement.

The emergence of newspaper offices as sites of political sociability in the 1820s is another good illustration of how the decline of salons simultaneously entailed a displacement of functions, the specializations of tasks, the search for organizational autonomy, and a growing separation of the sexes. The *bureau* of a journal was both a *lieu de rencontre* and a working enterprise: it was a voluntary union of stockholders and employees sharing similar opinions who brought technical and material assistance to the increasingly national political associations in whose direction they played a part. It was not necessarily the public nature of a newspaper office that separated it from salons as much as its orientation toward the accomplishment of specific tasks. During the electoral campaign of 1824, Rémusat and his friends had been meeting in the office of Jacques Coste's *Tablettes universelles* but found it too open in the face of government persecution to serve as a safe venue for "the daily conferences demanded by the always slightly confidential preparations for an election." As a result, they established a sort of roving "états généraux de la gauche" in the homes of Jacques Lafitte, Gévaudan, and Bourgeois to coordinate liberal electoral activity around the country, an operation that was both private and internally specialized, with an executive officer, legal counselors, a paid secretary, an operating budget, and a committee of journalists charged with distributing articles to various newspapers. Salons could structure the sociability of elite political factions, but they could not handle the publicity for a liberal parliamentary system — the public was simply too big and the growing complexity of political life necessitated an elaborate division of labor. When the liberals wanted to address "the most popular electoral class" in 1828, they mounted "the hustings of Westminster" in the grand rotunda (ironically called the Salon de Mars) at the *rond-point* of the Champs-Elysées; a room in a nearby café was rented from which to run the event, an account of which appeared the next day in the liberal press.[27] Institutions of elite sociability, even those extended by newsletters and epistolary exchange, could only be considered as adequate means of communication by those who had to (or wished to) address themselves to a world closed in on itself by elitism or state repression, which is why the defense of salons was so closely linked to publics circumscribed by the Republic of Letters or the Restoration's *pays légal*.

The functionalist approach to the decline of salons explains how salons were superseded, but it does not account for why they failed to adapt and become more internally specialized themselves. This would appear to have been a legacy of the salon's aristocratic identity, which made it an institution suited to those with the leisure to socialize and the *aisance* to meet and converse effortlessly with a variety of people. The modern world was slowly killing the amateur, the *homme non-spécialisé*, whose extinction signaled the erosion of a way of life founded on pure sociability and reflection rather than professional responsibility. Guizot considered the change in political life to have been especially pronounced because it entailed the transformation of a passion into a necessity. In the eighteenth century, he wrote, men occupied themselves with politics by taste and devoted all of their efforts to its intellectual rather than its practical side. In the nineteenth century, however, "Politics, real, practical politics, absorbed them; all their thoughts, all their energy was incessantly engaged, [with] no time for meditation, no leisure, only activity and work, and still more work and activity." As politics became a job, salons could still handle its meditative aspect, but conversation and the spirit of society suffered from a surfeit of work. "The yoke of political business weighed heavily upon the freedom of thought," Charles de Rémusat observed in

1834. Under such conditions, the reading of newspapers was a poor substitute for leisurely reflection: more information was available, but there was less time to study it; men offered opinions about things they barely understood; and society became less "spirituelle" for being "très occupé." Rémusat noted in particular a low level of education and a great deal of "insipid conversation" among lawyers, notaries, and businessmen, but he did not think that aristocrats were entirely immune to the spirit of the time.[28]

The diminishing importance of salons was an episode in the battle of the sexes occasioned by modernity—the inferior status with which women entered the modern era left them powerless to take advantage of the contraction of leisure and the professionalization of work. At the same time, the emergence of politics as a vocation for upper-class men undermined the shared idleness that had made the life experiences of aristocratic men and women more similar than was the case in other social categories, where inherited gender distinctions joined with material needs to place the sexes in radically different circumstances. The salon was a multifunctional informal institution associated with pleasure, family, and the private sphere; it was ill suited to the rigors of modern life. But its failure to adapt had at least as much to do with the preferences of salonnières. Men wanted institutions of political sociability that could be coordinated and used for increasingly diverse tasks; they wanted the autonomy to reinforce the internal organization of associations geared toward partisan activity on a national scale. Women, by contrast, wanted salons, and therefore devoted themselves to upholding the traditions of French sociability. On the one hand, salons called on to perform a multitude of political functions in a world that required continual political engagement would have given men control and made salons nothing more that political organs. On the other hand, salons devoted to recreation where politics was treated as a matter of abstract reflection would have become increasingly remote from the practical business of political life. The stresses that arose from such crosscurrents embroiled salons in a lopsided power struggle in which the purposes of political sociability were essentially at stake, one from which men could walk away to pursue other goals, while women were left with nowhere else to go.

II

Sociological change and the gendering of the public sphere were not the only factors responsible for the salon's decline. There were also those that pertained to the salon's internal life, and most particularly to the ideology of salonnières, which held that salons were a remedy for the very partisanship women blamed for ruining traditional sociability. Salonnières consistently expressed the conviction that conversation between political adversaries could dispel prejudices and reveal a basis for common ground. Many argued that political disputes were the product of short-sighted or egoistical judgments that would wither in the face of sustained contact, self-examination, and honest mutual disclosure.[29] Salonnières believed that the pacification of political conflict was their most important political task. In troubled times, wrote the duchesse de Maillé, "one must place oneself on the terrain of general interest so that the parties can be reconciled with one another." Delphine de Girardin went even further, arguing that those who could hold opposing forces in a state of competitive equilibrium would ultimately improve society. Salons arranged encounters that induced progress because salonnières ameliorated hatred and prevented the final and fatal victory of either side. In the end, this sort of creative rivalry would strengthen France: the "two enemies would perfect themselves," aristocrats would become more democratic, and democrats more civilized.[30]

The most prominent salonnières of the early nineteenth century were constitutional monarchists, tending toward the Right or Center-Right of the French political spectrum. The hallmarks of their liberalism mirrored the amicability and moderation implicit in traditional politesse: a respect for all opinions, a refusal to prejudge, and a distaste for orthodoxies of all kinds. As much a temperament as a set of ideas, the ideology of salonnières combined an almost reflexive hatred for violent partisanship with a preference for parliamentary institutions. The contemporaries of the duchesse de Duras considered her exemplary of this political sensibility, with her openness to all subjects and her willingness to entertain the unconventional — even Stendhal called her salon "a *trait d'union* between the liberal ideas that were developing everyday and the suspicions still current in the upper classes of society."[31] At the same time, it was a liberalism overtly committed to saving the Restoration and all the social and political arrangements that made it advantageous to the pays légal. Montcalm, who deplored seeing political passions divide the men she esteemed, believed that she was acting as a patriot in the interest of the public good when she tried to patch things up between her brother and Hyde de Neuville. Maillé blamed the Revolution of 1830 on Charles X and the ultras, who had repelled the country with their bigotry and fanaticism. "If I had directed the Restoration," she wrote, "I would have wanted the government to reassure all interests, and the court to take responsibility for calming and reassuring people's vanity." Ancelot agreed, explaining that the July Revolution would never have occurred if Charles X had embraced "the new principles" and appointed a few liberal ministers.[32]

Such support for judicious compromise had a distinctly anti-democratic social dimension, which Madame de Boigne made clear in noting that the English-style political moderation she recommended as an alternative to French combativeness inspired respect not only for liberty but for "les grandes existences sociales." The liberalism of the salonnières was an ideology of class solidarity, which equated sociability with the stability of the Restoration and presented itself as a defense of the common good. It revealed an absolute loyalty to an aristocratic social affiliation largely indifferent to the other fissures dividing the nation, including those that separated rich and poor and that erected barriers between women in general. It was in the name of elite solidarity that a number of legitimist women were willing to set aside their scruples about the oath to the July Monarchy. Montcalm, who thought that such "religious acts" had no place in politics, told the comtesse d'Orglandes in 1831 that women ought not be unjust or severe toward men who took the oath, because many did so for worthy motives — to condemn them would not change a thing. Women, she wrote, had "no sacrifices to make or examples to give" and could easily stand on principle, but men had to consider whether it might be unwise to retire from politics "and let themselves be replaced by republicans." Boigne suggested to Chateaubriand that it would be "more prudent to join those in possession of power, in view of the fact that they might be able to prevent the anarchical calamities which are not unreasonably to be expected."[33]

Salonnières held to their convictions in the face of relatives and husbands who were often considerably more conservative, willing to defy fashionable opinion for the sake of courtesy or reject intransigence out of esteem and sympathy for those who held opposing ideas.[34] The liberalism of salonnières belies the image of women as ideologically vacuous, inconsequential in their approach to public affairs, and focused on persons and formalities over substance, but it also made them partisans of a certain political vision. It is easy to understand why they would want to hold together a world in which they played an important role, but neither their ideas nor their interventions were politically neutral. Salonnières thought that salon conversation elevated participants above the considerations of everyday life, where they could contemplate the good and the beautiful, but this mythology fared badly in the context of early nineteenth-century politics, when partisanship undermined efforts at reconciliation, and when those favoring change understood harmony to be a pillar of the status quo. Boigne acknowledged her inability to keep the salon's two principal functions in balance when she admitted to being partisan in spite of herself, wondering in retrospect whether "[w]hen things quiet down, it will be curious to observe how the force of circumstances always pushed me to be partisan in earlier times, whereas, by instinct, taste, and reason, I have detested partisanship and I have indicated calmly enough the errors and the follies to which it leads."[35] Such candor was very rare among Boigne's female contemporaries, many of whom became involved in politics by expressing their distaste for its contestatory aspects and who therefore found it hard to conceive of neutrality, inclusion, and pacification as ideological positions. What if men did not want to be reconciled? What if they considered the political stakes too high to warrant compromise? What if liberals and conservatives saw no common ground upon which to settle their differences?

Newspaper offices and political clubs were expected to reflect the full range of ideological alternatives, but salons were obliged to cultivate diversity while making guests agreeable to one another. In the interest of suppressing acrimony, sometimes on pain of expulsion, salonnières were compelled to minimize antagonisms and give every side its due. Mondanité prized moderation, encouraged compromise, and was mainly concerned with facilitating social intercourse, but the politics of irreconcilable differences did not regard all opinions as equal, tolerated aggression in the name of principle, and refused to naturalize opinions considered inimical to the public good. Guizot pointed to the sexual dimension of this confrontation of values when he told the princesse de Lieven that the demands of politics created a gulf between men and women:

> Between ourselves, I have more than once regretted not being able to be as cordial and kind with my political adversaries as I feel inclined to be. I know more than one of them in whom, politics apart, I could perhaps find a friend, or at least a smooth and comfortable relationship. But the cares of personal dignity, duty to the cause, the exigencies and suspicions of partisanship, all that throws between men a coldness and a hostility, often without individual or personal motives. One must resign oneself to this; it is the law of this war, because it is a war. But you, Madame, should profit, and profit always from your privilege as a woman; be equitable toward all, good to all, amicable to those who merit it from you. Such equity and friendship is something beautiful and rare.[36]

Guizot insisted that Lieven was the more fortunate of the two, but by drawing a sharp distinction between politics and *amitié*, he was denying the salutary influence of women and contesting an older aristocratic consensus on the political efficacy of feminine virtue that had sustained a public role for salons. The representation of politics as war turned the public sphere into an arena of male rivalry in which a masculine code of honor was called upon to settle disputes that were not susceptible to feminine adjudication.[37] In such circumstances, salonnières began to regret the general deterioration of conditions favoring feminine conciliation, while men questioned aspects of salon etiquette and accused salonnières of suppressing freedom of speech. Philarète Chasles considered Madame Récamier's salon at the Abbaye-aux-Bois to be stiffly formal; Lamartine described it a monarchy and compared it to "an Academy holding its meetings in a monastery." Michelet refused Ballanche's invitation to go there, fearing that its "arranged and conventional" nature "would civilize me too much," and that its "vapid atmosphere" would deprive him of the ability to speak his mind. The aristocratic salonnières in Stendhal's novels counter boredom by exquisitely punishing offenders and compensate for the mere illusion of power by aspiring to be goddesses surrounded by a crowd of votaries—like Mathilde de la Molé in *Scarlet and Black*, they all excel at dominating those around them. Haussonville first encountered Madame de Montcalm as a "formidable power," under whose discipline "one does not quiet feel free":

> One found her only at home, stretched out on a chaise longue, wrapped in a shawl carelessly thrown over her shoulders like a cape. She rose for neither men nor women. With a gesture, she would invite the person entering to sit down on one of the armchairs or sofas that she designated among the seats arranged like a fan around a sort of throne, or better yet, *lit de justice*, on which she was nonchalantly situated. If by the expression "to hold a circle" one wanted to indicate the sort of empire exercised by a mistress of a house over the habitués who frequented it, the expression would be very correctly applied to Madame de Montcalm, who *held her circle* quite firmly. One did not talk aimlessly, going on about this or that, following the caprice of the audience.
>
> Madame de Montcalm did not hold the dice in conversation for too long. She hardly spoke. But she understood how to orchestrate things in her own way. She carefully guarded the children in her care, giving the signal for someone to speak, for another to be quiet; one would have said that she held on to them as with so many bell-pulls. No one dared to take the floor from her, nor to chat freely with a neighbor.[38]

Dena Goodman contends that charges of despotism against salonnières in the eighteenth century masked a desire for "an idyllic world of male companionship," free from the constraints of feminine governance. She bases her argument on Rousseau's complaint that the philosophes had been emasculated by pandering to women in salons.[39] Republicans and democrats in the nineteenth century might have recapitulated aspects of Rousseau's animus toward aristocratic women, but Orleanists and conservatives usually did not. Men of the Left had inherited notions of civic virtue from the Revolution that envisioned a wholly masculine fraternity sealed by allegiances that transcended the attachments of private life, but men of the Right had nothing to say about the immorality of salons and directed their denunciations of women at those they associated with revolutionary disorder, from Madame de Staël to the *pétroleuses* of 1871. Liberal royalists attacked court favorites like the comtesse de Cayla as secretive and ambitious but they did not stop attending salons. By contrast, Madame de Chastenay noticed among men with "the most advanced opinions" a marked displeasure at the renewed visibility of society women after 1815.[40] The anxieties and resentments common at the end of the eighteenth century, noted by Goodman and many others, appeared at a time when women's power was perceived to be on the rise, which could hardly have been said of the 1830s. The salons of the early nineteenth century gave men no reason to fear emasculation, if indeed we are to warrant Rousseau's paranoia only for the sake of argument.[41] Men in high society did carp about the freedom to broach sensitive subjects or to speak softly to one's neighbor, but their complaints about the despotism of salonnières did not amount to a critique of gender mixing per se. Guizot considered Madame de Rumford to have been "brutal [and] despotic" in her leadership, but he praised Madame d'Houdetot's way of directing a conversation. Gabriel Pailhès believed that the duchesse de Duras's contemporaries considered her a *présidente modèle* who knew how to guide a conversation without regimenting or enslaving it, suggesting that men at the time combined their enjoyment of salons with reservations about certain styles of feminine authority.[42]

Talk of despotism in the drawing room and intimations of a desire for independence were symptomatic of three sorts of problems that upper-class men involved in public life had with salons, all of which had to do less with women than with the politically or socially undesirable ways in which salons operated as institutions. The first was most common among liberals and concerned the salon's association with political conservatism and aristocratic domination. The second and third had essentially to do with the salon's status as an institution of mondaine sociability: the former related to the salon's tradition of offering amusement, which made it at times an inappropriate venue for conducting political business; the latter was linked to the pressures of the star system, which opened the salon to the whims and priorities of Tout-Paris, making it too permeable and socially heterogeneous.

French salons accommodated the ideological reaction against 1789 and became symbols of aristocratic arrogance and political conservatism during the Restoration. French liberals, in the tradition of the Madame de Staël, had hoped to preserve the salon as a site of enlightened sociability, but the Revolution and the emigration turned the nobility to the right and reinforced the association of salons with their aristocratic antecedents. Instead of weaning the nobility away from its social prejudices through contact with progressive forces in the worlds of government, commerce, and the arts, the salon became a congenial home for elitism, royalism, and the fashionable anti-materialism of the romantic intelligentsia. The aristocratic identity of the nineteenth-century salon allowed the institution to confer elite status on those able to enter by virtue of merit or birth, but it also came to stand for the privilege of unilateral and gratuitous condescension.[43] The power of aristocratic salons to legitimize access gave the aristocracy symbolic control over an essential rite of passage for those at the top of the social hierarchy and created an implicit inequality in high society between nobles, for whom confidence and security were *droits acquises*, and parvenus, whose insecurity and consequent vanity became a ubiquitous literary cliché, filling the works of Balzac and Stendhal with *routiers* anxious to be received and businessmen's wives convinced that only nobles could lend prestige to their salons.[44] Mondanité exuded disdain for bourgeois values and mores and subjected those of inferior status to a thousand tiny humiliations: Charles de Damas called the philosophes "the filth of society" when Villemain tried to insist that they had been received in the best company; the Orleanist aristocracy embraced Thiers but refused to open its salons to his wife and mother-in-law; the princesse Lieven bid adieu to the son-in-law of a former minister who had accompanied her all the way from Paris to the entrance of a German spa because her position did not permit her to present him to her society. In this context, criticism of salons converged easily with opposition to the persistence of aristocratic power and became a constituent part of bourgeois identity.[45]

Such attitudes became quite explicit during the 1840s in the controversy surrounding the liaison between Guizot and the princesse de Lieven. A protégée of the mother of Czar Paul I, Lieven made numerous contacts in the worlds of international diplomacy and high society as a friend of Metternich and the wife of Russia's ambassador to London from 1812 to 1834, where she was "adopted" by the British aristocracy. She was, in her own words, "a very great lady" in her own country, "the first in my rank, by my place at the palace, and more still because I am the only lady of the empire who may be counted as having lived intimately with the emperor [Nicholas I] and the empress." When her husband was recalled to Russia in 1835, she refused to go, despite the czar's insistence. Unable to remain in London for diplomatic reasons, she moved to Paris and eventually established a salon that took on the consistent role of bringing together the divided factions of the political Right in the name of the status quo, a task she continued to perform during the Second Empire, long after Guizot's disgrace, when her salon became a meeting place for Bonapartists and Orleanists. Before Guizot became her principle guest in 1837, her salon made the aging Talleyrand the central figure in gatherings of diplomats, Carlists, and government officials anxious see the July Monarchy accepted by the conservative monarchies of Europe — according to Apponyi, the main topic of conversation at the time was the possible marriage of the duc d'Orléans to a princess of one of the great courts. Guizot saw Lieven as a political neutral and judged that "in matters of government, she had ideas more practical than exacting and preoccupied herself much more with what was necessary and possible in the present than with aspirations or chances in the future."[46] Lieven inducted Guizot into the world of the cosmopolitan European aristocracy and helped him learn the ins and outs of international relations in what was still the Age of Metternich. As foreign minister and president of the French cabinet, he benefited from her experience, took advantage of her contacts, and got to hobnob with the best of French and international high society. It was a shrewd alliance on both sides: he put her back on the political map after she separated from her husband, and she eased his way into a diplomatic world still dominated by aristocrats — in relocating her salon to an apartment in the Hôtel de Talleyrand on the rue Saint-Florentin two years after their liaison began, she was perhaps trying to lend him an aura equal to that of the Austrian chancellor. When Guizot first starting coming to her house, she recalled, all his work was "directed towards the internal affairs of his country" so that "[m]y conversations, and that of my salon, were something quite new to him." In short order, she adapted him to what Rémusat called "the cosmopolitan diplomacy of the congresses of the Restoration," where he found himself by the mid 1830s among "a coterie that still found Metternich fashionable and that defended royal authority against the domination of orators and journalists."[47]

Why would Guizot seek out a vagabond princess, regarded by many in French society as a harpy, to invest him with "superiority," as Martin-Fugier contends?

And why, too, would a man who had already held ministerial office on a number of occasions and who had access to the king need Lieven's help in gaining "proximity to the centers of power," which was the other "essential point" in the relationship, according to Martin-Fugier?[48] On one level, Guizot was investing in social prestige when he frequented Lieven's salon, but he was also inaugurating a whole strategy of government designed to absolve the bourgeoisie of the crimes of the Revolution. In the early years of the Restoration, Guizot thought that the political triumph of the middle classes would result from a succession of elites, as the old nobility made way for the bourgeoisie. By the 1830s, however, he had concluded that only a fusion of old and new elites would allow the bourgeoisie to rule politically without abdicating to the forces of reaction in the face of the mounting democratic threat. Such a fusion would require a great historical compromise: the aristocracy would cede actual power to the bourgeoisie in exchange for a recognition of its cultural superiority; the bourgeoisie would abandon the class struggle, renounce revolutionary violence, and combine the principles of meritocracy and aristocracy to produce a new amalgamated ruling class whose manifest superiority would be sufficient to guarantee order in a free society.[49]

Since the Revolution, "*philosophes* of the second generation" had lost contact with la bonne compagnie, acquired coarse manners, and had forgotten how to benefit from unhurried and aimless conversation; they were more independent than those of an earlier generation, but they had also become a mistrustful and envious coterie, "unsociable toward whoever did not accept their yoke." Meanwhile, the aristocracy had preserved the sociable traditions of the Old Regime but had abandoned its former "libéralité de coeur" and its taste for intellectual progress. The role of salons, according to Guizot, was to reunite these two vanguard elites, much as the salons of the eighteenth century had, in the interest of creating an enlightened society that combined innovation with what was best in the past—hence his 1841 eulogy of the salon of Madame de Rumford, where he had first encountered people of distinction and seen "the last glimmers of the elegant, spiritual, and easy sociability of the last century."[50] Lieven's salon in the 1840s was a microcosm of Guizot's version of elite fusion, with the grandees of French high society and European diplomacy playing court to a Calvinist bourgeois minister under the auspices of an aristocratic grande dame. The key for Guizot was to convince the liberal bourgeoisie that it could hold its own in the coalition, maintain its fundamental principles, and emerge the stronger partner. Much has been made of Lieven's unwillingness to marry the French premier because she did not, as she told the comtesse de Nesselrode, want to be "announced as Madame Guizot," which is presumably meant to suggest that it was the calculating aristocrat rather than the bourgeois widower who emerged from the liaison with dignity intact. Both Guizot and Lieven knew that theirs was a pragmatic alliance, despite whatever real affection they felt for each other: she had to think of her children's name and of her ties with Russia, and he knew perfectly well that she was an aristocratic snob — she once told the duchesse Decazes that ministers without titles could never amount to very much. He even warned her of the myopia of "the upper regions of European society" when he observed that it had no contact with either the dynastic opposition or the democrats, leaving it ignorant of one of "the greatest influences of our time." She told him in 1838 that her absolute indifference to the affairs of the United States resulted from that fact that she was only interested in monarchies. "I am neither a puritan nor a democrat," wrote Guizot in the 1840s. "I have no more scorn for titles than for all other outward signs of grandeur. Neither scorn, nor appetite. I value and desire only two things: while living, my political strength; after me, the honor of my name."[51] What worried Guizot's former liberal colleagues was not his desire for frivolous distinctions but his pretension in thinking that his alliance with the aristocracy gave him the political strength to guarantee liberalism the upper hand. "I no longer believe," wrote Rémusat, "that Mme. de Lieven betrayed Guizot, either for Emperor Nicholas, or for any cabinet."

> She harmed him precisely by rendering to him the services he expected from her. She put the finishing touches on his entry into the diplomatic world. She made him known there by her correspondence. She saddled herself with errands. She fully satisfied this juvenile ambition, which Guizot never abandoned, to see himself incorporated into the clique of the Metternichs of every country, without ceasing to be a bourgeois, an intellectual, an orator, and a puritan. His way of being counted by the men of state of the old school as a peer, if not as a master, separated him more and more from his antecedents, his former opinions, and his relations, sinking him further and further into a mean and conservative politics, to which he prostituted a spirit and a talent made for great things.[52]

In a political world structured by the sociability of salons, a change of society meant a change of political orientation. Rémusat thought he and Guizot might have done important things together "if our intimacy had lasted," but the latter's acclimation to Lieven's salon constituted a form of "abdication." Martin-Fugier argued that Rémusat feared Lieven's "bad influence," but he blamed neither the princess nor her salon — she conducted herself as he expected. Instead, he pointed to the faults of Guizot himself, a man who liked "to succeed among his entourage" and was therefore particularly susceptible to his milieu.[53]

Was it possible to attend salons without risking ideological capitulation? Stendhal, for one, thought not, insisting that salon sociability took place on the aristocracy's turf, where an unspoken devotion to political and religious orthodoxies made visitors "afraid of saying anything that might lay them under suspicion of having a thought of their own." The "very best of society," he wrote, regarded all innovation as "an exterior sign of Jacobinism" and was anxious to suppress anything that cast the upper classes in a negative light; it hid a desire for absolute conformity beneath "a dexterity in conversation" that extinguished energy, discounted originality, and turned a once venerable French tradition into "a *corvée* from which one hoped to be delivered." During the eighteenth century, the aristocracy retained the "privilege to judge of what is *correct*," but "since it has believed itself attacked," it exceeded its authority by condemning as "coarse and disagreeable" that which "it considers harmful to its interests."[54] Although Stendhal sometimes cast the aristocratic women in his novels as ideological zealots, he was not inclined to blame them for the collapse of enlightened sociability, arguing instead that their subordination left them bored, isolated, and susceptible to political and religious fanaticism. During the Old Regime, when gender attitudes were more relaxed, women were amiable and conversation was gay; since the Restoration, however, the times "favored a purity of mores," women became prudish, and society turned flat. In such circumstances, women who tried to succeed through intelligence, like Madame de Staël, were held up for ridicule, leaving the acquisition of "an illustrious friendship" or "a lofty and sublime piety" as the only ways for women to gain influence.[55]

For Rémusat, ideological contamination was less important than the more general problem of mixing "political activity" with "the careless pleasures of a radiant and indulgent world." He praised salon life for the access it provided to the political world, but he came to regard it as the principal cause of the complacency, intellectual timidity, and social isolation of the French elite. Whether he attributed such consequences to the presence of women or to the evolution of historical circumstances is hard to know: on the one hand, he considered the discussion of political matters in salons to have been appropriate to a time when politics was a matter of pure speculation; on the other hand, the presence of women was a constant feature of salon sociability both before and after the Revolution, when the discursive politics of the Enlightenment gave way to a politics that was interested in getting things done. Like most men at the time,

Rémusat accepted the exclusion of women from the actual business of political life, so that neither their direct participation in politics nor the persistence of gender mixing in le monde was at issue in his critique of salons. Rather, it was the link between politics and mondanité, the persistence of traditional political sociability, that he called into question.

Salons, he argued, were obsolete in an era that required elites to translate ideas into reality; men responsible for public affairs in a parliamentary system had to be eloquent, but they also had to learn how to establish institutions, organize elections, campaign for office, and regulate the press. The political sociability inherited by Rémusat and his cohorts had been invented in the eighteenth century by a generation that had criticized despotism but had been "forbidden to concern itself with social realities." The trauma of the Revolution had made it doubt its convictions and had rendered it impotent in the face of Napoleonic despotism, while Napoléon's own preference for an essentially frivolous sociability was embraced by the debris of the Old Regime and communicated to the grand monde of the Restoration. The political convictions of gens du monde were largely beside the point — what blocked understanding of the need for new forms of political action were the habits contracted during a life that was too easy and too sequestered from "contact with the real world [*le gros du monde*]." A tendency to "traiter les affairs par la conversation," according to Rémusat, had become one of the greatest faults of the postrevolutionary generation. Pure conversation, he wrote, created a world unto itself, whose pleasures and enticements favored a disassociation between ideas and consequences. "*Gens d'esprit* are inclined to permit themselves a great deal in conversation, provided that *everything happens within conversation.*" A politics conducted in this manner was one that mistook words for actions, satire for criticism, and power for its external effects; it was an irresponsible politics that was subject to abuse, used to obfuscate real differences, wound opponents, or impress by flourishes that were neither calculated to convince nor supportive of the clarity of principles. For Rémusat, who was anxious to "establish a certain concert between the generals and soldiers of liberalism," conversational politics was simply a waste of time better reserved for reflection and action. It was impotent to respond to contemporary challenges because it was self-referential, conducive to the politics of coteries, and suitable for the purposes of an occult government or to a small number of initiates whose voices were imperceptible beyond "a circle of one hundred people." During the crisis leading up to the Revolution of 1830, Rémusat was dining with Madame de Rumford, who made a few negative remarks about the ordinances, and then went on to other things. The marquis de Mun was there to relax and was very pleased to learn from Rémusat that the streets of Paris seemed ordinary. "For the few hours we spend in the world of the salons, we acquire a disposition and a singular facility for not getting excited and for not conjecturing anything at all regarding what might be happening in public." When the meal ended, Rémusat went to the office of the *National* and signed the protest against the actions of Charles X.[56]

Rémusat was critical of aristocratic women for placing too much stock in decorum, and of bourgeois women for lacking talent, cultivation, and taste. But he reserved his harshest words for a whole style of politics that he identified with those who frequented salons. He detected the same insouciance, isolation, and preoccupation with internal stratagems in the Chamber of Deputies in 1848, when members amused themselves with "the little parliamentary war while civil war was at the door." Although he considered opposition newspapers like the *Globe* to have allowed young liberals to think more clearly about public affairs, he found that the *Globe*'s articles recommended the same alternatives he had heard discussed in Madame de Broglie's salon, where a spirit of accommodation, intellectual hesitation, and a passion for "vain and irrelevant details" clouded a clear sense of what to do. He contrasted his own determination to be a man of action with the affable and artificial world of his parents, and he liked to see himself as an outsider, isolated from his pleasure-seeking contemporaries and indifferent to society's allures, like a member of the *noblesse de robe* amid the *noblesse de cour*.[57]

Martin-Fugier explains Rémusat's critique of salons as an expression of the growing separation of work and leisure, but that only meant that he was being disingenuous when he distinguished politics from mondanité by associating the former with a set of specialized tasks. To characterize as obsolete an institution that could not escape the growing separation of spheres was to make a self-reinforcing argument in which existing gender arrangements did the work of assuring the incompatibility of salons and politics.[58] Salons had rarely been used for political action, either before or after the Revolution. It would have been considered quite pedestrian for a politician or an official to discuss questions related directly to the conduct of his office or even the general management of public affairs. As Adeline Daumard has pointed out, salon conversation recoiled from professional preoccupations so that all guests would be free to engage in more free-ranging political discussions that did not require knowledge of a particular job, just as it discouraged partisanship in circumstances where not all guests shared the same opinion. It was only when men involved in public affairs became concerned with parliamentary strategy, organizational questions, and the need for regular deliberations that they developed a *political* critique of salons and began searching for exclusively male forms of political sociability.[59]

At the same time, women's distaste for political discord and men's desire for a refuge from the escalating demands of work conspired to pull the treatment of politics in salons even further away from the preoccupations of public life. Balabine found under the July Monarchy that conversations in salons most associated with the centers of power, like those of Castellane and Lieven, had to be maintained at a certain "niveau mondain" because the frequent presence of "diverse interests" and prominent foreigners obliged the maîtresse de maison to uphold standards of good taste and attend to all the diplomatic niceties. In many aristocratic precincts of le monde, politics was considered tediously poor amusement, an inconvenient and unbearable distraction from what Cardinal de Bausset called the "preeminence of spirit and taste."[60] Elsewhere, its importance was lost in a style of conversation that was typically impromptu and kaleidoscopic, "always galloping from subject to subject, passing from politics to literature, from literature to foolish prattle, and from prattle to slander." In the salon of Comtesse Merlin, the events of the day provided the fodder for drawing-room farce, with *hommes politiques* acting the part of *hommes du monde*, setting aside their official preoccupations to read a part in a play, recite a fable, or compose a short story on a subject selected by the hostess. Bassanville described one such evening as follows:

> [C]harades would alternate with more important works, and I remember, among others, one evening that took place a short time after one of the summer riots in which Marshal de Lobau had so handily dispersed the insurgents with the help of fire hoses; people recalled this incident there in a charade that was most amusing.
>
> The word was *Jacqueminot*, and General [Jean-François] Jacqueminot, then a colonel in the National Guard, figured among the players. For the first clue, people mimed a pilgrimage to Santiago de Compostela [Saint-Jacques de Compostelle], for the second, a scene with a grain dealer [*minotier*], and for the finale, a riot.
>
> Quite naturally, M. Berryer was the leader of the royalists, just as Arnauld commanded the republicans, and I truly believe that they had so well entered into the spirit of their roles that they were actually hitting each other with their fists when the door opened to a great fuss and the colonel himself, wearing a great uniform and carrying in his hand the instrument that caused Pourceaugnac such a terrible fright,[61] mounted the shoulders of an immense engineering officer dressed as a bear and made his triumphal entry into the salon, amid the most Homeric bursts of laughter.

On May 19, 1847, Apponyi dined with the princesse de Beauvau, who wore the uniform of a Spanish officer for the occasion and had as her guest of honor a forty-two-year-old dwarf who was appearing in a passing circus.[62]

Insider complaints about the salon's decline registered a whole series of criss-crossing developments that were converging around the time of the July Revolution. The gendering of the public sphere tended to assimilate salon culture with leisurely preoccupations just as the ascent of the bourgeoisie to wealth and power encouraged the democratization of le monde. Habermas has argued that the expansion of the public sphere in western Europe entailed a loss of coherence and social exclusiveness as traditional institutions of sociability were increasingly called upon to adjudicate conflicts that would eventually be handled by public institutions designed to produce compromise among competing private interests.[63] Martin-Fugier sketches out another aspect of this transformation in her study of "the formation of Tout-Paris," showing how a social world centered primarily on the court and its aristocratic acolytes in Faubourg Saint-Germain gave way to a more anonymous style of sociability, oriented toward spectacles and celebrities and centered not only in salons but on *le Boulevard*, where shopping, the café, and the activities of a whole constellation of new and exclusive social clubs accommodated a larger and more heterogeneous society. Once again, the July Revolution marked a decisive turning point: "Until 1830," Roger Boutet de Montvel observes, "it appeared that the faubourg set the tone, but subsequently, many changes occurred. Henceforth, it was in the restaurants, the cercles, and the theater that *la vie parisienne* began to take off in full swing."[64]

To lament the decline of salons was to object to the salon's alignment with Tout-Paris, even though that alignment was all but assured by the salon's prior installation in la vie mondaine. As salons evolved to encompass the mondanité of a diverse elite, those nostalgic for the past began to bemoan the loss of intimacy and attacked the newfound taste in French society for big English-style parties (generally called *raouts*), which were denounced as too crowded, too difficult to navigate, and too socially diverse.[65] The anonymity of the new mondanité made it possible for anyone with wealth to receive, so that the equation between lavish parties and the new power of money was easy for traditionalists to make. Legitimists especially liked to note that it was bankers and millionaires who received most ostentatiously, and who thereby turned sociability into a means of display rather than an end in itself. Devotees of the classic salon also pointed out that the rising number of large gatherings was killing the art of conversation: on the one hand, a salon that was turned into a *salle de spectacle* for the purpose of a performance or the adoration of a celebrity was one in which guests were forced to endure the smell of body odor mixed with the scent of flowers while standing silently in the same place for three to five hours; on the other hand, guests avid to attend many parties in one night had no time to discuss the news, tell a story, or express a thought. "In these times," declared Custine, "there is a public but no society" because conversation required the freedom of expression born of intimacy in a socially uniform group.[66]

According to Delphine de Girardin, the problem with the new mondanité was not the disappearance of salons but "the abundance of insignificant relations." She told readers who insisted on the death of salons that what they were actually seeing were the effects of there being too many, so that their influence had become "dispersed." In the past, she explained, a Parisian had "limited himself to living in the circle of his friends; he chose them wisely, and was content with their society." Today, however, "people want to go everywhere" and were "consumed by the desire to be introduced to people they have never seen, by people they do not know." Far from stimulating the art of conversation, such habits made it impossible, since everyone had become "nomadic talkers," repeating tired clichés as they hastily reached for their coats in preparation for the next event. Big parties eroded social skills even further by giving everyone a slew of casual acquaintances ready to interrupt or drain the life out of those conversations that managed to get off the ground. As a result, Paris ended up with two kinds of salons: those at which one posed and those at which people shouted at one another, with guests constantly going from one to the other in order to alternate between "the stormy amusements of a boisterous salon" and "glacial solemnities" of a majestic one.[67]

At the same time, salonnières were finding the pleasures of Tout-Paris irresistible, refusing to stay home, and exposing salons in general to competition from the facile amusements of the city. Theaters, the races, carnival balls, gardens, spas, cafés, and clubs gained favor, especially among the young and nouveaux riches who were not well integrated into high society or who wanted to leave the partisanship of restricted circles behind. Many of the institutions of Tout-Paris were public and commercial; their proprietors had an interest in democratizing a lifestyle that helped sustain the retail sector of a growing metropolis. As Paul Gerbod has shown, the conviviality of French thermal spas escaped the etiquette that made sociability in Paris and other large cities more constraining, allowing middle-class professionals to "insert themselves into the life of mondaines relations, to rub shoulders effortlessly with the celebrities of the day, or to create useful social contacts." By the 1860s, according to Sylvie Aprile, the salon had ceased to be "the apanage of the aristocracy," its continued "efflorescence" reflecting "the accession to the leisure life of the great mass of Parisian bourgeois."[68]

Salonnières used the star system to make their salons relevant to Tout-Paris, inviting the rich and famous to assure themselves an outstanding place in the mondaine geography of Paris.[69] Under the July Monarchy, when large-circulation newspapers like *Le Siècle*, *La Presse*, and *Le Temps* tied Tout-Paris and salons together by offering society news that surveyed the vast landscape of Parisian mondanité, a few salonnières became adept at collaborating with journalists to amplify the prestige of the celebrities they recruited, thereby creating a star system that used publicity to reach well beyond the confines of traditional high society. Delphine de Girardin was the first woman to accomplish this synthesis after her marriage to Emile de Girardin gave her access to *La Presse*, founded in 1836 as a relatively inexpensive daily aimed at a large audience. Delphine estimated that "[n]othing would be easier for a young man of talent than to make a name for himself in the newspapers" because there were over one hundred rival journals and *revues* appearing each week, avid for something to print and only too happy to receive "a few amusing pages for nothing." Although she used her own column, the "Courier de Paris," to publicize news of le monde rather than to promote individuals, she saw journalists as potential kingmakers, calling them "ces aristocrates du jour," and was baffled by their apparent contempt for salons, believing that the most brilliant men of the era were also *hommes des salons*, and that salonnières and journalists alike had a common mission to destroy the prejudice against intelligence. From 1836 to 1841, Delphine's salon was located on the rue de Saint-Georges, across the street from the offices of *La Presse*; her intimate guests included a few nobles along with a large number of the period's most prominent writers (Hugo, Dumas, Balzac, Musset, Mérimée, and more)—Théophile Gautier, one of her most reliable habitués, was *La Presse*'s theater critic for twenty years. Delphine's salon, according to Alton-Shée, was a "meeting point" for those whose talent or ideas the Girardins wished to launch. It was especially known in this regard for its association with the literary and political success of Lamartine, whom Delphine had met in Italy in 1825, and who by the early 1840s had broken with the Right to become the star of her salon and the most celebrated political figures in the social world of the opposition.[70] In subsequent years, Marie d'Agoult took the collaboration between press and salon even further, not only by inviting opinion makers (like Emile de Girardin himself) to what journalists were calling "the Abbaye-aux-Bois of democracy," but by letting her salon be used in the 1850s as an editorial office for the *Revue germanique et française*, whose co-founder, Auguste Nefftzer, hoped to make German artists (including Richard Wagner) better known in France. This evolution was later taken to its logical conclusion by Juliette Adam, whose salon had its own organ, the *Nouvelle Revue*, which she edited, and by Marguerite Eymery (also known as Rachilde), who co-administered the *Mercure de France* with her husband, Alfred Wallette, and whose salon served explicitly to mediate between her semi-monthly review and the literary world.[71]

Privacy and institutional tradition had given salonnières a certain autonomy; their desire for notoriety allowed them to influence the composition of le monde, so that the rise of Tout-Paris could only have made salons more socially diverse. Aristocrats who wanted a less open and more regulated form of sociability responded by creating the Jockey Club, the Union, the Cercle agricole, and other socially exclusive (and exclusively masculine) associations, which met in rented (or purchased) spaces, screened aspirants, and required a membership fee. There is no reason to assume that men who met in clubs ceased entirely to frequent salons, but it seems clear that clubs were designed to allow them to escape the company of women. Clubs represented a form of sociability that men could control, one that could be insulated from the dictates of the star system, the requirements of political mingling, and the pressures of Tout-Paris. But the desire for control is not in itself a sufficient explanation: clubs did not admit women even after members had enacted rules of selective admission, just as Rémusat did not expect women to be present at the businesslike strategy sessions he seems to have had in mind. Whether the aristocratic critics of salons were liberals who complained about the restrictions of propriety or conservatives who accused salonnières of failing to uphold traditional standards of decorum, it was always women who were blamed for the disadvantages of the old sociability.

The English-style upper-class clubs that emerged in the 1830s were not only bastions of male sociability, they were also exclusively aristocratic and predominantly legitimist. Conservatives anxious to separate the sexes were also hoping to shield sociability from the democratization of le monde. If Rémusat thought that salons were careless of events and too insular to provide a basis for political sociability, the men who founded the Jockey Club, the Union, and the Cercle agricole believed they were too socially diverse and politically contentious. Alton-Shée, who became a member of the Jockey Club in 1835, argued that the organization had been created two years earlier "to elevate a barrier against the invasion of the unsavory people [*la mauvaise compagnie*]" who had been slipping into dining and gambling circles meeting at the Café de Paris. The Jockey Club was open only to those who had previously been admitted to the Société d'encouragement pour l'amélioration de la race des chevaux en France. Membership required an entry fee of 450 francs and yearly dues of 300 (the Cercle de l'Union required 500 francs upon admission and yearly dues of 250). Aristocrats with a family legacy or a distinguished sponsor could be admitted without formality; others typically needed two sponsors and had to submit to a vote, in which they could be black-balled by more than one in six (or one in twelve) members, depending on club rules. Such procedures replaced the inclusive monarchical discretion of the salon-nière with the restrictive democratic will of the majority, allowing legitimists to exclude anyone they did not like. According to Charles Yriarte, the royalists who dominated the Union and the Cercle agricole used *ballotage* as a "safety value" through which to vent their political frustrations: "[T]he admissions vote, a simple formality, was elevated to the level of a profession of faith and a declaration of principles, and, gathered around the urns, these patricians abandoned them-selves to the malicious pleasure of pitilessly refusing all those attached to the new party."[72] Political prejudices enforced by rules of exclusion produced an unusually rarified clientele, consisting of "an aristocracy in the aristocracy." Alton-Shée testified that the Jockey Club simply catered to "la jeunesse inoccupée," but Christophe Charle argued that nobles from less ancient or illustrious families were not likely to be admitted to such precincts. Charles Yriarte endorses this opinion, noting the absence of new money and the middle classes, and charac-terizing the members of the clubs as those generally possessing "the privileges of birth" and representing "the most elevated and most interesting society," includ-ing "the great names" in the world of legitimism and sport, factory owners, the old financial aristocracy, ambassadors, and foreign ministers.[73]

Men believed that clubs had certain advantages over salons and cafés. The latter were open venues that prevented patrons from dining, gambling, reading the newspaper, or talking with "the assurance of being in contact only with men of good company." Clubs, by contrast, were private, they provided a comfortable and luxurious setting, and offered meals that were healthier than restaurant fare and cheaper than the finest cuisine. Alton-Shée liked to gamble without the distractions of the Café de Paris or the clandestine gambling dens, where he often encountered cheaters, half-hearted players, and house rules designed to maxi-mize profit, as if the *maison de jeu* were a bank. Clubs had better food than salons, and members believed they could talk about any subject to whomever they pleased. At the Jockey Club, according to Yriarte, men liked to discuss public affairs among people with similar opinions or related professional experience; they also liked talking about nothing at all from time to time, and not to feel obliged to speak to their neighbors.[74]

Before 1830, men had frequented salons believing that feminine modulation would ensure harmony and repose. Now, convinced that salons had become disputatious in an era rife with political partisanship and boisterous in conjunction with Tout-Paris, they went to clubs in search of a peaceful and relaxing alternative. The Cercle de l'Union offered such an escape by means of a radical exclusivism that made it politically homogeneous and sheltered it from the parvenus, artists, and other interlopers who were invading Faubourg Saint-Germain. Political animosity was banished by the predominance of conservative opinion and by the sense of belonging to a selective aristocracy. "The conditions required for admission," Yriarte observes, "were such that each member could be sure of his neighbor, resulting in a sense of casual security and freedom not found in any Parisian salon or other such crowded associations." In contrast to the salonnière's desire to adorn society with variation, the Union preferred to admit only legitimists with historic names and Orleanists from good stock; there were few liberal nobles like Rémusat, Broglie, or Noailles, and few of the artists who had already become welcome in salons. Millionaires like Baron de Rothschild and Henri Hottinguer were members by virtue of their right-wing opinions, Thiers, Guizot, and Barrot because of their affiliation with the diplomatic corps, and Hugo, Musset, and Delacroix because they had seats in the Academy.

The Jockey Club, the Union artistique, and the Cercle des Chemins de Fer, by contrast, sought to maintain internal harmony by eschewing politics and organizing sociability around a common avocation. Members admitted to the Jockey Club came from a variety of political and social backgrounds but were united by great wealth, equestrian skills, and a love of horses. As a consequence, the Jockey Club was larger, more diverse, and more liberal than the other aristocratic clubs. But its liberalism was not threatening. Although the Jockey Club placed no limit on the size of its membership, its uncontrollable expansion was checked by the enforcement of class and gender restrictions that shielded it from the very pressures to which the larger public sphere was exposed. Members of the Jockey Club were convinced that the old politesse of private and intimate salons no longer sufficed as a means of fusion in a large and diverse association, which is why they were proud to emphasize masculine honorability and the enthusiasm of a shared interest as the basis for a new elite solidarity.[75]

Such bonds might have been enough to maintain the peace, but they provided a weak foundation for conversation, which in aristocratic clubs was not generally known for its brilliance and usually amounted to little more than a convivial buzz, configured in an unfocused manner around diverse preoccupations rather than directed toward intellectual matters by a salonnière. The various salons of the Jockey Club were set aside for smoking and drinking coffee, betting, or playing billiards; members assembled in one room after returning from the theater to trade stories about the *cancans* they had seen and to talk about a dancer's legs. Immersion in the public sphere encouraged men to speak of sports, money, and taxes; their camaraderie was too goal-oriented and too dependent on loyalty and mutual admiration to produce the kind of concentrated intensity and creative tension that had become the hallmark of French salons. When Charles X authorized the Cercle de l'Union in 1828, he had no reservations about its political goals, but he feared that the substitution of a sexually segregated institution imported from England for the mondanité of the Old Regime would be "the death of French society."[76]

III

In the spring of 1837, it seemed to Madame de Girardin that everyone in high society had a cold. Two balls held in early March were charming, the women were pretty in their fresh and elegant gowns, but there was a noticeable shortage of men. Since Girardin was certain that mondains would rather risk their health than stay home, she was forced to conclude that many of the men were at clubs, where they could meet in street clothes and without ceremony, undistracted by a minor illness. The occasion pointed to a much more general condition, which Balzac called the end of women's reign, in which men willingly left behind "the most noble and beautiful creatures for the delights of the cigar and whist" by going to "salons without maîtresses de maison." While in London, the duchesse de Dino heard from Comte Paul Médan in September 1831 that "[e]verything is unrecognizable; dress, manners, tone, morals and language — all is changed. The men spend their whole lives in the cafés and the women have vanished." Ten years later, Rémusat noted that Madame de Castellane had very few hommes politiques among her "old society." By the 1860s, wrote Ancelot, "the club was substituted for the salon" and conversation was being "organized in magnificent apartments, where [women] were not even permitted to enter."[77]

Agulhon's study of cercles in early nineteenth-century France suggests that their proliferation during the July Monarchy entailed the rise of a purely masculine sociability at the expense of a sociability that included both sexes. This occurred because the Revolution of 1830 brought about "the victory of a social system that allowed the separation [of men and women]," so that the triumph of the bourgeoisie "involved the passage — or the tendency to pass — from the salon to the cercle." Salons embodied the sociability of an idle aristocracy in which men and women shared similar cultural preoccupations. Bourgeois sociability, by contrast, eroded gender mixing: women were confined to the domestic sphere, while men were active in politics and business, with the sexes culturally estranged from each other because of the middle class's unwillingness or inability to educate girls. Noëlle Dauphin's explanation of the same process is less explicitly sociological, because it blames "the development of clubs" and "the exclusion of women from ruling circles" on the politicization of high society and the interior emigration of Faubourg Saint-Germain.[78]

These sorts of interpretations are sound in a general sense, but there are problems of chronology and detail that are significant enough to call their accuracy into question. Not all forms of political sociability were exclusively masculine, and the growing importance of politics did not lessen the number of salons prior to 1848. The politicization of high society predated the Revolution of 1830, which itself did not sweep salons from the scene. Aristocratic salons persisted and continued to be used as sites of political reconciliation, despite the rise of sexual segregation in bourgeois institutions of sociability. There is no doubt that the number of clubs grew in the early nineteenth century — the July Monarchy authorized more than 2,000 — but this growth did not necessarily come at the expense of salons. Clubs met outside the home, on their own premises, so that the sociability they encompassed was separate from the arrangements of the private sphere, to which salons were mostly confined. The Jockey Club, for example, met in a rented town house on the corner of the boulevard des Capucines and the rue Scribe, between the Opera and the place Vendôme in Faubourg Saint-Honoré. Its clientele included men who were mondains only part of the time and were engaged in a number of other activities for which they found the salon unsuitable. They were also more affluent than the middle-class men who gathered in the cercles Agulhon studied, and who were prevented by material circumstances from meeting in their homes.[79]

Clubs were rare during the Restoration, when elite sociability took place almost exclusively in salons and cafés. The small number that did exist had a tentative legal status and were still considered by many to be exotic foreign imports. Agulhon attributed their emergence to the idleness of the rich following the arrival of peace in 1815, the increasing demand for establishments catering to socializing, gambling, the reading that came with "the intensity of the new intellectual life," and the fondness many émigrés had acquired for the English lifestyle while living in London. Their rapid growth occurred only in the early 1830s, when a rentier and professional middle class entered politics and began reading the mass press, and when the development of the bureaucracy produced a greater number of men working away from home. According to Madame Dash, men "still spent time with women, and people would not have consented to deprive themselves of their company for the major part of the evening." Marie d'Agoult recalled in 1827 that "cercles and clubs [had] not yet been introduced among us." When Tocqueville was a *juge auditeur* at Versailles during the last years of the Restoration, all his friends, noble and bourgeois, met in salons.[80]

Early nineteenth-century forms of sociability were often hard to distinguish from one another. The earliest réunions of parliamentary factions met in the homes of Decazes, Ternaux, and Pierre Piet-Tardiveau, where like-minded deputies gathered with their wives to hold political discussions. In Lafitte's salon, to which the liberals moved in 1820, political meetings among deputies alternated with regular Thursday receptions that included dancing and general conversation. Apolitical sociability at the time also retained links to the drawing room: public sessions of the Literary Society, founded in 1821 by Fontanes, Chateaubriand, and Berryer, were very popular among society women; the Archeological Society of the South of France was formed in Toulouse in the salon of the marquis de Castellane; and the Cercle agricole, created in 1835, had a more homogeneous composition and a less distinct purpose than would eventually be the case. When the directors of the Cercle français envisioned "a commodious and agreeable meeting place, where one might be sure to find good company," they were hoping to supplement la vie mondaine by extending it into the summer and fall, when the salons were closed.[81]

Political sociability began to undergo a process of specialization in the 1820s, which tended to move practical political matters out of salons and into réunions, conferences, and clubs, although legal circumstances and the hybrid nature of sociability sometimes made the process much less linear than Agulhon suggests. Benjamin Constant was dissatisfied with parliamentary réunions and concluded that deputies ought to meet on their own in conferences, where too many invitations and the presence of women would not inhibit "regular deliberations." In the 1820s, he and his collaborators on *Le Constitutionnel* began using the Athénée, a learned society founded during the Consulate, to discuss pending legislation. In

1818, the duc de Broglie tried to form a Freedom of the Press Society "to discuss the conditions of good press legislation" but was forced by a hostile political climate to hold weekly réunions in his wife's salon. The Jockey Club was founded in 1833 as an alternative to cafés, according to Alton-Shée, but members who also sat in the Chamber of Peers found it necessary to form a réunion in the salon of the duc de Crillon in order to discuss ways of using the Upper House to effectively oppose government-sponsored legislation. Debating societies, or *parlottes*, organized by law students to help them prepare for a career in the Chamber or at the bar were transformed into more formal conferences by Emmanual Bailly, who turned the salon of his *pension* into a "veritable *salle de tribunal*" so that young men could practice public speaking. As such conferences proliferated and began to admit lawyers, deputies, businessmen, and government officials, they retained their original purpose but became more like clubs, where young men could make connections with deputies eager to prepare votes and resolutions in advance of the legislative calendar.[82]

The lack of clear differentiation among various forms of sociability, political or otherwise, meant that salons coexisted with clubs and cercles almost from the moment that the public sphere became relatively free. This had been the case in the early 1790s, and it was even truer between 1815 and 1848, when a protracted period of parliamentary government allowed the number and variety of sociable and political institutions to grow as never before. Frédéric Ozanam thought that conferences and salons had complementary roles to play in a young man's education, the first teaching jurisprudence and the second offering instruction in the ways of the world. Girardin believed that salons benefited from occupying the same social landscape as clubs, since the latter absorbed all the fanatics and bores who "would encumber conversation."[83] Specialization among institutions of sociability neither eliminated salons nor ended gender mixing, but it separated politics from mondanité, deprived salons of their multifunctionality, and left women to preside over a sociability of leisure that was increasingly marginal to public life. The private sphere to which women had already been confined was now drained of its relative political importance. Women were not entirely excluded from the new sociability — a few were admitted to learned societies, some became corresponding members, and many attended public lectures — but they entered this world largely as spectators and had lost the power to invite.[84]

The women of Parisian high society waged a vigorous rhetorical battle against the new institution, just as Englishwomen had denounced the rise of coffeehouses in the previous century. Women were among the first critics to take aim at the paraphernalia of the new sociability, whether it be sports jargon, billiards, horses, whist, or cigars. It was above all this last fixture of masculine culture that became the supreme symbol of club life. At the Jockey Club, the smoking of cigars was a ritual that invariably followed dinner and coffee. Members of the Cercle agricole spent 2,600 francs on cigars in 1855 and 6,225 francs in 1858.[85] Reputed to be unhealthy and vulgar, cigars were also evocative of the segregation of the sexes; women held them responsible for disrupting high society and reducing the quality of conversation. Cigars were rarely smoked in front of women; at dinner parties, men who wanted to indulge followed the English custom of retreating into the *fumior*. Smoking at an exclusively male club was, therefore, regarded as an act of masculine autonomy, like the ability to speak freely in the absence of a salonnière. Girardin saw cigars as symbolic of an alternative social bond, signifying the replacement of cultural refinement among men and women of rank with a masculine egalitarianism embodied by an etiquette that allowed any man to ask another for a light. At the same time, she equated cigars with the degradation of sociability, recounting a story about two friends who each thought the other had not been coming to the club, because they could never see each other though the thick fog in the establishment's smoking den. In a salon, the hostess could ask guests not to smoke, but no one was likely to make the same request of dues-paying members in a club. In that sense, smoking in clubs pointed to the salonnière's loss of authority. It also signaled a loss of respect for women in general: "Our young gentlemen do not always burn their incense (from Havana) at the feet of [society women]. Poor society women! Men waste such time smoking with so much devotion and indulgence, just to leave the women smoldering by themselves."[86]

Like clubs, smoking was one of those reprehensible "Anglo-American habits" that threatened French culture and Western civilization. To defenders of a fading aristocratic cultural preeminence, cigar smoking was indicative of a general decadence, in which aristocracy was replaced by democracy, intelligence succumbed to newspapers, mondanité gave way to camaraderie, and salons fell before the allure of billiards, cards, and sports. For Girardin, cigars were a plague, but they also held out the possibility that women would one day return to power. In the course of fifty years, she predicted, the immoderate use of tobacco would make men so careless and stupid that women would be forced to take control of everything; she recommended giving smoking accessories as gifts.[87]

CHAPTER SEVEN

Nostalgia, or The Limits of Aristocratic Feminism

By 1848, the collapse and resurrection of la vie mondaine had become an established pattern of French social and political history. Like the successive revolutions that brought this pattern into being, the cycle of destruction and revival became accelerated, as if habit had made the reenactment much easier to choreograph than the founding event.

Two great society balls scheduled for the evening of February 23 had to be suspended. At the Austrian embassy, elaborate preparations were well under way when serious fighting broke out at the Porte Saint-Martin. According to Count Rudolf Apponyi, both the ambassador and society at large were determined to see the ball take place, despite the gravity of events. In the end, however, the minister of the interior having refused his authorization, reasoning that it would be imprudent to have hundreds of women in satin and diamonds milling around under exterior galleries constructed to facilitate the circulation of the crowd, the festivities were canceled and food prepared for the occasion was distributed to the poor in the surrounding neighborhood. The grand ball at the Belgian embassy actually got under way, but the route to the Hôtel Flahaut was obstructed by the famous banquet, and only a handful of guests arrived, among whom waltzers were outnumbered by those hotly discussing the contents of the *Moniteur parisien*. By midnight, the salons were deserted, political preoccupations having prevailed over the desire for pleasure.[1]

In retrospect, the changes brought about by the temporary collapse of la vie mondaine in 1848 seemed to observers to have had a finality about them that was absent from accounts of 1792 and 1830. The comtesse d'Agoult readily acknowledged that the Second Empire "restored luxury and fêtes" but insisted that "customs had entirely changed, and that nothing will be more impossible than reviving in France the ancient French spirit" because the aristocracy had lost the power to arrest the evolution of mores. Madame Ancelot saw the advent of the Second Republic as marking the final disappearance of the edifice of the Old Regime. In the three months following the February Revolution, according to Madame de Girardin, the richest neighborhoods of the capital "resembled a city of the damned, a menaced Gomorrah, having secretly received the warning of its coming destruction" — the grands hôtels were deserted and there were few salons; here and there, an elegantly dressed man or women could be seen crossing the Champs-Elysées, but there were no fine carriages in sight. On March 6, Apponyi found Madame de Rambuteau barricaded at the Hôtel Sinet with all her furniture, clothes, and silver plate shoved up against the windows. The Tuileries had become a hospital for wounded insurrectionists and the salons of the new ministers had been invaded by "a sordid mob."[2]

Among the wives of the new republican leaders, only Madame de Lamartine had a salon, the others having "neither the leisure nor the skill to improvise" one. Madame de Girardin began to receive again on March 3, but few followed her example; most *soirées intimes* took place with family among gens du monde worried about the future and divided about public affairs. Although sad to see the passing of the salons of her youth, the comtesse d'Agoult could not conceal her sense of 1848 as just retribution: "After the proclamation of the democratic republic," she wrote, "the salons of the 'juste milieu' took the attitude that the salons of Faubourg Saint-Germain had taken after the proclamation of the bourgeois royalty: people sulked; they were frightened; they curtailed their expenses."[3] Once again, politics had determined the history of salons.

I

High society began to revive very soon after the February Revolution in an atmosphere initially tinged with shock and uncertainty. When the Girardins' salon opened eight days after the crisis had started, receptions at their hôtel on the corner of the rue de Chaillot were guarded by armed workers from the offices of *La Presse*, the municipal guard having been called away from its regular police duties. Despite the fears habitually associated with republican government among the rich, the new regime turned out to be "harmless," according to the comtesse de Bassanville, who reported that all the salons had reopened by the winter of 1849. Although aware that "times of trouble are not very favorable to the amiable pleasures of an easygoing conversation," Ancelot nevertheless continued to receive habitués once the initial storm had passed, reasoning that revolutions always "excite the mind in a lively manner" and that her friends would consequently need a place to communicate what they knew of events and share the ideas to which new experiences had given rise. "During its short life," wrote Beaumont-Vassy, "the Second Republic did not appreciably modify the social habits of the reign of Louis-Philippe." The election of Louis-Napoléon Bonaparte as president on December 10, 1848, reassured Parisian society and guaranteed that the winter social season of 1849 would begin "under favorable auspices" — with commerce on the mend and the theaters taking in their highest receipts in years, the new prefect of the Seine, M. Berger, inaugurated the *saison dansante* with a grand ball at the Hôtel de Ville, attended by 3,000 guests.[4] The Austrian ambassador began receiving again as early as March 3, Apponyi having attended several réunions the evening before with the duchesse de Maillé, the duchesse de La Trémoïlle, and the comtesse de Beaumont. Receptions hosted by the Girardins hinted at those of the Directory, with the duchesse de Maillé being announced as *la citoyenne*, and the daughter of Madame Tallien appearing in a headdress festooned in the national colors, like the one the painter David had once persuaded her mother to wear. In the winter of 1849, the newly elected prince-president began to gather "the best company of all the societies" at the Elysée Palace, while the princesse de Lieven, back from a brief stay in England, did "her best as formerly to attract every shade of political color to her house," where she presided over a salon wearing a bonnet in the style of Madame du Deffand.[5]

High society over the next two decades saw the consolidation of tendencies evident under the July Monarchy within a general framework that loosely replicated aspects of the transition from republic to empire a half century earlier. The political salons of the previous regime, in which prominent politicians held court in the homes of aristocratic grandes dames, gave way to "little groups" or "little committees," where gens du monde gathered to share news and comment on the events of the day in an atmosphere of seriousness that was punctuated now and then by an amusing anecdote. One such "little conventicle" began in the salon of Beaumont-Vassy and evolved in 1850 into a committee that worked to organize a petition for the revision of the constitution. Made up of conservative men who sided with Louis-Napoléon in the constitutional struggles that eventually destroyed the Republic, the committee was for Beaumont-Vassy the most useful and rational form a salon could take "in these times of political instability." It quickly evolved from an informal réunion into a full-blown organization, with an elected executive council, a headquarters on the rue Neuve-Sainte-Augustin, a staff, and departmental correspondents to ensure that the petition was "morally and materially supported by numerous adherents." At various points in its development, members tried but failed to extend the organization's responsibilities by suggesting that it publish a newspaper or serve as an electoral committee for the Party of Order. When Beaumont-Vassy helped organize a committee to reelect Louis-Napoléon in 1851, he did not even bother to refer to it in its initial stage as a salon, calling it successively an association, an organization, a réunion, and a *centre d'action* instead.[6]

The elite political sociability that took place in salons during the Second Republic was more male-dominated and more bifurcated between talk and action than ever before. Informal gatherings of like-minded men involved in public affairs quickly evolved into agencies of electioneering and propaganda; in the evening, men and women gathered in salons, but politics took center stage as colleagues from the National Assembly developed new constitutional theories or discussed legislative projects.[7] Such salons, however, were now far less important on the right than the Cercle constitutionnel and the Committee of the rue de Poitiers, which emerged in 1849 to chart parliamentary strategy, influence the press, and organize electoral campaigns on a national scale. Nothing similar to the rue de Poitiers had existed among conservatives during the Restoration and the July Monarchy, when such institutions were fledgling at best and when political sociability took place mostly in salons. The advent of such committees represented the definitive schism between political action and causal political talk in the milieu in which political salons endured the longest. At a time when Thiers presided over his salon on the place Saint-Georges as the leader of the moderate party, receiving solicitors, giving interviews, writing letters, and supporting campaigns, the princesse de Lieven could neither reassemble her old society nor build a salon de fusion for the benefit of the president of the Republic, despite making frequent visits in the hope of obtaining "an obligation of reciprocity from those she sought out." Ancelot's salon during these years consisted mostly of writers and artists, who apparently spent a great deal of time reminiscing about the past.[8]

Louis-Napoléon imitated the *politique mondaine* of the First Consul by "trying to attract as much as possible of what people see fit to call polite society" to the Elysée Palace, creating something akin to a second consular court. The president's first ball, held on February 15, 1849, was crowded, but was less well attended than the grand occasions that had marked Louis-Philippe's years in the Tuileries, a structure considerably larger than the presidential palace. Although it was a "gathering of all classes and opinions," according to Madame Dosne, "the flower of the aristocracy of the various groups in society that give charm and grace to fêtes could not be seen there," the guest list having been assembled haphazardly by a staff that "did not yet know the best of Parisian society." The next great ball, held one month later, was a resounding success: the women of Faubourg Saint-Germain, meeting in the salon of the duchesse de Chevreuse, had decided that each would be free to attend the president's balls, despite the threat of being compromised by an expected imperial restoration; as a consequence, the faubourg "made an act of adhesion by accepting invitations," and "[t]he legitimists throng[ed] his rooms," so that "after the ball nothing could be heard but the shouts of servants — 'The carriage of Madame la Duchesse, of M. le Prince,' etc."[9] The ralliement of 1849 was no less calculated than that of 1800, but it was much quicker, helped along by what Dino called "a complete reaction in favor of order and prosperity." Subsequent soirées at the Elysée, according to Madame Dosne, were aristocratic reunions distinguished from those of Louis-Philippe by the absence of "the women attached to the House of Orléans" in favor of "Russians and the women of Faubourg Saint-Germain." During a concert at the palace in 1849, Lady Ailesbury whispered to Apponyi that she would give him two hundred écus for every republican he could show her in the salon. Although she insisted that the president had failed to attract the majority of Faubourg Saint-Germain, she acknowledged that he had done well enough, pointing out that "he was anxious to see in his salon all the conservative parties of every nuance" and would be "satisfied if the great names gathered there [as long as] other opinions were equally represented." In other words, like his uncle, Louis-Napoléon hoped to use his burgeoning court as an instrument of political consolidation and conservative fusion. "The organization of mondaine sociability around the presidency," Martin-Fugier observes, "was one of the means by which he prepared the coup d'état and the reestablishment of the Empire."[10]

The structure of salon sociability under the Second Empire echoed that of the

First. The most prominent, well-attended, and extravagant salons belonged to the official world, and all the famous women of the Empire were either members of the imperial family, courtiers, the wives of ministers, or *les ambassadrices*, like the comtesse Walewska, the comtesse de Castiglione, and the duchesse de Morny. Writers and artists mingled with gens du monde under the regime's auspices at the Palais-Royal, where Prince Napoléon frequently threw lavish parties or gathered "des cercles intimes," and in the salon of the comte de Nieuwerkerke, the *surintendant des Beaux-Arts*, who sponsored musical and artistic soirées in his apartments in the Louvre.[11] The most notable salonnière of the period was the emperor's first cousin, Princesse Mathilde, who presided over the salons of the Elysée Palace, and whose receptions at her hôtel on the rue de Courcelles were "the most *recherchées* in Parisian society." According to Pascal Ory, the "ideological significance" of Mathilde's salon was "ambiguous." Contemporaries, however, noted that she detested political discussions and tolerated no overt criticism of the emperor (Hippolyte Taine, a habitué, was dismissed for having published an unflattering portrait of Napoléon III in the *Revue des deux mondes*). Her receptions were brilliant but formal, "the conversation always remained within the limits of propriety," and her artistic tastes favored established painters at the expense of the impressionists. Each week, she gave dinners for a collection of the most famous sculptors, writers, scientists, and orators of the day, surrounding her cousin's regime with the country's most eminent stars. "The emperor did justice to her abilities," Victor du Bled observed, "and knew that without her many artists and writers would have gone into the opposition."[12]

The other salons of the Second Empire fell into one of three categories: those of the opposition; those of foreigners; and those that sought to fuse legitimists and Orleanists into a single opposition.

Since the society of Faubourg Saint-Germain rallied more completely to the Second Empire than to any regime since the Revolution, with legitimists considering service in the army and the diplomatic corps as neutral, the salons of the opposition were more estranged from the centers of power than had been the case under Napoléon I and Louis-Philippe, the first having courted the royalists, and the second having had to compete with salons generally regarded as more desirable than those of his own supporters.[13] Although Madame de Pourtalès tried to reconcile intransigent Orleanists and legitimists with the regime, most salons belonging to the monarchist Right constituted voluntary enclaves in "disdainful isolation," from which royalists derided the Empire, with the women often displaying the most uncompromising attitude. Armaillé testified that the opposition salons of Faubourg Saint-Germain reinforced their attachment to the Bourbons by "preserving an independence that was as complete as possible." Among them, the duchesse de Galliéra's salon attracted monarchists of all stripes and was a destination of choice for nobles leaving the Tuileries after attending court. At the same time, notwithstanding the princesse de Lieven's success in attracting a few of Guizot's friends, Duc Victor de Persigny refused invitations to visit her salon because "he detested salons that did only harm to the government" and did not want to be obliged to speak to "old fogies" (*les Burgraves*). The frankly royalist salon of Madame d'Osmond was "very politely" persuaded to close its doors during the coup d'état, after which the comtesse left for Florence.[14]

The salons of the liberal opposition, those of Thiers, Broglie, the duchesse de Noailles, the princesse Grassalkowich, and Madame de Le Redorte, were filled with hatred for Louis-Napoléon and "consumed with revelations and forecasts of all sorts of iniquities and foolishness about which those in power had mostly never thought." Cut off from the official world, the liberal opposition was badly informed, and those who pretended to know what the government was doing tended to exaggerate or cast everything in a negative light. Orleanists especially felt repugnance at the thought of going to the Elysée or the Tuileries; those in power returned the compliment by avoiding their salons. In the salon of Paul de Ségur, where Thiers was the dominant figure, the *monde impéraliste* was represented by the nephew of the marquis de Cadore, whose wife Armaillé suspected of conveying news of what happened there to the imperial police. Some diplomats regularly attended, she wrote, but "the evening dinners were essentially Orleanist."[15]

In such circumstances, it was the foreign embassies that remain best equipped to serve as neutral terrain, where government officials and politicians from various camps mixed with les mondains at embassy balls and state dinners. Thiers hoped to use the salon of the duchesse Colonna to organize "a small group hostile to the Empire," but the hostess refused, believing that foreigners ought not exhibit any political preference whatsoever.[16] Meanwhile, salons de fusion like those of the duchesse de Doudeauville, the duchesse de Polignac, and the comtesse de Pozzo di Borgo provided venues for negotiations designed to address the dynastic issues that divided the partisans of the comte de Paris and the comte de Chambord. In general terms, elite political sociability during the Second Empire was bifurcated between official salons and the *salons particuliers* of a marginalized liberal and royalist opposition. The former overshadowed the latter, but divisions were such that salons close to the court and the government had a difficult time establishing outposts in the world of the opposition, while salons geared toward conversation — the high-minded consideration of ideas — were rarer than in the past.[17]

Paul Gerbod notes that the democratization of forms of sociability that originated with the aristocracy reached a critical stage during the Second Empire, when a national rail network facilitated the rise of the tourist industry and institutions such as thermal spas gained a largely bourgeois clientele.[18] The same was true of Parisian mondanité, which by the 1860s had seen the effacement of Faubourg Saint-Germain by the world of the high finance and officialdom, surrounded by the now permanent spectacle of Tout-Paris. The capital, wrote Beaumont-Vassy, had become more than ever "a city of luxury and pleasure." The rhythms of the traditional social season gave way to a perpetual fête; instead of disappearing into the countryside toward the middle of May, a good portion of high society stayed in Paris through spring, turning its attention to horse racing and to new occasions for leisure and socializing made possible by the proliferation of clubs, concerts, theaters, and cafés. The court, which had once defined le monde, became its emanation. The ostentatious *raouts* that were fashionable among the rich were amplified at the Tuileries, where a grand ball could consist of more than 2,000 guests, entail the construction of exterior rooms and hallways, and cost 60,000 francs. Princesse Mathilde's residence harbored not a salon so much as a virtual entertainment center, with rooms for music, billiards, reading, and dining. The costume balls that were "the ruinous mania of modern official society" were also "so numerous and so frequent" in le monde "that they become monotonous."[19]

For a traditionalist like Ancelot, the noisy and congested sociability of the Second Empire substituted the anonymity of crowds for the simplicity of relations available in a "more calm, more equitable, and more compact society." Being in society was like being in a public place, where conversation was lacking, where bonds failed to develop with those one encountered, and where "one never finds true friendship." As the new sociability removed le monde from the jurisdiction of the grandes dames, discernment was no longer practiced, forms of distinction once cultivated in salons were cheapened, and salonnières no longer fulfilled their public charge. After the coup d'état, wrote d'Agoult in 1867, "one perceived suddenly that the society of the past, 'the arbiter of elegance,' no longer existed, and that, neither in the salons nor in the châteaux, was any aristocratic power henceforth capable of arresting the new change of mores." Political agitation had stirred the social pot; vanities, interests, ambition had made it impossible for "the most pure and the best" to rise to the surface, and "false great men" with "a modest little particle" in their bourgeois names triumphed over the truly superior. The rich, who had once made the cultivation of excellence a habit, now conserved their money in order to give only a few soirées and dinners during the winter, so that they could display the greatest luxury and "make a noise in the papers." Even Faubourg Saint-Germain succumbed to the habit of holding big parties, its inhabitants preferring *l'ennui en commun* to *l'ennui solitaire* in an intellectually vacuous era.[20]

The history of mondanité in France is punctuated with times in which society seems to have preferred easy pleasure to the challenge of intellectual pursuits. Accusations of frivolity and extravagance made under the Regency and repeated in the era of Marie-Antoinette were echoed by critics of the mindless formality of the First Empire and the ostentatious materialism of the Orleanist bourgeoisie. Those who made such claims about the Second Empire, however, evinced a more far-reaching pessimism about the future, as if society's frenetic embrace of profligacy announced a permanent change. In one respect, the altered tone of mondanité merely reflected a new political reality in which the general depoliticization of the 1850s made for less politicized salons. For Armaillé, the "imperial orgy" was a "relatively happy" phase, during which "rich families" waited calmly for a restoration while assisting "at the spectacle by following it with interest and by participating in its advantages." A few soirées and balls had a "slightly political character," but most were agreeable, benevolent, and gay, "the violent hatreds of the time of the July Monarchy [having] passed." Music and spiritualism provided ways "to pass the evening and get away from mondaine and political conversations," and the salon itself "offered a distraction, an always new occupation for middle-aged women and for men."[21]

But salons requiring music for animation suggested an entirely different form of sociability, in which the silence and immobility of guests mirrored the mental inhibitions imposed by a dictatorial regime. Under such circumstances, political conversations became platitudinous and insignificant, nourished only by the intrigue, rumors, and exaggerations induced by the fear and ignorance associated with a secretive government. Rémusat was so disgusted with "the mediocrity of the political milieux" in France that he decided to go to England in 1853 to escape. Tocqueville deplored the salons of the Second Empire, contrasting their intellectual level unfavorably with the brilliant society of his youth and telling Madame de Circourt that if she excluded "well-meaning fools" and "witty rogues" from a typical salon, there would hardly be anybody left. In the absence of civic preoccupations, the intellectual condition of society declined. Madame de Staël had already made the case for this argument during the reign of Napoléon I, pointing to the integral relationship between the ability to enter public life and the possession of resources for serious conversation. Once public affairs ceased to be a matter of private interest, impersonal subjects could no longer be discussed, and conversation was reduced to the commonplace. "The new political society," wrote Rémusat in 1852, "was composed of covetous epicureans who thought only of their own pleasure and their affairs and very little of public affairs." This, he continued, was one of their motives for supporting the Second Empire, a regime that allowed them to dispense with the necessity of thinking in favor of indulging their curiosity for "the ordinary chronicle of absolute monarchies: palace anecdotes, the gossip of the antechamber."[22]

Ancelot analyzed the feminine side of this phenomenon by pointing to the inverse relationship between intelligent conversation and the augmentation of a woman's toilette. According to her theory, "witty words" and provocative ideas diminished in proportion to the mass of colored ribbons, flowers, and gaudy accessories. If mental poverty and elaborate dress went hand in hand, conversely, the rebirth of the salon required that the vanity of parvenus be mitigated and "the display of luxury" demoted. In 1886, Kathleen O'Meara made a similar equation with reference to the salon of Melanie Waldor Mohl, arguing that "the decadence of conversation" could be blamed on crinoline, which "invaded [women's] moral life, debased their character by destroying their influence, reduced their field of action, and narrowed the terrain of their ambition." According to O'Meara, crinoline distracted a woman from the task of governing and inspiring men by increasing her vanity and focusing her mind on her toilette, "imposing itself like a despot even on the most reasonable." The argument may seem trivial, but it forms part of a long-standing polemic against authoritarian government, a sort of feminist corollary to the denunciation of bread and circuses that is the essence of the progressive side of the political history of salons, a history in which the existence of salons encouraged the characteristics of a liberal society: human rights, parliamentary government, and educated women. During the Second Empire, women were "[t]oo absorbed in preparing to produce an outward effect" to have time "to prepare their conversations." The sexes continued to mix in society, but men no longer frequented salons to polish a speech for the Chamber, develop the subject of a new book, or discover the theme for a politically explosive pamphlet.[23]

II

If we separate the salon from the eulogistic tone with which traditionalists like Ancelot surrounded the institution's slow anachronization, it becomes possible to make a few tentative observations about its persistence after the middle of the nineteenth century. Political salons continued to play a role in structuring political sociability in elite circles. In the 1860s, when political opposition became possible once again, salons reemerged more partisan than ever, registering various shades of public opinion, and helping legitimists, liberals, and republicans to define their ideological identities. It was the "Roman Question" — the pope's opposition to Napoléon III's Italian policy — more than anything else that revived the opposition of Faubourg Saint-Germain, where Madame de Lamoricière and the widows of Castelfidardo were celebrated before the embarrassed silence of the imperial court.[24] On the left, the salon of Comtesse d'Agoult (who wrote novels under the pseudonym Daniel Stern) was torn by the generational and ideological divisions to which 1848 had given rise among the elite of the republican bourgeoisie, after which the young moderates coalesced in several new republican salons around 1865, led by Léon Laurent-Pichat, Madame Hérold, and Juliette Adam, the "*égérie*" of the Third Republic." After 1871, the republican salons divided further along factional lines, with Adam's salon on the boulevard Poissonnière organizing the partisans of Léon Gambetta and the marquise de Arconati-Visconti's providing a base for the radicals. According to Emile de Marcère, a member of the Center-Right, the deputies of the National Assembly quickly "met one another in the places where group meetings were held by habit, but with a preference for salons, as was natural. The diverse parties corresponded almost without exception to the different social categories." The friends and colleagues of President Thiers met in the salon of Madame de Valon, the supporters of monarchical fusion gathered in the salon of the vicomtesse de Renneville, and the intransigent "chevau-légers" made the home of the duchesse de Bisaccia their *lieu de ralliement*. Once the republicans triumphed definitively, a united royalist opposition emerged in the salon of the comtesse de La Ferronays, while the Bonapartists rallied around the comtesse de Pourtalès. Such divisions carried over into the 1880s and 1890s, when opportunists, radicals, Dreyfusards, anti-Dreyfusards, and nationalists all had their own salons.[25] Of the latter, the salon of the comtesse de Loynes was the most famous, serving as the original base for the Ligue de la Patrie française, an organization founded by such habitués as

Jules Lemaître, Maurice Barrès, and Léon Daudet at a dinner party given by Loynes on January 13, 1899 (the Ligue's first official meeting took place at the Salle des Agriculteurs on the following Thursday). Like many of the political salons of the Third Republic, hers was associated with the nationalist press and either spawned or contributed to a political organization, as if salons needed links to modern political institutions in order to be relevant. Besides presiding over the birth of the Ligue de la Patrie française, the comtesse subsidized *La France* and *Le Petit Journal* and helped launch *L'Eclair* and *L'Action française*. Juliette Adam, meanwhile, founded a political and literary periodical called the *Nouvelle Revue* in 1879 to which she contributed an unsigned column entitled "Lettres sur la politique extérieure," where she advocated revenge against Germany.[26]

When high society formed the core of the pays légal, or when a dictatorial regime required a limited public to address itself to the administration and the chief of state, salons mattered, the government took pains to monitor them, and politicians curried favor with them. In an age of universal suffrage, however, the confinement of salons to the world of high society was a recipe for irrelevance. Political salons in the latter half of the nineteenth century lavished attention on a narrow range of preoccupations: dynastic alliances, right-wing politics, diplomacy, and elections to the Academy. Although they still served to structure political sociability and reinforce ideological identity at the upper echelons of French public life, their political functions had little to do with shaping agendas and winning elections. Nothing prevented the salonnières of the Third Republic from having parties at which guests held forth on political matters, but the separation of politics and mondanité gave such conversations little resonance in the wider world. Beaumont-Vassy distinguished the opinion of *les salons* from that of *le peuple* and *la bourgeoisie* when discussing reactions to Louis-Napoléon's coup or his marriage to Eugénie de Montijo. The duc de Gramont, Napoléon III's foreign minister in 1870, had little difficultly convincing the emperor that the renunciation of the Hohenzollern candidacy for the Spanish throne was nothing more than a "Sadowa of the salons," and that a real diplomatic victory would require the French government to step up pressure on Prussia in order to satisfy the xenophobia that was rampant in the streets. The contrast between the influence of Maurrassian ideas among cultural and political elites from the turn of the century to the eve of the Popular Front and the failure of the Action française as an electoral force during the same period had a great deal to do with the fact that integral nationalism had its ideological base in the world of the salons, a part of French culture that Pascal Ory calls "académique," concerned only with the intellectual preoccupations of the conservative establishment. According to Sylvie Aprile, the sociability of the republican salons of the 1860s and 1870s would have suited the ultras and was limited to a "republican aristocracy" in search of prestige and respectability. To say after 1870 that something had occurred "in the salons" was to be dismissive of it in a way that would not have made sense during the First Empire or the Restoration.[27]

In the long run, artistic, literary, and musical salons fared better than political salons. When Princesse Mathilde reopened a salon on the rue de Berri after the fall of the Second Empire, she avoided politics and focused on literature and the arts in order to ensure her salon's longevity. Of course, literature was not neutral, and the princesse's sympathy for the military began to affect the composition of her society during the Dreyfus Affair, but her salon was no longer hitched to the fortunes of a particular regime. Apoliticism might very well have sheltered a few salons from the vicissitudes of events. The salon of Nina de Vallard, which consisted mostly of celebrities in the worlds of music, literature, and art, lasted for twenty years, from 1863 to 1882, unperturbed by the prevailing political turmoil.[28] In the 1890s, many Parisian salons were still being run by comtesses, duchesses, and princesses. By contrast, in the decade or so before World War I, a number of them were directed by male writers, actors, and composers (Alexandre Singer, Auguste Dorchaine, Henri Germain, Jacques Normand) who were more interested in the salon's literary vocation than in the political one it had acquired in 1789.[29]

The French salon persisted as an institutional form long after it ceased to matter politically. "If they have lost a great part of their political influence," Victor du Bled wrote in 1900, "the salons of the nineteenth century remained to some extent what they were in the past: schools of civilization, where the art of conversation produced a charming *douceur de vivre*, thanks to women." Literary salons continued to enhance reputations, highlight celebrities, and promote candidates for election to the Academy. As long as women were prevented from achieving literary fame, heading museums, managing publishing houses, or directing important periodicals, the salon remained virtually the only institution through which a woman could exercise significant influence in the world of high culture. Before World War I, Margherita Safatti used her connections among the Milanese industrial bourgeoisie to turn her salon into a powerful engine of artistic patronage. In the 1920s, her relationship with Mussolini brought her to Rome, where she edited two important literary magazines, supported Corrado Alvaro in his bid to secure a generous literary prize for his novel *Gente in Aspro-*

monte, and maintained a salon that helped win sympathy for Il Duce among Italy's cultural elite.[30]

In the contemporary era, the question of the salon's persistence becomes one of qualifications. The contraction of leisure, the entry of women into the professions, and the emergence of new modes of communication eroded the salon's sociological and technological foundations and cut it off from the conditions that authorized its appearance. When is a salon no longer a salon? How much of its original form would have to vanish before we could say that the institution has literally ceased to exist? In the nineteenth century, the salon was still associated with a set of specific attributes: an intimate society meeting in a room under the presidency of a skilled salonnière. Ancelot and d'Agoult believed that this arrangement had a certain national specificity, requiring openness and amiability among culturally compatible participants who desired to possess some of the charms and delicate intimacies of *French* conversation. In our own day, the salon has been kept alive as pure cultural legacy, detached from its institutional properties and its social moorings. Rose Fortassier sees its continuation in an "attitude of mondanité" that "perpetually ris[es] from the ashes" every time one wants to seem polite, belong to an elite, or distinguish oneself from the commonplace. Mona Ozouf and Elizabeth Badinter locate the spirit of the salon in the realm of values, where France still abhors "the war of the sexes or their physical separation."[31] To say, as we would today, that the salon is "in the culture," is to suggest that it has ceased to be an object with a specific social relevance. When I asked the public relations department at *Salon* magazine (by way of electronic mail) why the editors had chosen this historical reference for the title of their publication, I was told that a salon is nothing more than "the regular exchange of ideas," as if physical space and face-to-face encounters were not essential to its very existence. The salon has survived, in whatever form, because of its simplicity.

III

Was it premature for Ancelot to characterize salons as "foyers éteints" in 1858? Maurice Agulhon notes that the aristocratic model of mondaine sociability was being contested in the 1820s, long before its monopoly was shaken under the Second Empire. At the same time, the regular and unanimous proclamation of the salon's decline never recorded its actual extinction.[32] Perhaps we should ask, not whether salons disappeared (they exist today), but why they ceased to matter.

Salons proved to be of limited political value under the conditions created by universal suffrage, because the logic of democratic politics effaced most of the advantages the salon had possessed in the age of the censitary monarchies. The politicization of the 1820s and 1830s had not necessarily been harmful to salons; it might have undermined their internal harmony, but it complemented their ability to organize political sociability in a way that reinforced ideological solidarity in a context that did not require elites to address a wider constituency. Universal suffrage, by contrast, threw up alternative institutions with a much wider recruitment, while forcing traditional ones to focus more narrowly on electoral politics and on the coordination of departmental and local organizations.[33] In the first years of the Third Republic, the legitimist and Orleanist aristocracy used salons to organize its representatives in the National Assembly, and Juliette Adam assured Gambetta that he would have to be a member of high society if he wanted to be a member of the government. By the decisive elections of 1876 and 1877, however, the monarchist parties were being hamstrung by the habits contracted in salon society, where they learned nothing about addressing the masses, while the principal republican salons had become part of a larger electoral apparatus, including newspapers and fund-raising committees, that served primarily to put a network of political allies and financial backers at a candidate's disposal. Political salons continued to exist on both sides in the 1880s, but cercles, which had expanded rapidly, had taken over the management of elections. As the Right faltered at the polls and struggled unsuccessfully to cobble together an effective democratic political organization, the republicans built a national machine of provincial electoral committees that undermined Paris's traditional status as the nation's political epicenter.[34]

Agulhon argues that the rise of cercles and the decline of salons logically duplicated two larger processes: the displacement of "Old France" by "bourgeois France," and the shift from a "vertical-hierarchical" society to a "horizontal-egalitarian" one. In response to this formulation, Aprile tries to show that during the first decades of the Third Republic, the number of salons rose, along with the number of cercles, that both began to decline in the 1890s, and that "[t]he presence of cercles cannot therefore be a major reason for the effacement of salons as places of political sociability." But whether cercles displaced salons or followed a similar evolutionary chronology may be less important than the fact that the rise of cercles put salons on the Right in French political lexicography, sealing their fate as anachronisms, and associating them forever with legitimism, aristocracy, and reaction. Marie d'Agoult gave expression to this definitive semantic realignment when she wrote with reference to 1848 that "democratic egalitarianism . . . discredited the spirit of the salons." Since the 1820s, those who have identified with French political traditions hostile to the legacy of Old Regime have presumed that salons belong to an enemy camp, defined by their devotion to hierarchy, intolerance, and anti-democratic institutions. Pascal Ory has gone so far as to insist that "this type of sociability was ipso facto under the jurisdiction of the right wing," whose spirit "was at ease" in such places. It is a perception not entirely divorced from reality.[35]

Like the aristocratic society of which it was a part, the salon has been under severe stress since the middle of the nineteenth century. Holding a salon typically required considerable wealth and an elegant hôtel or apartment. Although many noble families had rebuilt and even modernized their fortunes after the Revolution, many were forced to economize more than had been customary in the eighteenth century. Competition from new wealth and the increasing cost of entertaining brought about by economic growth and the tendency toward ostentation and big parties during the Second Empire made it harder than ever for aristocratic families to keep up appearances. "The richness of dress became so exaggerated that a woman no longer dared to go to a soirée unceremoniously wearing a dress that would have been very suitable for the receptions of Queen Marie-Amélie," Kathleen O'Meara wrote in 1886; as a result, "receptions became onerous to those who accepted them and to those who gave them," so that the only hostesses continuing to receive were women who could spend a lot or who did not worry about expense. According to Beaumont-Vassy, the habits of the grand monde were changed dramatically during the Second Empire by the need for people at all levels of Parisian society to spend more than they earned. Some were ruined by this "immense social peril," while others either curbed their extravagant lifestyle or made economies elsewhere.[36] In the 1850s, Armaillé characterized as severe and austere the habits of Faubourg Saint-Germain, where "phalansteries" of old legitimist families kept servants on as long as possible, maintained antique carriages, and dressed modestly. Having embraced abstemiousness as both a religious virtue and a financial necessity, the women of the district were scandalized when the duchesse d'Uzès showed up at a retreat at the Convent of the Sacred Heart wearing a velour jacket hemmed with chinchilla. In the aftermath of World War I, when inflation and an agricultural depression dealt a blow to *propriétaires* and stockholders alike, many in the French nobility saw their net worth decline even further. The comtesse Benoist d'Azy, conceding to circumstances, admitted: "We are no longer the reigning goddesses of the land and the châteaux: we are the administrators of our houses, and we follow the fluctuations of the Bourse with attention. If money becomes rare, it is illusory to try to continue to live as before: mondanité is like war; it requires money, money, money."[37]

Economic pressures arose at a time when political and sociological changes favored the triumph of alternative forms of sociability. After 1880, once the cause of royalism came to depend more on ideological combat than on the cultivation of prestige or the exercise of social power, newspaper offices, Catholic associations, and *sociétés savantes* replaced salons as the principal institutions of political sociability on the Right, where leaders were less interested in social co-optation than in the diffusion of ideas. At the same time, salons were suffering from the progressive disestablishment of aristocratic *oisiveté* as the ideal basis for a public career. During the Restoration, salons brought together men who lived off income from their lands and, inasmuch as they were not heavily taxed by civilian and military responsibilities, were free to devote themselves to mondaine pursuits and disinterested scholarship. By the 1840s, however, politics, scholarly work, and the escalating pace of urban life took men of the same milieux further and further from the world of their parents and their youth. Guizot thought that the men of his generation lacked patience and were always in a hurry; having no leisure, they had no taste for conversation, lectures, visits, and all the other aimless diversions with which the older generation had passed the time.[38] Restlessness therefore went hand in hand with the erosion of a shared space for communication, where the requisite commonality of tastes and knowledge was threatened by social differences, material concerns, and occupational professionalization. As elite sociability became a counterpart to work rather than a feature of idleness, it became more varied and specialized, with the advent of clubs for everyone from horse enthusiasts to friends of the *chemins de fer*. In the 1860s, Beaumont-Vassy noted the "great progress" of sport in France by pointing to the rise of new associations dedicated to various English pastimes, including rowing, the chase, and cricket. By the 1890s, visitors to the spas at Vichy found many new activities, including bicycle races, velocipede rentals, croquet, *boules*, and target practice, with which to supplement the bathing, gambling, billiards, and conversation that usually filled their time. Meanwhile, the requirements of the elegant life and the position of the salonnière ran up against two emerging feminine ideals: the "femme chrétienne," busy with charity work and piety, threatened to displace the traditional grande dame among the aristocracy, while the duties of the modern wife competed with those of the maîtresse de maison among the bourgeoisie. According to Armaillé, the older women of the aristocracy still went into society in the 1850s, but they disapproved of its new pleasures. "A certain number of pious and austere people," she continued, "followed the existence widows would have been expected to follow in the past."[39]

The old customs of daily life persisted in Faubourg Saint-Germain long after the aristocracy ceased to set an example for elite society as a whole. A lifestyle whose rituals had once resonated widely among the upper classes more and more became habits associated with a particular set of domestic arrangements, in which the members of interrelated extended families often lived under the same roof, received one another three or four times a week, and took regular promenades in the Bois de Boulogne.[40] To be sure, these families occupied the pinnacle of the well-born and were able to gather around them intellectual, artistic, and political celebrities, as well as an endless parade of cultivated idlers. But the time had already come when aristocratic disdain for modernity had ceased automatically to reinforce the mystique that had allowed the old nobility to establish norms of superiority, savoir faire, and disinterested culture. At that moment, the world of the salons became the world of Proust, an elitist refuge, isolated, self-referential, seeing in its own class prejudice an honorable disregard for public opinion. Having ceased to represent power, the nobility of the faubourg could represent only itself, its mondanité reduced to the impeccable exercise of aristocratic precedent and etiquette. The duc de Guermantes regarded his mandate as a deputy as worthless and wanted to be nothing more than a grand seigneur and homme du monde. For Christian de Bartillat, such behavior was frivolous at best, the conservation of elegance and politesse being "paltry occupations when they become the principal ones in a life of which they ought only to be the accessory."[41]

Critics of le monde were already complaining in the 1820s that the old sociability served to support an aristocratic monopoly that had become an anachronism. In *Lucien Leuwen*, Stendhal's title character worries that contact with the friends of his aristocratic mistress will prevent him from acquiring "nineteenth-Century virtues," and compares the elegance of the "youthful inhabitants of the Faubourg Saint-Germain" to "an orange tree planted in the middle of the Compiègne Forest — pretty, but out of place in our age."[42] During the July Monarchy, a rising chorus declared that the salons of Paris had become sterile and lethargic, with some blaming the aristocracy's lack of energy while others disparaged the intellectual inferiority of the Orleanist bourgeoisie.[43] Meanwhile, salonnières like Madame de Girardin and Comtesse Dash worried that theirs was becoming a lost art and began offering advice to women on everything from the proper arrangement of chairs to strategies for sustaining conversations among different sorts of guests. In the 1850s, William Duckett and Louis Louvet compiled a *Dictionnaire de la conversation* in fifty-two volumes, designed to provide gens du monde with a useful repertoire "of the most indispensable general knowledge," as if to illustrate the principle that customary practices begin to fade at the point of their explicit reiteration.[44]

The word *salon* began to be used consistently in the Napoleonic era to designate an institution and a set of practices that had taken shape since the middle of the seventeenth century. By the end of the Second Empire, it had become increasingly common to speak of a salon as simply a reception room, or to replace the word in the political lexicon of the day with a more appropriate alternative, like *réunion, comité,* or *association.* It was about the same time that the word *société* began to acquire its modern meaning, so that Madame Ancelot was forced in 1866 to clarify when she was speaking of a group of friends and when she was referring to "the whole of the country."[45] During this process of linguistic slippage, the salon became the object of a nostalgic discourse that consolidated its status as a *lieu de mémoire.* For Marc Fumaroli, this process occurred under a cloud of doubt and mourning representative of the darkening and starching of conversational conventions in the hands of a busy, graceless bourgeoisie, giving every reconstituted salon of the nineteenth century a slightly funereal and historiographical quality, like "a commemoration, a perpetual anniversary mass."[46] But nineteenth-century salons had a vitality all their own, occasioned by their politicization, and a specificity that came from the fact that their reconstitution entailed the invention of the traditions we habitually associate with the French salon. Moreover, the salon was the site of a variety of distinctive memories — liberal, conservative, aristocratic, and feminine — which Fumaroli ignores by locating the origins of these traditions in the Grand Siècle in order to reinforce its association with the exceptional nature of French sociability.

It was the doctrinaires of the Restoration who invented the nineteenth-century salon as the embodiment of the spirit of the eighteenth century, which Sainte-Beuve called a "[h]appy time, [w]hen life as a whole revolved around sociability; when everything was arranged for the sweetest commerce of the mind and the best conversation." For Guizot, the salon of Madame de Rumford perpetuated this spirit by combining "gracious and noble mores" with "so much intellectual activity" and "a lively taste for the progress of civilization."[47] At the same time, Restoration aristocrats made the salons of both past and present a salutary feminine dominion, with aristocratic grandes dames as royalty. Beginning in 1825 with Comte Roederer's *Mémoire pour servir à l'histoire de la société polie en France*, dedicated to the glory of Madame de Rambouillet, and culminating under the Second Empire with the Goncourts's *La Femme au dix-huitième siècle*, a vast literature on the salonnières of the Old Regime mythologized French conversation and contributed to the consolidation of the main lines of an aristocratic feminism, suggestively associating the salon with feminine political power. Ancelot, who contributed to this genre with a comedy entitled *L'Hôtel de Rambouillet*, called the legendary marquise "our only hope" and made clear her interest in finding queens for salons of the elite, "cet empire de l'intelligence." In her *Essai sur l'éducation des femmes*, published in 1824, Madame de Rémusat paints a distressing portrait of a girl's life at court under Louis XV but pays tribute to the grace and tone of eighteenth-century conversation, created and codified by women to fulfill "one of the basic needs of the French."[48]

Both bourgeois liberals and aristocrats agreed that the intellectual quality of salon conversation declined in the nineteenth century; the former tended to blame society's abandonment of progressive ideas, while the latter asserted that egalitarianism and materialism hindered the continual production of great salonnières. Guizot argued that the philosophes would hardly have been able to find an example of "noble and liberal sociability" had they come back to life in the 1830s.[49] By contrast, d'Agoult thought that le monde disappeared in the first half of the nineteenth century because "the 'milieu' no longer gave this delicate flower, the grande dame, the aristocratic leisure without which there can be no exquisite society." Bassanville came to a similar conclusion, declaring in the 1860s that the "old dowagers" of the Restoration were "witty, distinguished, and had a degree of influence over the judgments of le monde that the present generation could not imagine." In her opinion, people judged the Restoration too harshly and never understood its "better aspects" or its appeal to women:

> They have seen its frivolous surface, and they have not wanted to lift the veil of frivolity to discover its heart. . . . One should have tried at least to save the women from [the] universal cataclysm [of its disappearance]. But alas! The civil code placed over their heads the standard of its articles, and the grande dame was dead; she disappeared with the crown she received from the past, with the powder, the beauty marks, the heeled slippers, the bodices embellished with knotted ribbon, pompons, lace, and all the things finally that women seek to recover today, but that very few know how to wear.[50]

Despite her republican sympathies, Marie d'Agoult preferred the mores of her youth to those of "our revolutionary generation," which was suspicious of noble traditions, annoyed by courtesy, quick to see hypocrisy in politeness, and inclined to view "the influence of women in salons as a violation of the law." "Democratic France honors mothers and wives in principle and print," she observed in 1877, "but in reality, they are subalterns in their own homes, with no other countenance than that of a housewife. At present, the women of democracy know neither what they can be nor what they ought to do."[51]

In memoirs written during the Second Empire, many aristocratic women born around the turn of the nineteenth century, now aging, bored, and nostalgic for their youth, expressed unanimous regret at the passing of the Restoration. Ancelot recalled it as a time filled with youthful potential, when liberty had been new, government stable, literature as yet unspoiled by commercialism, and everything worthwhile happened in salons. Girardin wrote of the Restoration that "no era of French society ever possessed a more complete and truly agreeably varied collection of interesting storytellers and intelligent conversationalists" — high praise indeed from one who helped mythologize the sociability of the Old Regime. Her mother, Sophie, simply remarked that it was the era "of our dreams."[52]

In 1862, Madame de Boigne sat down to write histories of the last days of Madame Adélaïde, Louis XV's daughter, and the July Monarchy "in order to ward off the idleness of the present," which she characterized as "somber and monotonous." In retrospect, it was politics, being at the center of things, that had made her life memorable and exciting. In the winter of 1821, when Chateaubriand was busy with ministerial duties, Madame de Duras told him that she was anxious to overcome an illness that kept her from receiving: "Give me voice, so that I can carry myself well, so that I have an indefatigable throat, so that I can give parties, dinners, so that people talk politics with me. Then I would be the fabled field mouse, the lions would consider me worthy, and you would return."[53]

IV

Salon nostalgia in the mid nineteenth century was a reactionary gesture, a way of facing a disappointing future by looking backwards. Girardin responded to the Second Republic's neglect of women with the language of counterrevolution, demanding not political rights but "ancient rights" closely associated with those of the salonnière: the right to be decorous, to have authority over hearth and home, and to govern the abode. Bassanville believed that the well-educated women of the 1860s, who knew several languages and read serious books, were worse off than the women of 1800, who "hardly knew how to spell" — the former were always surrounded by men, while the latter had been left alone, excluded from the places where men gathered, "thus proving to women that they should not demand to share in [men's] work, but to distract them from it, [and] that formal education for them is a luxury, while what is necessary is grace, sweetness, and affability, which nothing can replace."[54] Nostalgia also contained an element of self-doubt, expressing the sense that women were primarily responsible for the salon's demise: if only they had retained their prestige by remaining hostesses and muses, by acting respectably and avoiding decadent habits; if only they had remained aloof from politics, they would not have allowed clubs to take the place of salons. In 1834, the duchesse de Périgord told Rudolf Apponyi that the partisan fury of ultraroyalist women had crippled the influence of aristocratic high society: "Nous ne sommes plus ce que nous étions autrefois; nous sommes détrônées."[55]

Upper-class women had reason to regret the salon's decline. More than just a means of occupying a sedentary life, the salon offered friendship, intellectual stimulation, access to politics, and even celebrity. As Chastenay put it, a salonnière was "accustomed to conversation about everything that is most remarkable, to intimate society, [and] to the habitual confidence of men who have the most to say."[56] But the salon was neither a feminist institution nor logically pointed toward the goals of modern feminism. Contemporary scholars nevertheless continue to suggest otherwise, speaking of the salon as a power center and of the salonnière as an influential broker, even while recognizing the institution's archaic qualities, its constraints, and its limitations. The latest work to hint at the real effectuality of decision making in "the unofficial sphere" is Catherine Allgor's study of "parlor politics" in Washington, D.C., from the early days of the American Republic to the Jacksonian Era, which "may have been the zenith of wealthy women's strength in American politics."[57] The importance of salons has always been exaggerated, either by those who have wanted to flatter women (including women themselves), or by those who have waxed hysterical about women's illegitimate power in order more effectively "to put them in their place." It would be well to remember that the history of salons, like that of women in the modern era, is largely one of vulnerability. The functions salons provided writers and politicians were grounded in shifting gender norms and class prejudices; they were not guaranteed by right and could therefore be appropriated or obtained elsewhere.[58]

The salon, in short, was a historical cul-de-sac. The political roles women played there, whether as mondaine hostesses, confidantes, couriers of information, or referees, varied little from the eighteenth century to the Third Republic, or from aristocratic to republican milieux, because they responded to the needs of men who withheld the power of decision from them. Girardin found this arrangement acceptable, noting that "women are not made to act, but to command, which is to say to inspire: to council, hinder, ask, [and] obtain." Montcalm, who scoffed at the celebrity of muses and who thought it dangerous to give women a "deliberative voice," did not, fearing that persons exalted by their social position but without governmental experience would be tempted to talk about things they did not understand. "Today," she wrote in 1817, "I would perhaps choose the existence of a prefect's wife, because it is nearly the only one in which one could enjoy the good one could do; one's action becomes more direct within well-defined limits, and a woman busying herself with the direction of a hospital, or with alleviating misery, can hope to make her action useful without men reproaching her for seeking importance or fame."[59]

Once the salon ceased to be a feminocentric institution in the seventeenth century, it involved women in two forms of isolation. The first related to the salonnière's centrality among a group of men, which deprived her of individual autonomy and the sociability of other women. Since French high society was not monosexual, women had few places of their own in which to form relationships of friendship and solidarity. In the salon, a woman could preside over men in an authoritative manner, but mostly to facilitate the easy flow of a conversation that manifested the group's social, intellectual, or political aspirations, leaving her with neither an independent identity nor an autonomous voice. With few occasions for the sort of preliminary or alternative sociability available to men, in schools, in the military, in parliament, or in clubs, women in salons could neither win their autonomy, strive to achieve personal goals, nor protest collectively against their general condition, all of which would in any case have been entirely at odds with the principles of feminine honnêteté and politesse.[60] The second kind of isolation derived from the salonnière's status as a extraordinary woman, whose power could not be universalized and therefore did not threaten to metamorphose into equality and emancipation. Geneviève Fraisse and Eric Fassin have argued that exceptional women who were tolerated under the Old Regime became intolerable once "revolutionary logic" made the exception the rule. But exceptional women were more closely associated with social hierarchy than with women's equality, which is why nineteenth-century elites heaped praise on salonnières, who upheld traditional arrangements and were consequently less caricaturized (as Fraisse would have it) than mythologized after 1800. One has only to think of Madame de Staël, a staunch supporter of the liberal French Revolution, who regarded herself as a being apart, above simple mortals, and who became an iconic figure during the Restoration.[61]

Nineteenth-century salonnières aspired to individual power in traditional institutions; insofar as Frenchwomen aspired to be salonnières, they rarely became suffragettes. Even Juliette Adam, a republican, advocated not suffrage for women in general but for exceptional women alone, who would join men in provincial councils to select members of the upper house.[62] As Jolanta Pekacz observes, "the emancipation of women and their increasing participation in things public towards the end of the nineteenth century was not an outcome of the experience of salonnières, but of developments taking place outside of salons." An early public embodiment of women's putative civilizing mission, the logic of the salon pointed more toward patrician philanthropy and social work in the modern era than toward women's political power. Many nineteenth-century feminists, like Jeanne Deroin, applied traditional notions of femininity to politics by arguing that feminine opinion in public life would help make the public sphere more civil, peaceful, and altruistic. But the obstacles that prevented its effective expression in nineteenth-century France, like the law of July 28, 1848, that excluded women from participation in clubs, pointed to the need for concrete changes that implied the actual presence of women in journalism and government. After insisting on the real power of politicians' wives in the early American Republic, Allgor advises today's female students "to go run their own corporations" and "embrace the official sphere of power."[63]

V

During the last days of the Paris Commune, the home of the marquise de Blocqueville on the quai Malaquais was accidentally bombarded by government troops serving under General d'Auerstädt and General du Cissy. The next morning, her chambermaid entered her bedroom and announced in a bewildered fashion that a company of *fédérés* wanted to fire out of the windows of her salon, which was on the upper floor of the building. The marquise told the maid to let them in and that she would receive them herself. Appearing at the threshold of her salon, holding a fan, she greeted the soldiers as she would have greeted her guests: "I salute you, Messieurs. And I should hope that my salon might serve you as a refuge after the defeat, rather than as a citadel during the battle. My trinkets, which you will take heed to respect, my *chinoiseries*, my old porcelain, and yourselves will be better off that way."[64]

The salon has always had an ambivalent relationship with politics. In 1789, Madame de Staël hoped for the fusion of politics and polite conversation under the direction of women, in whose presence nobles and talented men of the bourgeoisie would engage in the enlightened discussion of important issues for the benefit of the common good.[65] But the Staëlian formula proved very difficult to achieve in the nineteenth century, when bitter partisanship made ideological consensus and social amalgamation unworkable, and when women grew disillusioned with having to choose between the excitement of the public sphere and the viability of an ideal sociability. In theory, the salon ought to have been able to unite the intellectualism of the Enlightenment with the politics of a liberal society, because upper-class women were ideally situated between the public and private spheres, where private aspirations mingled with the challenges of the outside world. In practice, however, it was very hard for the salon to be both a literary Arcadia and a space for careerism, propaganda, and negotiation: political divisiveness undercut the feminine qualities that supposedly elevated the salon above the fray and made it a civilizing institution. Salons and politics existed in a state of permanent tension. In his article "Salon," written for the *Grand Encyclopédie* of 1890, Philippe Berthelot wrote that "affairs have left little room for the disinterested cult of things of the spirit." Daniel Gordon concludes that there could be "no philosophical space for the ideal of politeness" in the modern political era, in which salons continued to exist but lost their "universal significance."[66]

The early nineteenth century was the era of political salons par excellence; it was also the era during which salonnières and habitués began to contemplate a return to the salon's prepolitical ideal. The perfect salon was imagined to be a space for commodious conversation among educated amateurs, conducted in the absence of material concerns, social distinctions, and political preoccupations. As Fumaroli points out, "All the literary myths that form the symbolic architecture of salon society — the Islands of Fortune, the Arcadia, the Platonic banquet — are myths of a life of noble leisure, removed from business and public affairs." In 1841, Guizot insisted on the superiority of eighteenth-century sociability, arguing that it had been a time of meditation that had given more scope to the human spirit than the politicized nineteenth century, which was "attached to ideas only in their relation with social facts and in order to apply them." Similarly, Ancelot remembered her favorite salons of the Restoration as apolitical, where guests met in the total absence of material preoccupations. Listening to Chopin playing the piano in a salon, Delphine de Girardin was moved to suggest that only serious art could restore the salon's transcendent mission:

Bourgeois existence seemed thoroughly sullen the day after [one of] these beautiful poetic fêtes. The ideal discourages real life. But such pleasures ought not cause alarm. Yes! Few Parisian salons resemble this little salon where we have spent this fine evening. It is an asylum open to all parties, a fresh oasis that makes you smile and attracts you in this arid desert, dried up by the wind of pride, which we call le grand monde. There, mediocrities do not sermonize, they are judged; great talent is not slandered, it is respected. It is a port surrounded by protective rocks, against which the waves of envy break; it is an arsenal where weapons of all kinds find themselves assembled, without anger, ostentation, or bravado, always ready to defend the worthy against the worthless.[67]

The transcendent salon of the nineteenth-century imagination was an expression of the desire to protect endangered traditions, on the assumption that it was better to be marginal but pure. What did it matter if the salon occupied a little corner of the world, as long as it remained a place in which to search for the good and the beautiful; why should salons embrace modernity if every compromise would be a sort of profanation? At the same time, distance from prevailing customs was what had originally given the salon its radical potential, a potential associated, not only with separation from the world, but with the violation of convention and the primacy of women. Even in the nineteenth century, the aristocratic salons of Paris contributed to the success of new tendencies in literature and art. What better way to recapture the contestatory nonconformism that characterized the salon's emergence than to separate it from the social and political pressures that made it an accomplice of reaction or a pillar of the established order? Something of this spirit reigned in the Parisian salon of Nathalie Barney, which became a safe harbor for lesbians and radical intellectuals in the early twentieth century. In the *Utne Reader*, a contemporary American lifestyle magazine that claims to bring together "the best of the alternative press," salon conversation has been characterized as hip and compared to conceptual jazz. Salons themselves are recommended as an antidote to our "atomized and overmediated" society that could revive "the endangered art of conversation" and "start a revolution in your living room."[68]

And yet there is a case to be made for the central importance of politics in both the history and vitality of salons. The right to talk politics at home among friends was not some blight visited upon the French upper classes by the Revolution; it was the accomplishment of freedom in private life, a freedom for which eighteenth-century elites had struggled and that nineteenth-century notables were happy to preserve, at least for themselves. It was what made salons controversial and relevant, both before and after 1789; it was what visited upon them the ire of both Napoleonic tyrannies and the admiration of those who continued to think about the achievement of a liberal society compatible with the fears born of revolutionary disorder. In the long run, the slow separation of politics and mondanité did more to marginalize salons than to invigorate their creativity. Jules Barbey d'Aurevilly tried to make the case for the lighter side of salon sociability ("at bottom, a very legitimate order of preoccupations, since they correspond to real needs"), but in imagining a salon without serious conversation, he reduced mondanité to card parties, storytelling, and sexual flirtation.[69] The more the men of the nineteenth century sought refuge from politics in salons, the more everyone complained about the decline of conversation. Under the Second Empire, the duchesse Colonna called the salon "a cage, a gilded aviary" and concluded that a woman interested in politics ought not have one. "The big problems, the serious questions, that preoccupy humanity," she wrote, "are dealt with elsewhere."[70]

Conclusion

Aristocratic conceptions of the social and political roles of women formed a sort of enduring class consensus that was the foundation of the salon's survival in an era of rising domesticity and increasing hostility to feminism. The hardiness of this consensus suggests why neither Rousseauists nor revolutionaries could kill the salon. As an aristocratic institution, the salon was vulnerable not to the ideology of the enemies of aristocratic power, but only to aristocrats themselves; consequently, the authority of salonnières was not subject to masculinist assumptions associated historically with the Left.[1] To be sure, the salon was a fragile institution, but it was socially insulated from the disapproval of Jacobins and their political progeny, who could ban salons by outlawing them and close them down by exiling and executing their habitués, but who could not eliminate them by boycotting a society to which they did not belong or by setting up cercles or clubs in which aristocratic men showed no interest. In the nineteenth century, however, the social coherence, cultural influence, and political utility of salons were threatened on all sides, by every historical development that gave wealthy, powerful men reason or occasion to associate independently of women. The decline of the salon was thus not a question of the motives of its critics, but of those of its clientele.

The aristocratic consensus that made possible the persistence of salons was reinforced and complemented by the ability of salonnières to transform conventional attitudes about gender into social and political assets. In the postabsolutist public sphere, and more firmly after 1815, attributes traditionally assigned to women were politicized in salons and made to serve the collective needs of public men. This was especially true under the conditions created by the Restoration and the July Monarchy, when the return of court life and the reestablishment of aristocratic high society coincided with the advent of a parliamentary regime in which a small but homogeneous elite, fearful of renewed upheaval but gratified to be free of dictatorship, sought a framework for political life that would allow for partisan organization while providing an antidote to the destructive factionalism of the recent past. In such circumstances, salonnières gained access to public life, but they were also made vulnerable to political criticism. Restoration elites turned salons into instruments of aristocratic power and co-optation, inviting attacks on them from liberals eager to free themselves from a system of political sociability that tended to shore up existing social hierarchies. Restoration salons structured the political world in a way that required members of the bourgeoisie either to put their talents at the service of social superiors, in whose homes they met, or found their own institutions, whose all-male composition reflected a contempt for the privileges of aristocratic women that was an invidious by-product of liberalism's struggle to extricate itself from dependence on the past. Hostility to ultraroyalists, the Bourbon monarchy, and legitimists was unfortunately (but inevitably) directed at social arrangements identified with publicly prominent women, who were accused by the Left of upholding royalist political orthodoxies. Under the July Monarchy, it was the turn of the socially conservative aristocrats, who accused salonnières anxious to conform to the new social realities of undermining the exclusivity of high society by welcoming parvenus into their salons. Gendered language, and gender itself, therefore became political weapons in the battles over democratization that were at the heart of French politics from 1815 to 1848, just as the construction of women's inferiority during the age of Enlightenment reflected a general rejection of aristocratic cultural domination.

The survival of salons depended not on the fortunes of an ideology of domesticity that aristocrats hesitated to embrace but on the factors that supported their political and social utility. This suggests that there were social and political causes (the rise of mass media, the growing separation of work and leisure) for the decline of salons, and that the rise of modern bourgeois politics was not essentially about gender, although women were certainly among the losers.[2] Salons continued to exist throughout the nineteenth century, but their political utility declined because the widening electoral franchise, the rise of liberalism, and the emergence of new forms of political sociability destabilized high society as a framework for elite politics and weakened the connections between politics and mondanité. Liberals who viewed salonnières as symbols of royalism and aristocratic social predominance also favored a system of elite recruitment based on individual masculine achievement and came to view mondanité as a frivolous distraction. Conditions supporting the existence of political salons eroded as the institutional features of modern political life emerged and as a discourse that held participation in public life responsible for inculcating public virtue assigned an increasingly marginal role to the civilizing functions of traditional sociability. In short, modernity invented alternatives for many of the things salons did.

The political history of salons illustrates how gender is implicated and deployed in the formation of our social practices, cultural perceptions, and political institutions. It does not, however, demonstrate conclusively that all modern constructs of gender are intrinsically exclusionary or that they are always deployed against women acting in public. Modern gender conceptions are historically constructed and therefore malleable: they have been made compatible, for example, with French salons and a women's right to vote. The French Revolution was hostile to attempts by women to act publicly, but that was not necessarily a threat to the survival of salons. At the time, the threat to salons came from the Revolution's scattering of its clientele and from its labeling of polite society as counterrevolutionary. But the Revolution also opened up lines of communication between state and society in a way that gave private persons who met to discuss public affairs access to power. Political salons emerged, along with other channels connecting state and society, when the ability to act in public created the opportunity to marry ideas to institutions and policies. The question, therefore, is not how salons disappeared along with the Old Regime but how and why they made the transition from absolutist to postrevolutionary politics, and under what conditions they survived alongside other forms of political sociability. The answer has everything to do with the fact that the salon was an aristocratic form of sociability rooted in a premodern universe of political communications. As long as the aristocracy predominated among those privileged to act publicly, salons continued to matter.

Upper-class women in France had a unique presence in political life between 1815 and 1848 (aside from the aborted precedent of 1789–91) because in that period a socially circumscribed public successfully claimed power through representative institutions and used salons to structure and modulate partisan competition. Salons arose historically from the organization of the aristocratic household and remained anchored in the private sphere once they became arenas of political discussion among those in a position to exercise power. In other words, the salons of the Restoration and the July Monarchy occupied the crossroads where social interests and political power intersected. Before 1815, the salon had faced a wall when turned toward the state; after 1848, it faced too many competitors when it turned toward society, and it thereby lost its privileged social and political location.

Biographical Appendix

ABRANTÈS, LAURE JUNOT, DUCHESSE DE (1784–1838). Born in Montpellier to a Corsican mother and a wealthy father, who made a fortune as an army contractor during the War of American Independence. She attended boarding school at Paris during the Jacobin phase of the Revolution, while her parents escaped to Toulouse, and after the fall of Robespierre, she lived with her mother at the Hôtel de la Tranquillité on the rue des Filles-Saint-Thomas in the Chaussée d'Antin, where Napoléon Bonaparte was a frequent guest. In 1800, she married General Jean-Andoche Junot, one of Napoléon's aides-de-camp, who served as governor of Paris and ambassador to Portugal. She received lavishly during the Empire and was friends with Joséphine de Beauharnais. Junot's suicide in 1813 and the fall of the Empire wrecked her finances and forced her to supplement her income by writing.

AGOULT, MARIE-CATHERINE DE FLAVIGNY, COMTESSE D' (1805–1876). Born at Frankfurt-am-Main. Her father was an officer in the army of Louis XVI who emigrated to Coblenz, fought in the army of the exiled princes, and married Marie-Elizabeth Bethmann, the Protestant daughter of an official of the Holy Roman Empire. She moved to France in 1809, grew up in the countryside near Tours, and was broadly educated in German and French. After the Bourbon Restoration, she lived amid her father's ultraroyalist society and continued her education in Frankfurt and in the Convent of the Sacré-Coeur. She married Comte Charles d'Agoult in 1827 and became a prominent salonnière in Faubourg Saint-Germain. Intellectual curiosity and romantic involvement with Franz Liszt led her to Switzerland and away from the world of the old aristocracy. She befriended Georges Sand, lived throughout Europe, became a noted writer, and embraced liberal republicanism. Under the pseudonym Daniel Stern she wrote a history of the Revolution of 1848, as well as a number of other works.

ANCELOT, MARGUERITE-LOUISE CHARDON (1792–1875). Daughter of an old parliamentary family from Dijon. Ancelot became a painter, writer, and playwright. She was the wife of novelist and playwright Jacques-Arsène-François Ancelot and hostess of an influential literary salon on the rue de Seine in Paris from 1824 to 1866.

BAGRATION, CATHERINE SKAVRONSKA, PRINCESSE DE (1783–1857). In 1800, Skavronska married Prince Peter Bagration, who was killed at Bordino in 1812. In 1830, she married Sir John Hobart Caradoc (Lord Howden), an English colonel.

BELGIOJOSO, CHRISTINA TRIVULZIO, PRINCESSE DE (1808–1871). Trivulzio married the Prince Barbiano Belgiojoso in 1824. She settled in Paris after the Treaty of Vienna, opened a salon, and published a four-volume work entitled *An Essay on the Formation of Catholic Dogma* in 1846. An opponent of Austrian rule in Lombardy, she rushed to Milan in 1848 to support the nationalist cause but was deprived of her property by Austria and exiled to Paris, where she lived primarily by her writing.

BOIGNE, LOUISE-ELÉONORE D'OSMOND, COMTESSE DE (1781–1866). Known primarily for her famous memoirs of the Restoration and the July Monarchy, originally entitled *Récits d'une tante*. She was born at Versailles and married during the emigration to a wealthy Savoyard soldier named Benoît de Boigne, who treated her scandalously and left her in England. He eventually redeemed himself by giving her liberty and a considerable pension. She was a friend of Queen Marie-Amélie and a liberal monarchist. Her Paris salon at the Hôtel de Lannion, rue de Bourbon, and her Sunday dinners at Châtenay attracted important writers, politicians, and diplomats.

BROGLIE, ALBERTINE DE STAËL HOLSTEIN, DUCHESSE DE (1797–1838). Born Albertine de Staël, daughter of Madame de Staël and granddaughter of Suzanne Necker. Married Duc Achille-Léon-Victor de Broglie, a leading doctrinaire and liberal, and presided over a political salon during the July Monarchy. An austere Protestant, she wrote *Fragments sur divers sujets de religion et de morale*, first published in 1840.

CONDORCET, MARIE-LOUISE SOPHIE DE GOUCHY, MARQUISE DE (1764–1822). Daughter of François-Charles, comte de Gouchy, and Marie-Gilberte Freteau, whose father was a *conseiller* at the parlement of Paris. She married Condorcet in 1786 and had a salon at the Hôtel des Monnaies that was frequented by the philosophes. To safeguard her liberty and her property, she divorced Condorcet shortly before his arrest and execution during the Terror. In 1795, she reestablished her salon on the rue de Matignon, where she hosted the idéologues. She lived in retirement under the Restoration. She edited her husband's *Esquisses d'un tableau historique des progrès de l'esprit humaine* and translated Adam Smith's *The Theory of Moral Sentiments* into French.

DEFFAND, MARIE DE VICHY CHAMROND, MARQUISE DU (1697–1780). Born the daughter of Gaspard de Vichy, comte de Chamrond. Married the marquis du Deffand in 1718 but separated from him as soon as she could. Mistress of the historian and poet Charles Hénault until his death in 1770. Her salon on the rue Saint-Dominique, in the former Couvent des Filles de Saint-Joseph, was frequented by writers, artists, and noblemen. She corresponded extensively with Horace Walpole and Voltaire.

DINO, DOROTHÉE DE COURLANDE, DUCHESSE DE (1792–1862). Daughter of Anne-Charlotte Dorothée de Médem and Pierre de Courlande, whose quasi-independent duchy had been eliminated by the third partition of Poland in 1791. Educated by private tutors, she started her career as a salonnière at age thirteen or fourteen, when she and her mother began to receive guests in Berlin. At seventeen, she entered into an arranged marriage with Comte Edmond de Périgord, Talleyrand's nephew, a compulsive gambler, from whom she separated in order to live with her uncle, over whose salon she presided during the Congress of Vienna. After returning to Paris in 1815, she took up residence in the Hôtel de Talleyrand, on the rue Saint-Florentin, before purchasing the Château de Rochecotte on the banks of the Loire. She directed Talleyrand's household and facilitated his political comeback in the wake of the July Revolution by introducing him to the society of the statesmen of the Holy Alliance.

Dosne, Sophie Matheron (1794–1869). Daughter of a Paris merchant. In 1811, she married Alexis-André Dosne, a stockbroker who was appointed *receveur général* at Brest in 1830. When her daughter Elise married Adolphe Thiers in 1833, the latter was twenty years older than his wife and only thirteen years younger than his mother-in-law, with whom he forged a close bond. Madame Dosne furnished Thiers with the financial means to be elected to the Chamber of Deputies and presided over his political salon in a house she built on the place Saint-Georges. Her memoirs demonstrate her close political collaboration with Thiers.

Duras, Claire de Coetnempren de Kersaint, duchesse de (1777–1829). She was the daughter of Comte Guy de Kersaint, a Breton noble and member of the Legislative Assembly and the Convention who was guillotined in December 1793. Claire left France and spent the rest of the Revolution in Philadelphia, Martinique, and England, where she married Amédée de Durfort, the duc de Duras. She returned to France under the Consulate but avoided the imperial court and spent much of her time at the château d'Ussé in Touraine. When the Bourbons returned, the duc de Duras was made a peer and entered the royal household. Duras's salon met at the couple's apartment in the Tuileries. She wrote the novels *Ourika* and *Edouard*, corresponded with Madame de Staël, and was closely associated with René de Chateaubriand.

Genlis, Caroline-Stéphanie du Crest de Saint-Aubin, comtesse de (1746–1830). Wife of the comte de Genlis and niece of Madame de Montesson. She was appointed governess of the children of the duc d'Orléans (later known as Philippe Egalité) before the French Revolution. Exiled in 1792, she returned to France after the 18th Brumaire coup, corresponded with Napoléon on court etiquette, and held a literary salon at the Bibliothécaire de Arsenal. She wrote extensively on education.

Geoffrin, Marie-Thérèse Rodet (1699–1777). Born in Paris and married at fourteen with a substantial dowry to the director of the glassworks at Saint-Gobain. She frequented the salon of Madame de Tencin and began her own salon before the latter's death in 1749. Her guests included mostly artists and men of letters, and she corresponded with the king of Poland, Stanisław August Poniatowski.

GIRARDIN, DELPHINE GAY DE (1804–1855). Born in Aix-la-Chapelle. Journalist and poet, daughter of Sophie Gay. Married Comte Emile de Girardin, founder of the modern French press and a deputy from Bourganeuf (Creuse). From 1834 to 1839, her salon attracted the principal romantic authors in France.

GONTAUT-BIRON, JOSEPHINE-LOUISE, DUCHESSE DE (1772–1857). Governess of the children of the royal family during the Restoration. She followed the Bourbons into exile in 1830 and is known principally through her memoirs.

HELVÉTIUS, ANNE-CATHERINE DE LIGNEVILLE (1720–1800). Married Claude Adrien Helvétius, *fermier général* and philosophe. At their salon on the rue Sainte-Anne, the Helvétiuses received the intellectual celebrities of the eighteenth century. When her husband died in 1771, she lived on the rue d'Auteuil, where she hosted the idéologues.

LA BRICHE, ADÉLAÏDE-EDMÉE PRÉVOST DE LA LIVE DE (1755–1844): She was the daughter of Bon Prévost, *receveur général des fermes* for the duchy of Lorraine, who died when she was six. She was raised by her uncle, Jean Le Maistre de La Martinière, general treasurer of fortifications, and married in 1780 to Alexis-Janvier La Live de La Briche, who served in the household of Queen Marie-Antoinette. Her husband's relations, and his death in 1785, made her rich and gave her access to high society. Her sister-in-law, Madame Houdetot, introduced her to the philosophes and other gens de lettres. Deciding not to remarry, she dedicated herself to her salon on the rue de la Ville-l'Evêque, which outlasted the Revolution, the Empire, and the Restoration. Her daughter married Comte Mathieu Molé, a French politician.

LESPINASSE, JULIE-JEANNE DE (1732–1776). Born at Lyon, the illegitimate daughter of the comtesse d'Albon. In 1754, the aging Madame du Deffand (then almost 60) invited the 22-year-old Lespinasse to live with her, where she then made her debut in the drawing room. After a falling out with Deffand, she started her own salon in 1765 at the Hôtel Hautefort, on the rue Saint-Dominique. Associated with the *Encyclopédistes*, she presided over one of the most celebrated philosophical salons of the eighteenth century.

LIEVEN, DOROTHEA CHRISTOPHORONA VON BEKENDORF, PRINCESSE DE (1785–1857). Born in Riga and married to Prince Christophe de Lieven, who served as the Russian ambassador to London from 1812 to 1834. She presided over an important political and diplomatic salon in London during her husband's tenure. She abandoned her unhappy marriage in 1835 in defiance of the orders of Czar Nicholas I and moved to Paris, where she opened a diplomatic salon in the mezzanine of the Hôtel Talleyrand on the rue Saint-Florentin. With François Guizot as her principal guest, she received important diplomats, members of the Academy, and Orleanist politicians.

MONTCALM-GOZON, ARMANDE-MARIE DE VIGNEROT DU PLESSIS DE RICHELIEU, MARQUISE DE (1777–1832). Eldest sister of the duc de Richelieu, who served as French prime minister from 1816 to 1818, and again in 1821. She was a hunchback in constant bad health, who almost never left home and received guests wrapped up in shawls to hide her deformity. She entered a loveless marriage in 1800 only to separate from her husband in 1808, after which she was free to devote her energy to her salon and her brother's career.

NECKER, SUZANNE CURCHOD (1739–1794). Daughter of a Swiss Calvinist pastor from the village of Crassier and wife of Jacques Necker, a banker from Geneva and Louis XVI's minister of finance, whom she married in 1765. Her salon began in Lausanne and continued in Paris when the Neckers moved to France in 1790. She was the mother of Anne-Louise Germaine Necker, later Madame de Staël.

RÉCAMIER, JEANNE-FRANÇOISE BERNARD (1777–1849). Married a wealthy banker at the age of fifteen and became a well-known Parisian hostess and salonnière during the Directory. Banished from Paris during the Consulat for her association with Madame de Staël, she was best know for her salon at the Abbaye-au-Bois, where René de Chateaubriand was the principal guest.

RUMFORD, MARIE-ANNE DE (1766–1836). Born Marie-Anne Pirette Paulze. Wife of the chemist Antoine-Laurent Lavoisier, who died on the scaffold in 1794, leaving her a wealthy widow. She subsequently married the British-American scientist Benjamin Thompson, who had entered the service of the elector of Bavaria and became a count of the Holy Roman Empire, adopting the title Count Rumford. After separating from Rumford, she presided over a salon for liberals and intellectuals..

STAËL-HOLSTEIN, ANNE-LOUISE-GERMAINE DE, BARONNE DE (1766–1817). Writer, daughter of Jacques Necker. The most celebrated salonnière in Europe from the late 1790s until her death during the early years of the Restoration. Before the Revolution, her salon was at the Swedish embassy in the Hôtel de Salm on the rue de Lille. The Revolution and Napoléon obliged her to flee Paris between 1792 and 1814. She spent much of her time at the Château de Coppet, the family's estate in Switzerland, where she assembled a brilliant collection of European guests.

Notes

INTRODUCTION: The Persistence of Salons

1. Stendhal, *Esquisses de la société parisienne de la politique et de la littérature: Chroniques, 1825–1829* (Paris, 1983), 2:155, 271.

2. Rudolf Apponyi, *Vingt-cinq ans à Paris (1826–1850): Journal du Comte Rodolphe Apponyi, attaché de l'ambassade d'Autriche-Hongrie à Paris* (Paris, 1913–26), 3:73–75.

3. Sébastien-Roch-Nicolas Chamfort, *Maxims et pensées: Anecdotes et caractères* (Paris, 1968), 61.

4. A critique of this literature can be found in Henri Rossi, *Mémoires aristocratiques féminins* (Paris, 1998). The words *salon* and *salonnière* seem to have come into general use in France in the nineteenth century, the former much earlier than the latter. *Le Grand Robert* dates the use of salon in the sense of "lieu de réunion, dans une maison où l'on reçoit régulièrement" to the works of Madame de Staël during the Napoleonic era. Emile Littré sites its earliest use in *Corinne* (1807), and uses it retrospectively to refer to "le salon de Mme Geoffrin, de la marquise du Deffant ont été célèbres au XVIIIe siècle." Prior to the early nineteenth century, the interior meeting places of an aristocratic hôtel in which people gathered for conversation were variably called *alcôves*, *ruelles*, or *chambres*. In more modest homes, the word *cabinet* was common. In the eighteenth and nineteenth centuries, the drawing-room was often next to an adjoining bedroom, which retained its older function as a reception room and was complementary to the salon. Although Littré identified *salonnière* as a neologism in 1873, Le Grand Robert defines the term (along with *salonnarde*) as "une femme qui fréquente les salons" and dates its earliest usage as such to Maupassant in 1880. The masculine form *salonnier* had been used in the 1870s to mean "un journaliste, critique qui rend compt des réunions mondaines." The *Oxford English Dictionary* attributes the use of *salonnière* in the sense of "a woman who holds a salon; a society hostess" to T. S Eliot's *Waste Land Drafts*, written in 1922. *Salonnière* has acquired this sense in the contemporary English-language scholarship on French sociability, and it is how I have used the term throughout. See Joan DeJean, *Tender Geographies: Women and the Origins of the Novel in France* (New York, 1991), 20–21; Benedetta Craveri, *Madame du Deffand and Her World*, trans. Teresa Waugh (Boston, 1994), 70–71; Emile Littré, *Dictionnaire de la langue française* (Paris, 1873), 1812–13; *Le Grand Robert de la langue française*, 12th ed. (Paris, 1985), 559.

5. Our contemporary understanding of French salons is based largely on the following works: Carolyn C. Lougee, *Le Paradis des Femmes: Women, Salons, and Social Stratification in Seventeenth-Century France* (Princeton, 1976); Dena Goodman, *The Republic of Letters: A Cultural History of the French Enlightenment* (Ithaca, N.Y., 1994); Jolanta Pekacz, *Conserva-*

tive Tradition in Pre-Revolutionary France: Parisian Salon Women (New York, 1999); Erica Harth, *Cartesian Women: Versions and Subversions of Rational Discourse in the Old Regime* (Ithaca N.Y., 1992); Jürgen Habermas, *The Structural Transformation of the Public Sphere: An Inquiry into a Category of Bourgeois Society*, trans. Thomas Berger (Cambridge, Mass., 1992).

6. On the historical study of sociability, see Maurice Agulhon, "Introduction: La Sociabilité est-elle objet d'histoire?" in *Sociabilité et société bourgeoise en France, en Allemagne et en Suisse, 1750–1850*, ed. Etienne François (Paris, 1986), 16–17. On political sociability, see Agulhon's *La République au village* (Paris, 1970) and *Le Cercle dans la France bourgeoise* (Paris, 1977). Freemasonry is discussed in Ran Halévi, *Les Loges maçonniques dans la France d'Ancien Régime: Aux origines de la sociabilité démocratique* (Paris, 1984). On sociability in student life and in the working-class café, see Olivier Galland, Mireille Clémençon, Patrick Le Gallès, and Marco Oberti, *Le Monde des étudiants* (Paris, 1995) and Scott Haine, *The World of the Paris Café: Sociability Among the French Working Class, 1789–1914* (Baltimore, 1996). Raymond Huard has looked at traditional institutions of sociability to study the birth of political parties in France, but he does not discuss salons. See Raymond Huard, *La Naissance du parti politique en France* (Paris, 1996).

7. Balzac's views on high society are discussed in Rose Fortassier, *Les Mondains de la Comédie humaine: Etude historique et psychologique* (Paris, 1974), 39, 192, 340. Alfred de Musset, *The Confessions of a Child of the Century*, trans. Kendall Warren (New York, 1892), 12–13.

8. Stendhal, *Scarlet and Black*, trans. Margaret R. B. Shaw (Harmondsworth, UK: Penguin Books, 1953), 266; Marcel Proust, quoted by Pascal Ory, "Le Salon," in *Histoire des droites en France*, ed. Jean-François Sirinelli (Paris, 1992), 2:114. Both Stendhal and Proust elsewhere suggest that the contrary was true, the former by writing as a literary correspondent that the men of Restoration high society were so preoccupied with "their political education that they had forgotten gallantry and paid little attention to women in the salons," and the latter by explaining in *Le Côté de Guermantes* that Madame de Villeparisis's salon was more celebrated in retrospect than Madame Leroi's because it contained more political celebrities. Stendhal, *Esquisses*, 2:250, 295; Marcel Proust, *Remembrance of Things Past*, trans. C. K. Scott Moncrieff (New York, 1934), 1:854.

9. See, e.g., Honoré de Balzac, *The Secrets of La Princesse de Cardignan*, trans. James Waring (Philadelphia, 1899); Victor Hugo, *Les Misérables* (New York, 1938), 3:54. Lamartine, quoted in Edouard Herriot, *Madame Récamier*, trans. Alys Hallard (New York, 1926), 1:177.

10. Virginie Ancelot, *Un Salon de Paris, 1824 à 1864* (Paris, 1866), 148–49. See also Madame Emile de Girardin, *Le Vicomte de Launay: Lettres parisiennes* (Paris, 1869), 1:43; 3:267; 4:82–83.

11. See Adeline Daumard, "La Vie de salon en France dans la première moitié du XIXe siècle," in *Sociabilité et société bourgeoise en France, en Allemagne et en Suisse, 1750–1850*, ed. Etienne François (Paris, 1986), 84.

12. Victor de Balabine, *Paris de 1842 à 1852: La Cour, la société, les moeurs. Journal de Victor de Balabine, secrétaire de l'ambassade de Russie* (Paris, 1914), 104; Vicomte de Beaumont-Vassy, *Les Salons de Paris et la société parisienne sous Louis-Philippe* (Paris, 1866), 258–59.

13. See Guillaume de Bertier de Sauvigny, "L'Aristocratie et monarchie dans la vie culturelle au temps de Louis XVIII et de Charles X," in *Hof, Kultur und Politik im 19. Jahrhundert*, ed. Karl Ferdinand Werner (Bonn, 1985), 64.

14. Fortassier, *Mondains*, 339.

15. Comtesse de Bassanville, *Salons d'autrefois: Souvenirs intimes* (Paris, 1862–66), 2:107.

16. Maurice Agulhon, "Vers une histoire des associations," *Esprit* 6 (1978): 15.

17. Honoré de Balzac, quoted in Fortassier, *Mondains*, 327.

18. See esp. Anne Martin-Fugier, *La Vie élégante, ou la formation de Tout-Paris, 1815–1848* (Paris, 1990), 228.

19. Charles de Rémusat, *Mémoires de ma vie* (Paris, 1959), 3:14, 60–63.

20. Daumard, "Vie de salon," in *Sociabilité et société bourgeoise*, 84.

21. Arno Mayer, *The Persistence of the Old Regime: Europe to the Great War* (New York, 1981); Charles Morazé, quoted in Agulhon, *Cercle*, 18; Edward Berenson, review of *The Invisible Code*, by William Reddy, *American Historical Review* 130, no. 2 (April 1998): 528–29; Otto Dann, "Sociabilité et association," in *Sociabilité et société bourgeoise en France, en Allemagne et en Suisse, 1750–1850*, ed. Etienne François (Paris, 1986), 317.

22. Lougee, *Paradis des Femmes*, 136–69.

23. Elizabeth Goldsmith, *Exclusive Conversations: The Art of Interaction in Seventeenth-Century France* (Philadelphia, 1988), 7–8; Norbert Elias, *The Court Society*, trans. Edmund Jephcott (New York, 1983), 94–95; Goodman, *Republic of Letters*, 117; Pierre Serna, "The Noble," in *Enlightenment Portraits*, ed. Michel Vovelle, trans. Lydia G. Cochrane (Chicago, 1997), 78.

24. Lougee, *Paradis des Femmes*, 51–54, 212.

25. Goldsmith, *Exclusive Conversations*, 8–9; Daniel Gordon, *Citizens Without Sovereignty: Equality and Sociability in French Thought, 1670–1789* (Princeton, 1994), 92–93.

26. David Higgs, *Nobles in Nineteenth-Century France: The Practice of Inegalitarianism* (Baltimore, 1987), 181–82; Mayer, *Persistence of the Old Regime*, 107; Christophe Charle, "Noblesse et élites en France au début du XIXe siècle," in *Les Noblesses européennes au XIXe siècle* (Paris, 1988), 42; Guy Chaussinand-Nogaret, "Le Pouvoir des signes," in *Histoire des élites en France du XVIe au XXe siècle: L'Honneur, le mérite, l'argent*, ed. id. et al. (Paris, 1991), 315.

27. Elias, *Court Society*, 112–13.

28. Habermas, *Structural Transformation*, 30, 127. For an alternative view of the periodization of the salon, see Joan B. Landes, *Women and the Public Sphere in the Age of the French Revolution* (Ithaca, N.Y., 1988), 23; Goodman, *Republic of Letters*, 233–80.

29. Elias, *Court Society*, 1, 50–51; Suzanne Fiette, *La Noblesse française des Lumières à la Belle Epoque* (Paris, 1997), 226.

30. Marie de Flavigny, comtesse d'Agoult (Daniel Stern), *Mémoires, souvenirs et journaux de la comtesse d'Agoult* (Paris, 1990), 206–7. See Noémi Hepp, "La Galanterie," in *Les Lieux de mémoire*, ed. Pierre Nora (Paris, 1992), 3, 2:748–49; Marc Fumaroli, "La Conversation," in ibid., 679–743.

31. See, e.g., Joseph-Alexandre Ségur, *Women, Their Condition and Influence in Society* (London, 1803), 1:v–vi, xii–xiii. At a time when Napoléon's jurists were codifying separate spheres and women's inferior status, Ségur wrote that the "reign of terror was, in France, the production of men alone. The women were only its victims. Robespierre found among them neither a mistress nor a friend; and it is to the courageous arm of a woman that France owes the happiness of being delivered from the horrible monster Marat." Ibid., 10–11, 230–31.

32. Fiette, *Noblesse française*, 40, 223; Jolanta Pekacz, "Whose Muses? Parisian Salon Women from the French Revolution to 1848" (MS), 2–3.

33. Huard, *Naissance du parti politique*, 28–29, 360–61; Augustin Challamel, *Les Clubs contre-révolutionnaires: Cercles, comités, sociétés, salons, réunions, cafés, restaurants et librairies* (Paris, 1895), 498–500.

34. Huard, *Naissance du parti politique*, 42–45.

35. Etienne-Denis Pasquier, *A History of My Time: Memoirs of Chancellor Pasquier*, ed. Duc d'Audiffret-Pasquier, trans. Charles E. Roche (London, 1894), 1:522–23.

36. Many historians see a more decisive connection between the Napoleonic Code and women's political status, insisting that the exclusionary impulses that deprived women of political rights "dated from the Napoleonic years," or that the Napoleonic Code "firmly excluded women" from participation in politics (as if they had been participating before), or that it "consecrated and aggravated" the work of the Revolution with regard to women's status, or that it "extended . . . and made more systematic" the accomplishments of the Jacobin Republic. See William M. Reddy, *The Invisible Code: Honor and Sentiment in Postrevolutionary France, 1814–1848* (Berkeley, Calif., 1997), xi, 69, 229; Bronislaw Baczko, "Femmes: Une Singularité française," *Le Débat* 87 (1995): 119; Keith Michael Baker, "Defining the Public Sphere in Eighteenth-Century France: Variations on a Theme by Habermas," in *Habermas and the Public Sphere*, ed. Craig Calhoun (Cambridge, Mass., 1992), 200–201.

37. The conventional account of women's exclusion from the public sphere and the end of salon culture at the time of the French Revolution is most closely associated with the work of Dena Goodman and Joan Landes. See Goodman, *Republic of Letters*, 233–80; Landes, *Women and the Public Sphere*. For an alternative analysis, see Steven D. Kale, "Women, the Public Sphere, and the Persistence of Salons," *French Historical Studies* 25, no. 1 (Winter 2002): 115–48.

CHAPTER ONE: Between the Republic of Letters and the *Grand Monde*

1. Henriette Lucie Dillon, marquise de La Tour du Pin Gouvernet, *Memoirs of Madame de La Tour du Pin*, trans. Felice Harcourt (New York, 1969, 1971), 17.

2. Joan DeJean, "Amazons et femmes des lettres: Pouvoirs politiques et littéraires à l'âge classique," in *Femmes et pouvoirs sous l'Ancien Régime*, ed. Danielle Haase-Dubose and Eliane Viennit (Paris, 1991), 156–57; Joan DeJean, "Salons, 'Preciosity,' and Women's Influence," in *A New History of French Literature*, ed. Denis Hollier (Cambridge, Mass., 1994), 301; Claude Dulong, "From Conversation to Creation," in *A History of Women*, vol. 3: *Renaissance and Enlightenment Paradoxes*, ed. Natalie Davis and Arlette Farge (Cambridge, Mass., 1993), 405–6.

3. On the salon's "Cartesian moment," see Harth, *Cartesian Women*, 33, 64–65, 139.

4. Ibid., 33, 54–65, 135–39, 149; Dulong, "From Conversation to Creation," 407; DeJean, "Amazons," 161–62; Joan DeJean, "(Literary) World at War, or What Can Happen When Women Go Public," in *Going Public: Women and Publishing in Early Modern France*, ed. Elizabeth C. Goldsmith and Dena Goodman (Ithaca, N.Y., 1995), 118; DeJean, *Tender Geographies*, 21; Lougee, *Paradis des femmes*, 70–71.

5. DeJean, "Salons, 'Preciosity,' and Women's Influence," 299–300; Landes, *Women and the Public Sphere*, 54; Erica Harth, "The Salon Woman Goes Public . . . or Does She?" in *Going Public: Women and Publishing in Early Modern France*, ed. Elizabeth C. Goldsmith and Dena Goodman (Ithaca, N.Y., 1995), 179–93; Harth, *Cartesian Women*, 149; Madelyn

Gutwirth, *The Twilight of the Goddesses: Women and Representation in the French Revolutionary Era* (New Brunswick, N.J., 1991), 90.

6. Dena Goodman, "Seriousness of Purpose: Salonières, Philosophes, and the Shaping of the Eighteenth-Century Salon," *Proceedings of the Annual Meeting of the Western Society for French History* 15 (1988): 111; Dena Goodman, "Enlightenment Salons: The Convergence of Female and Philosophic Ambitions," *Eighteenth-Century Studies* 22 (1989): 332; Goodman, *Republic of Letters*, 74–76, 89.

7. The evolutionary, or progressive, model is especially pronounced in Roger Picard's *Les Salons littéraires et la société française, 1610–1789* (New York, 1943), 136–47.

8. Goodman, *Republic of Letters*, 89, 90–91; Goodman, "Enlightenment Salons," 335; Fumaroli, "Conversation," 706; Suzanne Delorme, "Le Salon de la marquise de Lambert, berceau de *l'Encyclopédie*," in *L'Encyclopédie et le progrès des sciences et techniques*, ed., René Taton and Suzanne Delorme (Paris, 1952), 21; Marguerite Glotz and Madeleine Marie, *Salons du XVIIIe siècle* (Paris, 1949), 14; Comte d'Haussonville, *The Salon of Madame Necker*, trans. Henry M. Trollop (London, 1882), 1:110–11.

9. Ancelot, *Salon de Paris*, 95; Charlotte Louise d'Osmond, comtesse de Boigne, *Memoirs of the Comtesse de Boigne (1781–1830)*, ed. Charles Nicoullaud (London, 1913), 1:ix, xviii; 2:296.

10. Goodman, "Enlightenment Salons," 183–99; Gordon, *Citizens Without Sovereignty*, 191; Benedetta Craveri, *Madame du Deffand and Her World*, trans. Teresa Waugh (Boston, 1982), 64.

11. Agoult, *Mémoires*, 266; Duras to Staël, September 3, 1816, in Joseph d'Haussonville, *Femmes d'autrefois, hommes d'aujourd'hui* (Paris, 1912), 212; Bassanville, *Salons d'autrefois*, 1:3.

12. Goodman presents a salonnière's apprenticeship as a sort of scholarly training involving "careful study" with a mentor and leading to "mastership." Goodman, *Republic of Letters*, 74–76.

13. Margaret Darrow, "French Noblewomen and the New Domesticity, 1750–1850," *Feminist Studies* 5, no. 1 (Spring 1979): 45; Evelyn G. Bodek, "Salonniers and Bluestockings: Educated Obsolescence and Germinating Feminism," *Feminist Studies* 3 (Spring 1976): 186; Marie d'Agoult, *Mes souvenirs, 1803–1833* (Paris, 1877), 113–14, 346–47.

14. Craveri, *Madame du Deffand*, 66; Goodman, "Enlightenment Salons," 333.

15. Charles de Rémusat, *Mémoires*, 2:80–81; Victor de Broglie, *Souvenirs, 1785–1870* (Paris, 1886), 2:9; Charlotte d'Osmond, comtesse de Boigne, *Mémoires de la comtesse de Boigne: Récits d'une tante*, ed. Jean-Claude Berchet (Paris, 1986), 2:301–2; Sylvie Aprile, "Bourgeoise et républicaine, deux termes inconciliables," in *Femmes dans la cité, 1815–1871*, ed. Alain Corbin et al. (Grâne, 1997), 220.

16. Boigne, *Mémoires*, 3:2; Charles de Rémusat, *Mémoires*, 1:174; 2:81; Gilbert Stenger, *La Société française pendant le Consulat* (Paris, 1903–5), 3:379, 396–97.

17. Daumard, "Vie de salon," in *Sociabilité et société bourgeoise*, 89.

18. Marmontel, quoted in Chartier, "The Man of Letters," in *Enlightenment Portraits*, ed. Michel Vovelle, trans. Lydia G. Cochrane (Chicago: University of Chicago Press, 1997), 155; Kathleen O'Meara, *Un Salon à Paris: Madame Mohl et ses intimes* (Paris, 1886), 162; Ancelot, *Salon de Paris*, x.

19. Craveri, *Madame du Deffand*, 89; Sophie Gay, *Salons célèbres* (Paris, 1882), 3; Ancelot, *Salon de Paris*, 174.

20. Boigne, *Mémoires*, 2:6.

21. Villemain, quoted in Gabriel Pailhès, *La Duchesse de Duras et Chateaubriand d'après des documents inédites* (Paris, 1910), 148–49, 277; Dorothée Dino, *Memoirs of the Duchesse de Dino, 1836–1850*, ed. Marie Radziwill (New York, 1910), 3:178; Marmontel, quoted in Chartier, "Man of Letters," 157.

22. See comments by Marmontel, Morellet, and Friedrich Melchior Grimm on the restrictive nature of conversation in the salons of Madame Geoffrin and Madame Necker in Jean-François Marmontel, *Mémoires*, ed. John Renwick (Clermont-Ferrand, 1972), André Morellet, *Mémoires sur le dix-huitième siècle et sur la Révolution* (Paris, 1988), and Friedrich Melchior Grimm, *Les Salons de Paris sous la Révolution* (Paris, 1900).

23. Baron de Staël, quoted by E. Lairtullier, *Les Femmes célèbres de 1789 à 1795, et leur influence dans la Révolution* (Paris, 1840), 109.

24. Thomas, quoted in Daniel Gordon, "Philosophy, Sociology, and Gender in the Enlightenment Conception of Public Opinion," *French Historical Studies* 17, no. 4 (Fall 1992): 907; Staël, quoted in Lairtullier, *Femmes célèbres*, 109.

25. Goodman, *Republic of Letters*, 5–6, 57–60, 91, 100–101; Goodman, "Governing the Republic of Letters," 187. Goodman takes issue with Alan Kors's *D'Holbach's Coterie: An Enlightenment in Paris* (Princeton, 1976), 92–97, and Daniel Roche's "Salons, lumières, engagement politique," in *Les Républicains des lettres: Gens de culture et lumières au XVIIIe siècle* (Paris, 1988), 247–48. Kors and Roche fail to demonstrate that salons embodied the triumph of style over substance, but Goodman forgets that the philosophes were willing to make sacrifices in exchange for an audience in le monde.

26. Jolanta Pekacz, "Political Correctness for Polite Society: Pro-Monarchical Ideas of *Honnêteté* in Seventeenth- and Eighteenth-Century France" (MS), 6; Harth, *Cartesian Women*, 191; Harth, "Salon Woman Goes Public," in *Going Public*, 192.

27. Lougee, *Paradis des Femmes*, 52, 211–13.

28. Goodman, *Republic of Letters*, 114.

29. Stéphanie Félicité Genlis, *Memoirs of the Comtesse de Genlis, Illustrative of the History of the Eighteenth and Nineteenth Centuries* (New York, 1825), 1:42, 86–87, 319–20. Fumaroli, "Conversation," 706.

30. Goodman and Landes argue that the acquisition of manners by bourgeois intellectuals was an act of "usurpation" or "appropriation" that transferred control over the definition of social status from the nobility to the bourgeoisie. Goodman elaborates on this point by asserting that men of letters took only the rule-making aspect of aristocratic politesse to bring order to their normally disputatious deliberations. She also insists that the philosophes needed salons to be "upwardly mobile" but that they "now sought entry [into] the new Republic of Letters" rather than the "old aristocracy." But why would men of letters need to define social status in order to enter a Republic of Letters to which they already belonged? And how could they have usurped only the rule-making aspect of politesse if they continued to attend salons in which salonnières had the power to insist upon civility? Goodman uses various arguments about the discursive aspects of salon sociability in order to claim that the Republic of Letters gained its autonomy from le monde. I find this argument unconvincing. See Goodman, *Republic of Letters*, 97, 113, Goodman, "Enlightenment Salons," 330, and Landes, *Women and the Public Sphere*, 24, 55.

31. Duclos and d'Alembert quoted in Craveri, *Madame du Deffand*, 60–61.

32. Landes, *Women and the Public Sphere*, 24.

33. Ségur, *Women*, 2:227–28; Genlis, *Memoirs*, 1:320. See also Lougee, *Paradis des Femmes*, 170 and Fiette, *Noblesse française*, 32. Goldsmith says that in the seventeenth

century, "when traditional signs of social status were becoming less rigid, the norms for behavior in polite society were becoming more hierarchical." Goldsmith, *Exclusive Conversations*, 4.

34. Our conceptual language is almost always inadequate, especially, perhaps, with regard to class and culture, in light of the failure of a variety of applications of Marxist categories of analysis. Salons were aristocratic not because all salonnières and their guests were nobles (although many were) but because it is conceptually fruitful to see the attitudes, purposes, and practices with which they are associated as aristocratic. Many well-known eighteenth-century salonnières were grandes dames who belonged to the *noblesse d'épée* and whose families held a high rank at court (Mesdames de Lambert, d'Aiguillon, du Deffand, de Robecq). Others hailed from the *grande bourgeoisie* (Helvétius, Geoffrin, Necker) or were patronized by nobles (Lespinasse, Graffigny). All had or acquired the resources to possess a suitable space. If anything, nineteenth-century salonnières seem even more often to have been of noble birth, although the social, political, and ideological diversity of the French nobility and the intensity of its interactions with other classes makes this sort of sociological roll call seem pretty pointless. Thinking about the salon as an aristocratic institution has the greatest explicative capacity.

35. For an alternative view, see the work of Daniel Gordon, who argues that the habit of eschewing "the hierarchical distinctions and deferential norms stemming from corporate life" in polite society complemented an effort by its participants "to define a sphere of practice that was based on the egalitarian premises of natural law." Gordon, *Citizens Without Sovereignty*, 30, 68–69, 93, 111; id., "Philosophy, Sociology, and Gender," 905.

36. Genlis, *Memoirs*, 1:330; Boigne, *Memoirs*, 2:147–49.

37. Gutwirth, *Twilight of the Goddesses*, 98. On this point, see also Agulhon, "Vers une histoire des associations," 16, Agulhon, *Cercle*, 25–29, and Elias, *Court Society*, 62.

38. On the "courtly art of observing people," see Elias, *Court Society*, 104–7. On Deffand's prose portraits, see Craveri, *Madame du Deffand*, 71–72.

39. This point has often been made too emphatically. See, e.g., Picard, *Salons littéraires*, 52, Roger Chartier, *The Cultural Origins of the French Revolution*, trans. Lydia G. Cochrane (Durham, N.C., 1991), 22, and Fumaroli, "Conversation," 695.

40. La Tour du Pin, *Memoirs*, 82; A. Morellet, *Eloges de Madame Géoffrin, contemporaine de Madame du Deffand* (Paris, 1812), v–vi.

41. Goodman, *Republic of Letters*, 75–76, 103–5; Goodman, "Enlightenment Salons," 332–33.

42. See Daniel Gordon, "Beyond the Social History of Ideas: Morellet and the Enlightenment," in *André Morellet (1727–1819) in the Republic of Letters and the French Revolution*, ed. Jeffrey Merrick and Dorothy Medlin (New York, 1995), 50–51, Craveri, *Madame du Deffand*, 89, and Olwen Hufton, *The Prospect Before Her: A History of Women in Western Europe* (New York, 1996), 1:435.

43. Goodman, *Republic of Letters*, 75. Harth comments that eighteenth-century salonnières presided over a "masculine star system." Harth, *Cartesian Women*, 33.

44. Grimm, *Salons de Paris*, 17. According to Goodman, the argument that Enlightenment salonnières formed salons "to gain fame and power through associations with brilliant and powerful men" was put forward by the same brilliant and powerful men who frequented salons. Goodman, *Republic of Letters*, 75.

45. Horace Walpole, quoted in Glotz and Marie, *Salons du XVIIIe siècle*, 19; Picard, *Salons littéraires*, 156; Craveri, *Madame du Deffand*, 164–65; Jules de Goncourt and Ed-

mond de Goncourt, *The Woman of the Eighteenth Century, Her Life, from Birth to Death, Her Love and Her Philosophy in the Worlds of Salon, Shop and Street*, trans. Jacques Le Clercq and Ralph Roeder (New York, 1927), 56–57.

46. Dale Van Kley, "In Search of Eighteenth-Century Parisian Public Opinion," *French Historical Studies* 19, no. 1 (1995): 225.

47. Lougee, *Paradis des Femmes*, 170; Elias, *Court Society*, 78–79; Goncourt, *Woman of the Eighteenth Century*, 41; *Lettres de Monsieur le Chevalier de Méré*, quoted in Gordon, *Citizens Without Sovereignty*, 101–2.

48. Landes, *Women and the Public Sphere*, 23–25; Gordon, *Citizens Without Sovereignty*, 141, 192; Goodman, *Republic of Letters*, 95–97; Dena Goodman, "Public Sphere and Private Life: Toward a Synthesis of Current Historiographical Approaches to the Old Regime," *History and Theory* 31, no. 1 (1992): 17–18. Ironically, Habermas never made a sharp distinction between "good society" and the court, preferring instead to see the former as a "free-floating . . . sphere" bifurcated into "a vehicle for the representation of the monarch" and "an enclave . . . separating itself from the state." Habermas's characterization of the "early public" as "compris[ing] both court and 'town' " is closer to Fumaroli's image of a nearby court as the object but not the theater of conversation and Goldsmith's conception of a free passage between two worlds distinguished by degrees of hospitality and exclusivity. Salon life, Goldsmith says, "was thought to be sheltered from the distractions of courtly politics, while very much committed to cultivating ideal courtly behavior." Habermas, *Structural Transformation*, 10–11; Fumaroli, "Conversation," 694; Goldsmith, *Exclusive Conversations*, 7, 44.

49. La Tour du Pin, *Memoirs*, 81–82, 341–42.

50. Ségur, *Women*, 233.

51. Boigne, *Memoirs*, 1:17, suggested that social leveling in le monde toward the end of the eighteenth century encouraged increased discrimination: "The increase of wealth among the middle classes had induced all of inferior rank to adopt the manners and customs of high society, and, not withstanding the absurd regulation which demanded proof of nobility in the case of any would-be officer, anyone who had wealth and education could enter the service. Rank and wealth were thus hand-in-glove, both in garrison and in all Paris society, but the balls of Versailles restored the line of demarcation in the most uncompromising manner."

52. René Dujarric de la Rivière, *Dames de la Révolution* (Périgueux, 1963), 10–11; Helen Clergue, *The Salon: A Study of French Society and Personalities in the Eighteenth Century* (New York, 1907), 98–99; Boigne, *Memoirs*, 1:42; La Tour du Pin, *Memoirs*, 109; Fiette, *Noblesse française*, 31–32; Léon Abensour, *La Femme et le féminisme avant la Révolution* (Paris, 1923), 136–37.

53. La Tour du Pin, *Memoirs*, 109.

54. Saint-Simon, quoted in Picard, *Salons littéraires*, 62; Galiani, quoted in Goodman, *Republic of Letters*, 89.

55. Genlis, *Memoirs*, 1:321.

56. Baron Auguste-François Fauveau de Frénilly, quoted in Christian de Bartillat, *Histoire de la noblesse française, 1789–1989* (Paris, 1988), 1:45; Stenger, *Société française*, 3:312; Goncourt, *Woman of the Eighteenth Century*, 41; Pasquier, *History of My Time*, 1:19. Pasquier suggested that there were more than thirty salons that were open to him, not that there were a total of thirty in the world of the Paris magistracy. His colleagues had "the habit of meeting frequently and of exchanging ideas."

57. Goodman, *Republic of Letters*, 233, 274. On the proliferation of salons in the eighteenth century, see Fumaroli, "Conversation," 687; Dulong, "From Conversation to Creation," 416; and Daniel Mornet, *La Vie parisienne au XIXe siècle: Leçons faites à l'Ecole des hautes études sociales* (Paris, 1914). On the limited place of Enlightenment salons in le monde and the vast dimensions of "the world on the Seine," see Robert Forster, *The House of Saulx-Tavanes: Versailles and Burgundy, 1700–1830* (Baltimore, 1971), 117, and id., review of *The Republic of Letters*, by Dena Goodman, *Journal of Modern History* 71, no. 1 (March 1999): 214–15.

58. Agoult, *Mémoires*, 163.

59. La Tour du Pin, *Memoirs*, 17.

60. Virginie Ancelot, *Les Salons de Paris: Foyers éteints* (Paris, 1858), 26–27; Craveri, *Madame du Deffand*.

61. Paul de Zurich, *Une Femme heureuse: Madame de La Briche (1755–1844)* (Paris, 1934), 251–55.

62. "Les salons se sont multipliés et diversifiés" in the eighteenth century, Jacqueline Hellegouarc'h observes. "Ce ne sont seulement les nobles et les parlementaires de haut rang qui tiennent cercle." Hellegouarc'h, *L'Esprit de société: Cercles et "salons" parisiens au XVIIIe siècle* (Paris, 2000), 23.

63. Details drawn from the following sources: Jules Bertaut, *Les Belles émigrés* (Paris, 1948), 84–87; Laure d'Abrantès, *Salons révolutionnaires* (Paris, 1989), 141; Henri d'Alméras, *La Vie parisienne sous la Révolution et le Directoire* (Paris, 1925), 290; Agénor Bardoux, *La Comtesse Pauline de Beaumont* (Paris, 1889), 62–64; Challamel, *Clubs contre-révolutionnaires*, 554–56; Goncourt, *Woman of the Eighteenth Century*, 327–28; Edmond de Goncourt and Jules de Goncourt, *Histoire de la société française pendant la Révolution* (1864; reprint, Geneva, 1971), 17; Vicomte de Reiset, *Les Reines de l'émigration: Louise d'Esparbès, Comtesse de Polastron* (Paris, 1907), 65–67.

64. Goodman argues that the Republic of Letters appropriated the salon to create a new form of cultural practice and to gain "the independent ground" from which to challenge the monarchy and the aristocracy. She also estimates that salons served this function for less than two decades, from roughly 1765 to the mid 1780s. See Goodman, "Governing the Republic of Letters," 184; id., *Republic of Letters*, 3, 24, 41, 83, 91, 95–99, 118–19, 238, 242; id., "Enlightenment Salons," 330–31, 336–39.

65. Auguste-François Fauveau de Frénilly, *Mémoires, 1768–1828: Souvenirs d'un ultra-royaliste* (Paris, 1987), 92.

66. Tocqueville, *The Old Regime and the French Revolution*, trans. Stuart Gilbert (New York, 1955), 142; Victorine de Chastenay, *Mémoires, 1771–1815* (Paris, 1987), 28.

67. Pasquier, *History of My Time*, 1:19–20; Anne Goldgar, *Impolite Learning: Conduct and Community in the Republic of Letters, 1680–1750* (New Haven, 1995), 230–31, 238; Malesherbes quoted in Craveri, *Madame du Deffand*, 61.

68. Goodman, *Republic of Letters*, 56; Goodman, "Governing the Republic of Letters," 188; Craveri, *Madame du Deffand*, 182–83; Chartier, "Man of Letters," 153–54, 160; Kors, *D'Holbach's Coterie*, 214–16; Francis Steegmuller, *A Man, a Woman, and Two Kingdoms: The Story of Madame d'Epinay and the Abbé Galiani* (New York, 1991), 143–44; Robert Darnton, *The Literary Underground of the Old Regime* (Cambridge, Mass., 1982), 4.

69. Landes, *Women and the Public Sphere*, 57; Darnton, *Literary Underground*, 1–7, 23–24, 40. Goodman asserts that Darnton is betraying "masculinist assumptions that mask the role of women in the cultural practices of the French Enlightenment" in arguing that the

philosophes were "domesticated" by le monde. See Goodman, *Republic of Letters*, 71–73, 99–100.

70. Tocqueville, *Old Regime*, 142. François Furet makes Tocqueville's paradox seem all the more perplexing by insisting that the Enlightenment provided many nobles with "the century's political alternative." Furet, *Interpreting the French Revolution*, trans. Elborg Forster (Cambridge, 1981), 114.

71. See Guy Chaussinand-Nogaret, *The French Nobility in the Eighteenth Century: From Feudalism to Enlightenment*, trans. William Doyle (Cambridge, 1985), 129.

72. Tocqueville, *Old Regime*, 142.

73. Fiette, *Noblesse française*, 49–51. For contrary views, see Chartier, *Cultural Origins*, 31, 37; Goodman, *Republic of Letters*, 118.

74. Fiette, *Noblesse française*, 10, 23; Chaussinand-Nogaret, *Histoire des élites*, 258–59; Reddy, *Invisible Code*, 10.

75. Serna, "The Noble," in *Enlightenment Portraits*, 54–57, 77–78; Chaussinand-Nogaret, *French Nobility*, 73–74, 129; La Tour du Pin, *Memoirs*, 95.

76. Edward Butler Lytton and Mrs. Trollope, quoted in A.-D. Toledano, *La Vie de famille sous la Restauration et la Monarchie de Juillet* (Paris, 1943), 80–81.

77. Goncourt, *Woman of the Eighteenth Century*, 243–51, 250, 330–31; id., *Histoire de la société française pendant la Révolution*, 1–2.

78. See, e.g., Abensour, *Femme*, 72, which recapitulates themes that go back to Montesquieu's *Persian Letters*, in which Rica finds that no business whatsoever can be contracted in France without " a woman through whose hands all favors . . . have to pass." When Rousseau arrived in Paris, Père Castel told him: "One does nothing [here] without women." Montesquieu, *Persian Letters* (New York, 1973), 92; Glotz and Marie, *Salons du XVIIIe siècle*, 12.

79. Abensour, *Femme*, 70–71, 82, 303, 461; Goncourt, *Woman of the Eighteenth Century*, 56, 244, 297–98; Gay, *Salon célèbres*, 10.

80. See esp. Landes, *Women and the Public Sphere*, 20–24; Lougee, *Paradis des Femmes*, 5; Gutwirth, *Twilight of the Goddesses*, 86; Michelle Perrot, "Un Histoire sans affrontements," *Le Débat* 87 (November–December 1995): 131; DeJean, "Salons, 'Preciosity,' and Women's Influence," 298; Geneviève Fraisse, *Reason's Muse: Sexual Difference and the Birth of Democracy*, trans. Jane Marie Todd (Chicago, 1994), 95; Sara Maza, "Women's Voices in Literature and Art," in *A New History of French Literature*, ed. Denis Hollier (Cambridge, Mass., 1994), 623.

81. See Mona Ozouf, *Women's Words: Essay on French Singularity*, trans. Jane Marie Todd (Chicago, 1997), 229–83; Elizabeth Badinter, *De l'identité masculine* (Paris, 1992); Gutwirth, *Twilight of the Goddesses*, xv. Goodman's work represents a qualified exception. Although she agrees that France's "extreme sociability" and the public role it accorded women distinguishes France from other countries, she objects to fact that in the eighteenth century "salonnières were often tarred with the same brush as women of the court." Goodman is mostly interested in defending the boundary between "Habermas's two public spheres," the absolutist and the authentic, but in doing so, she correctly removes salonnières from "the secrecy of court politics," where they are "reduced to intriguers and influence peddlers." Goodman, "Governing the Republic of Letters," 194; id., *Republic of Letters*, 5; id., "Public Sphere and Private Life," 16–18.

82. Haussonville, *Salon of Madame Necker*, 1:105; Genlis, *Memoirs*, 2:243–44.

83. Under what definition of the political could salons be considered part of the political sphere? Chaussinand-Nogaret argues that politics could only have been "effective" at court until the system established by Louis XIV "fell apart" in the eighteenth century. By contrast, Chartier suggests that salons were political by nature because their "individualistic and egalitarian modes of operation" defied the society of orders at the representational level and because they provided a place in which autonomous individuals could make rational judgments about the state. For Goodman, salonnières were not involved in courtly politics but acted politically by shaping public opinion; for Gordon, they helped invent an alternative to absolutism by investing the acts of private life with public significance, which is close to the notion of the political elaborated by Maza, who tried to show that a repressive regime forced the French to use their private lives to air political disputes. Susan Conner, however, insists that political intervention be defined "as activities that take place either within formal government institutions or through informal channels to power" that consciously and purposefully put pressure "on the governing group" in an organized manner. On the one hand, Conner's definition would bar from consideration all political activities that did not take place either at court or through modern political institutions — like parties or unions — that had not yet been created. On the other hand, Maza's much broader sense of "public affairs," while more conceptually fruitful with regard to the Old Regime, makes everything that took place in private potentially political. Chaussinand-Nogaret, *French Nobility*, 9–10; Chartier, *Cultural Origins*, 16, 162; Goodman, *Republic of Letters*, 12, 139, 303; Gordon, *Citizens Without Sovereignty*, 3, 112, 137, 243; Sara Maza, *Private Lives and Public Affairs: The Causes Célèbres of Prerevolutionary France* (Berkeley, Calif., 1993); Susan P. Conner, "Women and Politics," in *French Women in the Age of Enlightenment*, ed. Samia I. Spenser (Bloomington, Ind., 1984), 50.

84. Abensour, *Femme*, 154–56; La Tour du Pin, *Memoirs*, 92.

85. Fumaroli, "Conversation," 695.

86. Picard, *Salons littéraires*, 342; Simone Balayé, *Madame de Staël: Lumières et liberté* (Paris, 1979), 12–13; Madelyn Gutwirth, *Madame de Staël, Novelist: The Emergence of the Artist as Woman* (Urbana, Ill., 1978), 29.

87. Haussonville, *Salon of Madame Necker*, 2:67–68, 159–60.

88. Balayé, *Madame de Staël*, 24; Pekacz, "Political Correctness for Polite Society," 5; Picard, *Salons littéraires*, 350.

89. Haussonville, *Salon of Madame Necker*, 1:110; 2:118–20, 182–83.

90. Boigne, *Memoirs*, 1:29; La Tour du Pin, *Memoirs*, 95.

91. René de Chateaubriand, *Mémoires d'outre-tombe* (Paris, 1910), 1:277; Laure d'Abrantès, *Histoire des salons de Paris* (Paris, 1837–38), 2:375; Habermas, *Structural Transformation*, 14.

92. La Tour du Pin, *Memoirs*, 61; Pasquier, *History of My Time*, 1:20, 57–58, Zurich, *Femme heureuse*, 112.

93. Habermas, *Structural Transformation*, 70; Challamel, *Clubs contre-révolutionnaires*, 3.

94. Keith Michael Baker, "Politics and Public Opinion Under the Old Regime: Some Reflections," in *Press and Politics in Pre-Revolutionary France*, ed. Jack Censer and Jeremy D. Popkin (Berkeley, Calif., 1987), 209, 212–13.

95. Chastenay, *Mémoires*, 54; Haussonville, *Salon of Madame Necker*, 2:148; Abrantès, *Salons révolutionnaires*, 39–40.

CHAPTER TWO: Liberals and Emigrés (1789–1799)

1. Habermas, *Structural Transformation*, 69–70; Chateaubriand, *Mémoires d'outre-tombe*, 2:293–94; *Atlas de la Révolution française*, vol. 4: *Les Sociétés politiques*, ed. J. Boutier et al. (Paris, 1992).

2. Jules Bertaut, *Les Parisiens sous la Révolution* (Paris, 1952), 27–29; Joseph Turquan, *Les Femmes de l'émigration, 1789–1815* (Paris, 1911–12), 10; Mme. Lenormant, *Quatre femmes au temps de la Révolution* (Paris, 1872), 313; François Guizot, *Madame de Rumford (1758–1836)* (Paris, 1841), 10; Goncourt, *Histoire de la société française pendant la Révolution*, 15; Fiette, *Noblesse française*, 107–8.

3. Agulhon, *Cercle*, 70.

4. Bertaut, *Parisiens*, 34; Challamel, *Clubs contre-révolutionnaires*, 553–55.

5. Victor Du Bled, *Le Rôle social et mondaine de la femme depuis le Moyen Age*, vol. 4 of *La Femme dans la nature, dans les moeurs, dans la legende, dans la société* (Paris, 1908), 89; Challamel, *Clubs contre-révolutionnaires*, 11–12, 555; Chateaubriand, *Mémoires d'outre-tombe*, 1:296–97; Goncourt, *Histoire de la société française pendant la Révolution*, 15; Chastenay, *Mémoires*, 81.

6. See the testimony in Frénilly, *Mémoires*, 91; Chastenay, *Mémoires*, 85–86; Bertaut, *Parisiens*, 35. Upon returning from Russia in 1791, Comte Louis-Philippe de Ségur found Parisian society transformed: "I spent my evenings traveling through the various circles of the capital to see once again the social gatherings that had given my youth such charm, but political passions had invaded them and had turned them into Roman forums, where the most opposed opinions collided and clashed ceaselessly. People no longer discussed. They argued, and they argued uniquely and eternally about politics." Ségur, quoted in Antoine Guillois, *Le Salon de Madame Helvétius: Cabanis et les Idéologues* (New York, 1971), 79.

7. Jacques de Saint-Victor, "L'Action parlementaire et les clubs contre-révolutionnaires," in *La Contre-Révolution*, ed. Jean Tulard (Paris, 1990), 36.

8. Huard, *Naissance du parti politique*, 27; Fiette, *Noblesse française*, 88; Saint-Victor, "Action parlementaire," 36, 51; Henri d'Alméras, *La Vie parisienne sous la Révolution et le Directoire* (Paris, 1926), 78–79.

9. Saint-Victor, "Action parlementaire," 52; Challamel, *Clubs contre-révolutionnaires*, 132–33; Abrantès, *Histoire des salons*, 2:39.

10. Frénilly, *Mémoires*, 92; Challamel, *Clubs contre-révolutionnaires*, 555, 558–59; Bertaut, *Parisiens*, 35.

11. Joseph Weber, *Mémoires concernant Marie-Antoinette* (London, 1804–9), 2:61; Alméras, *Vie parisienne sous la Révolution*, 78; Saint-Victor, "Action parlementaire," 36–38, 51–53.

12. Abrantès, *Salons révolutionnaires*, 47, 51; id., *Memoirs of Madame Junot (Duchesse d'Abrantès)* (London, 1910), 1:80; 2:172; id., *Histoire des salons*, 2:209, 217, 375; 4:115.

13. See La Tour du Pin, *Memoirs*, 107; Pasquier, *History of My Time*, 1:61; Ségur, quoted in Du Bled, *Rôle social et mondaine de la femme*, 111–12; Chastenay, *Mémoires*, 112–13.

14. Bertaut, *Belles émigrés*, 100; Zurich, *Femme heureuse*, 261, 283; Jules Bertaut, *Egéries du XVIIIe siècle* (Paris, 1928), 56–57; Vicomte Hervé de Broc, *Dix ans de la vie d'une femme pendant l'émigration: Adélaïde de Kerjean, marquise de Falaiseau d'après des lettres inédites et des souvenirs de famille* (Paris, 1893), 26.

15. Madame de Staël, *Considérations sur la Révolution française* (Paris, 1818), 1:199–200.

Madame de La Tour du Pin described Staël in this period as "at the full height of her youthful enthusiasm, interested alike in politics, science, learning, intrigue, and love." La Tour du Pin, *Memoirs*, 188.

    16. Tocqueville, *Old Regime*, 145–46.

    17. Abrantès, *Histoire des salons*, 2:394; Balayé, *Madame de Staël*, 32; Madame de Staël, *Des Circonstances actuelle qui peuvent terminer la Révolution et des principes qui doivent fonder la République en France* (Paris, 1979), 19.

    18. Habermas, *Structural Transformation*, 99; Balayé, *Madame de Staël*, 96.

    19. Abrantès, *Histoire des salons*, 2:391.

    20. See G. E. Gwynne, *Madame de Staël et la Révolution française: Politique, philosophie, littérature* (Paris, 1969), 13–21; Balayé, *Madame de Staël*, 34–43. Balayé stresses that Staël "occupe dans la société une place exceptionnelle" as the daughter of a minister and the wife of an ambassador, but there were minister's daughters who were neither salonnières nor politically famous. She also points out that Staël "a fourni très peu de reseignements sur sa conduite personnelle" during this period. Sophie Gay judged her salon on the rue du Bac more "influent" than the ones she held under the Directory and the Restoration, which might well be true given the volume of bitter attacks, caricatures, and nasty newspaper articles to which she was subjected before leaving for Coppet in 1792. Abrantès called the early Revolution "Le moment le plus lumineux pour la conversation dans le salon de madame de Staël," and Herriot placed her "on the very foreground of the stage upon which the destinies of France were being played." Her critics (Sénac de Meilhan, Deperret) fantasized about her ideological fanaticism and the aggressiveness with which she expressed her views. Gutwirth, oddly enough, highlighted her relationship with Narbonne and her efforts to advance his career. Balayé, *Madame de Staël*, 3, 36, 42; Gay, *Salons célèbres*, 5; Abrantès, *Histoire des salons*, 2:389; Herriot, *Madame Récamier*, 1:35; Bertaut, *Parisiens*, 30; Challamel, *Clubs contre-révolutionnaires*, 568; Gutwirth, *Madame de Staël*, 72.

    21. Elisabeth Badinter and Robert Badinter, *Condorcet (1743–1794): Un Intellectual en politique* (Paris, 1988), 284–85, 327, 377, 384, 474; Abrantès, *Salons révolutionnaires*, 46, 144; Challamel, *Clubs contre-révolutionnaires*, 560, 563; Guillois, *Salon de Madame Helvétius*, 80–81; Stenger, *Société française*, 3:417.

    22. Abrantès wrote: "Il est à remarquer que dans ces réunions du soir chez madame Roland il n'y avait aucune femme. . . . [E]lle y était seule." Abrantès, *Salons révolutionnaires*, 88.

    23. Dominique Godineau, "The Woman," in *Enlightenment Portraits*, ed. Michel Vovelle, trans. Lydia G. Cochrane (Chicago, 1997), 419; Gita May, *Madame Roland and the Age of Revolution* (New York, 1970), 183; Abrantès, *Salons révolutionnaires*, 87. The Goncourts situated Roland's salon in a "société bourgeoise" that "avait tenté, la société du dix-huitième siècle morte, non de lui succéder, mais de vivre après elle. C'était une société de part, fort affairée, fort grave, presque toute girondine, et semblait un complot d'honnêtes gens." Patrice Hignonnet refused to count as a Girondin anyone who was not an habitué. Goncourt, *Histoire de la société française pendant la Révolution*, 355; Mona Ozouf, "Girondins," in *A Critical Dictionary of the French Revolution*, ed. François Furet and Mona Ozouf, trans. Arthur Goldhammer (Cambridge, Mass., 1989), 353.

    24. Ozouf, *Women's Words*, 60; May, *Madame Roland*, 68, 184.

    25. May, *Madame Roland*, 212–13, 230.

    26. Abrantès, *Salons révolutionnaires*, 87; Jeanne-Marie Roland de La Platière, *Mémoires de Mme. Roland*, ed. Claude Perroud (Paris, 1905), 1:200–202; May, *Madame Roland*, 184.

27. Paule-Marie Duhet, ed., *Les Femmes de la Révolution, 1789–1794* (Paris, 1989), 77–78; Anne Sporani, *La Révolution et les femmes* (Paris, 1988), 45.

28. Abrantès, *Salons révolutionnaires*, 68, 87, 90; Gutwirth, *Twilight of the Goddesses*, 245; Godineau, "Woman," in *Enlightenment Portraits*, 419; Ozouf, "Girondins," in *Critical Dictionary*, 353; Challamel, *Clubs contre-révolutionnaires*, 471–73.

29. Badinter, *Condorcet*, 385–86; Challamel, *Clubs contre-révolutionnaires*, 471–78.

30. Chastenay, *Mémoires*, 107, 114.

31. Alméras, *Vie parisienne sous la Révolution*, 92; Challamel, *Clubs contre-révolutionnaires*, 554, 559.

32. Chateaubriand, *Mémoires d'outre-tombe*, 2:14; Sporani, *Révolution et les femmes*, 123; Gwynne, *Madame de Staël*, 26; Bertaut, *Belles émigrés*, 102–3; Abrantès, *Salons révolutionnaires*, 144; Guillois, *Salon de Madame Helvétius*, 100–102. According to Stenger, Madame d'Houdetot "traversa les mois de la Terreur, sans rien changer à sa vie, donnant des fêtes en son hôtel, au moment le plus terrible des émeutes populaires" because of her liaison with Rousseau. Stenger, *Société française*, 3:378–79.

33. Ghislain de Diesbach, *Histoire de l'émigration, 1789–1814* (Paris, 1984), 231; Bertaut, *Parisiens*, 200.

34. Chastenay, *Mémoires*, 136; Zurich, *Femme heureuse*, 325.

35. Abrantès, *Memoirs*, 1:80, 90; id., *Salons révolutionnaires*, 105; Du Bled, *Rôle social et mondaine de la femme*, 114.

36. Alméras, *Vie parisienne sous la Révolution*, 210–13, 293–94; Goncourt, *Histoire de la société française pendant la Révolution*, 396–97; Abrantès, *Histoire des salons*, 3:9–10.

37. Camille Desmoulins wrote of Roland's salon that "il ne faut pas croire qu'il ait à table du ministre que des députés gourmands, et que la Circé du lieu ne sache que changer en pourceaux les compagnons de Barbardoux. Elle a recours à d'autres enchantements, qui à son âge et avec si peu de beauté supposent une bien plus grande magicienne." Saint-Just called one of the receptions in the salon of Madame de Sainte-Amaranthe a "souper conspirateur." *Moniteur*, September 29, 1792, quoted in Sporani, *Révolution et les femmes*, 130; Challamel, *Clubs contre-révolutionnaires*, 563.

38. The phrase is Danton's, quoted in Challamel, *Clubs contre-révolutionnaires*, 561. See also Mona Ozouf, "Girondins," in *Critical Dictionary*, 353; and Goncourt, *Histoire de la société française pendant la Révolution*, 358. In contrast to the Jacobins, who saw Roland's salon as an indication of the Girondins' attachment to the Old Regime, the *Actes des Apôtres*, a leading royalist newspaper, attacked Madame de Condorcet in 1791 as an adulteress who could not be received at court. Badinter, *Condorcet*, 342.

39. See Benjamin Nathans, "Habermas's 'Public Sphere' in the Era of the French Revolution," *French Historical Studies* 16, no. 3 (1990): 642; Patrice Gueniffey and Ran Halévi, "Clubs and Popular Societies," in *A Critical Dictionary of the French Revolution*, ed. François Furet and Mona Ozouf, trans. Arthur Goldhammer (Cambridge, Mass., 1989), 467–68.

40. Abrantès, *Histoire des salons*, 3:58.

41. These stories were taken from various sources, including the *Mémoires sur les Prisons*, De Lescurf's *L'Amour sous la Terreur*, the *Almanach des prisons*, and Olivier Blanc's *La Dernière lettre*. They appear in Goncourt, *Histoire de la société française pendant la Révolution*, 322–25; Bertaut, *Parisiens*, 160–61; Alméras, *Vie parisienne sous la Révolution*, 345–46; and Bartillat, *Histoire de la noblesse*, 1:90–91.

42. Duc de Castries, *La Vie quotidienne des émigrés* (Geneva, 1979), 37, 82–84; La Tour du Pin, *Memoirs*, 318.

43. See Diesbach, *Histoire de l'émigration*, 383–99; Fernand Baldensperger, *Le Mouvement des idées dans l'émigration française (1789–1815)* (New York, 1968), 1:119, 140–69; Castries, *Vie quotidienne des émigrés*, 40–41, 214; Forster, *House of Saulx-Tavanes*, 173.

44. See Broc, *Dix ans de la vie d'une femme*, 63; Jean Vidalenc, *Les Emigrés français, 1789–1825* (Caen, 1963), 226–29; La Tour du Pin, *Memoirs*, 153; Stenger, *Société française*, 1:19; Diesbach, *Histoire de l'émigration*, 27.

45. Chastenay, *Mémoires*, 108; Vidalenc, *Emigrés français*, 226–31; Chateaubriand, *Mémoires d'outre-tombe*, 1:391–92; La Tour du Pin, *Memoirs*, 169.

46. Baldensperger, *Mouvement des idées*, 1:122–23; Vidalenc, *Emigrés français*, 237; Joseph d'Haussonville, *Ma jeunesse, 1814–1830: Souvenirs* (Paris, 1885), 31; Louis de Rochechouart, *Souvenirs sur la Révolution, l'Empire et la Restauration* (Paris, 1889), 18–20.

47. Broc, *Dix ans de la vie d'une femme*, 269.

48. Baldensperger, *Mouvement des idées*, 1:118, 140–41; Bertaut, *Belles émigrés*, 111–13; Turquan, *Femmes*, 62, 113.

49. Bertaut, *Belles émigrés*, 122–23.

50. Reiset, *Reines de l'émigration*, 253–58; Bertaut, *Belles émigrés*, 107; Broc, *Dix ans de la vie d'une femme*, 63–5, 78–81.

51. Rochechouart, *Souvenirs sur la Révolution*, 20; Haussonville, *Ma jeunesse*, 43. See Diesbach, *Histoire de l'émigration*, 397–99, 508–9, on émigrés in Russia and the United States.

52. Bertaut, *Belles émigrés*, 8–10; Chastenay, *Mémoires*, 471.

53. Broc, *Dix ans de la vie d'une femme*, 81, 268; Vidalenc, *Emigrés français*, 231, 238.

54. Vidalenc, *Emigrés français*, 231.

55. Broc, *Dix ans de la vie d'une femme*, 80.

56. Louis de Bouillé, *Souvenirs et fragments pour servir aux mémoires de ma vie et de mon temps* (Paris, 1906–8), 2:19. Castries stresses the theme of adversity in *Vie quotidienne des émigrés*, 215.

57. See, e.g., Diesbach, *Histoire de l'émigration*, 212; Joseph Turquan, *Le Monde et le demi-monde sous le Consulat et l'Empire* (Paris, 1900), 1; Baldensperger, *Mouvement des idées*, 1:12, 118; Bertaut, *Belles émigrés*, 10.

58. La Tour du Pin, *Memoirs*, 153.

59. Diesbach, *Histoire de l'émigration*, 161, 289, 415–16.

60. See Turquan, *Femmes*, 62–65, 152–56; Jean Harmand, *Madame de Genlis: Sa Vie intime et politique, 1746–1830* (Paris, 1912), 340–43; Bertaut, *Belles émigrés*, 111–13, 170–71; Vidalenc, *Emigrés français*, 229.

61. See Diesbach, *Histoire de l'émigration*, 250, 383–84; Baldensperger, *Mouvement des idées*, 1:140–41; Bartillat, *Histoire de la noblesse française*, 1:113–15.

62. See Diesbach, *Histoire de l'émigration*, 154–63, 212 and Stenger, *Société française*, 1:19–20.

63. Haussonville, *Ma jeunesse*, 115; Broc, *Dix ans de la vie d'une femme*, 146; Pailhès, *Duchesse de Duras et Chateaubriand*, 24.

64. Baldensperger, *Mouvement des idées*, 1:120.

65. La Tour du Pin, *Memoirs*, 318; Baldensperger, *Mouvement des idées*, 1:124–25; Harmand, *Madame de Genlis*, 290–91; Bertaut, *Belles émigrés*, 111–13, 171.

66. See Diesbach, *Histoire de l'émigration*, 546–49 and Bartillat, *Histoire de la noblesse française*, 1:149–50.

67. Abrantès, *Histoire des salons*, 5:2–3; Staël, *Considérations*, 1:302. "Insensiblement,"

wrote Abrantès, "la société s'effaça en France . . . on en perdit jusqu'au souvenir . . . on ne reçut plus, et lorsque madame de Fontenay, après le 9 Thermidor, voulut avoir *une maison* à Chaillot, à ce qu'on nommait *la Chaumière*, elle eut une peine extrême à la former." Abrantès, *Salons révolutionnaires*, 133.

68. Abrantès, *Histoire des salons*, 3:227–29; Duc de Raguse, cited in L. Gastine, *Madame Tallien* (London, n.d.), 186–87; Chastenay, *Mémoires*, 216, Bartillat, *Histoire de la noblesse française*, 1:150.

69. Bertaut, *Parisiens*, 234; Edmond de Goncourt and Jules de Goncourt, *Histoire de la société française pendant le Directoire* (2d ed., Paris, 1855; reprint, Paris, 1992), 129–30; Arthur Léon Imbert de Saint-Amand, *Citizeness Bonaparte*, trans. Thomas Sergeant Perry (New York, 1900), 217.

70. Constant, quoted in Chateaubriand, *Mémoires d'outre-tombe*, 4:376–79; Chastenay, cited in Bartillat, *Histoire de la noblesse française*, 1:150; *Memoirs of Madame Junot*, 2:172. Stenger thought there were few salons under the Directory because the nouveaux riches were socially inept and constantly left the theaters too late to make it home for supper. At least, he consoled himself, "on ne se tutoyait plus." Frénilly says that when "les débris éparpillés de la bonne compagnie commencèrent à rentrer au colombier . . . [l]e suprême bon ton était d'être ruiné, d'avoir été suspect, persécuté, emprisonné surtout." Stenger, *Société française*, 1:56; Frénilly, *Mémoires*, 151.

71. Jules Bertaut, *La Duchesse d'Abrantès* (Paris, 1949), 36; Imbert de Saint-Amand, *Citizeness Bonaparte*, 217–18; Abrantès, *Memoirs of Madame Junot*, 2:172; Staël, *Considérations*, 1:302; Chastenay, *Mémoires*, 218–19; Diesbach, *Histoire de l'émigration*, 548; Abrantès, *Salons révolutionnaires*, 162–63; Frénilly, *Mémoires*, 151. Abrantès does not record the admission requirements for the *bals des victimes* but other sources mention that guests had to be related to at least one victim of the Terror. Bassanville reported that one had to have lost at least three relatives, but most other sources speak of only one relative or simply "un membre de sa famille." See Henriette Tassé, *Salons française du XIXe siècle* (Montreal, 1952), 22; Bassanville, *Salons d'autrefois*, 2:20.

72. Ouvrard, cited in Gastine, *Madame Tallien*, 231. See also Gastine, *Madame Tallien*, 127–29, Marie-Hélène Bourquin, *Monsieur et Madame Tallien* (Paris, 1987), 272–75, and François Gendron, *La Jeunesse dorée: Episodes de la Révolution française* (Montreal, 1979), 55.

73. Bassanville, *Salons d'autrefois*, 2:21–22.

74. Abrantès, *Histoire des salons*, 4:100, 229–31 (emphasis in the original).

75. Abrantès, *Memoirs of Madame Junot*, 2:247–48; Zurich, *Femme heureuse*, 341–54.

76. Abrantès, *Histoire des salons*, 3:374–75; 4:100; Pasquier, *History of My Time*, 3:218, 246; Fernand Bassan, *Politique et haute société à l'époque romantique: La Famille Pastoret d'après sa correspondance (1788 à 1856)* (Paris, 1969), 24–25; Bartillat, *Histoire de la noblesse française*, 1:153; Ancelot, *Salons de Paris*, 34; Bertaut, *Egéries du XVIIIe siècle*, 179.

77. Imbert de Saint-Amand, *Citizeness Bonaparte*, 218.

78. Louis Lacour, *Grand monde et salons politiques de Paris après la Terreur: Fragments précédés d'une étude sur la société avant 1789* (Paris, 1859), 59–60; Zurich, *Femme heureuse*, 315; Imbert de Saint-Amand, *Citizeness Bonaparte*, 217, 222.

79. Lacour, *Grand monde et salons politiques*, 59. On the Directory's surveillance of royalist clubs and salons, see Challamel, *Clubs contre-révolutionnaires*, 484–501.

80. Madame de Bawr, *Mes souvenirs* (Paris, 1853), 100; Challamel, *Clubs contre-révolutionnaires*, 564–67.

81. La Tour du Pin, *Memoirs*, 306. On Staël's political views at the time, see especially

her *Réflexions sur la paix intérieure*. In *Considérations sur la Révolution française*, she lamented the separation between high society and the governing class under the Directory: "La société de Paris était d'autant plus libre, que la classe des gouvernants n'en faisait pas partie. Cette separation avait et devait avoir sans doute beaucoup d'inconvénients à la longue." Staël, *Considérations*, 1:308.

82. Pasquier, *History of My Time*, 1:136–37; Gwynne, *Madame de Staël*, 31–39; Challamel, *Clubs contre-révolutionnaires*, 507–11.

83. Bardoux, *Comtesse de Beaumont*, 245. See also Armand François d'Allonville, *Mémoires secrets de 1770 à 1830* (Paris, 1838–45), 4:134.

84. See esp. Gwynne, *Madame de Staël*, 31–34; Balayé, *Madame de Staël*, 62–63.

85. Staël, *Considérations*, 1:302. See, e.g., the descriptions by an English traveler cited in A. Babeau, *La France et Paris sous le Directoire* (Paris, 1888), 71, and by Pasquier in *History of My Time*, 1:135–36. Lacour called the Luxembourg "les Tuileries du nouveau roi," and Constant wrote that power at the "cour du Directoire" was "tout à la fois terrible et familier, inspirant la crainte sans échapper au mépris." Lacour, *Grand monde et salons politiques*, 65; Constant cited in Chateaubriand, *Mémoires d'outre-tombe*, 4:377. According to Chastenay, Treilhard also received visitors at the Luxembourg, but "Le directeur Larevellière ne voyait à peu près personne; les directeurs Rewbel et Merlin ne recevaient guère, sauf à certains jours, et seulement leurs familles et leurs intimes amis." Chastenay, *Mémoires*, 256.

86. Imbert de Saint Amand, *Citizeness Bonaparte*, 187–88.

87. During the Consulate, both Lebrun and Cambacérès held numerous receptions in their official salons. Napoléon held receptions at the Tuileries that helped him build the foundations of a new court. See Chapter 3.

88. Barbara C. Pope, "Revolution and Retreat," in *Women, War, and Revolution*, ed. Carol R. Berkin and Clara M. Lovett (New York, 1980), 228–29.

89. Abrantès, *Histoire des salons*, 3:247; 5:2.

CHAPTER THREE: *Ralliés* and Exiles (1799–1815)

1. Gueniffey and Halévi, "Clubs and Popular Societies," in *Critical Dictionary*, 470–71.

2. Abrantès, *Memoirs of Madame Junot*, 3:24–25, 43–44, 48, 163; Chastenay, *Mémoires*, 319; Baronne de Vaux, *Souvenirs d'une dame du palais impérial* (Paris, 1830), 76; Chateaubriand, *Mémoires d'outre-tombe*, 2:242.

3. See Fiette, *Noblesse française*, 145.

4. Paul Gautier, *Madame de Staël et Napoléon* (Paris, 1903), 103.

5. Charles de Rémusat, *Mémoires*, 1:171.

6. Chastenay pointed out that younger nobles who disregarded the distinctions and rivalries nurtured by their elders often bent the rules of the past regarding whose society to frequent. Salons that brought together old and new elites at the time included those of Madame Permon, Madame Récamier, Madame de Souza (previously Flahaut), the princesse de Vaudémont, and Madame de La Briche. Charles de Rémusat described the latter's salon as diverse and "almost unique." Chastenay, *Mémoires*, 292–94, 312–13; Rémusat, *Mémoires*, 1:171.

7. Duchesse de Saulx-Tavanes, *Sur les routes de l'émigration: Mémoires de la duchesse de Saulx-Tavanes (1791–1806)* (Paris, 1934), 143.

8. Turquan, *Monde*, 88–89; Stenger, *Société française*, 4:144–45.

9. Saulx-Tavanes, *Sur les routes de l'émigration,* 157; Arthur Léon Imbert de Saint-Amand, *The Wife of the First Consul* (Paris, 1900), 109. Napoléon granted her a marriage settlement of 160,000 livres as a princess of the blood.

10. Abrantès, *Histoire des salons,* 4:16.

11. Imbert de Saint-Amand, *Wife of the First Consul,* 109. See Charles-Otto Zieseniss, *Napoléon et le Cour Impériale* (Paris, 1980), 28–31, for a good description of Montesson's role during the Consulate.

12. Abrantès, *Histoire des salons,* 5:4–5.

13. Gautier, *Madame de Staël et Napoléon,* 107.

14. Napoléon, quoted in Pope, "Revolution and Retreat," 221. See also Abrantès, *Histoire des salons,* 5:50–51.

15. See, e.g., Jules Bertaut, *Le Faubourg Saint-Germain sous l'Empire et la Restauration* (Paris, 1949), 85; Bartillat, *Histoire de la noblesse,* 1:174.

16. Abrantès, *Histoire des salons,* 5:5–6, 51–52n.

17. Haussonville, *Ma jeunesse,* 69; Abrantès, *Histoire des salons,* 4:241; 5:7n; Claire Elisabeth Jeanne Gravier de Vergennes, comtesse de Rémusat, *Memoirs of Madame de Rémusat,* 2:2:273–74.

18. Staël, *Considérations,* 2:2:42.

19. Claire de Rémusat, *Memoirs,* 2:245–46.

20. Chastenay, *Mémoires,* 319; Broc, *Dix ans de la vie d'une femme,* 312–13. See also Staël, *Considérations,* 2:6.

21. See Charles-Otto Zieseniss, *Napoléon et la cour impériale* (Paris, 1980), 74–75; Abrantès, *Memoirs of Madame Junot,* 1:177; 2:410; Henri d'Alméras, *La Vie parisienne sous le Consulate et l'Empire* (Paris, 1923), 368n; Harmand, *Madame de Genlis,* 396–97.

22. Claire de Rémusat, *Memoirs,* 1:29; La Tour du Pin, *Memoirs,* 341–43; Pasquier, *History of My Time,* 1:135. *Radiation* was the process by which names were erased from the *liste des émigrés,* thus allowing those who fled to return without fear of prosecution.

23. Imbert de Saint Amand, *Wife of the First Consul,* 183–84; Gay, *Salons célèbres,* 187–89, 197–98; Stenger, *Société française,* 4:13–17; Claire de Rémusat, *Memoirs,* 1:xv, 9; Imbert de Saint Amand, *Citizeness Bonaparte,* 4–5, 222–24. *Le Mémorial de Sainte-Hélène,* quoted in id., *Citizeness Bonaparte,* 108.

24. Abrantès, *Memoirs of Madame Junot,* 2:208–9; 3:167–68, 174; id., *Histoire des salons,* 5:33–36; Claire de Rémusat, *Memoirs,* 1:8; 2:276–77. In April 1802, Madame de Staël quipped in a letter to Madame Récamier that there was "[n]othing fresh in Paris as regards society events. Duroc is to marry Mlle. d'Ervas; Mad. Grand they say is to be married to M. de Talleyrand. Bonaparte would like everyone to marry, bishops, cardinals, &c." Staël to Récamier, 13 Floréal, Year X, in Herroit, *Madame Récamier,* 1:79.

25. Turquan, *Monde,* 244; Imbert de Saint Amand, *Wife of the First Consul,* 43–44; Abrantès, *Histoire des salons,* 4:153, 188–89; 5:33.

26. Boigne, *Mémoires,* 1:1:152; Imbert de Saint Amand, *Wife of the First Consul,* 179. The expression is Talleyrand's.

27. Chastenay, *Mémoires,* 321. "A cette époque," wrote Madame de Saulx-Tavanes of the Consulate, "on était rappelé par un voeu unanime et spontané; le besoin de réparer les maux passés se faisait sentir avec toute l'énergie d'impression récentes." Saulx-Tavanes, *Sur les routes de l'émigration,* 153.

28. On nobles in the imperial household, see Philip Mansel, *The Court of France, 1789–1830* (Cambridge, 1988), 82–86, Louis Bergeron, *France Under Napoleon,* trans. R. R. Palmer (Princeton, 1981), 66–67, and Zieseniss, *Napoléon et la cour impériale.*

29. Jean Tulard, "Problèmes sociaux de la France impériale," *Revue d'histoire moderne et contemporaine*, special issue (July–September 1970): 639–63; Bartillat, *Histoire de la noblesse*, 1:185. See also Philip Mansel, "How 'Forgotten' Were the Bourbons in France, 1812–1814," *European Studies Review* 13, no. 1 (January 1993): 20. On the nobles who resisted Napoléon's offers of employment, see Mansel, *Court of France*, 81–82.

30. Bartillat, *Histoire de la noblesse*, 1:175; Boigne, *Memoirs*, 1:172–73; Abrantès, *Histoire des salons*, 6:3.

31. Abrantès, *Histoire des salons*, 6:165. On Staël's salon and her political activity during the Consulate, see Balayé, *Madame de Staël*, 78–89, Gautier, *Madame de Staël et Napoléon*, 66–68, 129–31, 392–93, and Dennis Wood, *Benjamin Constant: A Biography* (London, 1993), 153–56.

32. Françoise Wagener, *Madame Récamier: 1777–1849* (Paris, 1986), 123; Claire de Rémusat, *Memoirs*, 2:409; 3:615; Gautier, *Madame de Staël et Napoléon*, 393.

33. Gautier, *Madame de Staël et Napoléon*, 393.

34. Guillois, *Salon de Madame Helvétius*, 182–78, 242–44.

35. See Harmand, *Madame de Genlis*, 402, and Gautier, *Madame de Staël et Napoléon*, 129–31.

36. Challamel, *Clubs contre-révolutionnaires*, 571; Abrantès, *Histoire des salons*, 4:139; Claire de Rémusat, *Memoirs*, 2:352; Guillois, *Salon de Madame Helvétius*, 175–76.

37. Guillois, *Salon de Madame Helvétius*, 164; Staël, *Considérations*, 2:42; Gautier, *Madame de Staël et Napoléon*, 255.

38. Bartillat, *Histoire de la noblesse*, 1:207; Norvins's *Mémorial* and Metternich's *Mémoires*, quoted in Gautier, *Madame de Staël et Napoléon*, 103, 255.

39. Balayé, *Madame de Staël*, 92–93. According to Madame de Rémusat, Napoléon once said that she "teaches people to think who have never thought before, or who had forgotten how to think." She also testified that Napoléon "was very gracious to artists of any distinction [and] he encouraged them in his liberality and his praise; provided, however, that they were always willing to dedicate their art to his praises, or to the furtherance of his projects." Claire de Rémusat, *Memoirs*, 2:408, 3:615.

40. Carla Hesse, "French Women in Print, 1750–1850: An Essay in Historical Bibliography," *Studies on Voltaire and the Eighteenth Century* 359 (Oxford, 1998): 68–83. See also id., *The Other Enlightenment: How French Women Became Modern* (Princeton, 2001).

41. Louis de Villefosse and Janine Bouissounouse, *The Scourge of the Eagle: Napoleon and the Liberal Opposition*, trans. Michael Ross (London, 1972), 202, 220.

42. Villefosse, *Scourge of the Eagle*, 54; Claire de Rémusat, *Memoirs*, 2:408; Gay, *Salons célèbres*, 5, 12–13.

43. Villefosse, *Scourge of the Eagle*, 152–53, 224, 229–30; *Cahiers de Sainte-Hélène*, quoted in Gutwirth, *Madame de Staël*, 287; Abrantès, *Memoirs of Madame Junot*, 3:92.

44. Staël, *Considérations*, 2:42.

45. Napoléon commented that Staël's house was "not a salon, but a club" in a conversation with Regnault de Saint-Jean d'Angély. Staël herself would have rejected the label out of hand because she maintained a distinction between clubs and salons based on differences of function and class: salons were nonpartisan gatherings of enlightened elites that gave rise to an "opinion that makes itself felt everywhere, but resides in no particular body"; clubs, by contrast, were partisan and popular — they aspired to be "ces autorités en dehors," criticizing the existing order while "giving laws to the Assembly," coveting power without taking responsibility. Staël, *Considérations*, 1:207–8. Fraisse discusses the distinction between clubs and salons in *Reason's Muse*, 104, 124.

46. On Madame Récamier in 1803, see Herriot, *Madame Récamier*, 1:84–106, and Wagener, *Madame Récamier*, 122–25.

47. Chateaubriand, *Mémoires d'outre-tombe*, 4:398–401; Stendhal, quoted in Herriot, *Madame Récamier*, 1:107.

48. Claire de Rémusat, *Memoirs*, 2:298. See also Wagener, *Madame Récamier*, 86, 122–27, and Jeanne Récamier, *Memoirs and Correspondence of Madame Récamier*, trans. Isaphene M. Luyster (Boston, 1867), 21. When Madame de Boigne attended a ball given by Madame Récamier, she found "a large number of specimens of the new Empire [and] and great number of the old nobility, of returned *émigrés*, high financial authorities, and many foreigners." Napoléon tried to attract Récamier to court by offering her a position in Josephine's service, but she refused. "L'indépendance de son caractère l'éloignait de la cour de Napoléon dont elle avait refusé de faire partie," Constant observed. Boigne, *Memoirs*, 1:1:169; Constant, quoted in Chateaubriand, *Mémoires d'outre-tombe*, 4:399.

49. Boigne, *Mémoires*, 1:1:180; Chastenay, *Mémoires*, 467–68; Claire de Rémusat, *Memoirs*, 2:273–74, 404–5; 3:265. Staël wrote of the impression made by her exile in *Considérations*, 2:40–42, and *Ten Years' Exile, or, Memoirs of That Interesting Period of the Life of the Baroness de Staël-Holstein*, ed. Margaret Crosland (Fontwell, Sussex, UK, 1968), 8. On the exile of nobles, see Bartillat, *Histoire de la noblesse*, 1:201–2.

50. Abrantès, *Memoirs of Madame Junot*, 4:203–4, 297; Claire de Rémusat, *Memoirs*, 2:273; Stenger, *Société française*, 1:337.

51. Claire de Rémusat, *Memoirs*, 1:8; 2:352, 405.

52. Mansel, *Court of France*, 188.

53. Chastenay, *Mémoires*, 386; Claire de Rémusat, *Memoirs*, 3:552–53, 567.

54. Claire de Rémusat, *Memoirs*, 2:198, 246–47, 350; Chastenay, *Mémoires*, 420; Mansel, *Court of France*, 74–81; Staël, *Considérations*, 2:89. For similar testimony, see Boigne, *Memoirs*, 1:160, 181; Claire de Rémusat, *Memoirs*, 3:470, 483, 522; Guizot, *Madame de Rumford*, 16–17, 31. Abrantès wrote that in 1809, "The drawing-rooms of Paris were . . . in a singular state of constraint [because] politics were an interdicted subject, except when spoken aside or mysteriously." Chastenay identified the period 1806–7 as "la dernière époque de l'indépendance de l'ancien monde." Abrantès, *Memoirs of Madame Junot*, 5:172; Chastenay, *Mémoires*, 380.

55. Martin-Fugier, *Vie élégante*, 392.

56. Broglie, *Souvenirs*, 1:246.

57. Abrantès, *Memoirs of Madame Junot*, 2:209; Stenger, *Société française*, 1:386–87; Bertaut, *Duchesse d'Abrantès*, 140–41; Chastenay, *Mémoires*, 368–70.

58. Broglie, *Souvenirs*, 1:131–32; Mansel, *Court of France*, 75–81.

59. Mansel, *Court of France*, 85–86; Broglie, *Souvenirs*, 1:246–47.

60. Abrantès, *Memoirs of Madame Junot*, 4:179; 5:43. Abrantès recalled an encounter with Napoléon in which he asked her to take care of an affair he considered unimportant, commenting, "I never like women to interfere in serious matters, because they are sure to be always intriguing!"

61. Claire de Rémusat, *Memoirs*, 2:201–2, 351; Abrantès, *Memoirs of Madame Junot*, 4:194–95; Frédéric Masson, *Napoléon et les femmes* (Paris, 1817), 174–75.

62. Claire de Rémusat, *Memoirs*, 1:8; 2:352; Staël, quoted in Gutwirth, *Twilight of the Goddesses*, 383; Chastenay, *Mémoires*, 346–47, 446.

63. Chastenay, *Mémoires*, 446; Abrantès, *Histoire des salons*, 5:350–53, 392.

64. Claire de Rémusat, *Memoirs*, 2:277; 3:529; Abrantès, *Histoire des salons*, 6:152–64.

65. Bartillat, *Histoire de la noblesse*, 1:178–81, 197–98; Claire de Rémusat, *Memoirs*, 1:xvi; 3:461, 506; Chastenay, *Mémoires*, 380–83; Mansel, *Court of France*, 82.

66. Villemain in *Le Correspondant* (1859), 220–21, quoted in Herriot, *Madame Récamier*, 1:133.

67. Mansel, *Court of France*, 81–82; Bertaut, *Faubourg Saint-Germain*, 96.

68. Boigne, *Memoirs*, 1:1:201; Alméras, *Vie parisienne sous le Consulat et l'Empire*, 49–50. For a discussion of the reconstitution of noble patrimony, see Adeline Daumard, "Noblesse et Aristocratie en France au XIXe siècle," in *Noblesses européennes au XIXe siècle* (Milan, 1988), 94–95.

69. For salacious rumors about Napoléon and his family, see Jacques Thomas Veneur, *L'Echo des salons de Paris depuis la Restauration, ou Recueil d'anécdotes sur l'ex-empereur Buonaparte, sa cour et ses agens* (Paris, 1814–15).

70. Claire de Rémusat, *Memoirs*, 2:345.

71. Recalling the years of the Consulate, Pasquier wrote, "Le grand charme de nos réunions était dans l'indulgence et la complète liberté qui y régnaient. Le bonheur de se retrouver rendait tout facile. On se pardonnait des nuances, des divergences d'opinion, qu'on aurait jamais supportées avant 1791: querelles oubliées ainsi que les rancunes et les haines qu'on devait retrouver si vivaces sous l'Empire et sous la Restauration." Pasquier, *History of My Time*, 1:206.

72. See Bertaut, *Faubourg Saint-Germain*, 83; Fiette, *Noblesse française*, 19. Bertaut argued that Faubourg Saint-Germain began to count as a "personne morale dès le premier Empire," and not after 1814. Under the Empire, he wrote, "il avait constitué sur la rive gauche un solide noyau." For a description of Saint Honoré in 1814, see Charles de Rémusat, *Mémoires*, 1:133–34. Balzac's use of mondain geography in *Scènes de la vie privée* to characterize different social types is discussed in Fortassier, *Mondains*, 65–66. According to Haussonville, the divisions characteristic of Parisian society under the Empire were echoed in the provinces. At Metz, "la société se divisait, comme celle de bien d'autres villes, entre une société aristocratique, un peu fermée et boudeuse, et un petit groupe de fonctionnaires." Haussonville, *Madame de Staël et M. Necker*, 382–83.

73. See, e.g., La Tour du Pin, *Memoirs*, 354; Frénilly, *Mémoires*, 297.

74. Boigne, *Mémoires*, 1:160–61, 190, 508–9; Chastenay, *Mémoires*, 446; Abrantès, *Histoire des salons*, 4:189; Chateaubriand, *Mémoires d'outre-tombe*, 4:80, 88; Claire de Rémusat, *Memoirs*, 3:507.

75. Armandine de Montcalm, *Mon journal, 1815–1818* (Paris, 1836), 284; Gutwirth, *Madame de Staël*, 281.

76. Claire de Rémusat, *Memoirs*, 2:409.

77. Montcalm, *Mon journal*, 201; Broglie, *Souvenirs*, 1:272–73.

78. Broglie, *Souvenirs*, 1:272–73; Victor de Pange, *The Unpublished Correspondence of Madame de Staël and the Duke of Wellington*, trans. Harold Kurtz (London, 1965), 40–53; Prosper Duvergier de Hauranne, *Histoire du gouvernement parlementaire en France, 1814–1848* (Paris, 1860–72), 4:97. Madame de Chastenay quipped during the allied occupation that England, France, and Staël's salon were the only three powers in Europe that mattered. Chastenay, *Mémoires*, 445.

79. Staël, *Considérations*, 2:145–46, 148, 150–53, 185.

80. Ibid., 1:112; Gautier, *Madame de Staël et Napoléon*, 202; Gwynne, *Madame de Staël*, 238–39.

81. Staël, *Considérations*, 2:150–54. See also the correspondence between Staël and the

duchesse de Duras that took place in 1814 and 1815 in Haussonville, *Femmes d'autrefois*, 201–5.

82. Staël to Constant, October 27, 1815, in Germaine de Staël, *Lettres de Mme de Staël à Benjamin Constant* (Paris, 1928), 261. Staël was especially critical of the ultras in this regard. See also Montcalm, *Mon journal*, 201; Staël to Duras, September 17, 1814, in Haussonville, *Femmes d'autrefois*, 204.

83. Staël, *Considérations*, 2:153–54.

84. On the theme of le monde's degeneration, see Martin-Fugier, *Vie élégante*, 179, 186–87.

85. Staël, *Considérations*, 2:170, 241; Ozouf, *Women's Words*, 79.

86. Letter to Madame Swetchine, November 19, 1817, in Pailhès, *Duchesse de Duras et Chateaubriand*, 424.

87. Astolphe de Custine, *Empire of the Czar: A Journey Through Eternal Russia* (New York, 1989), 58; Girardin, *Vicomte de Launay: Lettres parisiennes*, 1:128–29; 2:203; 3:258–59, 265.

88. François Villemain, *Souvenirs contemporaines d'histoire et de littérature* (Paris, 1854), 1:453.

89. Charles-Augustine Sainte-Beuve, *Portraits de femmes* (Paris, 1869), 63.

90. Pailhès, *Duchesse de Duras et Chateaubriand*, 400–401; Villemain, *Souvenirs contemporaine*, 1:471.

91. Boigne, *Mémoires*, 2:2:11; Chateaubriand, *Mémoires d'outre-tombe*, 3:458–59; Pailhès, *Duchesse de Duras et Chateaubriand*, 400.

92. Pailhès, *Duchesse de Duras et Chateaubriand*, 421; Broglie, *Souvenirs*, 1:217. The two women shared many of the same habitués, including Pozzo di Borgo, Humboldt, Barante, Madame Récamier, and Delphine Gay. Duras's salon tended to attract a number of ultras, like Bonald, Villèle, and Chateaubriand, who avoided Madame de Staël's, but both maintained assemblies that were ideologically mixed. Staël was also a frequent guest in Duras's salon.

93. Pailhès, *Duchesse de Duras et Chateaubriand*, 412, 416–17, 421; Agoult, *Mémoires*, 30.

94. Boigne, *Memoirs*, 1:1:311. Sainte-Beuve wrote that she wanted her salon to embody the transactions necessary to support the liberal royalism of her final years and consequently liked to have represented there "all the hues characteristic of the social phases through which she had passed." Sainte-Beuve, *Portraits de femmes*, 84.

95. Boigne, *Memoirs*, 1:311.

CHAPTER FOUR: *Le Pays féminin* (1815–1848)

1. Abrantès, *Memoirs of Madame Junot*, 6:130. Mansel argued that "the Bourbons were far from forgotten in France" despite widespread assertions to the contrary. See Mansel, "How Forgotten Were the Bourbons in France Between 1812 and 1814?" 13–37.

2. Bertaut, *Le Faubourg Saint-Germain*, 102–4; Bertaut, *La Duchesse d'Abrantès*, 250–51; Blanche-Joséphine de Maillé, *Souvenirs des deux Restaurations* (Paris, 1984), 183–84.

3. Staël, *Considérations*, 2:150; Montcalm, *Mon journal*, 88.

4. Bassanville, *Salons d'autrefois*, 2:1; Ancelot, *Salons de Paris*, 19; Ancelot, *Salon de Paris*, 57–59; Sainte-Beuve, *Portraits de femmes*, 62.

5. Villemain, *Souvenirs contemporains*, 1:464–65; Guillaume Bertier de Sauvigny, *The Bourbon Restoration*, trans. Lynn M. Case (Philadelphia, 1967), 260–61.

6. See Claire de Rémusat, *Memoirs*, 1:xl; Ancelot, *Salon de Paris*, xx, 59.

7. See Chastenay, *Mémoires*, 528, 598; Villemain, *Souvenirs contemporains*, 1:455.

8. Alphonse de Lamartine, *Nouvelles confidences* (Paris, n.d.), 326.

9. Karl Marx, *The Eighteenth Brumaire of Louis Bonaparte* (New York, 1963), 66; Beaumont-Vassy, *Salons de Paris sous Louis-Philippe*, 258.

10. See Martin-Fugier, *Vie élégante*, 228; Anne Martin-Fugier, "La Cour et la ville sous la Monarchie de Juillet d'après les feuilletons mondains," *Revue historique* 278, no. 1 (1987): 116.

11. See Pierre Rosanvallon, *Le Moment Guizot* (Paris, 1985), 25; Dominique Bagge, *Les Idées politiques en France sous la Restauration* (Paris, 1952), 22. The view that the Charter gained the general assent of Parisian high society under the Restoration was widely shared, especially among moderate royalists. See Villemain, *Souvenirs contemporains*, 1:460; Duras to Staël, September 1, 1814, in Haussonville, *Femmes d'autrefois*, 203; Maillé, *Souvenirs*, 227.

12. Haussonville, *Ma jeunesse*, 289; François Guizot, *Mélanges politiques et historiques* (Paris, 1869), cited in Bagge, *Idées politiques*, 20–21.

13. See Daumard, "Noblesse et aristocratie en France au XIXe siècle," in *Noblesses européennes*, 86; Fiette, *Noblesse française*, 223, 245.

14. Rosanvallon, *Moment Guizot*, 17, 20; Charles de Rémusat, *Mémoires* 1:234.

15. Bawr, *Mes souvenirs*, 94.

16. Emmanuel de Waresquiel, *Le Duc de Richelieu, 1766–1822: Un Sentimental en politique* (Paris, 1990), 275; Fumaroli, "Conversation," 734.

17. Villemain, *Souvenirs contemporains*, 1:454; Guizot, *Madame de Rumford*, 22; Staël, quoted in Wagener, *Madame Récamier*, 278; Saint-Beuve, *Causeries du lundi*, quoted in Herriot, *Madame Récamier*, 2:72.

18. On the evolution from informal to formal political sociability, see Huard, *Naissance du parti politique*, 16, 47–48; Agulhon, *Cercle*, 66.

19. For examples of the flexibility of salons, see Boigne, *Mémoires*, 1:348; 2:8; Noëlle Dauphin, "Les Salons de la Restauration: Un Influence spécifique sur les milieux dirigeants," in *Femmes dans la cité, 1815–1871*, ed. Alain Corbin et al. (Grâne, 1997), 253; Charles de Rémusat, *Mémoires*, 1:339; Apponyi, *Vingt-cinq ans à Paris*, 2:340; Ancelot, *Salons de Paris*, 19; Boigne, *Memoirs*, 2:183.

20. Maillé, *Souvenirs*, 10–11; Pasquier, *History of My Time*, 3:3, 64.

21. Maillé, *Souvenirs*, 19; Montcalm, *Mon journal*, 137. On the treatment of Bonapartist courtiers by royalist women, see Staël, *Considérations*, 2:150–51; Boigne, *Memoirs*, 1:284.

22. Françoise Waquet, *Les Fêtes royales sous la Restauration, ou l'ancien régime retrouvé* (Geneva, 1981), 141; Mansel, *Court of France*, 94, 109–10, 120–21. Louis XVIII implemented the new policy in the face of substantial opposition from within his own entourage. On the attitude of the ultras toward efforts to make court appointments more inclusive, see Staël, *Considérations*, 2:151–52; Maillé, *Souvenirs*, 19–20; Arthur Léon Imbert de Saint-Amand, *The Duchesse de Berry and the Court of Louis XVIII*, trans. Elizabeth Gilbert Martin (New York, 1890–95), 93; Mansel, *Court of France*, 189.

23. Mansel, *Court of France*, 109, 124–28, 134, 189. Ten of Napoléon's court officials

received court offices in 1820, including Comte Rapp, a Protestant aide-de-camp who had fought for the emperor during the Hundred Days, and General Reille, who was a *gentilhomme de la chambre*.

24. Bassanville, *Salons d'autrefois*, 1:153–54; Mansel, *Court of France*, 98–99, 138. Contemporary testimony supports Mansel's claim that the Tuileries contained a more diverse aristocratic society than the court of Versailles, and that its entertainments were less exclusive. See La Tour du Pin, *Memoirs*, 427; Boigne, *Memoirs*, 1:284; Hugo, *Misérables*, 3:54.

25. New financial arrangements limiting the court's ceremonial expenses prevented it from dominating the social life of the capital as thoroughly as had its predecessors. Funds allocated for "fêtes et spectacles" under the Restoration were considered personal expenses of the king and were therefore included in the civil list. Out of a budget of roughly 30 million francs for each reign, pomp and entertainment consumed no more than 13.7 percent. Consequently, the Restoration "did not have the means to conduct that same *politique festive* as the Old Regime." Waquet, *Fêtes royales*, 36–47.

26. See Bertier de Sauvigny, "Aristocratie et monarchie dans la vie culturelle au temps de Louis XVIII et de Charles X," in *Hof, Kultur und Politik*, 62; Mansel, *Court of France*, 135–36; Martin-Fugier, *Vie élégante*, 391.

27. Mansel, *Court of France*, 95, 120, 160–65, 189. On the court of the July Monarchy, see Martin-Fugier, *Vie élégante*, 111, 219–20; Anne Martin-Fugier, *La Vie quotidienne de Louis-Philippe et sa famille, 1830–1848* (Paris, 1992), 154–59; Suzanne d'Huart, "Le Cour de Louis-Philippe," in *Hof, Kultur und Politik*, 80–83; Comtesse d'Armaillé, *Quand on savait vivre heureux (1830–1860): Souvenirs de jeunesse* (Paris, 1934), 71; Charles de Rémusat, *Mémoires*, 3:99. Jo Burr Margadant has suggested that the Orleanist court failed to attract the attention of the public because the masculinization of politics had forced it to become more private and hence less interesting. But the court was already becoming domestic under the Restoration and the growing tendency of journalists to represent politics as an exclusively male arena did not prevent the female-governed salons of Paris from supplanting the court at the center of French social and political life. Under the Restoration, wrote Noëlle Dauphin, "[p]olitical groups were animated much less by the court, reputed to be tedious, than by a whole series of salons," where, according to Rémusat, "the court and the royal family would hardly ever occupy the conversation." Jo Burr Margadant, "Gender, Vice, and the Political Imaginary in Nineteenth-Century France: Reinterpreting the Failure of the July Monarchy, 1830–1848," *American Historical Review* 104, no. 5 (December 1999): 1488–89; Dauphin, "Salons de la Restauration," in *Femmes dans la cité*, 252; Charles de Rémusat, *Mémoires*, 1:235. The domestic habits of the royal family during the Restoration are discussed in Waquet, *Fêtes royales*, 150–51; Mansel, *Court of France*, 97–98, 138, 163; Boigne, *Memoirs*, 3:3:11–13; Bertier de Sauvigny, "Aristocratie et monarchie dans la vie culturelle au temps de Louis XVIII et de Charles X," in *Hof, Kultur und Politik*, 69–70; Maillé, *Souvenirs*, 4; Marie d'Agoult, *Mes souvenirs* (Paris, 1877), 272–74. On the eclipse of the Tuileries and the centrality of salons during the Restoration, see Bertier de Sauvigny, *Bourbon Restoration*, 260–61.

28. Habermas, *Structural Transformation*, 32.

29. Eurydice Dosne, *Mémoires de Madame Dosne, l'égérie de M. Thiers*, ed. Henri Malo (Paris, 1928), 2:88; Charles de Rémusat, *Mémoires*, 3:98, 339.

30. Bertier de Sauvigny, *Bourbon Restoration*, 261; Villemain, *Souvenirs contemporains*,

458. Stendhal reported that the society women who were frequently invited to His Majesty's card parties at Saint-Cloud in the 1820 "always return to Paris with the impression of having escaped the most tiresome place in the world." Stendhal, *Esquisses*, 144–45.

31. Martin-Fugier, *Vie élégante*, 392; Beaumont-Vassy, *Salons de Paris sous Louis-Philippe*, 236; Apponyi, *Vingt-cinq ans à Paris*, 1:405–6; Dino, *Memoirs*, 1:213–14; 3:19; Balzac quoted in Bartillart, *Histoire de la noblesse*, 1:257 and Fortassier, *Mondains*, 113.

32. Dino, *Memoirs*, 2:17–18.

33. Astolphe de Custine, *Ethel* (Paris, 1839), 1:308; Balabine, *Paris de 1842 à 1852*, 102. Musset characterized le monde in the 1830s as "merely a number of whirlpools, each one whirling independent of the others. [The people of this world] float about in groups like flocks of birds." Musset, *Confessions*, 109.

34. Martin-Fugier, *Vie élégante*, 393.

35. Beaumont-Vassy, *Salons de Paris sous Louis-Philippe*, 321.

36. Agoult, *Mémoires*, 204. Bertier de Sauvigny, "Aristocratie et monarchie dans la vie culturelle au temps de Louis XVIII et de Charles X," in *Hof, Kultur und Politik*, 60–62, endorsed d'Agoult's view of Faubourg Saint-Germain as "d'un sort de large famille, dont les membres ont entre eux des liens de parenté plus ou moins distants et qui se reconnaissent à une certaine communauté d'idées, de manières, de langage, de train de vie, et qui se retrouvent fréquemment les uns chez les autres." Etienne Jouy went so far as to insist that "chaque quartier" was "une nation à part." This seems to be an exaggeration, since residential mobility, social affiliations, and mondanité itself created a great deal of interaction. In any event, Christophe Charle has shown that the social composition of each neighborhood remained strikingly homogeneous in the early twentieth century: "le Faubourg Saint-Germain garde une réalité sociologique puisque près de 40% des nobles anciens y élisent domicile. L'aristocratie nouvelle, en revanche, suivant en cela le reste de la bourgeoisie, préfère nettement la rive droite (Faubourg Saint-Honoré et 8e arrondissement dans son ensemble) ou les nouveaux quartiers de l'ouest (16e et 17e arrondissements)." Of the recent nobles with domiciles in Paris at the time, almost 44 percent lived in the eighth arrondissement, while only about 10 percent lived in the seventh. It is credible, therefore, for Martin-Fugier to assert that "Les gens du monde se classeraient . . . selon les adresses de l'hôtel particulier qu'ils habitent." Etienne Jouy, *L'Hermite de la Chaussée d'Antin, ou observations sur les moeurs et usages parisiennes au commencement du XIXe siècle* (Paris, 1815), 3:293; Christophe Charle, "Noblesse et élites en France au début du XXe siècle," in *Noblesses européennes*, 428; Martin-Fugier, *Vie élégante*, 109. On the linguistic variations that distinguished each quartier, see Georges Matoré, *Le Vocabulaire et la société sous Louis Philippe* (Geneva, 1951), 51–57.

37. Charles de Rémusat, *Mémoires*, 1:133, 170.

38. Agoult, *Mémoires*, 204. See also Armaillé, *Quand on savait vivre heureux*, 157. See also Martin-Fugier, *Vie élégante*, 193; Bertaut, *Faubourg Saint-Germain*, 8.

39. Martin-Fugier, *Vie élégante*, 117–19; Agoult, *Mes souvenirs*, 257; Charle, "Noblesse et élites en France," 429–30; Girardin, *Vicomte de Launay: Lettres parisiennes*, 3:9, 193; Gay, *Salons célèbres*, 32–33.

40. On high society in Toulouse and Grenoble, see René de Belleval, *Souvenirs de ma jeunesse* (Paris, 1895), 7; Bernard Jacquier, *Le Légitimisme dauphinois, 1830–1870* (Grenoble, 1976). Balabine describes the mondain habits of Paris's Russian colony in his *Paris de 1842 à 1852*, 219.

41. Beaumont-Vassy, *Salons de Paris sous Louis-Philippe*, 321–24; Girardin, *Vicomte de Launay: Lettres parisiennes*, 2:261; Martin-Fugier, *Vie élégante*, 102, 110.

42. Charles de Rémusat, *Mémoires*, 3:99.

43. Girardin, *Vicomte de Launay: Lettres parisiennes*, 3:193; Staël, *Considérations*, 2:152; Agoult, *Mémoires*, 204. Stendhal mocked the tension in society between social exclusiveness and political pragmatism in *Armance, or, Scenes from a Parisian Salon in 1827*, trans. Gilbert Sale and Suzanne Sale (London, 1960).

44. Haussonville, *Ma jeunesse*, 246, 253; Boigne, *Memoirs*, 2:181–82; Maillé, *Souvenirs*, 51–53; Charles de Rémusat, *Mémoires*, 1:288, 353; Montcalm, *Mon journal*, 100, 149.

45. Guizot, *Madame de Rumford*, 31–32.

46. See Montcalm, *Mon journal*, 199; Boigne, *Memoirs*, 2:178–82; Zurich, *Femme heureuse*, 478. At the end of 1816, Montcalm had to begin asking guests who "had adopted a more resolute nuance of opinion" not to trouble her rest or disregard her hospitality by engaging in hurtful discussions. At the same time, Madame de Boigne, who was shunned by those who found her too supportive of Elie Decazes, had to begin avoiding sensitive topics of conversation whenever her ultraroyalist aunt, the vicomtesse d'Osmond, visited her salon.

47. Montcalm, *Mon journal*, 136; Frénilly, *Mémoires*, 347; Boigne, *Memoirs*, 2:111; Herriot, *Madame Récamier*, 2:136; Broglie, *Souvenirs*, 2:9–10.

48. Balabine, *Paris de 1842 à 1852*, 103; Girardin, *Vicomte de Launay: Lettres parisiennes*, 4:237, 267; Armaillé, *Quand on savait vivre heureux*, 69.

49. This was Bertier de Sauvigny's view as well: "Politics being the principal subject, along with literature, it is easy to imagine that these salons were characterized especially by their political color." Bertier de Sauvigny, *Bourbon Restoration*, 262.

50. Balabine, *Paris de 1842 à 1852*, 102–4; Villemain, *Souvenirs contemporains*, 1:465 (emphasis in the original). The Congrégation was a Catholic association of several hundred members, including a number of prominent ultraroyalists and politically active clergy. Liberals denounced it as an all-powerful secret society that controlled the state from behind the scenes.

51. Sainte-Beuve, *Portraits de femmes*, 62–63; Dino, *Memoirs*, 1:202, 213.

52. Apponyi, *Vingt-cinq ans à Paris*, 1:406; 2:285.

53. Charles de Rémusat, *Mémoires*, 1:340–41; Guizot, quoted in Stenger, *Grandes dames*, 367; Viel-Castel, *Faubourg Saint-Germain*, 6–7.

54. Villemain, *Souvenirs contemporains*, 1:454 (emphasis in the original); Beaumont-Vassy, *Salons de Paris sous Louis-Philippe*, 258–59. Chapter 5 discusses the various functions of political salons and examines the degree to which salonnières could be said to have exercised political influence.

55. Dauphin, "Salons de la Restauration," in *Femmes dans la cité*, 257; Balzac, *Secrets of La Princesse de Cardignan*.

56. Charles de Rémusat, *Mémoires*, 1:277, 361, 397; Herriot, *Madame Récamier*, 2:176–77; Tassé, *Salons française*, 37; Bassanville, *Salons d'autrefois*, 1:viii.

57. Dauphin, "Salons de la Restauration," in *Femmes dans la cité*, 254. For a similar analysis of the differences between the salons of the right and the left, see Martin-Fugier, "Cour et la ville," 120–21; Sylvie Aprile, "La République au salon: Vie et mort d'une forme de sociabilité politique (1865–1885)," *Revue d'histoire moderne et contemporaine* 38 (July–September 1991): 475.

58. Sainte-Beuve, *Portraits de femmes*, 63–64.

59. Guizot, *Madame de Rumford*, 7; Charles de Rémusat, *Mémoires*, 1:542.

60. This was the opinion of Delphine de Girardin in *Vicomte de Launay: Lettres parisiennes*, 2:259–60.

61. Jacques Vier, *La Comtesse d'Agoult et son temps* (Paris, 1955), 1:28; Dauphin, "Salons de la Restauration," in *Femmes dans la cité*, 257.

62. Stendhal, *Esquisses*, 30.

63. Agoult, *Mémoires*, 205; Bertaut, *Faubourg Saint-Germain*, 8.

64. Hugo, *Misérables*, 3:54. On political intolerance in ultraroyalist salons, see Stendhal, *Armance*, 47–49; Boigne, *Mémoires*, 2:16; Agoult, *Mémoires*, 205, 229, 233.

65. Balabine, *Paris de 1842 à 1852*, 110–11; Armaillé, quoted in Higgs, *Nobles in Nineteenth-Century France*, 212–13.

66. Agoult, *Mémoires*, 205; Stenger, *Grandes dames*, 117, 129; Boigne, *Mémoires*, 2:16.

67. Stenger, *Grandes dames*, 312, 332–33; Vier, *Comtesse d'Agoult*, 1:94–101. Stendhal wrote in 1826 that "High society is in the process of reviving the mores of the era of Louis XVI." Stendhal, *Esquisses*, 12.

68. Madame de La Briche to Frénilly, 1815, in Frénilly, *Mémoires*, 347n. Liberals widely blamed the ultras for their "exaggerated hatreds and violent opinions." See Staël, *Considérations*, 2:151; Agoult, *Mémoires*, 84; Boigne, *Mémoires*, 2:111; Duras to Roselie de Constant, 1823, in Pailhès, *Duchesse de Duras et Chateaubriand*, 277–78; Charles de Rémusat, *Mémoires*, 1:235; Boigne, *Mémoires*, 2:16.

69. Lamartine, quoted in Baron Arthur Léon Imbert de Saint-Amand, *The Duchess of Angoulême and the Two Restorations*, trans. James Davis (New York, 1900), 313–21, 352.

70. Waresquiel, *Duc de Richelieu*, 249, 294, 305, 388; Broglie, *Souvenirs*, 2:121.

71. Rosanvallon, *Moment Guizot*, 72, 107–15.

72. Charles de Rémusat, *Mémoires*, 1:370, 452; Guizot, *Madame de Rumford*, 7–8.

73. Bertant, *Faubourg Saint-Germain*, 156–58, 189–90; Charles de Rémusat, *Mémoires*, 1:361, 370, 451; Stenger, *Grandes dames*, 366–67. Salvandy called Broglie's salon "le canapé de la doctrine." Apponyi, *Vingt-cinq ans à Paris*, 3:57–58.

74. Frénilly, *Mémoires*, 347. See also Stenger, *Grandes dames*, 331; Bartillart, *Histoire de la noblesse*, 1:257; Maillé, *Souvenirs*, 206.

75. Ory, "Salon," 118.

76. Armaillé, *Quand on savait vivre heureux*, 211; Dino, *Memoirs*, 2:86.

77. Edmond de Lignères d'Alton-Shée, *Mes mémoires (1826–1848)* (Paris, 1869), 288; Dosne, *Mémoires*.

78. Guinot and Balzac, quoted in Martin-Fugier, "Cour et la ville," 110; Balabine, *Paris de 1842 à 1852*, 94; Beaumont-Vassy, *Salons de Paris sous Louis-Philippe*, 86.

79. André Jardin, *Tocqueville: A Biography*, trans. Lydia Davis (New York, 1988), 378–79; Jules Bertaut, *Le Faubourg Saint-Germain en 1835: Verité inédite* (Paris, 1935), 250–51, 280–81.

80. Apponyi, *Vingt-cinq ans à Paris*, 2:234, 301–2; 3:308; Balabine, *Paris de 1842 à 1852*, 90–94, 176, 280–81; Ancelot, *Salon de Paris*, 113.

81. Balzac warned that "le monde forgets those it does not see everyday and everywhere." Fortassier, *Mondains*, 39.

82. Boigne, *Mémoires*, 1:1:490–92. Rémusat, who insisted that he lost "half his political relations" when he stopped going to Madame de Castellane's, argued that his father had not been made a peer at the beginning of the Restoration because "he was forgotten in Paris" after having withdrawn from "salon society." Charles de Rémusat, *Mémoires*, 1:167.

83. Agulhon explained that "la vie de salon" had "ses cercles concentriques." On ordinary days, "le salon est relativement intime, réduit à une 'société' de famille élargie et d'amis proches." This is how Haussonville remembered the pattern of daily life in society during the Restoration: "On recevait alors beaucoup plus simplement que de nos jours. Un petit nombre de familiers étaient presque partout sur le pied de venir, sans invitation préalable et même sans prévenir, demander à dîner, quand cela leur convenait, aux ménages qui passaient pour avoir une bonne table et pour jouir d'une certaine aisance." Rémusat called the three salons he frequented in his youth "salons de fondation." Agulhon, *Cercle*, 25; Haussonville, *Ma jeunesse*, 240; Charles de Rémusat, *Mémoires*, 1:175.

84. Charles de Rémusat, *Mémoires*, 4:148. See Dauphin, "Salons de la Restauration," in *Femmes dans la cité*, 252. See Chapter 5 for a fuller treatment of these matters.

85. George Armstrong Kelly, *The Humane Comedy: Constant, Tocqueville, and French Liberalism* (Cambridge, 1992), 19. On the prevalence of kinship ties in the salons of Faubourg Saint-Germain and in Broglie's salon, see Haussonville, *Ma jeunesse*, 225, 256–57, 277; Broglie, *Souvenirs*, 1:9–10. Sylvie Aprile observes that republican society of the 1860s and 1870s had a similarly familial configuration because republicans "a su tisser autour des nouveaux hommes politiques la trame d'un réseau d'amitiés et d'alliances matrimoniales solide." Aprile, "République au salon," 482.

86. Haussonville, *Ma jeunesse*, 238–39; Charles de Rémusat, *Mémoires*, 1:173, 269; Apponyi, *Vingt-cinq ans à Paris*, 3:203.

87. André-Jean Tudesq, *Les Pairs de France au temps de Guizot* (Paris, 1956), 266.

88. Bertier de Sauvigny, *Bourbon Restoration*, 261.

89. Darrow, "French Noblewomen," 42–57.

90. Martin-Fugier, "Cour et la ville," 116; Martin-Fugier, *Vie élégante*, 216–18.

91. Boigne, *Memoirs*, 3:3:1; Charles de Rémusat, *Mémoires*, 4:211; Laure d'Abrantès, *Memoirs of the Duchess of Abrantès: 1830*, trans. Gerard Shelly (London, n.d. [1929?]), 37, 53.

92. Serna, "The Noble," in *Enlightenment Portraits*, 78. See also Chaussinand-Nogaret, *Histoire des élites*, 286–91; André-Jean Tudesq, "L'Elargissement de la noblesse en France dans la première moitié du XIXe siècle," in *Noblesses européennes au XIXe siècle* (Paris, 1988), 121–35.

93. See Christophe Charle, "Noblesse et élites en France," in *Noblesses européennes*, 432; Martin-Fugier, "Cour et la ville," 110; Martin-Fugier, *Vie élégante*, 392–93.

94. Girardin, *Vicomte de Launay: Lettres parisiennes*, 2:318; Balabine, *Paris de 1842 à 1852*, 113–14; Stendhal, *Lucien Leuwen*, trans. Louise Varèse (New York, 1950), 2:103.

95. On the authority of *les douairières*, see the now classic accounts in Agoult, *Mémoires*, 227–28; Comtesse Dash [Gabrielle Anna Poillow, vicomtesse de Saint-Mars], *Mémoires des autres* (Paris, 1896–97), 2:196; Guillelmine-Marie Ferrón de La Ferronnays, *Mémoires de Mme de La Ferronnays* (Paris, 1899), 329.

96. Gabrielle Houbre, "L'Entrée dans le monde: Le Jeune Homme et les femmes (première moitié du XIXe siècle)," in *Femmes dans la cité, 1815–1871*, ed. Alain Corbin et al. (Grâne, 1997), 261–62; Mayer, *Persistence of the Old Regime*, 13–14, 84–85; Dosne, *Mémoires*, 2:16–17.

97. Adeline Daumard, "L'Oisiveté aristocratique et bourgeoise en France au XIXe siècle: privilège ou malédiction?" in *Oisiveté et loisirs dans les sociétés occidentales au XIXe siècle. Colloque pluridisciplinaire, Amiens 19–20 novembre 1982* (Abbeville, 1983), 127; Martin-Fugier, "Cour et la ville," 132–33.

98. Viel-Castel, *Faubourg Saint-Germain*, xvii; Balabine, *Paris de 1842 à 1852*, 114.

99. Stendhal, *Esquisses*, 30, 118, 154–55; Stendhal, *Lucien Leuwen*, 2:102–5.

CHAPTER FIVE: Salons and *Salonnières* in the Politics of the Restoration and the July Monarchy

1. Beaumont-Vassy considered the salon of the Ministry of Foreign Affairs "the most interesting of all, especially because of the news and political information that one is certain to gather there." Beaumont-Vassy, *Salons de Paris sous Louis-Philippe*, 271.

2. Boigne, *Memoirs*, 3:236–37; Abrantès, *Memoirs of the Duchess of Abrantès*, 200–208.

3. See, e.g., Veneur, *Echo des salons*, 1:ix.

4. Dino, *Memoirs*, 3:60n. Salons that could be used to spread information could also be used to squelch it, as when the duc de Richelieu asked the duchesse de Duras to "impose silence" on those in her salon at the Tuileries who voiced outrage at the suppression of Chateaubriand's *La Monarchie selon la Charte*. Agénor Bardoux, *La Duchesse de Duras* (Paris, 1898), 196–99, 300.

5. Chateaubriand, *Mémoires d'outre-tombe*, 4:57–58; Récamier, *Memoirs and Correspondence*, 154–65. Claude-Isabelle Brelot argues that the salon's communicative functions turned society women into what he calls "managers of a political network" insofar as they were in a position to selectively transmit privileged information and were routinely asked to use their own discretion by those who requested their assistance. Chateaubriand repeatedly told Récamier to use her own judgment or "to make what use of it you choose" when he sent her personally advantageous news. Brelot, "De la tutelle à la collaboration: Une Femme de la noblesse dans la vie politique (1814–1830)," in *Femmes dans la Cité, 1815–1871*, ed. Alain Corbin, Jacqueline Lalouette, and Michèle Riot-Sarcey (Grâne, 1997), 244; Récamier, *Memoirs and Correspondence*, 161, 166.

6. See Pange, *Madame de Staël and the Duke of Wellington*, 36.

7. See Charles de Rémusat, *Mémoires*, 1:194, 405.

8. Haussonville, *Ma jeunesse*, 265, 275; Boigne, *Memoirs*, 2:296; Marie Joséphine Louise Gontaut-Biron, *Memoirs of the Duchesse de Gontaut*, trans. Mrs. J. W. Davis (New York, 1894), 136–37. De Gontaut (1773–1862) was the governess of the royal family's children during the Restoration.

9. Stendhal, *Esquisses*, 144, 155–56. Stendhal wrote that the newspapers of Paris held sway over public opinion only during the six months each year when high society retreated to the provinces.

10. Bassanville, *Salons d'autrefois*, 4:8.

11. When, in 1835, the press reported indecent behavior at Achille Vigier's home at Granvaux at which Thiers and Duchâtel were spending the night, Rémusat commented indignantly on "cette immixtion calomnieuse de la presse dans la choses de la vie privée." Charles de Rémusat, *Mémoires*, 3:148–49.

12. Récamier, *Memoirs and Correspondence*, 256. Madame de Vaudémont called M. de La Chaise "her thermometer," because she could read on his face "the variations of politics" more clearly than in all the newspapers available at the time: "I have only to ask him news of the ministers or of the men in power; right away, his nose goes up or down depending on the greater or lesser degree of favor they enjoy at the moment; and this nose is always so well informed that I could not truly say where it fishes up its news." Bassanville, *Salons d'autrefois*, 1:15.

13. On attitudes toward the press under the July Monarchy, see Reddy, *Invisible Code*, 210–14.

14. Ancelot, *Salon de Paris*, 61; Dino, *Memoirs*, 1:191–96; 2; Récamier, *Memoirs and Correspondence*, 303.

15. Genlis, *Memoirs*, 2:147–48; Girardin, *Vicomte de Launay: Lettres parisiennes*, 4:21819. On the practice of ghost-writing by politicians, see Charles de Rémusat, *Mémoires*, 3:357–59. The same suspicions of calculated and impersonal speech help explain the preference in high society for memoirs over history, the former being a record of intimate hopes and hidden deceptions, while the latter was an official portrayal of how men of state wished to appear.

16. Boigne, *Memoirs*, 2:296, 3:227; Apponyi, *Vingt-cinq ans à Paris*, 3:30–31; Dino, *Memoirs*, 3:292. Face-to-face interviews with Dino convinced Rémusat that "elle redoutait pour elle-même le rôle en grand de *Nièce du curé*, et la responsabilité d'une influence vraie ou supposée au coeur d'un gouvernement ouvert au jour et au bruit de la publicité." Charles de Rémusat, *Mémoires*, 2:577; emphasis in original.

17. Girardin, *Vicomte de Launay: Lettres parisiennes*, 2:91, 291; Kirsten Borg, "Princess Lieven: A New Interpretation of Her Role" (Ph.D. thesis, University of Illinois at Chicago, 1978), 209, 267; Ernest Daudet, *Une Vie d'ambassadrice au siècle dernier: La Princesse de Lieven* (Paris, 1910), 181–88; Apponyi, *Vingt-cinq ans à Paris*, 4:29–30.

18. See Martin-Fugier, *Vie élégante*, 268–69.

19. Récamier, *Memoirs and Correspondence*, 154–66, 322; Bardoux, *Duchesse de Duras*, 267–68, 300; Wood, *Benjamin Constant*, 217–18.

20. Brelot found this sort of role to be paramount in Céleste de Vaulchier's political collaboration with her husband. In addition to her duties as a salonnière in Paris and Besançon, Madame de Vaulchier served as M. de Vaulchier's "information agent," summarizing his correspondence to his local constituents, assessing the political climate in Paris, alerting him to rumors, and giving him advice about those with whom he should speak. Brelot, "De la tutelle à la collaboration," 244–45. See also Dosne, *Mémoires*, 1:xxv–xxvi.

21. François Guizot, *Lettres de François Guizot et de la Princess de Lieven, 1836–1846* (Paris, 1963), 2:20–21, 35, 67–68, 163, 261; Borg, "Princess Lieven," 270, 291–93, 270.

22. Chateaubriand, *Mémoires d'outre-tombe*, 3:498–99. Of Chateaubriand's fitness for political life, Maillé wrote, "J'étais convaincue que la belle imagination de M. de Chateaubriand et sa mobilité nuiraient à ses succès d'homme d'Etat, et qu'enfin, pour trancher le mot, il ne serait jamais dans les affaires qu'une cause d'agitation, autant son beau style, la chaleur de sa affections pour son pays le rendraient selon moi capable d'élever à la France un monument historique et littéraire qui fût digne d'elle. J'ai toujours cherché à le dégoûter de la carrière politique dans laquelle il est incapable de porter la justesse d'esprit et le sang-froid nécessaire, pour ramener à la littérature dont il tirera toujours sa véritable gloire." Maillé, *Souvenirs*, 90–91.

23. Bardoux, *Duchesse de Duras*, 185–86, 239, 250, 283–85, 392–93.

24. Dino, *Memoirs*, 1:79–80.

25. Balzac, who received his initiation under the tutelage of Madame de Berny observed: "*L'usage du monde*, when it is not a gift of high birth, constitutes an education that chance must second by a certain elegance of form, distinguished traits, and a timber of voice." Balzac, quoted by Fortassier, *Mondains*, 192. On the increased scrutiny of comportment in society, see Reddy, *Invisible Code*, 22–23.

26. Lougee, *Paradis des Femmes*, 211–13. See Houbre, "L'Entrée dans le monde," in *Femmes dans le cité*, 261–70.

27. Waresquiel, *Duc de Richelieu*, 231; Bardoux, *Duchesse de Duras*, 124–25, 171–77.

28. Charles de Rémusat, *Mémoires*, 1:456; Boigne, *Memoirs*, 3:308–12.

29. Récamier, *Memoirs and Correspondence*, 282–323; Herriot, *Madame Récamier*, 2:199; Balabine, *Paris de 1842 à 1852*, 292–93; Borg, "Princess Lieven," 269–80; Dosne, *Mémoires*, 1:xiv–xxvi.

30. Montcalm, *Mon journal*, 11.

31. Staël, *Ten Years' Exile*, 47.

32. Marquise de Montcalm, *Un Salon politique sous la Restauration: Correspondence de la marquise de Montcalm*, ed. Emmanuel de Lévis-Mirepoix (Paris, 1949), 25.

33. Charles de Rémusat, *Mémoires*, 3:98; Boigne, *Memoirs*, 2:297; Maillé, *Souvenirs*, 287–88; Daudet, *Vie d'ambassadrice*, 186; Borg, "Princess Lieven," 157.

34. Chateaubriand, *Mémoires d'outre-tombe*, 4:169; Ancelot, *Salon de Paris*, 68; Haussonville, *Ma jeunesse*, 274; Apponyi, *Vingt-cinq ans à Paris*, 4:112; Pailhès, *Duchesse de Duras et Chateaubriand*, 421; Guizot, *Lettres*, 1:115.

35. Récamier, *Memoirs and Correspondence*, 227, 256, 342; Etienne-Jean Delécluze and Sainte-Beuve, quoted in Wagener, *Madame Récamier*, 348; Cynthia Gladwyn, "Madame Récamier," in *Affairs of the Mind: The Salon in Europe and America from the Eighteenth to the Twentieth Century*, ed. Peter Quennell (Washington, D.C., 1980), 65; Herriot, *Madame Récamier*, 2:176.

36. Charles de Rémusat, *Mémoires*, 1:339.

37. Ancelot, *Salon de Paris*, 100, 108; Villemain, *Souvenirs contemporains*, 1:460, 465; Apponyi, *Vingt-cinq ans à Paris*, 3:204–7; Ancelot, *Salons de Paris*, 243–44.

38. Villemain, *Souvenirs contemporains*, 1:478–79; Pailhès, *Duchesse de Duras et Chateaubriand*, 407–8; Gay, *Salons célèbres*, 59, 140; Herriot, *Madame Récamier*, 2:176.

39. Bassanville, *Salons d'autrefois*, 2:135, 142–43; Vier, *Comtesse d'Agoult*, 2:11–43. The prominence and longevity of the salon founded by Marie d'Agoult upon her return to Paris in 1839 owed something to its status as a traditional bureau d'esprit and its association with the talent and the fortunes of Liszt. On musical salons, see Fortassier, *Mondains*, 72–73.

40. Bassanville, *Salons d'autrefois*, 4:145–46; Apponyi, *Vingt-cinq ans à Paris*, 3:8.

41. Agoult, *Mémoires*, 270. On the role of foreign hostesses in Parisian society, see Bassanville, *Salons d'autrefois*, 4:2–4; Turquan, *Monde*, 300–301; Bertier de Sauvigny, *Bourbon Restoration*, 262–63.

42. Beaumont-Vassy, *Salons de Paris sous Louis-Philippe*, 132–40; Martin-Fugier, *Vie quotidienne de Louis-Philippe*, 256.

43. Perrot, *Femmes publiques*, 64.

44. Girardin, *Vicomte de Launay: Lettres parisiennes*, 4:200–201.

45. J. E. Zimmerman, *Dictionary of Classical Mythology* (New York, 1971), 92; Dosne, *Mémoires*, 1:xii–xiii; Pailhès, *Duchesse de Duras et Chateaubriand*, 162, 397; Apponyi, *Vingt-cinq ans à Paris*, 4:20.

46. Girardin, *Vicomte de Launay: Lettres parisiennes*, 3:311; Balzac, quoted in Dosne, *Mémoires*, 1:xiii; *Dictionnaire de la conversation et de la lecture, inventaire raisonné des notions générales les plus indispensables à tous*, ed. William Duckett et al. 2d ed. (Paris, 1854–58), 15:298.

47. Guizot, *Lettres*, 1:121; Dino, *Memoirs*, 3:48; Balabine, *Paris de 1842 à 1852*, 22.

48. Girardin, *Vicomte de Launay: Lettres parisiennes*, 2:301–2, 3:245; Tassé, *Salons du XIXe siècle*, 66; Custine, *Empire of the Czar*, 382–83.

49. Bardoux, *Duchesse de Duras*, 170, 184, 343–44.

50. Montcalm, *Mon journal*, 252–55; Chateaubriand, *Mémoires d'outre-tombe*, 3:458–68.

51. Herriot, *Madame Récamier*, 2:73; Dino, *Memoirs*, 2:117; Turquan, *Femmes*, 8; Charles de Rémusat, *Mémoires*, 1:252; 2:567–68.

52. Apponyi, *Vingt-cinq ans à Paris*, 3:224–28; Balabine, *Paris de 1842 à 1852*, 105; Custine, *Empire of the Czar*, 383; Abrantès, *Memoirs of Madame Junot*, 5:43–44.

53. Stenger, *Grandes dames*, vii–viii.

54. Brelot, "De la tutelle à la collaboration," 274; Dosne, *Mémoires*, 2:16.

55. Montcalm quoted in Agoult, *Mémoires*, 230; Martin-Fugier, *Vie élégante*, 188; Daudet, *Vie d'ambassadrice*, 193.

56. Villemain, *Souvenirs contemporains*, 1:476; Agoult, *Mémoires*, 230–33. So reluctant was d'Agoult to renounce everything and devote herself fully to the cult of a great man that she refused to open a salon in the early 1830s, considering the vocation of salonnière at the time incompatible with her spirit, her character, and her ambitions. Ibid., 266–69.

57. Zurich, *Femme heureuse*, 464–77. The death or disgrace of a salon's principal male attraction commonly resulted in the forced retirement of the salonnière, perhaps in reference to the fate of Egeria herself, who was so heartbroken by Numa's death that she melted into tears and was changed into a fountain by Diana. Richelieu's death in 1822 forced his sister to withdraw from society. The same happened to the duchesse de Dino, whose salon lost its popularity and allure as her "political importance" seemed to vanish with Talleyrand's death in 1838. Lieven was twice cut adrift, once in England by the death of Canning and again in 1848, when Guizot fled into exile. On Montcalm's fate, see Villemain, *Souvenirs contemporains*, 1:479; Chateaubriand to Duras, 1822, in Bardoux, *Duchesse de Duras*, 321. On Dino, see Borg, "Princess Lieven," 206–7. Lieven's troubles are mentioned in Apponyi, *Vingt-cinq ans à Paris*, 1:143, Bassanville, *Salons d'autrefois*, 3:210–12, Dino, *Memoirs*, 3:279, and Balabine, *Paris de 1842 à 1852*, 292–93.

58. See, e.g., Borg, "Princess Lieven," 90; Apponyi, *Vingt-cinq ans à Paris*, 4:113; Chateaubriand, *Mémoires d'outre-tombe*, 4:249; Du Bled, *Rôle social et mondaine de la femme*, 108; Charles de Rémusat, *Mémoires*, 4:43; Custine, *Empire of the Czar*, 383; Stendhal, *Lucien Leuwen*, 1:32.

59. Borg, "Princess Lieven," 51, 76–77, 98–99.

60. Montcalm, *Mon journal*, 97, 107, 166; Waresquiel, *Duc de Richelieu*, 304, 314–17; Dauphin, "Salons de la Restauration," in *Femmes dans la cité*, 255.

61. Fraisse, *Reason's Muse*, 95.

62. Dino, *Memoirs*, 3:87, 292; Boigne, *Memoirs*, 3:80–81.

63. Stenger, *Grandes dames*, 98–99; Charles de Rémusat, *Mémoires*, 1:248; Harmand, *Madame de Genlis*, 455; Bardoux, *Duchesse de Duras*, 283–85, 392–93.

64. See Goodman, "Governing the Republic of Letters," 184–95; Gordon, "Philosophy, Sociology, and Gender," 906–7.

65. Girardin, *Vicomte de Launay: Lettres parisiennes*, 3:260; Ségur, *Women*, 1:vi; Bassanville, *Salons d'autrefois*, 3:2–10–12; Bertaut, *Faubourg Saint-Germain*, 190; Abrantès, *Histoire des salons*, 2:395. On the use of such metaphors by women, see Montcalm, *Mon journal*, 105; Dosne, *Mémoires*, 1:xxi; Zurich, *Femme heureuse*, 464; Herriot, *Madame Récamier*, 2:285; Gay, *Salons célèbres*, 59. The representation of salonnières as nurses seems to have

begun during the Restoration, when it became common to relate the ministrations of salonnières to the bloodletting of the Chamber. Sainte-Beuve, who wanted to place Duras in line with the salonnières of the past, called her "un chef d'orchestre" in his *Nouveaux lundis*. The twentieth century also seems to have preferred the language of an earlier time, perhaps to persuade women that they had more power in the past at a time when they were winning substantive political rights. See esp. Du Bled, *Rôle social et mondaine de la femme*, 10–13; Glotz and Marie, *Salons du XVIIIe siècle*, 13. Marmontel's metaphor has had a long shelf life: "a salon is like an instrument, a little like a symphony orchestra," Stephanie Mills writes in "Salons and Beyond," *Utne Reader* 44 (March–April 1991): 73.

66. Ancelot, *Salons de Paris*, 155; Chateaubriand, *Mémoires d'outre-tombe*, 4:188; Beaumont-Vassy, *Salons de Paris sous Louis-Philippe*, 259–63.

67. Abrantès, *Memoirs of the Duchess of Abrantès*, 118; Montcalm, *Mon journal*, 10; Waresquiel, *Duc de Richelieu*, 319; Villemain, *Souvenirs contemporains*, 1:477; Ancelot, *Salon de Paris*, 72–73, 78, 80.

68. Pailhès, *Duchesse de Duras et Chateaubriand*, 424–25, 432; Récamier, *Memoirs and Correspondence*, 122, 136, 232; Chateaubriand, *Mémoires d'outre-tombe*, 3:499, 517.

69. Charles de Rémusat, *Mémoires*, 3:62; Chateaubriand, *Mémoires d'outre-tombe*, 4:473.

70. On April 11, 1830, the duc de Montmorency wrote to Récamier to compliment her "on the fact that no new book appears which does not contain hymns of admiration for you. Everyone, without exception, is being insulted on one side or the other. You are the only person in France who is respected." Herriot, *Madame Récamier*, 2:227.

71. Wellington to Récamier, January 13, 1815, in Chateaubriand, *Mémoires d'outre-tombe*, 4:460; Abrantès, *Memoirs of the Duchess of Abrantès*, 118; Sainte-Beuve, quoted in Herriot, *Madame Récamier*, 2:72. Despite Récamier's studied political neutrality, liberals accused her of associating with ultras, while ultras denounced her for fraternizing with liberals.

72. Bawr, *Mes souvenirs*, 108–9; Dino, *Memoirs*, 2:123; Boigne, *Memoirs*, 1:1:178–79. On the phases of Récamier's life, see Wagener, *Madame Récamier*, 311–432.

73. Staël to Récamier, July 15, 1816, in Herriot, *Madame Récamier*, 2:19; Goethe and Montcalm quoted in Wagener, *Madame Récamier*, 294, 519; Boigne, *Mémoires*, 2:166–67; Agoult, *Mémoires*, 276.

74. Dino, *Memoirs*, 3:30; Bawr, *Mes souvenirs*, 311–12.

75. Borg, "Princess Lieven," 77. On this theme, see Girardin, *Vicomte de Launay: Lettres parisiennes*, 2:70–71.

76. Boigne, *Memoirs*, 3:3:308–9; Montcalm, *Mon journal*, 131, 140–45; Brelot, "De la tutelle à la collaboration," 242–43.

77. Girardin, *Vicomte de Launay: Lettres parisiennes*, 3:230; Bawr, *Mes souvenirs*, 7; Borg, "Princess Lieven," 187, 411; Viel-Castel, *Faubourg Saint-Germain*, 27.

78. Bardoux, *Duchesse de Duras*, 180; Boigne, *Mémoires*, 2:2:40; Broglie, *Souvenirs*, 2:146–47; Martin-Fugier, *Vie élégante*, 177.

79. Ancelot, *Salon de Paris*, viii. The reputations of Martignac, Salvandy, Raguse, La Ferronnays, and Pasquier are discussed in Maillé, *Souvenirs*, 261, 278; Balabine, *Paris de 1842 à 1852*, 189; Boigne, *Mémoires*, 2:2:158; Bassanville, *Salons d'autrefois*, 4:118.

80. Karl Mannheim, "The Problem of the Intelligentsia: An Inquiry into Its Past and Present Role," in *Essays on the Sociology of Culture* (London, 1956), 140.

81. Ancelot, *Salon de Paris*, 78–79, 128; Haussonville, *Ma jeunesse*, 240; Chateaubriand, *Mémoires d'outre-tombe*, 3:459.

82. Agulhon, *Cercle*, 27; Martin-Fugier, *Vie élégante*, 194–98; Dosne, *Mémoires*, 1:xi.

83. Hugo, *Misérables*, 3:55–56; Girardin, *Vicomte de Launay: Lettres parisiennes*, 4:216; Vier, *Comtesse d'Agoult*, 112–14. On the celebrity of Tocqueville and Villèle, see Récamier, *Memoirs and Correspondence*, 370; E. Gans, "Le Salon de Madame Récamier," *Revue de Paris*, February 7, 1836, 237–42; Martin-Fugier, *Vie élégante*, 219; Boigne, *Memoirs*, 2:2:204–5. Stendhal gives a fictional account of the salon's role in this quest for fame from the point of view of the old aristocracy (in *Armance*) and the wealthy bourgeoisie (in *Lucien Leuwen*).

84. Ancelot, *Salons de Paris*, 179; Girardin, *Vicomte de Launay: Lettres parisiennes*, 2:42.

85. Stendhal, *Lucien Leuwen*, 2:298; Agoult, *Mémoires*, 266.

86. Charles de Rémusat, *Mémoires*, 4:42, 136–39; Boigne, *Mémoires*, 2:2:167; Beaumont-Vassy, *Salons de Paris sous Louis-Philippe*, 7, 18–19.

87. Martin-Fugier, *Vie élégante*, 276–84; Montcalm, *Mon journal*, 200; Haussonville, *Ma jeunesse*, 276; Apponyi, *Vingt-cinq ans à Paris*, 3:224–25; 4:413; Borg, "Princess Lieven," 396. D'Agoult explained that the salonnières of her generation had a preference for "the most considerable, the most influential, and most illustrious men." Agoult, *Mémoires*, 266.

88. Martin-Fugier, *Vie élégante*, 20, 393.

89. Comtesse Dash (Gabrielle Anna Poillow, vicomtesse de Saint-Mars) cited in Bartillat, *Histoire de la noblesse française*, 1:400; Astolphe de Custine, *Ethel* (Paris, 1839), 1:308.

90. Girardin, *Vicomte de Launay: Lettres parisiennes*, 2:262. On "salons and their attractions," see Martin-Fugier, "Cour et la ville," 122–23. On lions and dandies in salons, see Martin-Fugier, *Vie élégante*, 355–59.

CHAPTER SIX: The Decline of Salons (1830–1848)

1. See Jouy, *Hermite de la Chaussée-d'Antin*, 1:134–35; Agoult, *Mémoires*, 201, 251–52; Fortassier, *Mondains*, 89.

2. See esp. Germaine de Staël, *De l'Influence des passions sur le bonheur des individus et des nations* (Paris, 1820), 162–75.

3. Montcalm, *Mon journal*, 89, 130, 144, 149; Guizot, *Madame de Rumford*, 4, 31–32. Such sentiments were commonplace by the 1820s. They were both a reaction to and an expression of the escalating politicization of high society. See Ancelot, *Salon de Paris*, 148–49; Gontaut-Biron, *Memoirs*, 1:48; Stendhal, *Esquisses*, 2:250; Custine, *Empire of the Czar*, 177–78; Dino, *Memoirs*, 2:68.

4. See, e.g., Montcalm, *Mon journal*, 208, 324; Ancelot, *Salons de Paris*, 16; id., *Salon de Paris*, 148–49; Dino, *Memoirs*, 1:213–14; Charles de Rémusat, *Mémoires*, 3:95; Girardin, *Vicomte de Launay: Lettres parisiennes*, 4:251.

5. Ancelot, *Salon de Paris*, 147; Maillé, *Souvenirs*, 293; Récamier, *Memoirs and Correspondence*, 369.

6. Armaillé, *Quand on savait vivre heureux*, viii, 60; Dino, *Memoirs*, 3:180; Ancelot, *Salons de Paris*, 72. The Pritchard affair, during which Guizot was attacked for doing too little to defend national honor, involved a quarrel over the expulsion of a British missionary, George Pritchard, from Tahiti by the French in November 1843.

7. Abrantès, *Salons révolutionnaires*, 51. For Ancelot, this was an old story: "In times of trouble," she wrote, "the voice of intelligent women ceases to be heard; like the song of birds vanishing in a storm, they lose this authority that leads the hearts of men to delicate things." Ancelot, *Salon de Paris*, 374.

8. Ancelot, *Salon de Paris*, 62; Charles de Rémusat, *Mémoires*, 3:88–89; Boigne, *Mémoires*, 2:252.

9. See André Jardin and Jean-André Tudesq, *Restoration and Reaction, 1815–1848*, trans. Elborg Forster (Cambridge, 1988), 73; Mansel, *Court of France*, 193; Chaussinand-Nogaret, *Histoire des élites*, 314.

10. Beaumont-Vassy, *Salons de Paris sous Louis-Philippe*, 3.

11. Maillé, *Souvenirs*, 391; Viel-Castel, *Faubourg Saint-Germain*, xxxvi.

12. On the reopening of Rumford's salon, see René Dujarric de la Rivière, *Dames de la Révolution* (Périgueux, 1963), 27. High society in the immediate aftermath of the Revolution of 1830 is characterized in Beaumont-Vassy, *Salons de Paris sous Louis-Philippe*, 3–6, 43–52; Dosne, *Mémoires*, 2:87; Boigne, *Mémoires*, 2:2:252; Bertaut, *Faubourg Saint-Germain*, 234.

13. Fortassier, *Mondains*, 113–14, 132–34; Herriot, *Madame Récamier*, 2:243; Apponyi, *Vingt-cinq ans à Paris*, 2:287–88.

14. See Apponyi, *Vingt-cinq ans à Paris*, 1:394–99; Agulhon, *Cercle*, 37; Bertaut, *Faubourg Saint-Germain*, 234–35.

15. Beaumont-Vassy, *Salons de Paris sous Louis-Philippe*, 33–34; Alméras, *Vie parisienne sous Louis-Philippe*, 436.

16. Apponyi, *Vingt-cinq ans à Paris*, 1:357–59, 401; Daumard, "Vie de salon," in *Sociabilité et société bourgeoise*, 87.

17. Apponyi, *Vingt-cinq ans à Paris*, 1:291; Agoult, *Mémoires*, 259.

18. On the role of the embassies, see Apponyi, *Vingt-cinq ans à Paris*, 2:114–319; Martin-Fugier, *Vie quotidienne de Louis-Philippe*, 254–55.

19. Boigne, *Mémoires*, 2:2:256; Dino, *Memoirs*, 1:24; Bertaut, *Faubourg Saint-Germain*, 2356–36; Apponyi, *Vingt-cinq ans à Paris*, 2:114–15, 314–17. The *bal de l'ancienne liste civile* is discussed in Martin-Fugier, "Cour et la ville," 129, and in Alméras, *Vie parisienne sous Louis-Philippe*, 436–38.

20. Apponyi, *Vingt-cinq ans à Paris*, 2:380–82; 3:8, 16, 84, 108; Dino, *Memoirs*, 1:34, 82; Beaumont-Vassy, *Salons de Paris sous Louis-Philippe*, 245–47.

21. Girardin, *Vicomte de Launay: Lettres parisiennes*, 1:42, 91; 2:11–12.

22. Beaumont-Vassy, *Salons de Paris sous Louis-Philippe*, 327; Balabine, *Paris de 1842 à 1852*, 113–19; Alton-Shée, *Mémoires*, 293–94. On the activities of Madame de Flahaut, see Dino, *Memoirs*, 3:19–23.

23. Agoult, *Mémoires*, 260. On generational change in society after 1830, see also Stendhal, *Armance*, 99–100; Haussonville, *Ma jeunesse*, 228, 320; Dujarric de La Rivière, *Dames de la Révolution*, 27.

24. Agoult, *Mémoires*, 260–62; Balabine, *Paris de 1842 à 1852*, 101; Dino, *Memoirs*, 1:245.

25. See Ancelot, *Salon de Paris*, 166–67; Balzac, *Autre étude de femme*, quoted in Matoré, *Vocabulaire*, 58; Ory, "Salon," 125.

26. Habermas, *Structural Transformation*, 65; Deborah Hertz, *Jewish High Society in Old Regime Berlin* (New Haven, 1988), 282.

27. Charles de Rémusat, *Mémoires*, 2:102–8, 215–16. See also André-Jean Tudesq, "Le Journal, lieu et lien de la société bourgeoise en France dans la première moitié du XIXe siècle," in *Sociabilité et société bourgeoise en France, en Allemagne et en Suisse, 1750–1850*, ed. Etienne François (Paris, 1986), 264–66; Huard, *Naissance de parti politique*, 55.

28. Guizot, *Madame de Rumford*, 4, 19; Charles de Rémusat, *Mémoires*, 3:88–89.

29. See Dino, *Memoirs*, 2:18; Boigne, *Mémoires*, 2:148.

30. Maillé, *Souvenirs*, 50; Girardin, *Vicomte de Launay: Lettres parisiennes*, 4:114–16.

31. Stendhal, *Esquisses*, 2:273. On Duras's liberalism, see Pailhès, *Duchesse de Duras et Chateaubriand*, 277–78, 425–38.

32. Montcalm, *Salon politique*, 25; Montcalm, *Mon journal*, 11; Ancelot, *Salon de Paris*, 60.

33. Boigne, *Mémoires*, 1:15, 220; Montcalm, *Mon journal*, 103; Montcalm, *Salon politique*, 91–98; Boigne, *Memoirs*, 3:311.

34. Boigne, *Memoirs*, 2:182; Ancelot, *Salon de Paris*, 78.

35. Boigne, *Mémoires*, 1:23.

36. Guizot to Lieven, July 14, 1837, in *Lettres*, 1:24.

37. On related themes, see Reddy, *Invisible Code*, 35, and Margadant, "Gender, Vice, and Political Imaginary," 1481.

38. Herriot, *Madame Récamier*, 2:177, 366–68; Bawr, *Mes souvenirs*, 106; Stendhal, *Scarlet and Black*, 319; id., *Armance*, 77–79; Haussonville, *Ma jeunesse*, 263–65 (emphasis in the original). Montcalm admitted that people with different opinions sometimes created irritation or constraint in her salon, but she often found the clash of ideas instructive, especially when someone of superior intellect led the conversation. Boigne thought she was "very exacting" because she wanted people to appreciate her mind, but d'Agoult found her extremely indulgent, subtly authoritative, and disinclined to intimidate anyone. When her godson, Armand Marquiset, visited her upon his arrival in Paris, she "received me as would a simple mortal, put me perfectly at ease, and questioned me with kindness for more than a hour about my mother, my family, and myself." Montcalm, *Mon journal*, 293; Boigne, *Memoirs*, 3:9; Agoult, *Mémoires*, 230–31; Armand Marquiset, quoted in Houbre, "L'Entrée dans le monde," in *Femmes dans le cité*, 265.

39. Goodman, *Republic of Letters*, 54–55, 234; id., "Governing the Republic of Letters," 189–90.

40. Stenger, *Grandes dames*, 400; Chastenay, *Mémoires*, 598. On gendered expressions of opposition to the Paris Commune, see Gay L. Gullickson, *Unruly Women of Paris: Images of the Commune* (Ithaca, N.Y., 1996).

41. On the "rise of women" under the Old Regime, see Gutwirth, *Twilight of the Goddesses*, 79.

42. Guizot to Lieven, October 29, 1839, *Lettres*, 1:310; Guizot, *Madame de Rumford*, 15; Pailhès, *Duchesse de Duras et Chateaubriand*, 413–14.

43. Stéphane Rials, "Le Cercle et le salon," in *Révolution et Contre-Révolution au XIX siècle* (Paris, 1987), 244–45. See also Martin-Fugier, *Vie élégante*, 214, 285–86.

44. The marquis de Custine explained that "[a] fixed security of position in society is the basis of courtesy in all its relations, and the source also of those sallies of wit that enliven conversation." D'Agoult recalled that a gentleman who frequented the salons of Faubourg Saint-Germain "n'avait ni vouloir ni pouvoir, comme il arrive en nos assemblées de parvenus, de se donner pour autre qu'il n'était, de paraître ce que ne l'avait pas fait sa naissance. Là aussi, contrairement à la vanité bourgeoise, les titres, les changes, les emplois, tous les accidents de la fortune ne comptaient guère, et l'on ne s'y réglait aucunement pour accroître ou diminuer l'honneur de l'accueil." Custine, *Empire of the Czar*, 178; Agoult, *Mémoires*, 206. On bourgeois anxieties of acceptance, see Stendhal's *Lucien Leuwen*. Stendhal reported to the English press in 1826 that "liberal writers" who had once criticized the style of the duchesse de Duras's novels had ceased to do so because "[i]ls craindraient de passer pour des gens qui n'ont pas leurs entrées dans la bonne compagnie." Stendhal, *Esquisses*, 2:30.

45. Bardoux, *Duchesse de Duras*, 309–10; Dosne, *Mémoires*, 1:xi; Daudet, *Vie d'ambassadrice*, 303.

46. Apponyi, *Vingt-cinq ans à Paris*, 3:224–28; Lieven to Guizot, September 25, 1837, in Guizot, *Lettres*, 1:121; Borg, "Princess Lieven," 401. The details of Lieven's life can be found in Daudet, *Vie d'ambassadrice*, and Borg, "Princess Lieven."

47. Borg, "Princess Lieven," 268; Charles de Rémusat, *Mémoires*, 3:143.

48. Martin-Fugier, *Vie élégante*, 212–14.

49. Rosanvallon, *Moment Guizot*, 117–18, 202–3.

50. Guizot, *Madame de Rumford*, 6–10; Guizot to Lieven, October 29, 1839, in Guizot, *Lettres*, 1:310.

51. Daudet, *Vie d'ambassadrice*, 259–60, 303; Borg, "Princess Lieven," 255; Guizot, *Lettres*, 1:xxxviii; Lieven to Guizot, October 23, 1838, in ibid., 223.

52. Charles de Rémusat, *Mémoires*, 4:40–43.

53. Ibid., 1:445; Martin-Fugier, *Vie élégante*, 181.

54. Stendhal, *Scarlet and Black*, 266; id., *Esquisses*, 2:42–43, 118, 273, 278–79; id., *Armance*, 77.

55. Stendhal, *Lucien Leuwen*, 1:32, 44–47, 350; 2:103–4, 328; id., *Esquisses*, 2:27–28, 59–61, 146–47, 250.

56. Charles de Rémusat, *Mémoires*, 1:181–82, 317–20, 354–55, 452; 2:88–91; 3:14 (emphasis in the original); Martin-Fugier, *Vie élégante*, 180–81, 393; Rosanvallon, *Moment Guizot*, 28, 146–49.

57. Charles de Rémusat, *Mémoires*, 1:252, 306, 320; 2:142–43, 272–73; 3:57, 97–99; 4:209–10.

58. Martin-Fugier, *Vie élégante*, 393.

59. Daumard, "Vie de salon," in *Sociabilité et société bourgeoise*, 91; Agulhon, *Cercle*, 68–69.

60. Balabine, *Paris de 1842 à 1852*, 104–5; Custine, *Empire of the Czar*, 383; Cardinal de Bausset, quoted in Montcalm, *Salon politique*, 172.

61. A reference to Molière's comédie-ballet *Monsieur de Pourceaugnac*, in which Pourceaugnac is attacked by a team of doctors looking to administer an enema.

62. Viel-Castle, *Faubourg Saint-Germain*, 10–13, 190; Bassanville, *Salons d'autrefois*, 2:115–18; Apponyi, *Vingt-cinq ans à Paris*, 4:119.

63. Habermas, *Structural Transformation*, 131–32.

64. Martin-Fugier, *Vie élégante*, 22–25, 325–27; Roger Boutet de Monvel, *Les Anglais à Paris, 1800–1850* (Paris, 1911), 242.

65. See *Annuaire de Lesur*, March 1, 1821, in Alméras, *Vie parisienne sous la Restauration*, 286–87; Montcalm, *Mon journal*, 324; Girardin, *Vicomte de Launay: Lettres parisiennes*, 4:81, 232, 250. D'Agoult recalled that *raouts* replaced the intimate gatherings of the Restoration when salons reopened in the aftermath of the crisis of 1830–32, but Madame de Staël wrote in 1817 that the greater mixing of ranks and parties was already leading society "to adopt the English method of numerous gatherings." D'Agoult, cited in Martin-Fugier, "Cour et la ville," 121; Staël, *Considérations*, 2:153.

66. Girardin, *Vicomte de Launay: Lettres parisiennes*, 4:81, 232, 250; Ancelot, *Salons de Paris*, 220–23; Custine, *Empire of the Czars*, 147. Girardin considered *les raouts* "very monotonous" and proclaimed that "what we like are *les réunions intimes.*"

67. Girardin, *Vicomte de Launay: Lettres parisiennes*, 2:277–78; 4:83–85, 153, 233.

68. Gay, *Salons célèbres*, 3–4; Paul Gerbod, "Une Forme de sociabilité bourgeoise: Le Thermalisme en France, en Belgique et en Allemagne, 1800–1850," in *Sociabilité et société*

bourgeoise en France, en Allemagne et en Suisse, 1750–1850, ed. Etienne François (Paris, 1986), 113–17; Aprile, "République au salon," 473.

69. See Ancelot, *Salon de Paris,* xxi, 70; Stendhal, *Lucien Leuwen,* 2:128.

70. Girardin, *Vicomte de Launay: Lettres parisiennes,* 1:127–28; 2:161, 261; Alton-Shée, *Mémoires,* 178.

71. Vier, *Comtesse d'Agoult,* 2:39–43; Aprile, "République au salon," 476, 484; Marie Gougy-François, *Les Grands Salons féminins* (Paris, 1965), 183–84; Claude Bellanger et al., *Histoire générale de la presse française* (Paris, 1969), 2:284.

72. Charles Yriarte, *Les Cercles de Paris, 1828–1864* (Paris, 1864), 4–5, 29, 46–47, 62–63, 164–65.

73. Alton-Shée, *Mémoires,* 135; Charle, "Noblesse et élites en France," 431; Yriarte, *Cercles de Paris,* 8, 46, 65, 164, 302.

74. Alton-Shée, *Mémoires,* 136, 142; Balabine, *Paris de 1842 à 1852,* 57–58; Yriarte, *Cercles de Paris,* 35, 65.

75. Yriarte, *Cercles de Paris,* 4–8, 29, 42, 62–65, 302–3; Martin-Fugier, *Vie élégante,* 336; Balabine, *Paris de 1842 à 1852,* 57.

76. Yriarte, *Cercles de Paris,* 104–8, 119; Agulhon, *Cercle,* 29.

77. Girardin, *Vicomte de Launay: Lettres parisiennes,* I 108; Balzac, quoted in Fortassier, *Mondains,* 137 and Matoré, *Vocabulaire,* 57n; Dino, *Memoirs,* 1:7; Charles de Rémusat, *Mémoires,* 4:140; Ancelot, *Salon de Paris,* 380. Fortassier points out that the word *club* was replacing the indigenous *cercle* in the 1830s.

78. Agulhon, *Cercle,* 28–29, 36–37, 51–53, 82; Dauphin, "Salons de la Restauration," in *Femmes dans la cité,* 258.

79. Yriarte, *Cercles de Paris,* 102; Agulhon, *Cercle,* 57. Agulhon writes: "On soupçonne qu'une relation de causalité réciproque était établie: l'inconfort des cafés conduisait la bourgeoisie à créer des cercles."

80. Agulhon, *Cercle,* 24–29, 40; Dash, quoted in Matoré, *Vocabulaire,* 57; Agoult, *Mémoires,* 180; Jardin, *Tocqueville,* 83.

81. Agulhon, *Cercle,* 26–28, 68–69; Charles de Rémusat, *Mémoires,* 1:277; Anne Martin-Fugier, "La Formation des élites: Les 'conférences' sous la Restauration et la Monarchie de Juillet," *Revue d'histoire moderne et contemporaine* 36 (April–June 1989): 211–41; Jean-Pierre Chaline, *Sociabilité et érudition: Les Sociétés savantes en France, XIXe–XXe siècle* (Paris, 1995), 123; Yriarte, *Cercles de Paris,* 162–63.

82. Frénilly, *Mémoires,* 369; Agulhon, *Cercle,* 68; Broglie, *Souvenirs,* 2:82–83; Alton-Shée, *Mémoires,* 135–36, 212; Martin-Fugier, *Vie élégante,* 226–28, 248–49. *Parlottes* and conferences are discussed in Martin-Fugier, "Formation des élites," 224–41.

83. Martin-Fugier, *Vie élégante,* 237–39; Girardin, *Vicomte de Launay: Lettres parisiennes,* 4:84–87.

84. Chaline, *Sociabilité et érudition,* 120; Yriarte, *Cercles de Paris,* 308–9.

85. Girardin, *Vicomte de Launay: Lettres parisiennes,* 1:82; Yriarte, *Cercles de Paris,* 118, 197.

86. Girardin, *Vicomte de Launay: Lettres parisiennes,* 1:82; 3:193; 4:104.

87. Agoult, *Mémoires,* 227; Ancelot, *Salon de Paris,* 382; Girardin, *Vicomte de Launay: Lettres parisiennes,* 105–6.

CHAPTER SEVEN: Nostalgia, or The Limits of Aristocratic Feminism

1. Apponyi, *Vingt-cinq ans à Paris,* 4:137; Beaumont-Vassy, *Salons de Paris sous Louis-Philippe,* 338–40.

2. Agoult, *Mémoires*, 201, 277; Ancelot, *Salon de Paris*, xv; Beaumont-Vassy, *Salons de Paris sous Louis-Philippe*, 338, 367; Girardin, *Vicomte de Launay: Lettres parisiennes*, 4:282–83; Apponyi, *Vingt-cinq ans à Paris*, 4:167.

3. Girardin, *Vicomte de Launay: Lettres parisiennes*, 4:282–83; Vicomte de Beaumont-Vassy, *Les Salons de Paris et la société parisienne sous Napoleon III* (Paris, 1868), 7–8; Agoult, *Mémoires*, 276–77.

4. Beaumont-Vassy, *Salon de Paris sous Louis-Philippe*, 367–68; Bassanville, *Salons d'autrefois*, 3:210; Ancelot, *Salon de Paris*, 157; Beaumont-Vassy, *Salons de Paris sous Napoléon III*, 6–7, 110, 118.

5. Apponyi, *Vingt-cinq ans à Paris*, 4:163; Beaumont-Vassy, *Salons de Paris sous Louis-Philippe*, 368–69; Dosne, *Mémoires*, 2:159; Dino, *Memoirs*, 3:279.

6. Beaumont-Vassy, *Salons des Paris sous Napoléon III*, 50–51, 154–58, 181–87.

7. Ibid., 118–21, 155.

8. Ancelot, *Salon de Paris*, 154–231. On Thiers's salon in 1848, see Charles de Rémusat, *Mémoires*, 4:372, and Dosne, *Mémoires*, 88–90. Lieven's fate is recounted in Bassanville, *Salons d'autrefois*, 3:210–12 and in Dino, *Memoirs*, 3:279, 283.

9. Beaumont-Vassy, *Salons des Paris sous Napoléon III*, 134; Dosne, *Mémoires*, 2:131–32, 147; Apponyi, *Vingt-cinq ans à Paris*, 4:248–49; Dino, *Memoirs*, 3:267.

10. Dino, *Memoirs*, 3:267; Dosne, *Mémoires*, 2:159; Apponyi, *Vingt-cinq ans à Paris*, 4:244, 249, 257, 264; Martin-Fugier, *Vie élégante*, 391.

11. Beaumont-Vassy, *Salons de Paris sous Napoléon III*, 241–43, 300–327; Louis Sonolet, *La Vie parisienne sous le Second Empire* (Paris, 1929), 41–55; Frédéric Loliée, *Les Femmes du Second Empire* (Paris, 1912), 310, 334.

12. Ory, "Salon," 119; Apponyi, *Vingt-cinq ans à Paris*, 4:379; Tassé, *Salons français*, 129–31; Loliée, *Femmes du Second Empire*, 91, 98, 101; Gougy-François, *Grands Salons*, 158–61. On Princesse Mathilde and her salon, see Jean Des Cars, *La Princesse Mathilde: L'Amour, la gloire et les arts* (Paris, 1988).

13. On the attitude of the legitimists toward imperial society, see Armaillé, *Quand on savait vivre heureux*, 155–65.

14. Loliée, *Femmes du Second Empire*, 310–11; Apponyi, *Vingt-cinq ans à Paris*, 4:447; Bassanville, *Salons d'autrefois*, 3:211–12.

15. Charles de Rémusat, *Mémoires*, V, 49; Dosne, *Mémoires*, 2:158; Armaillé, *Quand on savait vivre heureux*, 203–7, 212–13.

16. Armaillé, *Quand on savait vivre heureux*, 199; Beaumont-Vassy, *Salons de Paris sous Napoléon III*, 328–31; Loliée, *Femmes du Second Empire*, 80–81, 346–47. The Comtesse Le Hon, wife of the Belgian ambassador, was probably the most famous diplomatic hostess.

17. Ory, "Salon," 119; Armaillé, *Quand on savait vivre heureux*, 198–99; Beaumont-Vassy, *Salons de Paris sous Napoléon III*, 330–31. Armaillé reported that the court entrusted the duchesse d'Istrie with the mission of creating a salon "où la diplomatie et le monde pussent se rencontrer sans froisement" but "la cour impériale ne séduisait personne, à moins d'avoir besoin de places." The salon held receptions for a few week before the duchesse fell ill, after which the project had to be abandoned. Beaumont-Vassy mentioned the salons of the comte de Flavigny, Madame de Bouillé, the duc de Maillé, and General Trouche as the only ones "où l'on cause."

18. Paul Gerbod, "Loisirs et santé: Les Cures thermales en France (1850–1900)," in *Oisivité et loisirs dans les sociétés occidentales au XIXe siècle. Colloque pluridisciplinaire, Amiens 19–20 novembre 1982* (Abbeville, 1983), 198–200.

19. Louis Girard, "La Cour de Napoléon III," in *Hof, Kultur und Politik im 19. Jahr-*

hundert: Akten des 18. Deutsch-französischen Historikerkolloquiums, Darmstadt, vom 27.–30. September 1982, ed. Karl Ferdinand Werner (Bonn, 1985), 155; Martin-Fugier, *Vie élégante*, 391; Beaumont-Vassy, *Les Salons de Paris sous Napoléon III*, 154, 211, 241–43, 321; Armaillé, *Quand on savait vivre heureux*, 171; Daumard, "Vie de salon," in *Sociabilité et société bourgeoise*, 83; Apponyi, *Vingt-cinq ans à Paris*, 4:254–55; Loliée, *Femmes du Second Empire*, 102.

20. Ancelot, *Salon de Paris*, 226, 239–40, 247, 293, 297, 303–4, 307, 354–55; Agoult, *Mémoires*, 201.

21. Armaillé, *Quand on savait vivre heureux*, 156–57, 172–73, 186–87; Ancelot, *Salon de Paris*, 307.

22. Charles de Rémusat, *Mémoires*, 5:49–50; Tocqueville to Circourt, October 31, 1854, quoted in Jardin, *Tocqueville*, 477–78.

23. Ancelot, *Salon de Paris*, 297–98; O'Meara, *Salon à Paris*, 95–101, 196–98.

24. Armaillé, *Quand on savait vivre heureux*, 240–41.

25. Aprile, "République au salon," 476–79, 483; Ory, "Salon," 116–17, 120; Emile de Marcère, *L'Assemblée nationale de 1871* (Paris, 1907), 1:88; Tassé, *Salons français*, 148, 229–30.

26. Ory, "Salon," 120–24; Gougy-François, *Grands Salons*, 167; Tassé, *Salons français*, 188–90, 230. Born in 1837 to a textile worker in Reims, Jeanne Tourbet became a fixture of the Paris demimonde in the 1860s before marrying the comte de Loynes, a wealthy industrialist.

27. Beaumont-Vassy, *Salons de Paris sous Napoléon III*, 228; James F. McMillan, *Napoleon III* (London, 1991), 157–58; Ory, "Salon," 120; Aprile, "Bourgeoise et républicaine, deux termes inconciliables," in *Femmes dans la cité*, 211–24.

28. Perrot, *Femmes politiques*, 65–67; Ory, "Salon," 119; Gougy-François, *Grands Salons*, 152–53, 170–71.

29. Du Bled, *Rôle social et mondaine de la femme*, 127–28.

30. Ibid., 4:10–11; Adrian Lyttelton, "Il Duce's Other Woman," *New York Review of Books* 11, no. 13 (July 15, 1993): 1922.

31. Ancelot, *Salon de Paris*, 161; Agoult, *Mémoires*, 202–3; Fortassier, *Mondains*, 516–17; Elisabeth Badinter, "L'Exception française," *Le Débat* 87 (November–December 1995): 124.

32. Ancelot, *Salons de Paris*, passim; Agulhon, *Cercle*, 82.

33. See Raymond Huard, "Sociabilité et politique en Languedoc méditerranéen des lendemains de la Restauration à la fin de 1849," in *Sociabilité et société bourgeoise en France, en Allemagne et en Suisse, 1750–1850*, ed. Etienne François (Paris, 1986), 305–11; id., *Naissance du parti politique*, 83–94.

34. Aprile, "République au salon," 480–86. On the failure of legitimists to adapt to universal suffrage in the 1870s, see Steven D. Kale, *Legitimism and the Reconstruction of French Society, 1852–1883* (Baton Rouge, La., 1992), 329–35.

35. Agulhon, *Cercle*, 71, 83; Aprile, "République au salon," 485–86; Agoult, *Mémoires*, 201; Ory, "Salon," 116.

36. O'Meara, *Salon à Paris*, 96–98; Beaumont-Vassy, *Salons de Paris sous Napoléon III*, 338–40.

37. Armaillé, *Quand on savait vivre heureux*, 208–10; Comtesse Benoist d'Azy, quoted in Gougy-François, *Grands Salons*, 187.

38. Guizot, *Madame de Rumford*, 8.

39. Yriarte, *Cercles de Paris*, 278–79; Beaumont-Vassy, *Salons de Paris sous Napoléon III*, 331–32; Gerbod, "Loisirs et santé," 202–3. On the piety of legitimist women in the 1860s, see Armaillé, *Quand on savait vivre heureux*, 129, 216. M.-F. Lévy addressed the emerging feminine ideals in the nineteenth century in *De mères en filles: L'Education des Françaises, 1850–1880* (Paris, 1984), 151.

40. Armaillé, *Quand on savait vivre heureux*, 204–9.

41. Fortassier, *Mondains*, 290, 509; Bartillat, *Histoire de la noblesse*, 1:312.

42. Stendhal, *Lucien Leuwen*, 2:328–29. Visitors to the salon of the comtesse de Loynes in the 1890s were struck by what Ory called "son ambiance second Empire maintenue." Boni de Castellane recalled that she received everyday, from 5 o'clock to 7, "assise en douillette blanche dans un pouf rose de style Second-Empire, entourée de ses petits chiens favoris, un éventail à la main." Boni de Castellane, quoted in Ory, "Salon," 122.

43. See Stendhal's *Armance* and Charles de Rémusat, *Mémoires*, 3:98–100.

44. Girardin, *Vicomte de Launay: Lettres parisiennes*, 4:87–88; Comtesse Dash, *Comment on fait son chemin dans le monde* (Paris, 1868); *Dictionnaire de la conversation et de la lecture*, ed. Duckett et al.

45. Ancelot, *Salon de Paris*, 335. Beaumont-Vassy switched back and forth between designating particular salons and using expressions such as "je vins dans le salon où se trouvait le prince," or "le prince se dirigea vers la porte fermée du salon que j'ai mentionné tout à l'heure." Beaumont-Vassy, *Salons de Paris sous Napoléon III*, 186–87, 194–95.

46. Fumaroli, "Conversation," 718–19.

47. Charles-Augustin Sainte-Beuve, "Lettres de Mademoiselle de Lespinasse," in *Causeries du lundi* (Paris, 1862), 2:125; Guizot, *Madame de Rumford*, 32.

48. Fumaroli, "Conversation," 719; Madame Ancelot, *L'Hôtel de Rambouillet, comédie en trois actes mêlés de chants* (Paris, 1842), ix; Claire de Rémusat, *Essai sur l'éducation des femmes* (Paris, 1824), 35.

49. Guizot, *Madame de Rumford*, 9.

50. Agoult, *Mémoires*, 227; Bassanville, *Salons d'autrefois*, 1:1; 3:187; 4:129.

51. Agoult, *Mémoires*, 278.

52. Ancelot, *Salon de Paris*, 57, 147, 166, 227; Ancelot, *Salons de Paris*, 17–19; Girardin, *Vicomte de Launay: Lettres parisiennes*, 4:82; Gay, *Salons célèbres*, 17.

53. Boigne, *Mémoires*, 2:2:488; Duras to Chateaubriand, January 4, 1821, in Bardoux, *Duchesse de Duras*, 223.

54. Girardin, *Vicomte de Launay: Lettres parisiennes*, 4:276–77; Bassanville, *Salons d'autrefois*, 4:132.

55. Apponyi, *Vingt-cinq ans à Paris*, 2:467–68. Similar expressions of culpability can be found in Girardin, *Vicomte de Launay: Lettres parisiennes*, 2:301–4, Ancelot, *Salon de Paris*, 380, and Comtesse Dash, *Mémoires des autres*, 5:57.

56. Chastenay, *Mémoires*, 406.

57. Catherine Allgor, *Parlor Politics: In Which the Ladies of Washington Help Build a City and a Government* (Charlottesville, Va., 2000). See Allgor's comments in Jeff Sharlet, "Parlor Politics and Power: A New View of Washington Women," *Chronicle of Higher Education* 47, no. 16 (December 15, 2000): A16–18. I offer a more extended analysis of the salon's status as a feminist institution in Kale, "Women, the Public Sphere, and the Persistence of Salons," 137–40.

58. Daniel Gordon argues that the eighteenth-century case for the inclusion of women in the discussion of political affairs rested on shaky ground because any "theory emphasiz-

ing the positive *functions* of women in a particular domain of society is less likely to secure their status in that domain than a theory emphasizing their inherent *right* to participate in it in order to voice their particular interests" and "will carry little weight in the face of arguments that seem to prove that the participation of women will actually be dysfunctional." Gordon, "Philosophy, Sociology, and Gender," 904 (emphasis in the original).

59. Girardin, *Vicomte de Launay: Lettres parisiennes*, 2:302; Montcalm, *Mon journal*, 284, 295. On the "parallélisme frappant" of the roles of ultraroyalist and republican salonnières, see Odile Krakovitch, "De la sociabilité," in *Femmes dans la cité, 1815–1871*, ed. Alain Corbin et al. (Grâne, 1997), 207–8.

60. See Michelle Perrot, "Une Histoire sans affrontements," *Le Débat* 87 (November–December 1995): 134.

61. Geneviève Fraisse, "Rupture révolutionnaire," in *Femmes et pouvoirs sous l'ancien régime*, ed. Danielle Haase-Dubosc and Eliane Viennot (Paris, 1991), 295; Eric Fassin, "The Purloined Gender: American Feminism in a French Mirror," *French Historical Studies* 22, no. 1 (1999): 136.

62. Tassé, *Salons français*, 234.

63. Pekacz, "Whose Muses?" 4; Jeanne Deroin, quoted in Joan Wallach Scott, *Only Paradoxes to Offer: French Feminists and the Rights of Man* (Cambridge, Mass., 1996), 77; Sharlet, "Parlor Politics," A17.

64. Du Bled, *Rôle social et mondaine de la femme*, 128.

65. Staël, *Considérations*, 1:199.

66. Ory, "Salon," 125; Gordon, *Citizens Without Sovereignty*, 240.

67. Fumaroli, "Conversation," 695; Guizot, *Madame de Rumford*, 11–12; Ancelot, *Salon de Paris*, 95; Girardin, *Vicomte de Launay: Lettres parisiennes*, 4: 230–32.

68. Bonnie Smith, *Changing Lives: Women in European History Since 1700* (Lexington, Mass., 1989), 341; "Salons: How to Revive the Endangered Art of Conversation and Start a Revolution in Your Living Room," *Utne Reader* 44 (March–April 1991): 66–67.

69. Jules Barbey d'Aurevilly, *Dandyism*, trans. Douglas Ainslie (New York, 1988). See also Baldensperger, *Mouvement des idées*, 1:171–73; Girardin, *Vicomte de Launay: Lettres parisiennes*, 4:80–81.

70. Loliée, *Femmes du Second Empire*, 347.

Conclusion

1. Goodman argues that the legitimacy and authority of salonnières were "tenuous and temporary" because they were subject to the generalization of masculinist assumptions. Goodman, *Republic of Letters*, 6.

2. For a contrary view, see Landes, *Women and the Public Sphere*, 21–23.

Select Bibliography

PRIMARY SOURCES

Abrantès, Laure Junot, duchesse d'. *Histoire des salons de Paris: Tableaux et portraits du grand monde, sous Louis XVI, le directoire, le consulat et l'empire, la restauration, et le règne de Louis-Philippe Ier*. 6 vols. Paris: Ladvocat, 1837–38.
———. *Memoirs of Madame Junot (Duchesse d'Abrantès)*. 6 vols. London: Grolier Society, 1910.
———. *Memoirs of the Duchess of Abrantès: 1830*. Translated by Gerard Shelly. London: John Hamilton, n.d. [1929?].
———. *Salons révolutionnaires*. Paris: France-Empire, 1989.
Agoult, Marie de Flavigny, comtesse d' [Daniel Stern]. *Mémoires, souvenirs et journaux de la comtesse d'Agoult*. Edited by Charles F. Dupêchez. Paris: Mercure de France, 1990.
———. *Mes souvenirs, 1806–1833*. Paris: Calmann-Lévy, 1877.
Allonville, Armand François, comte d'. *Mémoires secrets de 1770 à 1830*. 6 vols. Paris: Werdet, 1838–45.
Alton-Shée, Edmond de Lignères, comte d'. *Mes mémoires (1826–1848): Première partie (1826–1839)*. Paris: Librairie internationale, 1869.
Ancelot, Virginie. *Les Salons de Paris: Foyers éteints*. Paris: Jules Tardieu, 1858.
———. *Un Salon de Paris, 1824 à 1864*. Paris: E. Dentu, 1866.
Apponyi, Rudolf. *Vingt-cinq ans à Paris (1826–1852): Journal du Comte Rodolphe Apponyi, attaché de l'ambassade d'Autriche-Hongrie à Paris*. 4 vols. Paris: Plon, 1913–26.
Armaillé, comtesse d'. *Quand on savait vivre heureux (1830–1860): Souvenirs de jeunesse*. Edited by Pauline de Broglie, comtesse Jean de Pange. Paris: Plon, 1934.
Balabine, Victor de. *Paris de 1842 à 1852: La Cour, la société, les moeurs. Journal de Victor Balabine, secrétaire de l'ambassade de Russie*. Paris: Emile-Paul Frères, 1914.
Balzac, Honoré de, *The Secrets of La Princesse de Cardignan*. Translated by James Waring Philadelphia: Gebbie, 1899.
Barante, Amable-Guillaume, baron de. *Souvenirs du baron de Barante, de l'Académie française, 1782–1866*. Edited by Claude de Barante. 8 vols. Paris: Calmann-Lévy, 1890–1901.
Barbey d'Aurevilly, Jules. *Dandyism*. Translated by Douglas Ainslie. New York: PAJ Publications, 1988. Originally published Caen: B. Mancel, 1845–61. Reprinted as *Du dandysme et de George Brummell* (Paris: Balland, 1986).
Bassan, Fernand, ed. *Politique et haute société à l'époque romantique: La Famille Pastoret d'après sa correspondance (1788 à 1856)*. Paris: Minard, 1969.
Bassanville, Anaïs Lebrun, comtesse de. *De l'Education des femmes*. Paris: C. Douniol, 1861.

————. *Les Salons d'autrefois: Souvenirs intimes.* 4 vols. Paris: H. Anière, 1862–66.

Bawr, Alexandrine-Sophie de. *Mes souvenirs.* Paris: Passard, 1853.

Beaumont-Vassy, Edouard-Ferdinand de la Bonninière, vicomte de. *Les Salons de Paris et la société parisienne sous Louis-Philippe.* Paris: F. Sartorius, 1866.

————. *Les Salons de Paris et la société parisienne sous Napoléon III.* Paris: F. Sartorius, 1868.

Boigne, Charlotte-Louise d'Osmond, comtesse de. *Mémoires de la comtesse de Boigne, née d'Osmond: Récits d'une tante.* Edited by Jean-Claude Berchet. Le Temps retrouvé, 23. 2 vols. Paris: Mercure de France, 1986.

————. *Memoirs of the Comtesse de Boigne (1781–1830).* Edited by Charles Nicoullaud. 3 vols. London: William Heinemann, 1907–8.

Bouillé, Louis-Joseph Amour, marquis de. *Souvenirs et fragments pour servir aux mémoires de ma vie et de mon temps.* 2 vols. Paris: A. Picard, 1906–8.

Broc, Hervé, vicomte de. *Dix ans de la vie d'une femme pendant l'émigration: Adélaïde de Kerjean, marquise de Falaiseau, d'après des lettres inédites et des souvenirs de famille.* Paris: Plon-Nourrit, 1893.

Broglie, Victor, duc de. *Souvenirs, 1785–1870.* 3 vols. Paris: Calmann-Lévy, 1886.

Castelbajac, Léontine Villeneuve, comtesse de. *Mémoires de l'occitanienne: Souvenirs de famille et de jeunesse.* 6th ed. Paris: Plon, 1927.

Chastenay, Victorine de. *Mémoires, 1771–1815.* Paris: Perrin, 1987.

Chateaubriand, René de. *Mémoires d'outre-tombe.* 1848–50. 6 vols. Paris: Garnier Frères, 1910.

Colnet, M. *L'Hermite du faubourg Saint-Germain, ou observations sur les moeurs et les usages français au commencement du XIXe siècle.* 2 vols. Paris: Pillet, 1825.

Correspondence and Conversations of Alexis de Tocqueville with Nassau Senior, from 1834 to 1859. Edited by Mary Charlotte Mair. 2 vols. New York: H. S. King, 1872.

Custine, Astolphe, marquis de. *Empire of the Czar: A Journey Through Eternal Russia.* Edited by Daniel J. Boorstin. New York: Doubleday, 1989.

————. *Ethel.* 2 vols. Paris: Lavocat, 1839.

Dash, Comtesse [Gabrielle Anna Poillow, vicomtesse de Saint-Mars]. *Comment on fait son chemin dans le monde.* Paris, 1868.

————. *Mémoires des autres.* 6 vols. Paris: Lévy Frères, 1896–97.

Dictionnaire de la conversation et de la lecture, inventaire raisonné des notions générales les plus indispensables à tous, par une société de savants et de gens de lettres. Edited by William Duckett et al. 16 vols. 2d ed. Paris: Aux comptoirs de la direction, 1854–58.

Dino, Dorothée, duchesse de, *Memoirs of the Duchesse de Dino (afterwards Duchesse de Talleyrand et de Sagan), 1836–1840.* Edited by Marie Radziwill. 3 vols. New York: Charles Scribner's Sons, 1910.

Dosne, Eurydice Sophie Matheron. *Mémoires de Madame Dosne, l'égérie de M. Thiers.* Edited by Henri Malo. 2 vols. Paris: Plon, 1928.

Duvergier de Hauranne, Prosper. *Histoire du gouvernement parlementaire en France, 1814–1848.* 10 vols. Paris: Michel Lévy, 1860–72.

Frénilly, Auguste-François Fauveau de. *Souvenirs du Bon de Frénilly, pair de France (1768–1828).* Edited by Arthur Chuquet. Paris: Plon-Nourrit, 1908. Reprinted under the title *Mémoires, 1768–1828: Souvenirs d'un ultraroyaliste.* Paris: Perrin, 1987.

Gay, Sophie. *Salons célèbres.* Paris: Calmann-Lévy, 1882.

Genlis, Stéphanie Félicité, comtesse de. *De l'esprit des étiquettes de l'ancienne cour et des usages du monde de ce temps.* Paris: Mercure de France, 1996.

————. *Memoirs of the Countess de Genlis, Illustrative of the History of the Eighteenth and Nineteenth Centuries.* 2 vols. New York: Wilder & Campbell, 1825.

Girardin, Madame Emile de. *Le Vicomte de Launay: Lettres parisiennes.* 4 vols. Paris: Michel Lévy Frères, 1857–68.

Goncourt, Jules de, and Edmond de Goncourt. *La Femme au dix-huitième siècle.* Rev ed. Paris: Firmin-Didot, 1887.

————. *Histoire de la société française pendant le Directoire.* 2d ed. Paris: E. Dentu, 1855. Reprint. Paris: E. Dentu, 1992.

————. *Histoire de la société française pendant la Révolution.* Paris: Flammarion, 1864. Reprint. Geneva: Slatkine, 1971.

————. *The Woman of the Eighteenth Century, Her Life, from Birth to Death, Her Love and Her Philosophy in the Worlds of Salon, Shop and Street.* Translated by Jacques Le Clercq and Ralph Roeder. New York: Minton, Balch, 1927.

Gontaut-Biron, Marie Joséphine Louise de Montaut de Navailles, duchesse de. *Memoirs of the Duchesse de Gontaut, Gouvernante to the Children of France During the Restoration, 1773–1836.* Translated by Mrs. J. W. Davis. New York, Dodd, Mead, 1894.

Grimm, Friedrich Melchior. *Les Salons de Paris sous la Révolution.* Paris: H. Gautier, 1900.

Guizot, François. *Lettres de François Guizot et de la Princesse de Lieven, 1836–1846.* 3 vols. Edited by Jacques Naville. Paris: Mercure de France, 1963.

————. *Madame de Rumford (1758–1836).* Paris: Crapelet, 1841.

————. *Mélanges politiques et historiques.* Paris: M. Lévy, 1869.

Haussonville, Joseph de Cléron, comte d'. *Femmes d'autrefois, hommes d'aujourd'hui.* Paris: Perrin, 1912.

————. *Ma jeunesse, 1814–1830: Souvenirs.* Paris: Calmann-Lévy, 1885.

————. *Madame de Staël et M. Necker, d'après leur correspondance inédite.* Paris: Calmann-Lévy, 1925.

————. *The Salon of Madame Necker.* Translated by Henry M. Trollope. 2 vols. London: Chapman & Hall, 1882.

Herpin, Clara Adele Luce. *Memoirs of the Princess de Ligne.* London: R. Bentley & Son, 1887.

Hugo, Victor. *Les Misérables.* Translated by Lascelles Wraxall. 5 vols. New York: H.M. Cadwell, 1938.

Jouy, Etienne. *L'Hermite de la Chaussée-d'Antin, ou observations sur les moeurs et les usages parisiens au commencement du XIXe siècle.* 4 vols. Paris: Pillet, 1815.

Lacour, Louis. *Grand monde et salons politiques de Paris après la Terreur: Fragments précédés d'une étude sure la société avant 1789.* Paris: A. Claudin, 1859.

La Ferronnays, Guillelmine-Marie Ferrón de. *Mémoires de Mme de La Ferronnays.* 2d ed. Paris: Librairie Paul Ollendorff, 1899.

Lamartine, Alphonse de. *Les Nouvelles confidences.* Paris: Furne, 1875.

La Tour du Pin Gouvernet, Henriette Lucie Dillon, marquise de. *Memoirs of Madame de La Tour du Pin.* Edited and translated by Felice Harcourt. With an introduction by Peter Gay. New York: McCall, 1969, 1971.

Maillé, Blanche-Joséphine Le Bascle d'Argenteuil, duchesse de. *Souvenirs des deux Restaurations: Journal inédit.* Edited by Xavier de La Fournière. Paris: Perrin, 1984.

Marcère, Emile de. *L'Assemblée nationale de 1871.* 2 vols. Paris: Poln-Nourrit, 1907.

Marmontel, Jean-François. *Mémoires.* Edited by John Renwick. 2 vols. Clermont-Ferrand: G. de Bussac, 1972.

May, Lewis J., ed. *The Unpublished Correspondence of Hornoré de Balzac and Madame Zulma Carraud, 1829–1850.* London: John Lane, 1937.

Montcalm, Armandine, marquise de. *Mon journal, 1815–1818.* Edited by Sébastien Charléty. Paris: Grasset, 1936.

——. *Une Salon politique sous la Restauration: Correspondence de la marquise de Montcalm.* Edited by Emmanuel de Lévis-Mirepoix. Paris: Editions du Grand siècle, 1949.

Montesquieu, Charles Louis de Secondat, baron de. *Persian Letters.* Translated by C. J. Betts. Baltimore: Penguin Books, 1973.

Morellet, André. *Eloges de Madame Géoffrin, contemporaine de Madame du Deffand.* Paris: H. Nicolle, 1812.

——. *Mémoires de l'Abbé Morellet sur le dix-huitième siècle et sur la Révolution.* Paris: Mercure de France, 2000.

Musset, Alfred de. *The Confessions of a Child of the Century.* Translated by Kendall Warren. New York: Charles H. Sergel, 1892.

Pailhès, Gabriel. *La Duchesse de Duras et Chateaubriand d'après des documents inédites.* Paris: Perrin, 1910.

Pange, Victor de. *The Unpublished Correspondence of Madame de Staël and the Duke of Wellington.* Translated by Harold Kurtz. London: Cassell, 1965.

Pasquier, Etienne-Denis, duc de. *A History of My Time: Memoirs of Chancellor Pasquier.* Edited by the duc d'Audiffret-Pasquier. Translated by Charles E. Roche. 3 vols. London: T. F. Unwin, 1893–94.

Proust, Marcel. *Remembrance of Things Past.* Translated by C. K. Scott Moncrieff. 2 vols. New York: Random House, 1934.

Récamier, Jeanne Françoise Julie Adélaïde Bernard. *Memoirs and Correspondence of Madame Récamier.* Translated by Isaphene M. Luyster. Bonton: Knight & Millet, 1867.

Rémusat, Charles de. *Mémoires de ma vie.* Edited by Charles H. Pouthas. 5 vols. Paris: Plon, 1959.

Rémusat, Claire Elisabeth Gravier de Vergennes, comtesse de. *Essai sur l'éducation des femmes.* Paris: Ladvocat, 1825.

——. *Memoirs of Madame de Rémusat, 1802–1808.* Translated by Mrs. Cashel Hoey and John Lillie. 3 vols. New York: D. Appleton, 1880.

Rochechouart, Louis Victor, comte de. *Souvenirs sur la révolution, l'empire et la restauration.* Paris: Plon-Nourrit, 1889.

Roland de La Platière, Jeanne-Marie. *Mémoires de Madame Roland.* Edited by Claude Perroud. 2 vols. Paris: Plon-Nourrit, 1905.

Sainte-Beuve, Charles-Augustin. *Causeries du lundi.* 16 vols. Paris: Garnier Frères, 1852.

——. *Portraits de femmes.* Paris: Garnier Frères, 1869.

Saint-Surin, Rosalie Richard de Cendrecourt, dame de. *Miroir des salons: Scènes du monde.* Paris: Maignaud, 1831.

Saulx-Tavanes, Aglaé-Marie de Choiseul-Gouffier, duchesse de. *Sur les routes de l'émigration: Mémoires de la duchesse de Saulx-Tavanes (1791–1806).* Paris: Calmann-Lévy, 1934.

Ségur, Alexandre Joseph Pierre, vicomte de. *Women, Their Condition and Influence in Society.* 3 vols. London: T. N. Longman & O. Rees, 1803.

Staël, Anne-Louise-Germaine de. *Considérations sur la Révolution française.* 2 vols. Paris: Bibliothèque Charpentier, 1818.

——. *Corinne, or Italy.* Translated by Avriel H. Goldberger. New Brunswick, N.J.: Rutgers University Press, 1987.

————. *De la littérature considérée dans ses rapports avec les institutions sociales*. 2 vols. Geneva: Droz, 1959.

————. *De l'influence des passions sur le bonheur des individus et des nations*. Paris: Treuttel & Würtz, 1820.

————. *Des circonstances actuelles qui peuvent terminer la Révolution et des principes qui doivent fonder la République en France*. Geneva: Droz, 1979.

————. *Germany*. Translated by O. W. Wight. 2 vols. New York: Hurd & Houghton, 1871.

————. *Ten Years' Exile, or, Memoirs of That Interesting Period of the Life of the Baroness de Staël-Holstein*. Edited by Margaret Crosland. Fontwell, Sussex, UK: Centaur Press, 1968.

Stendhal. *Armance, or, Scenes from a Parisian Salon in 1827*. Translated by Gilbert Sale and Suzanne Sale. London: Merlin Press, 1960.

————. *Esquisses de la société parisienne de la politique et de la littérature: Chroniques, 1825–1829*. 2 vols. Paris: Le Sycomore, 1983.

————. *Lucien Leuwen*. Translated by Louise Varèse. 2 vols. New York: New Directions, 1950.

————. *Scarlet and Black*. 1830. Translated by Margaret R. B. Shaw. Harmondsworth, UK: Penguin Books, 1953.

Stern, Daniel. See Agoult, Marie de Flavigny.

Tocqueville, Alexis de. *The Old Regime and the French Revolution*. Translated by Stuart Gilbert. Garden City, N.J.: Doubleday, Anchor Books, 1955.

Vaux, Marie-Constance, baronne de. *Souvenirs d'une dame du palais impériale*. Paris: n.p., 1830.

Veneur, Jacques Thomas. *L'Echo des salons de Paris depuis la Restauration, ou Recueil d'anecdotes sur l'ex-empereur Buonaparte, sa cour et ses agens*. 6 vols. Paris: Delaunay, 1814–15.

Viel-Castel, Horace de. *Le Faubourg Saint-Germain*. Paris: Ladvocat, 1837.

Vigée-Lebrun, Louise-Elisabeth. *Souvenirs de Madame Vigée-Lebrun*. 2 vols. Paris: Charpentier, 1869.

Villemain, François. *Souvenirs contemporains d'histoire et de littérature*. 2 vols. Paris: Didier, 1854.

SECONDARY SOURCES

Abensour, Léon. *La Femme et le féminisme avant la révolution*. Paris: Leroux, 1923.

————. *Le Féminisme sous le règne de Louis-Philippe et en 1848*. Paris: Plon, 1913.

Agulhon, Maurice. *Le Cercle dans la France bourgeoise, 1810–1848: Etude d'une mutation de sociabilité*. Paris: Armand Colin, 1977.

————. "Vers une histoire des associations." *Esprit* 6 (1978): 13–18.

Allgor, Catherine. *Parlor Politics: In Which the Ladies of Washington Help Build a City and a Government*. Charlottesville: University of Virginia Press, 2000.

Alméras, Henri d'. *La Vie parisienne sous la Révolution et le Directoire*. Paris: Albin Michel, 1925.

————. *La Vie parisienne sous la Restauration*. Paris: Cercle du Bibliophile, 1968.

————. *La Vie parisienne sous le Consulat et l'Empire*. Paris: Cercle du Bibliophile, 1968.

————. *La Vie parisienne sous le règne de Louis-Philippe*. Paris: Albin Michel, 1923.

Aprile, Sylvie. "Bourgeoise et républicaine, deux termes inconciliables." In *Femmes dans la cité, 1815–1871,* edited by Alain Corbin, Jacqueline Lalouette, and Michèle Riot-Sarcey. Grâne: Créphis, 1997.

———. "La République au salon: Vie et mort d'une forme de sociabilité politique (1865–1885)." *Revue d'histoire moderne et contemporaine* 38 (July–September 1991): 473–87.

Atlas de la Révolution française. Vol. 6: *Les Sociétés politiques.* Edited by J. Boutier, P. Boutry, and S. Bonin. Paris: Ecole des hautes études en sciences sociales, 1992.

Badinter, Elisabeth. "L'Exception française." *Le Débat* 87 (November–December 1995): 123–26.

Badinter, Elisabeth, and Robert Badinter. *Condorcet (1743–1794): Un Intellectuel en politique.* Paris: Fayard, 1988.

Bagge, Dominique. *Les Idées politiques en France sous la Restauration.* Paris: Presses universitaires de France, 1952.

Baker, Keith Michael. *Inventing the French Revolution: Essays on French Political Culture in the Eighteenth Century.* Cambridge: Cambridge University Press, 1990.

———. "Politics and Public Opinion Under the Old Regime: Some Reflections." In *Press and Politics in Pre-Revolutionary France,* edited by Jack R. Censer and Jeremy D. Popkin, 204–46. Berkeley: University of California Press, 1987.

Balayé, Simone. *Madame de Staël: Lumières et liberté.* Paris: Klincksieck, 1979.

Baldensperger, Fernand. *Le Mouvement des idées dans l'émigration française (1789–1815).* 2 vols. New York: Burt Franklin, 1968.

Bardoux, Agénor. *La Comtesse Pauline de Beaumont.* Paris: Calmann-Lévy, 1889.

———. *La Duchesse de Duras.* Paris: Calmann-Lévy, 1898.

Bartillat, Christian de. *Histoire de la noblesse française, 1789–1989.* 2 vols. Paris: Albin Michel, 1988.

Bergeron, Louis. *France Under Napoleon.* Translated by R. R. Palmer. Princeton: Princeton University Press, 1981.

Berkin, Carol R., and Clara M. Lovett, eds. *Women, War, and Revolution.* New York: Holmes & Meier, 1980.

Bertaut, Jules. *Les Belles émigrés.* Paris: Flammarion, 1948.

———. *La Duchesse d'Abrantès.* Paris: Flammarion, 1949.

———. *Le Faubourg Saint-Germain sous l'Empire et la Restauration.* Paris: Tallandier, 1949.

———. *Egéries du XVIIIe siècle: Madame Suard, Madame Deille, Madame Helvétius, Madame Diderot, Mademoiselle Quinault.* Paris: Plon, 1928.

———. *Madame de Genlis.* Paris: B. Grasset, 1941.

———. *Les Parisiens sous la Révolution.* Paris: Amiot-Dumont, 1952.

Bertier de Sauvigny, Guillaume de. "Aristocratie et monarchie dans la vie culturelle au temps de Louis XVIII et de Charles X." In *Hof, Kultur und Politik im 19. Jahrhundert: Akten des 18. Deutsch-französischen Historikerkolloquiums, Darmstadt, vom 27.–30. September 1982,* edited by Karl Ferdinand Werner. Bonn: L. Röhrscheid, 1985.

———. *The Bourbon Restoration.* Translated by Lynn M. Chase. Philadelphia: University of Pennsylvania Press, 1967.

Bodek, Evelyn G. "Salonieres and Blue Stockings: Educated Obsolescence and Germinating Feminism." *Feminist Studies* 3 (Spring–Summer 1976): 185–99.

Borg, Kirsten Elizabeth Aida. "Princess Lieven: A New Interpretation of Her Role." Ph.D. thesis, University of Illinois at Chicago, 1978.

Bourquin, Marie-Hélène. *Monsieur et Madame Tallien.* Paris: Perrin, 1987.

Brelot, Claude-Isabelle. "De la tutelle à la collaboration: Une Femme de la noblesse dans la vie politique (1814–1830." In *Femmes dans la Cité,* 1815–1871, edited by Alain Corbin, Jacqueline Lalouette, and Michèle Riot-Sarcey. Grâne: Créphis, 1997.

Bronislaw, Baczko. "Egalité et exclusions." *Le Débat* 87 (November–December 1995): 118–23.

Calhoun, Craig, ed. *Habermas and the Public Sphere.* Cambridge, Mass.: MIT Press, 1992.

Castries, René de la Croix, duc de. *La Vie quotidienne des émigrés.* 1966. Reprint. Geneva: Famot, 1979.

Chaline, Jean-Pierre. *Sociabilité et érudition: Les Sociétés savantes en France, XIXe–XXe siècles.* Paris: Editions du C.T.H.S., 1995.

Challamel, Augustin. *Les Clubs contre-révolutionnaires, cercles, comités, sociétiés, salons, réunions, cafés, restaurants et librairies.* Paris: L. Cerf, 1895.

Chartier, Roger. *The Cultural Origins of the French Revolution.* Translated by Lydia G. Cochrane. Durham, N.C.: Duke University Press, 1991.

Chartier, Roger, ed. *A History of Private Life.* Vol. 3: *Passions of the Renaissance.* Translated by Arthur Goldhammer. Cambridge, Mass.: Harvard University Press, 1989.

Chaussinand-Nogaret, Guy. *The French Nobility in the Eighteenth Century: From Feudalism to Enlightenment.* Translated by William Doyle. Cambridge: Cambridge University Press, 1985.

Chaussinand-Nogaret, Guy, J. M. Constant, C. Durandin, and A. Jouanna, eds. *Histoire des élites en France au XVIe au XXe siècle: L'Honneur, le mérite, l'argent.* Paris: Tallandier, 1991.

Clergue, Helene. *The Salon: A Study of French Society and Personalities in the Eighteenth Century.* New York: Burt Franklin, 1907.

Cohen, Paul. *Freedom's Moment: An Essay on the French Idea of Liberty from Rousseau to Foucault.* Chicago: University of Chicago Press, 1997.

Coignard, Sophie, and Marie-Thérèse Guichard. *Les Bonnes Fréquentations: Histoire secrète des réseaux d'influence.* Paris: Bernard Grasset, 1997.

Corbin, Alain, Jacqueline Lalouette, and Michèle Riot-Sarcey, eds. *Femmes dans la cité, 1815–1871.* Grâne: Créphis, 1997.

Craveri, Benedetta. "Conqueror of Paris." *New York Review of Books* 39, no. 12 (December 17, 1992): 63–68.

———. *Madame du Deffand and Her World.* Translated by Teresa Waugh. Boston: David R. Godine, 1994.

Dann, Otto. "Sociabilité et association." In *Sociabilité et société bourgeoise en France, en Allemagne et en Suisse, 1750–1850,* edited by Etienne François, 313–14. Paris: Recherche sur les Civilizations, 1986.

Darnton, Robert. *The Literary Underground of the Old Regime.* Cambridge, Mass.: Harvard University Press, 1982.

Darrow, Margaret. "French Noblewomen and the New Domesticity, 1750–1850." *Feminist Studies* 5, no. 1 (Spring 1979): 41–65.

Daudet, Ernest. *Une Vie d'ambassadrice au siècle dernier: La Princesse de Lieven.* 1903. Reprint. Paris: Plon, 1910.

Daumard, Adeline. "Noblesse et Aristocratie en France au XIXe siècle." In *Les Noblesses européennes au XIXe siècle: Actes du colloque organisé par l'Ecole française de Rome et le Centro per gli studi di politica estera e opinione pubblica de l'Université de Milan (Rome 21–23 novembre 1985),* 81–104. Milan: Ecole française de Rome, 1988.

———. "L'Oisiveté aristocratique et bourgeoise en France au XIXe siècle: Privilège ou malédiction?" In *Oisiveté et loisirs dans les sociétés occidentales au XIXe siècle. Colloque pluridisciplinaire, Amiens 19–20 novembre 1982*, 127–33. Abbeville: F. Paillart, 1983.

———. "La Vie de salon en France dans la première moitié du XIXe siècle." In *Sociabilité et société bourgeoise en France, en Allemagne et en Suisse, 1750–1850*, edited by Etienne François, 81–94. Paris: Recherche sur les Civilisations, 1986.

Dauphin, Noëlle. "Les Salons de la Restauration: Un Influence spécifique sur les milieux dirigeants." In *Femmes dans la cité, 1815–1871*, edited by Alain Corbin, Jacqueline Lalouette, and Michèle Riot-Sarcey, 251–60. Grâne: Créphis, 1997.

Davis, Natalie Zemon, and Arletta Farge, eds. *A History of Women in the West.* Vol. 3: *Renaissance and Enlightenment Paradoxes.* Cambridge, Mass.: Harvard University Press, 1993.

DeJean, Joan. *Tender Geographies: Women and the Origins of the Novel in France.* New York: Columbia University Press, 1991.

Delorme, Suzanne. "Le Salon de la marquise de Lambert, berceau de *l'Encyclopédie.*" In *L'Encyclopédie et le progrès des sciences et techniques*, edited by René Taton and Suzanne Delorme. Paris: Presses universitaires de France, 1952.

Desan, Suzanne. "What's After Political Culture? Recent French Revolutionary Historiography." *French Historical Studies* 23, no. 1 (2000): 163–96.

Des Cars, Jean. *La Princesse Mathilde: L'Amour, la gloire et les arts.* Paris: Editions j'ai lu, 1988.

Diesbach, Ghislain de. *Histoire de l'émigration, 1789–1814.* Paris: Perrin, 1984.

Du Bled, Victor. *Le Rôle social et mondain de la femme depuis le Moyen Age.* Vol. 4 of *La Femme dans la nature, dans les moeurs, dans la legende, dans la société.* Paris: Bong, 1908.

———. *La Société française du XVIe siècle au XXe siècle.* 9 vols. Paris: Perrin, 1900–1913.

Duhet, Paule-Marie, ed. *Les Femmes de la Révolution, 1789–1794.* Paris: Gallimard, 1989.

Dujarric de la Rivière, René. *Dames de la Révolution.* Périgueux: Pierre Fanlac, 1963.

Dulong, Claude. *La Vie quotidienne des femmes au Grand Siècle.* Paris: Hachette, 1984.

Elias, Norbert. *The Civilizing Process: The History of Manners.* Translated by Edmund Jephcott. New York: Urizen Books, 1978.

———. *The Court Society.* Translated by Edmund Jephcott. New York: Pantheon Books, 1983.

Fassin, Eric. "The Purloined Gender: American Feminism in a French Mirror." *French Historical Studies* 22, no. 1 (Winter 1999): 113–38.

Fiette, Suzanne. *La Noblesse française des Lumières à la Belle Epoque: Psychologies d'une adaptation.* Paris: Perrin, 1997.

Forster, Robert. *The House of Saulx-Tavanes: Versailles and Burgundy, 1700–1830.* Baltimore: Johns Hopkins University Press, 1971.

Fortassier, Rose. *Les Mondains de la Comédie humaine: Etude historique et psychologique.* Paris: Klincksieck, 1974.

Fraisse, Geneviève. *Reason's Muse: Sexual Difference and the Birth of Democracy.* Translated by Jane Marie Todd. Chicago: Chicago University Press, 1994.

———. "Rupture révolutionnaire." In *Femmes et pouvoirs sous l'Ancien Régime*, edited by Danielle Haase-Dubosc and Eliane Viennot, 291–305. Paris: Rivages, 1991.

François, Etienne, ed. *Sociabilité et société bourgeoise en France, en Allemagne et en Suisse, 1750–1850.* Paris: Recherche sur les Civilisations, 1986.

Fumaroli, Marc. "La Conversation." In *Les Lieux de Mémoire*, edited by Pierra Nora, vol. 3: *Les Traditions*, 2:679–743. Paris: Gallimard, 1992.

Furet, François. *Interpreting the French Revolution.* Translated by Elborg Forster. Cambridge: Cambridge University Press, 1981.

Furet, François, and Mona Ozouf, eds. *A Critical Dictionary of the French Revolution.* Translated by Arthur Goldhammer. Cambridge, Mass.: Harvard University Press, 1989.

Galland, Olivier, Mireille Clémençon, Patrick Le Gallès, and Marco Oberti. *Le Monde des étudiants.* Paris: Presses universitaires de France, 1995.

Gans, E. "Le Salon de Madame Récamier." *Revue de Paris,* February 7, 1836, 237–42.

Gastine, Louis. *Madame Tallien, Notre Dame de Thermidor, from the Last Days of the French Revolution until her Death as Princess de Chimay in 1835.* New York: John Lane, 1913.

Gendron, François. *La Jeunesse dorée: Episodes de la Révolution française.* Sillery, Quebec: Presses de l'Université de Québec, 1979.

Gerbod, Paul. "Une Forme de sociabilité bourgeoise: Le Thermalisme en France, en Belgique et en Allemagne, 1800–1850." In *Sociabilité et société bourgeoise en France, en Allemagne et en Suisse, 1750–1850,* edited by Etienne François, 105–22. Paris: Recherche sur les Civilisations, 1986.

———. "Loisirs et santé: Les Cures thermales en France (1850–1900)." In *Oisiveté et loisirs dans les sociétés occidentales au XIXe siècle. Colloque pluridisciplinaire, Amiens 19–20 novembre 1982, 195–206.* Abbeville: F. Paillart, 1983.

Girard, Louis. "La Cour de Napoléon III." In *Hof, Kultur und Politik im 19. Jahrhundert: Akten des 18. Deutsch-französischen Historikerkolloquiums, Darmstadt, vom 27.–30. September 1982,* edited by Karl Ferdinand Werner, 155–68. Bonn: L. Röhrscheid, 1985.

Gladwyn, Cynthia. "Madame Récamier." In *Affairs of the Mind: The Salon in Europe and America from the Eighteenth to the Twentieth Century,* edited by Peter Quennell. Washington, D.C.: New Republic Books, 1980.

Glotz, Marguerite, and Madeleine Maire. *Salons du XVIIIe siècle.* Paris: Nouvelles Editions latines, 1949.

Godineau, Dominique. "The Woman." In *Enlightenment Portraits,* edited by Michel Vovelle, translated by Lydia G. Cochrane, 393–426. Chicago: University of Chicago Press, 1997.

———. *The Women of the French Revolution.* Translated by Katherine Streip. Berkeley: University of California Press, 1988.

Goldberger, Aviel H., ed. *Woman as Mediatrix: Essays on Nineteenth-Century European Women Writers.* New York: Greenwood Press, 1987.

Goldgar, Anne. *Impolite Learning: Conduct and Community in the Republic of Letters, 1680–1750.* New Haven: Yale University Press, 1995.

Goldsmith, Elizabeth C. *Exclusive Conversations: The Art of Interaction in Seventeenth-Century France.* Philadelphia: University of Pennsylvania Press, 1988.

Goldsmith, Elizabeth C., and Dena Goodman, eds. *Going Public: Women and Publishing in Early Modern France.* Ithaca N.Y.: Cornell University Press, 1995.

Goodman, Dena. "Enlightenment Salons: The Convergence of Female and Philosophic Ambitions." *Eighteenth-Century Studies* 22 (1989): 329–50.

———. "Governing the Republic of Letters: The Politics of Culture in the French Enlightenment." *History of European Ideas* 13, no. 3 (1991): 183–99.

———. "Public Sphere and Private Life: Toward a Synthesis of Current Historiographical Approaches to the Old Regime." *History and Theory* 31, no. 1 (1992): 1–20.

———. *The Republic of Letters: A Cultural History of the French Enlightenment.* Ithaca N.Y.: Cornell University Press, 1994.

————. "Seriousness of Purpose: Salonnières, Philosophes, and the Shaping of the Eighteenth-Century Salon." *Proceedings of the Annual Meeting of the Western Society for French History* 15 (1988): 111–18.

Gordon, Daniel. "Beyond the Social History of Ideas: Morellet and the Enlightenment." In *André Morellet (1727–1819) in the Republic of Letters and the French Revolution*, edited by Jeffrey Merrick and Dorthy Medlin. New York: Peter Lang, 1995.

————. *Citizens Without Sovereignty: Equality and Sociability in French Thought, 1670–1789*. Princeton: Princeton University Press, 1994.

————. "Philosophy, Sociology, and Gender in the Enlightenment Conception of Public Opinion." *French Historical Studies* 17, no. 4 (Fall 1992): 882–911.

Gougy-François, Marie. *Les Grands Salons féminins*. Paris: Debresse, 1965.

Guillois, Antoine. *Le Salon de Madame Helvétius: Cabanis et les Idéologues*. New York: Burt Franklin, 1971.

Gautier, Paul. *Madame de Staël et Napoléon*. Paris: Plon, 1903.

Gueniffey, Patrice, and Ran Halévi. "Clubs and Popular Societies." In *A Critical Dictionary of the French Revolution*, edited by François Furet and Mona Ozouf, translated by Arthur Goldhammer, 458–73. Cambridge, Mass.: Harvard University Press 1989.

Gutwirth, Madelyn. *Madame de Staël, Novelist: The Emergence of the Artist as Woman*. Urbana: University of Illinois Press, 1978.

————. *The Twilight of the Goddesses: Women and Representation in the French Revolutionary Era*. New Brunswick, N.J.: Rutgers University Press, 1992.

Gutwirth, Madelyn, Avriel Goldberger, and Karyna Szmurlo, eds. *Germaine de Staël: Crossing the Borders*. New Brunswick, N.J: Rutgers University Press, 1991.

Gwynne, G. E. *Madame de Staël et la Révolution française: politique, philosophie, littérature*. Paris: A.-G. Nizet, 1969.

Haase-Dubosc, Danielle, and Eliane Viennot, eds. *Femmes et pouvoirs sous l'Ancien Régime*. Paris: Rivages, 1991.

Habermas, Jürgen. *The Structural Transformation of the Public Sphere: An Inquiry into a Category of Bourgeois Society*. Translated by Thomas Burger. Cambridge, Mass.: MIT Press, 1989.

Haine, Scott W. *The World of the Paris Café: Sociability Among the French Working Class, 1789–1914*. Baltimore: Johns Hopkins University Press, 1996.

Halévi, Ran. *Les Loges maçonniques dans la France d'Ancien Régime: Aux origines de la sociabilité démocratique*. Paris: A. Colin, 1984.

Harmand, Jean. *Madame de Genlis: Sa Vie intime et politique, 1746–1830*. Paris: Perrin, 1912.

Harth, Erica. *Cartesian Women: Versions and Subversions of Rational Discourse in the Old Regime*. Ithaca, N.Y.: Cornell University Press, 1992.

Hellegouarc'h, Jacqueline. *L'Esprit de société: Cercles et "salons" parisiens au XVIIIe siècle*. Paris: Garnier, 2000.

Herriot, Edouard. *Madame Récamier*. Translated by Alys Hallard. 2 vols. New York: Boni & Liveright, 1926.

Hertz, Deborah. *Jewish High Society in Old Regime Berlin*. New Haven: Yale University Press, 1988.

Hesse, Carla. "French Women in Print, 1750–1800: An Essay in Historical Bibliography." *Studies on Voltaire and the Eighteenth Century* (Oxford: Voltaire Foundation) 359 (1998): 65–82.

———. *The Other Enlightenment: How French Women Became Modern*. Princeton: Princeton University Press, 2001.

Higgs, David. *Nobles in Nineteenth-Century France: The Practice of Inegalitarianism*. Baltimore: Johns Hopkins University Press, 1987.

Hollier, Denis, ed. *A New History of French Literature*. Cambridge, Mass.: Harvard University Press, 1994.

Houbre, Gabrielle. "L'Entrée dans le monde: Le Jeune Homme et les femmes (première moitié du XIXe siècle)." In *Femmes dans la cité, 1815–1871*, edited by Alain Corbin, Jacqueline Lalouette, and Michèle Riot-Sarcey, 261–78. Grâne: Créphis, 1997.

Huard, Raymond. *La Naissance du parti politique en France*. Paris: Presse de la Fondation nationale des Sciences politiques, 1996.

———. "Sociabilité et politique en Languedoc méditerranéen des lendemains de la Restauration à la fin de 1849." In *Sociabilité et société bourgeoise en France, en Allemagne et en Suisse, 1750–1850*, edited by Etienne François, 299–312. Paris: Recherche sur les Civilisations, 1986.

Hufton, Olwen. *The Prospect Before Her: A History of Women in Western Europe*. 2 vols. New York: Knopf, 1996.

Imbert de Saint-Amand, Arthur Léon, baron. *Citizeness Bonaparte*. Translated by Thomas Sergeant Perry. New York: Charles Scribner's Sons, 1900.

———. *The Duchesse de Berry and the Court of Charles X*. New York: Charles Scribner's Sons, 1900.

———. *The Duchesse de Berry and the Court of Louis XVIII*. Translated by Elizabeth Gilbert Martin. New York: Charles Scribner's Sons, 1900.

———. *The Duchesse of Angoulême and the Two Restorations*. Translated by James Davis. New York: Charles Scribner's Sons, 1900.

———. *The Wife of the First Consul*. Translated by Thomas Sergeant Perry. New York: Charles Scribner's Sons, 1900.

Jacquier, Bernard. *Le Légitimisme dauphinois, 1830–1870*. Grenoble: Centre de recherche d'histoire économique, sociale et institutionnelle, 1976.

Jardin, André. *Tocqueville: A Biography*. Translated by Lydia Davis. New York: Farrar Straus Giroux, 1988.

Jardin, André, and Jean-André Tudesq. *Restoration and Reaction, 1815–1848*. Translated by Elborg Forster. Cambridge: Cambridge University Press, 1988.

Jones, Colin. "The Great Chain of Buying: Medical Advertisement, the Bourgeois Public Sphere, and the Origins of the French Revolution." *American Historical Review* 101, no. 1 (February 1996): 13–40.

Kale, Steven D. *Legitimism and the Reconstruction of French Society, 1852–1883*. Baton Rouge: Louisiana State University Press, 1992.

———. "Women, the Public Sphere, and the Persistence of Salons." *French Historical Studies* 25, no. 1 (Winter 2002), 115–48.

Kelly, George Armstrong. *The Humane Comedy: Constant, Tocqueville, and French Liberalism*. Cambridge: Cambridge University Press, 1992.

Kors, Alan Charles. *D'Holbach's Coterie: An Enlightenment in Paris*. Princeton: Princeton University Press, 1976.

Krakovitch, Odile. "De la sociabilité." In *Femmes dans la cité, 1815–1871*, edited by Alain Corbin, Jacqueline Lalouette, and Michèle Riot-Sarcey, 205–10. Grâne: Créphis, 1997.

Lairtullier, E. *Les Femmes célèbres de 1789 à 1795, et leur influence dans la Révolution.* Paris: Chez France, 1840.

Landes, Joan B, ed. *Feminism, the Public, and the Private.* New York: Oxford University Press, 1998.

———. *Women and the Public Sphere in the Age of the French Revolution.* Ithaca, N.Y.: Cornell University Press, 1988.

La Vopa, Anthony J. "Conceiving a Public: Ideas and Society in Eighteenth-Century Europe." *Journal of Modern History* 64, no. 1 (March 1992): 79–115.

Lenormant, Madame. *Quatre femmes au temps de la Révolution.* Paris: Didier, 1872.

Lévy, Marie Françoise. *De Mères en filles: L'Education des Françaises, 1850–1880.* Paris: Calmann-Lévy, 1984.

Loliée, Frédéric. *Les Femmes du Second Empire.* Paris: Tallandier, 1912.

Lougee, Carolyn C. *Le Paradis des Femmes: Women, Salons, and Social Stratification in Seventeenth-Century France.* Princeton: Princeton University Press, 1976.

———. "Salons and Conversations: Comment on Papers by Goodman and Gordon." *Proceedings of the Annual Meeting of the Western Society for French History* 15 (1988): 119–21.

Mannheim, Karl. "The Problem of the Intelligentsia: An Inquiry into Its Past and Present Role." In *Essays on the Sociology of Culture.* London: Routledge, 1956.

Mansel, Philip. *The Court of France, 1789–1830.* Cambridge: Cambridge University Press, 1988.

———. "How Forgotten Were the Bourbons in France Between 1812 and 1814?" *European Studies Review* 13, no. 1 (June 1983): 13–37.

Margadant, Jo Burr. "Gender, Vice, and the Political Imaginary in Nineteenth-Century France: Reinterpreting the Failure of the July Monarchy, 1830–1848." *American Historical Review* 104, no. 5 (December 1999): 1461–96.

Martin-Fugier, Anne. "La Cour et la ville sous la Monarchie de Juillet d'après les feuilletons mondains." *Revue historique* 278, no. 1 (1987): 107–33.

———. "La Formation des élites: Les 'conférences' sous la Restauration et la Monarchie de Juillet." *Revue d'histoire moderne et contemporaine* 36 (April–June 1989): 211–41.

———. *La Vie élégante, ou la formation de Tout-Paris.* Paris: Fayard, 1990.

———. *La Vie quotidienne de Louis-Philippe et de sa famille, 1830–1848.* Paris: Hachette, 1992.

Marx, Karl. *The Eighteenth Brumaire of Louis Bonaparte.* 1852. New York: International Publishers, 1963.

Masson, Frédéric. *Napoléon et les femmes.* Paris: Ollendorff, 1911.

———. *La Société sous le Consulat.* Paris: Flammarion, 1937.

Matoré, Georges. *Le Vocabulaire et la société sous Louis-Philippe.* Geneva: Droz, 1951.

May, Gita. *Madame Roland and the Age of Revolution.* New York: Columbia University Press, 1970.

Mayer, Arno J. *The Persistence of the Old Regime: Europe to the Great War.* New York: Pantheon Books, 1981.

Maza, Sarah. *Private Lives and Public Affairs: The Causes Célèbres of Prerevolutionary France.* Berkeley: University of California Press, 1993.

———. "Women, the Bourgeoisie, and the Public Sphere: Response to Daniel Gordon and David Bell." *French Historical Studies* 17, no. 4 (Fall 1992): 935–50.

———. "Women's Voices in Literature and Art." In *A New History of French Literature,* ed. Denis Hollier, 623–27. Cambridge, Mass.: Harvard University Press, 1994.

McMillan, James F. *Napoleon III*. London: Longman, 1991.

Mills, Stephanie. "Salons and Beyond." *Utne Reader* 44 (March–April 1991): 68–86.

Montgomery, Hyde H. *La Princesse de Lieven, grande dame et coeur de femme*. Paris: Hachette. 1940.

Mornet, Daniel, *La Vie parisienne au XIXe siècle: Leçons faites à l'Ecole des hautes études sociales*. Paris: F. Alcan, 1914.

Nathans, Benjamin. "Habermas's 'Public Sphere' in the Era of the French Revolution." *French Historical Studies* 16, no. 3 (Spring 1990): 620–44.

Les Noblesses européennes au XIXe siècle: Actes du colloque organisé par l'Ecole française de Rome et le Centro per gli studi di politica estera e opinione pubblica de l'Université de Milan (Rome 21–23 novembre 1985). Milan: Ecole française de Rome, 1988.

Nora, Pierre, ed. *Les Lieux de Mémoire*. Vol. 3: *Les Traditions*. Paris: Gallimard, 1992.

O'Meara, Kathleen. *Un Salon à Paris: Madame de Mohl et ses intimes*. Paris: Plon, 1886.

Ory, Pascal. "Le Salon." In *Histoire des droites en France*, ed. Jean-François Sirinelli, 2:113–27. Paris: Gallimard, 1992.

Oisiveté et loisirs dans les sociétés occidentales au XIXe siècle: Colloque pluridisciplinaire, Amiens 19–20 novembre 1982. Abbeville: F. Paillart, 1983.

Ozouf, Mona. "Le Compte des jours." *Le Débat* 87 (November–December 1995): 140–46.

———. " 'Public Opinion' at the End of the Old Regime." *Journal of Modern History* 60, suppl. (September 1988): S1–S21.

———. *Women's Words: Essay on French Singularity*. Translated by Jane Marie Todd. Chicago: University of Chicago Press, 1997.

Pekacz, Jolanta. *Conservative Tradition in Pre-Revolutionary France: Parisian Salon Women*. New York: Peter Land, 1999.

———. "Political Correctness for Polite Society: Pro-Monarchical Ideas of *Honnêteté* in Seventeenth- and Eighteenth-Century France." MS.

———. "Gender as a Political Orientation: Parisian Salonnières and the *Querelle des bouffons*." *Canadian Journal of History* 32, no. 3 (December 1997): 405–14.

———. "Whose Muses? Parisian Salon Women from the French Revolution to 1848." Paper presented at Annual Meeting of the Society for French Historical Studies, Ottawa, Canada, 1998.

Perrot, Michelle. *Femmes publiques*. Paris: Textuel, 1997.

———. "Une Histoire sans affrontements." *Le Débat* 87 (November–December 1995): 130–34.

Picard, Roger. *Les Salons littéraires et la société française, 1610–1789*. New York: Brentano's, 1943.

Pope, Barbara C. "Revolution and Retreat." In *Women, War, and Revolution*, edited by Carol R. Berkin and Clara M. Lovett. New York: Holmes & Meier, 1980.

Quennell, Peter, ed. *Affairs of the Mind: The Salon in Europe and America from the Eighteenth to the Twentieth Century*. Washington, D.C.: New Republic Books, 1980.

Reddy, William. *The Invisible Code: Honor and Sentiment in Postrevolutionary France, 1814–1848*. Berkeley: University of California Press, 1997.

Reiset, Vicomte de. *Les Reines de l'émigration: Louise d'Esparbès, Comtesse de Polastron*. Paris: Emile-Paul, 1907.

Rials, Stéphane. *Révolution et contre-révolution au XIXe siècle*. Paris: D.U.C. / Albatros, 1987.

Roche, Daniel. *Les Républicains des lettres: Gens de culture et Lumières au XVIIIe siècle*. Paris: Fayard, 1988.

Rosanvallon, Pierre. *Le Moment Guizot.* Paris: Gallimard, 1985.

Rossi, Henri. *Mémoires aristocratiques féminins.* Paris: H. Champion, 1998.

Roy, Joseph Antoine. *Histoire du Jockey Club.* Paris: Marcel Rivière, 1958.

Scott, Joan Wallach, ed. *Feminism and History.* Oxford: Oxford University Press, 1996.

——. *Gender and the Politics of History.* New York: Columbia University Press, 1988.

——. *Only Paradoxes to Offer: French Feminists and the Rights of Man.* Cambridge, Mass.: Harvard University Press, 1996.

——. " 'Vive la différence.' " *Le Débat* 87 (November–December 1995): 134–40.

Serna, Pierre. "The Noble." In *Enlightenment Portraits,* edited by Michel Vovelle, translated by Lydia G. Cochrane, 30–84. Chicago: University of Chicago Press, 1997.

Showalter, English, Jr. "Madame de Graffigny and Her Salon." In *Studies in Eighteenth-Century Culture,* edited by Ronald C. Rosbottom, 6:367–81. Madison: University of Wisconsin Press, 1975.

Smith, Bonnie G. *Changing Lives: Women in European History Since 1700.* Lexington, Mass.: D.C. Heath, 1989.

Sonolet, Louis. *La Vie parisienne sous le Second Empire.* Paris: Payot, 1929.

Soprani, Anne. *La Révolution et les femmes, 1789–1796.* Paris: Emile Dubois, 1988.

Spencer, Samia I, ed. *French Women and the Enlightenment.* Bloomington: Indiana University Press, 1984.

Spitzer, Alan B. *The French Generation of 1820.* Princeton: Princeton University Press, 1987.

Steegmuller, Francis. *A Woman, a Man, and Two Kingdoms: The Story of Madame d'Epinay and the Abbé Galiani.* New York: Knopf, 1991.

Steinbrügge, Lieselotte. *The Moral Sex: Woman's Nature in the French Enlightenment.* New York: Oxford University Press, 1995.

Stenger, Gilbert. *Grandes dames du XIXe siècle: Chronique du temps de la Restauration.* Paris: Perrin, 1911.

——. *La Société française pendant le Consulat.* 5 vols. Paris: Perrin, 1903–5.

Tassé, Henriette. *Salons français du dix-neuvième siècle.* Montreal: Saint-Joseph, 1952.

Tenenbaum, Susan. "Liberal Heroines: Madame de Staël and the 'Woman Question' and the Modern State." *Annales Benjamin Constant* 5 (1985): 37–52.

Tolédano, A.-D. *La Vie de famille sous la Restauration et la Monarchie de Juillet.* Paris: Albin Michel, 1943.

Tudesq, André-Jean. "L'Elargissement de la noblesse en France dans la première moitié du XIXe siècle." In *Les Noblesses européennes au XIXe siècle: Actes du colloque organisé par l'Ecole française de Rome et le Centro per gli studi di politica estera e opinione pubblica de l'Université de Milan (Rome 21–23 novembre 1985),* 121–35. Milan: Ecole française de Rome, 1988.

——. "Le Journal, lieu et lien de la société bourgeoise en France dans la première moitié du XIXe siècle." In *Sociabilité et société bourgeoise en France, en Allemagne et en Suisse, 1750–1850,* edited by Etienne François, 261–74. Paris: Recherche sur les Civilisations, 1986.

——. *Les Pairs de France au temps de Guizot.* Paris: A Colin, 1956.

Tulard, Jean, ed. *La Contre-Révolution.* Paris: Perrin, 1990.

——. "Problèmes sociaux de la France impériale." *Revue d'histoire moderne et contemporaine,* special issue (July–September 1970): 639–63.

Turquan, Joseph. *Les Femmes de l'émigration, 1789–1815.* 2 vols. Paris: Emile-Paul, 1911–12.

———. *A Great Coquette: Madame Récamier and Her Salon*. Translated by Jeanne Bernard. New York: Brentano's, 1913.

———. *Le Monde et le demi-monde sous le Consulat et l'Empire*. Paris: Montgredien, 1900.

Van Kley, Dale K. "In Search of Eighteenth-Century Parisian Public Opinion." *French Historical Studies* 19, no. 1 (Spring 1995): 215–26.

Veauvy, Christiane, and Laura Pisano. *Paroles oubliées: Les Femmes et la construction de l'Etat-nation en France et en Italie (1789–1860)*. Paris: Armand Colin, 1997.

Vidalenc, Jean. *Les Emigrés français, 1789–1825*. Caen: Associations des Publications de la Faculté des Lettres et Sciences humaines de l'Université de Caen, 1963.

Vier, Jacques. *La Comtesse d'Agoult et son temps*. 2 vols. Paris: Armand Colin, 1955–59.

Villefosse, Louis de, and Janine Bouissounouse. *The Scourge of the Eagle: Napoleon and the Liberal Opposition*. Translated by Michel Ross. London: Sidgwick & Jackson, 1972.

Vovelle, Michel, ed. *Enlightenment Portraits*. Translated by Lydia G. Cochrane. Chicago: University of Chicago Press, 1997.

Wagener, Françoise. *Madame Récamier, 1777–1849*. Paris: J. C. Lattès, 1986.

Waquet, Françoise. *Les Fêtes royales sous la Restauration, ou l'Ancien Régime retrouvé*. Geneva: Droz, 1981.

Waresquiel, Emmanuel de. *Le Duc de Richelieu, 1766–1822: Un Sentimental en politique*. Paris: Perrin, 1990.

Weber, Joseph. *Mémoires concernant Marie-Antoinette*. 3 vols. London: L'auteur, 1804–9.

Werner, Karl Ferdinand. *Hof, Kultur und Politik im 19. Jahrhundert. Akten des 18. Deutsch-französischen Historikerkolloquiums, Darmstadt vom 27.–30. September 1982*. Bonn: Ludwig Röhrscheid Verlag, 1985.

Willms, Johannes. *Paris: Capital of Europe*. New York: Holmes & Meier, 1997.

Wood, Dennis. *Benjamin Constant: A Biography*. London: Routledge, 1993.

Yriarte, Charles. *Les Cercles de Paris, 1828–1864*. Paris: Dupray de la Mahérie, 1864.

Zieseniss, Charles-Otto. *Napoléon et la cour impériale*. Paris: Tallandier, 1980.

Zurich, Paul de. *Une Femme heureuse: Madame de La Briche (1755–1844)*. Paris: E. de Boccard, 1934.

Zimmerman, J. E. *Dictionary of Classical Mythology*. New York: Bantam Books, 1971.

Index